*The publisher gratefully acknowledges the
generous contribution to this book provided by
the Classical Literature Endowment Fund of
the University of California Press Foundation,
which is supported by a major gift
from Joan Palevsky.*

THE SEER IN ANCIENT GREECE

Michael Attyah
Flower   ·   THE SEER IN

ANCIENT GREECE

University of California Press

Berkeley   Los Angeles   London

University of California Press, one of the most
distinguished university presses in the United States,
enriches lives around the world by advancing scholarship in the humanities, social sciences, and natural
sciences. Its activities are supported by the UC Press
Foundation and by philanthropic contributions from
individuals and institutions. For more information,
visit www.ucpress.edu.

University of California Press
Berkeley and Los Angeles, California

University of California Press, Ltd.
London, England

Library of Congress Cataloging-in-Publication Data

Flower, Michael Attyah, 1956–.
    The seer in ancient Greece / Michael Attyah Flower.
       p.   cm.
    Includes bibliographical references and index.
    ISBN 978-0-520-25229-5 (cloth : alk. paper)
    1. Oracles, Greek.   2. Prophets — Greece.
3. Divination — Greece.   4. Greece — Religious life
and customs.   I. Title.
BF1765.F56   2008
133.30938 —dc22   2007004264

Manufactured in the United States of America

16 15 14 13 12 11 10 09 08 07
10 9 8 7 6 5 4 3 2 1

This book is printed on Natures Book, which contains
50% post-consumer waste and meets the minimum
requirements of ANSI/NISO Z39.48-1992 (R 1997)
(*Permanence of Paper*).

For Harriet Flower

CONTENTS

ILLUSTRATIONS

ACKNOWLEDGMENTS

When I began work on this book in 2000, I could not foresee when, or indeed if, I would finish it. In the interim other, shorter, projects required my attention, and personal matters also intervened. This book's completion is due, in no small measure, to the assistance of friends and colleagues in several different academic departments and institutions. Harriet Flower, as always, has been my greatest asset, and without her help and encouragement this book would never have been written. Despite the heavy demands on her time, she read the entire manuscript twice and made many improvements both great and small. Two colleagues at Franklin and Marshall College have influenced my approach to the subject. Misty Bastian encouraged my interest in using anthropological material and has been generous with her advice and knowledge. Ann Steiner helped me to think about the art historical dimensions of the subject.

My debts to colleagues and friends at Princeton are also important. William Childs assisted me in acquiring photographs and permissions, and Beate Pongratz-Leisten was willing to share her vast knowledge of the ancient Near East. Many of my students have contributed to this project in various ways. In the spring of 2002 I taught a graduate seminar on Greek divination to a group of excellent students, and that experience greatly advanced the writing of this book. And in the fall of 2005, in collaboration with John Gager, I offered a seminar called "Priests and Power in the Ancient World." No one can teach with John and not emerge a better scholar and teacher.

I am also indebted to scholars at other institutions. I have profited a great deal both from the writings of Kai Trampedach and from our conversations. At the beginning of this project I had a very valuable conversation with Heinrich von Staden about how to use Plato as a source for Greek society. Christopher Pelling has answered so many queries over the years on so many different subjects that it would be impossible for me to give an accounting of them. Daryn Lehoux kindly answered my questions about Near Eastern divination. My friends Joshua Katz, John Marincola, Olga Palagia, and Deborah Steiner have also been a great help to me in numerous conversations. I am especially grateful to John Dillery, who read the manuscript for the Press and who made many valuable suggestions for improvement. I also have debts of a different kind to acknowledge. Shari Kenfield and Donna Sanclemente kindly offered to scan several of the images, and my daughter, Isabel Flower, drew figure 9. I would like to thank Laura Cerruti, editor for the Press, for encouraging me to submit the manuscript and for correctly diagnosing my perfectionism. No author could hope for a more efficient and patient project editor than Cindy Fulton or for a more skilled copy editor than Marian Rogers, and their efforts have made this a much better book.

Two academic institutions provided generous financial support. I began this project while on sabbatical leave from Franklin and Marshall College. A grant from the Magie Fund of the Department of Classics at Princeton University was used to obtain the photographs for this book, and it also provided for professional indexing and proofreading.

Finally, I wish to express my gratitude to my colleague and friend Denis Feeney, who gave me the resources to finish this project and an example to imitate.

PREFACE

I conceived the idea of writing this book while engaged on another project, a commentary on book 9 of Herodotus's *Histories*. Seers play a fairly prominent role in Herodotus's account of the battles of Plataea and Mycale, and I soon discovered that there was no adequate treatment of the role, function, and representation of the seer in Greek society. Once the idea of a book on Greek seers struck me, I was immediately convinced of the importance of the topic and the need for a general study. It was also a topic that was, and is, particularly congenial to my own interests.

Ever since I began the study of classical antiquity as an undergraduate, I have been fascinated by oracles; and when I became a teacher of Greek history, I always had a great deal to say to my students about divination. Most of them found the Greek reliance on Delphi and on seers to be either bizarre or laughable, or both. I well remember an incident in a seminar that made a great impression on me at the time. A student of mine from India, who happened to be a practicing Hindu, said that he found nothing peculiar about accepting at face value the Delphic prophecies recounted by Herodotus; for it was simply the case that a god, whom the Greeks happened to call Apollo, was speaking through the priestess. The other students jeered terribly, and my attempts to defend the intellectual legitimacy of his point of view had little effect. What this incident impressed upon me was not the authenticity of Delphic prophecy, but rather the difficulty that many of us have in taking different systems of belief seriously on their own terms.

I think that in a book of this sort it is not out of place to reveal something of my own biases right at the beginning. The reader will not find any declarations as to the validity of divination. That is not to say that I believe in the power of the Pythia to predict the future or in the ability of seers to determine the divine will by examining the entrails of sacrificial animals. But it is to say that I am convinced that the vast majority of Greeks really believed in such things. They took their own religion seriously, and as a system of knowledge and belief it worked very well for them. It is methodologically inappropriate when modern scholars project their own views about religion onto the Greeks and sometimes even claim that the seers as a group were conscious charlatans who duped the superstitious masses. Such assertions fly in the face of work on divination by anthropologists, work that reveals a good deal about the mentality of diviner and client as well as about the social usefulness of divination.

When I was working on this book, an astrophysicist at the Institute for Advanced Study (where my wife was a member) inquired about my research and asked me a typical question. When the seers discovered that they could not make accurate predictions on the basis of looking at the entrails of sheep, why did they not just give up the practice? Well, I responded, it was because the system worked for them. Sacrificial divination worked for the Greek seers because they saw in the entrails what they needed to know in order to help them make decisions. Within their own system of belief, their methods of divination were successful; divination was a viable means of knowing about the world, and seers performed a fundamentally important social and religious function. Now I realize that this response of mine needs a great deal of explanation and qualification, for I certainly do not mean to imply that absolutely anything, even things that defy the laws of nature, is possible if people merely believe that it is. What I mean is that within a system of belief practices can be constructed and construed in such a way as to make them viable and socially useful. For a fuller exposition of my approach, one will need to read this book.

The chapters of the book are arranged so as to build on each other, but they also can be read separately. In order to allow each chapter to stand on its own, some repetition of material was necessary. So too some of the same passages from ancient authors reappear in different chapters; this is unavoidable because the many aspects of a particular passage can be relevant to several different topics. I have made a determined effort to keep all such repetitions to a minimum. The index locorum will guide the reader who wishes to read every discussion of a particular passage.

In a study such as this one, it is absolutely essential that translations be as accurate as possible, since an entire argument can hinge on the meaning of particular words and phrases. For that reason I have provided my own translations of Greek and Latin texts. That is not to say that I have not made any errors, but only that I would rather that such errors that do exist be mine rather than someone else's. I will claim, however, that I have never deliberately falsified a translation in order to strengthen my own argument, just as I have not consciously omitted passages from discussion that seem to contradict my own theories. Citations of Greek and Latin have been kept to a bare minimum, and what does appear is always accompanied by a translation. Classical Greek has been transliterated, except for the very few phrases that appear in the text and footnotes. All quotations from the Hebrew Bible have been taken from *The Harper Collins Study Bible*, edited by Wayne A. Meeks et al. (San Francisco, 1997). Various editions and translations of cuneiform texts are listed in the notes where appropriate.

Finally, I have generally cited other scholars in the footnotes, rather than in the main text. This might seem to be a rhetorical device aimed at privileging my own views, but it is actually done for the ease of the general reader, whose attention can only be distracted by wading through a sea of scholarly disputation. In other words, my principal rhetorical aim has been to make the reader participate in my own fascination with the topic of the Greek seer and of Greek divination generally. I have tried to put the study of the Greek seer into context by looking at seercraft in the ancient Near East as well as by making judicious use of modern scholarship in anthropology and ethnology. Those fields have vast bibliographies and cover wide expanses of time and space; and so, rather than confound the reader with an array of detailed case studies, I have attempted to draw generalizations that shed light on Greek practice and belief. There is always a danger of oversimplification or misunderstanding when one draws on fields outside of one's own immediate area of specialization, but the benefits strike me as far outweighing the risks.

I have cited only a few items published after 2005. This book does not replicate the detailed argumentation of my 2008 article on the mantic family of the Iamidae, since that piece is meant to stand on its own.

I have made every attempt to produce a narrative that will be accessible and interesting to readers who have no special training in classical studies. In particular, I am hoping that those with an interest in other religious systems, both ancient and modern, as well as in the anthropology and sociology of religion more generally, will find something of use and value in this study.

Although I have tried to gloss unusual terms where appropriate, one point of confusion might be my use of the name Lacedaemonian(s) where, less accurately, most modern writers might simply refer to Spartan(s). Although these terms are often used synonymously, the technical difference is that a Spartan (or, more correctly, Spartiate) is a full citizen with voting rights who had passed through a very rigid system of state education, whereas the term Lacedaemonian includes both the Spartiates themselves and the second-class members of their society called *perioeci* (who were freeborn but lacked voting rights). These two groups together formed the "Spartan" army and were collectively known as Lacedaemonians. As someone with a special interest in Spartan history and religion, I thought it best to reflect the usage of our sources.

ABBREVIATIONS

CAH^3 *Cambridge Ancient History.* 3d ed. Cambridge, 1975.

CEG   P. A. Hansen, ed. *Carmina Epigraphica Graeca.* Vol. 2, *Saeculi IV a.Chr.n.* Berlin and New York, 1989.

CVA   *Corpus Vasorum Antiquorum.*

Diels-Kranz   H. Diels. *Die Fragmente der Vorsokratiker.* 6th ed. Edited by W. Kranz. Berlin, 1952.

EGF   M. Davies, ed. *Epicorum Graecorum Fragmenta.* Göttingen, 1988.

EGM   R. Fowler, *Early Greek Mythography.* Vol. 1, *The Texts.* Oxford, 2000.

FGrH   F. Jacoby, ed. *Die Fragmente der griechischen Historiker.* Berlin and Leiden, 1923–58.

Fornara   C. W. Fornara, ed. and trans. *Archaic Times to the End of the Peloponnesian War.* 2d ed. Cambridge, 1983. [Cited by document number.]

GHI   P. J. Rhodes and Robin Osborne, eds. *Greek Historical Inscriptions, 404–323 B.C.* Oxford, 2003.

HCT   A. W. Gomme, A. Andrewes, and K. J. Dover. *A Historical Commentary on Thucydides.* 5 vols. Oxford, 1945–81.

IEG[2]	M. L. West, ed. *Iambi et Elegi Graeci.* 2d ed. Oxford, 1992.
Kannicht	R. Kannicht, ed. *Tragicorum Graecorum Fragmenta.* Vol. 5, Euripides (in two parts). Göttingen, 2004.
Kassel-Austin	R. Kassel and C. Austin, eds. *Poetae Comici Graeci.* Berlin and New York, 1983–.
LIMC	*Lexicon Iconographicum Mythologiae Classicae.* Zurich, 1981–.
ML	R. Meiggs and D. Lewis, eds. *A Selection of Greek Historical Inscriptions to the End of the Fifth Century B.C.* Oxford, 1969; corr. repr., 1975.
MW	F. Solmsen, ed. *Hesiodi Theogonia, Opera et Dies, Scutum.* R. Merkelbach and M. L. West, eds. *Fragmenta Selecta.* 3d ed. Oxford, 1990.
RE	A. von Pauly, G. Wissowa, and W. Kroll, eds. *Realencyclopädie der classischen Altertumswissenschaft.* Stuttgart, 1893–1980.
SEG	*Supplementum Epigraphicum Graecum.* Amsterdam, 1923–.
Smyth	H. W. Smyth. *Greek Grammar.* Cambridge, Mass. 1956. [Cited by section number.]

ONE · Problems, Methods, and Sources

Surprising as it may seem, the oracle's replies to
questions are rarely vague. . . . But I suppose that
it would be difficult for any scientific investigation
either to prove or disprove conclusively the validity
of his pronouncements.

HIS HOLINESS THE 14TH THE DALAI LAMA
TENZIN GYATSO, *Freedom in Exile*

One of the reasons for this neglect [by Assyriologists]
is perhaps the extraordinary monotony of the treatises
on divination that make up the principal pieces of the
dossier. But I wonder whether the main reason is not that
divination is considered, consciously or unconsciously,
to be a simple superstition, trivial, outdated, and not
really deserving of attention.

JEAN BOTTÉRO, *Mesopotamia: Writing, Reasoning,
and the Gods*

SETTING THE STAGE

When most of us think of Greek divination, the first thing that comes to mind is the
oracle of Apollo at Delphi, where the Pythia, possessed by the god, delivered oracles while seated on her tripod. Yet as famous as Delphi and the Pythia may be, due
in part to the large role that Delphi plays both in Greek tragedy and in the historical narrative of Herodotus, neither Delphi nor any other oracular center, nor even
all such centers collectively, could have constituted the major access to divination
in Greek society. At Delphi, prophecies were given only on the seventh of each
month, and not at all during the three winter months when Apollo was away.[1] Thus
very few Greeks were in a position to consult Delphi, and any consultations that did
occur needed to be planned out well in advance. And even if one appeared on the

---

1. Eur. *Ion* 93; Plut. *Mor.* 292d.

right day and could afford all of the preliminary sacrifices, there was no guarantee that one would get a turn to put one's question. This depended on the number of inquirers, some of whom may have enjoyed *promanteia* (the right of jumping the line). Yet, as we shall see, divination was a major system of knowledge and belief for the Greeks and was practiced in regard to every sort of important question.

So if the Greeks were not constantly making hasty trips to Delphi, how did they access divine knowledge? There were many less prominent oracular sites in Boeotia; but these would have been denied to Athenians during the long periods of war between them and the Boeotians. Greeks from the Peloponnese would also have found the trek to Delphi expensive and inconvenient. The most authoritative oracle in the Peloponnese was at Olympia, and this would have seen heavy use and long lines, especially at the time of the Olympic games. The oracle of Zeus at Dodona in Epirus was located in a remote part of Greece and, moreover, was far from the sea.[2] In any case, the individual who faced an unexpected decision or the commander in the field who wanted to know whether it was a good day to fight needed a more immediate access to divine knowledge and guidance than oracular consultation could possibly provide. This immediate access was provided by the class of individuals known as seers.[3]

The ancient Greek word for "seer" is *mantis,* and the plural is *manteis.* Rather than attempt to introduce a new word into English usage, I will use the translation "seer" throughout this book. Seers played a fundamental role in Greek culture. In fact, their presence was pervasive. We know the names of about seventy "historical" seers (as opposed to mythical/legendary ones), some of whom were individuals of considerable influence. Many more seers are left anonymous by our sources, even when their presence and contribution were crucial to the matters at hand. This anonymity contributes to the false modern sense that seers merely validated decisions that had already been made by their superiors and employers. Part of my task is to restore the seer to his, and her, appropriate place of prominence in archaic and classical Greek society.

This is intended to be an innovative book, but not in the sense of promoting some outlandish thesis or advancing arguments that are based on either a misuse or a par-

---

2. Most of the lead tablets from Dodona, on which inquirers wrote their questions, are written in Northwest Greek, although others are in a variety of dialects. See Parke 1967: 101 and Christidis, Dakaris, and Vokotopoulou 1999: 67–68.

3. A point well made by Parker (2005: 118–19).

tial use of evidence. Rather, this study has as its aim to stimulate further discussion and to place the person of the seer in its appropriate historical context. Seers were far more important in Greek society than the scattered evidence explicitly indicates. They are always lurking just beneath the surface of historical texts; they rear their heads only when they are involved in some extraordinary action. The most famous example is arguably Tisamenus of Elis, the seer who helped the Spartans to win their decisive victory over the Persians at Plataea in 479 B.C.[4] It would have been easy enough for Herodotus to narrate the events of that campaign without ever mentioning the name of Tisamenus or the fact that Plataea was merely the first of five famous victories that he won. How many other seers who played prominent roles in the battles of ancient Greece, as well as in other areas of life, went unmentioned? They make their appearance in Herodotus and Xenophon when their actions seemed unusually noteworthy or when the author had a particular literary or rhetorical purpose in mind.

Various aspects of this subject have been dealt with in articles and monographs, but there has never been a book-length study of Greek seers in any language.[5] Nor has there been a comprehensive and synthetic treatment of Greek divination as a whole since the nineteenth century.[6] This book is about the role and function of seers in Greek society, the techniques of their art, and the system of belief within which they operated. Part of the purpose of this study is to recover as far as possible who seers were and what activities they engaged in. Another purpose, however, is to retrieve the image and representation of the seer. Just as important as what historical seers actually said and did is the way that society imagined the seer and the way in which seers represented themselves. Representation is not always, or even usually, identical with reality, but the relationship between representation and reality can tell us a great deal about a society's values and beliefs. Questions of belief

---

4. Hdt. 9.33–36.

5. The most thorough studies are Kett 1966 (in German and largely a prosopography), Pritchett 1979: 47–90 (very technical), Roth 1982 (a PhD thesis), and Burkert 1992 (on the archaic age). Two often cited articles dealing with seers are Bremmer 1993 and 1996, although I find myself in disagreement with his views. Dillery (2005) makes many interesting suggestions and observations. Parker (2005: 116–22) gives a succinct account of seers at Athens.

6. The most complete study of Greek divination in its various forms is Bouché-Leclercq 1879–82. Volume 1 deals with the various types of divination in Greece. Bloch 1984 and 1991 are very succinct introductions. Dream interpretation is well surveyed by Näf (2004), who provides a comprehensive bibliography on this topic. Johnston (2005) gives a concise survey of the modern study of Greek and Roman divination.

are also important here because belief conditions perception and the perception of a seer's clients in turn necessarily conditioned his own conception of his role.[7]

I am limiting myself principally to the period 800–300 B.C., for that is where most of the evidence lies. The treatment is synthetic, rather than diachronic. We simply do not have the evidence to write an account of Greek religion that posits a devolution of mantic authority from a time when mantic power and royal power were concentrated in the same person, the king, to later periods when the power of the king was divested into a number of less powerful functionaries.[8]

In my attempt to recover what it meant to be a seer and how a seer might represent himself, the following questions will be especially important: How did seers fashion an image for themselves? What kind of image was important? What was the relationship between image making and actual success in one's career? And given that the rituals of divination constituted a type of public performance, how did the seer go about scripting his own role? Our ancient sources do not address these types of questions directly, and so the answers must be inferred through a close reading of texts. Recent work on the anthropology of divination can provide both a theoretical framework and clues for how to read our sources.[9]

One of the most difficult mental exercises that the study of history requires is to think beyond established questions and even beyond the categories of experience and structures of thought that give rise to such questions. Some of the established questions concerning Greek divination are these: Did the Pythia really compose her own verse oracles, and, whatever forms her pronouncements took, were her consultants guided by them in any significant way? Did generals and statesmen really let their strategy and movements be dictated by omens? Did seers influence decision making, or were they merely pawns in the hands of their employers?

The answers to such questions often reveal more about the cultural assumptions of modern historians than about those of the Greeks. And so it is common to be told that the priests at Delphi, who knew the questions in advance, put into verse the inarticulate ramblings of the Pythia; that generals cynically (or at least consciously)

---

7. To adapt what McSweeney (1974: 6) says about priesthood.

8. Halliday (1913: 54–98) argues that the *mantis* is the descendant of the primitive medicine man and that the kings of the legendary past were *manteis*. His book was much influenced by the theory of the development of religion from magic in J. G. Frazer's famous, but now methodologically outdated, *Golden Bough* (first published in 1890 in two volumes, and then expanded into twelve volumes between 1906 and 1915).

9. Especially useful are Peek 1991a, LaGamma 2000, and Pemberton 2000, which explore both the social function of divination and the performative aspects of divinatory rituals.

manipulated the omens to suit their strategic needs or to boost the morale of their troops; and that seers told their employers precisely what they thought they wanted to hear. Since divination is a marginal practice in industrialized Western societies, such questions and answers are formed from the viewpoint that divination must have been an encumbrance to the Greeks, something that rational individuals either had to maneuver around or else had to manipulate for their own interests. Above all, to modern sensibilities, a random and irrational system of divination must not be seen as determining what the elite of the Greek world thought and did. In fact, it has been argued that the elite manipulated divination for their own ends, whether to exploit or to assist the uneducated masses. It is easy enough to validate this prejudice by appealing to the more "rational" segment in Greek society; for instance, by quoting isolated expressions of skepticism, such as the famous line attributed to Euripides that "the best seer is the one who guesses well."[10]

Our own biases can be hard to overcome. As the anthropologist Philip Peek has observed, "the European tradition tends to characterize the diviner as a charismatic charlatan coercing others through clever manipulation of esoteric knowledge granted inappropriate worth by a credulous and anxiety-ridden people." In reference to divination in sub-Saharan Africa he concludes: "Instead, we have found diviners to be men and women of exceptional wisdom and high personal character."[11] I am convinced that if we could go back in time and conduct the sort of fieldwork that a contemporary anthropologist is able to engage in, we undoubtedly would find that Peek's observation would hold true for the Greek seer as well.

The focus of this book is on how divination functioned as a respected access to knowledge both for individuals and for communities in the Greek world, and, in particular, on the role of the seers in making divination a viable and useful social practice. The practitioners, the seers, were not marginal characters on the fringe of Greek society. They were not like the mediums and palm readers in modern Western cities who generally inhabit the fringe both spatially and intellectually, and who ply their trade in the seedy sectors of the urban landscape. Rather, a significant

---

10. F 973 Kannicht.

11. Peek 1991b: 3. The negative bias of classical scholars is well illustrated by Lateiner (1993), who conflates seers, magicians, sorcerers, healers, and mediums under the general designation "preternaturalists." His study is further undermined by his transparent personal bias that most, if not all, such individuals were self-consciously fraudulent: he calls them "con-men" who sought to profit from the suffering of the spiritually and physically needy (194). Similarly, many historians have either neglected the historical significance of Native American prophets or dismissed them as sinister charlatans (see Nabokov 2002: 222–23).

proportion of them were educated members of the elite, who were highly paid and well respected. There were, to be sure, practitioners of a lower order; but the seers who attended generals and statesmen were often the wealthy scions of famous families. They were at the center of Greek society.

One question that I cannot address has to do with the objective truth of divination. Yet the questions "Can divination function effectively?" and "Can it accurately predict the future?" are actually quite distinct. A system of divination within a particular system of belief can work very well for its constituency, for divination is "a system of knowledge in action,"[12] which is a different, but not necessarily less valid, way of knowing than that of Western science. So divination can be a useful source of knowledge and a highly effective means of decision making without it also being, in Western scientific terms, an objectively valid system for discovering what is true about the world. In Western intellectual discourse truth is conceived of in terms of knowledge that can be verified by observation.[13] At all cost we must avoid the temptation to call divination "illogical" or "non-rational" simply because it does not adhere to Western positivist scientific principles.[14] The renowned anthropologist E. E. Evans-Pritchard himself shows how easy it is to adapt to other modes of decision making. As he confesses in his seminal study *Witchcraft, Oracles, and Magic among the Azande:* "I always kept a supply of poison for the use of my household and neighbours and we regulated our affairs in accordance with the oracles' decisions. I may remark that I found this as satisfactory a way of running my home and affairs as any other I know of."[15]

There may or may not be supernatural forces that inform the art of the seer; clairvoyance as a psychological attribute may or may not be a characteristic of some individuals. Unfortunately, the truth or falsity of such phenomena cannot be proven. The modern scholar can only reconstruct the claims that seers made for themselves, and what their contemporaries believed about those claims.[16] The famous classical scholar E. R. Dodds, who was in the habit of attending séances,

12. Peek 1991b: 3.
13. Shaw 1991: 137.
14. Peek 1991b: 11. See also Jules-Rosette 1978.
15. 1976: 126 (originally published in 1937).
16. Meier (1994: 509–17) discussses the historian's proper attitude toward reports of miracles. Johnson (1999) demonstrates that David Hume did not disprove the possibility of miracles or the rational credibility of reports of miracles. Moberly 2006 is a controversial attempt to establish criteria for distinguishing between those individuals who merely claim to speak for God and those who truly do.

wrote in his autobiography that he could not tell if the mediums were pretending to be in a state of trance or really were.[17] Even experts can be easily deceived. In 1932 the 13th Dalai Lama ordered the various oracles in Tibet to undergo a personal test, and a commission was formed for that purpose. One old woman went into a trance, answered all of the questions she was asked, and fooled the commission completely. She then confessed: "You see, this is how I make my living. I wasn't in trance, I was making it up."[18] Yet the existence of fake oracles in no way lessened the Tibetan belief in the existence of true ones. In connection with his consultation of the Nechung oracle, the 14th Dalai Lama writes in his autobiography: "Surprising as it may seem, the oracle's replies to questions are rarely vague. As in the case of my escape from Lhasa, he is often very specific. But I suppose that it would be difficult for any scientific investigation either to prove or disprove conclusively the validity of his pronouncements. The same would surely be true of other areas of Tibetan experience, for example the matter of *tulkus* [reincarnate lamas]."[19]

In 1871 the British ethnographer Henry Callaway asserted in a lecture before the Royal Anthropological Institute of Great Britain and Ireland that "there is a power of clairvoyance, naturally belonging to the human mind, or, in the words of a native [Zulu] speaking on this subject, 'there is something which is divination within man.'"[20] Some ancient Greek philosophers, particularly the Peripatetics and Stoics, believed that there was a prophetic element within the human soul that could be stimulated to foresee the future.[21] Such speculations, however, seem to postdate the fifth century B.C. During the archaic and classical periods most Greeks believed that the gods would speak directly through the mouth of a priest or priestess, or else that a religious specialist, who was able to detect and interpret the signs that the gods sent, could ascertain their intentions. Some of those specialists, primarily in myth, were given the gift of second sight, which in some way and to some degree they passed on to their descendants; but no classical author (apart from Plato, who claims

17. 1977: 97–111.

18. Lipsey 2001: 270–71.

19. 1990: 236.

20. 1871–72: 165, 168–69 (for the quotation); cf. Peek 1991b: 23–24. At least one person in the audience, a certain Mr. Dendy, was greatly offended: "The idea of spiritual influence over the true savage was an illusive fallacy, which no man of real science ought for a moment to entertain. . . . The anecdotes of the prophetic clairvoyance of the Kaffirs and the Zulu ought to raise a blush in those who cite them as spiritual phenomena; if we hear nothing from south-eastern Africa more rational, the sooner the district is tabooed the better" (184).

21. Cic. *Div.* 2.100; Plut. *Mor.* 431e–33.

that the liver is the seat of divination) speaks of a prophetic element being present within the soul of every mortal.

Leaving aside the question of its objective validity, can one really know what the majority of Greeks thought about divination? One must say "the majority" because there are always individuals who have views that run counter to popular sentiment. The sixth-century B.C. philosopher Xenophanes of Colophon repudiated divination altogether (Cic. *Div*.1.3.5), but he generally held radical beliefs about the gods. When one looks at the whole range of sources, both in verse and in prose, the picture that emerges is pretty clear. The vast majority of Greeks believed that the gods desired to communicate with mortals, that they did so through signs of various kinds, and that there were religious experts who could correctly interpret those signs. Divination was a primary means of bridging the gap between the known and unknown, the visible and the invisible, the past and the future, and the human and the divine. There were, to be sure, rival means, but none of them ever replaced or eclipsed the central role of divination. Divination was so vitally important to the Greeks that it was included, second only to medicine, among the *technai* (arts, skills, or crafts) that Prometheus gave to humankind. And thus Prometheus boasts in Aeschylus's play *Prometheus Bound* (484–99): "I set in order the many ways of the mantic craft." So too in Euripides' *Suppliants* (195–213), Theseus lists the capacity of seers to explicate the unknown as among the means that the gods gave to mortals for sustaining life.

On occasion, a piece of eyewitness testimony can tell us a great deal about what people were at least represented as thinking. The following two examples are worth considering, even if they date from the first century B.C. and the first century A.D., respectively. Deiotarus, the tetrarch of Gallograecia and king of Lesser Armenia, once told his guest-friend Quintus Cicero that he had abandoned a journey because of the warning given him by the flight of an eagle. Sure enough, the room in which he would have stayed, had he continued his journey, collapsed the very next night. After that he very often abandoned a journey, even if he had been traveling for many days. And even though he later suffered at the hands of Caesar, he did not regret that the auspices (bird signs) favored his joining Pompey in the Civil War that broke out in 49 B.C. He thought that the birds had counseled well, since glory was more important to him than his possessions (Cic. *Div*. 1.26–27). The story of Deiotarus provides a good example both of a genuine faith in the validity of divination and of how the rites of divination, even when proven wrong in the event, cannot easily be discredited in the eyes of a true believer.

Pliny the Younger, writing around A.D. 100, reports in one of his letters (2.20) the machinations of the legacy hunter M. Aquilius Regulus. On one occasion he convinced a wealthy woman, Verania, that she would recover from a serious illness first by forecasting her horoscope and then by confirming the findings through extispicy (the examination of the entrails of a sacrificed animal). She lived just long enough to add Regulus to her will as a legatee. Despite the fact that Regulus duped this woman, he was nonetheless a genuine believer in divination. He boasted to Pliny that when he performed extispicy in order to discover how soon his fortune would reach 60 million sesterces, he discovered that the victim had a double set of entrails, which portended that he would acquire 120 million. This appears to be a clear case of someone who selfishly and consciously manipulated divinatory rites for his own ends and yet also genuinely believed in the validity of those same rites. Although the example comes from Rome and is from a much later period, the psychology revealed must have been, and surely still is, common enough.

METHODOLOGICAL PROBLEMS

There are several dangers inherent in a study of this kind. First of all, since the evidence for seers is fragmentary and must be extracted from an extremely wide variety of sources, there is a temptation to ignore the context in which individual references are imbedded. Thus it is crucial not to rip references to seers out of their literary matrix and then stitch them together out of context, for that is merely to create an artificial construct that is likely to be false in its conclusions. While it is useful to construct this type of artificial narrative in order to make sense of and give order to hundreds of discrete pieces of evidence, it is necessary to be aware of an item's context and logic within its original narrative. Nevertheless, it is by bringing disparate pieces of evidence together that the whole becomes greater than the parts and new insights are gained. It obviously requires a good deal of scholarly discretion to strike the right balance between investigating the context of individual passages in detail and combining several such passages in interesting ways.

Second, because there are significant gaps in our evidence for seers, it is tempting to fill those gaps by recourse to historical and anthropological studies of other societies. These range in time and space from China during the Shang dynasty to contemporary sub-Saharan Africa and include all of the types of divination as practiced in Greece, from burning the hides of animals to spirit possession. The danger in misusing such evidence is obvious; but, if handled properly, there are also real benefits. The parallels between the Delphic Pythia and the Chief State Oracle of Tibet are so striking that it should be possible to enhance our understanding of the former by reference to the fuller documentation for the latter. There are classical scholars who feel uncomfortable with the use of comparative evidence, on the grounds that it is not legitimate to compare the Greeks, who had reached the level of state formation, with so-called primitive peoples who have not. There is an assumption that Greek society was more complex, more sophisticated, and more self-reflective than the societies to which it is compared. Whether that supposition is true or false (and it is surely false when the comparison is with ancient China or twentieth-century Tibet), it does not preclude judicious use of comparative material.[22] I am convinced that ethnographic evidence is relevant precisely because it can be used to flesh out and confirm cultural phenomena that otherwise appear only in a literary context.

Third, it is a commonplace that inquirers into another culture are biased by their own experiences and worldviews, and that this bias inevitably influences both observation and interpretation. In the case of literary texts, and even of monuments, this is not entirely problematic, for texts and monuments have a meaning for each and every reader and viewer that transcends their original meanings. Yet in the study of religion nothing is so pernicious as the projection onto others of one's own beliefs. Ironically, the most perverse form of this is to deny the concept of religious belief altogether to the Greeks by claiming that their religion was exclusively concerned with ritual.[23] Belief was as important an aspect of religion to the ancient Greeks as it is to the adherents of monotheistic religions today—it is just that the Greeks believed in different things.

Belief, of course, is a tricky concept, and competing theories of belief have been, and currently are, held by philosophers.[24] For our purposes, a commonsense

---

22. I have particularly profited from Evans-Pritchard's classic study of the Azande (1937); the commonly cited abridged edition (1976) is useful for students, but much of interest for the study of Greek seers has been omitted. Peek 1991a is fundamental not only for the study of divination in sub-Saharan Africa, but for anthropological theory on divination in general (with criticisms of Evans-Pritchard's methodology). Two useful surveys of divination in world cultures are Caquot and Leibovici 1968 and Loewe and Blacker 1981. Vernant 1974 is a collection of articles surveying divination in antiquity (his own contribution on Greek divination is reprinted in Vernant 1991).

23. See the excellent discussion by Harrison (2000: 18–22), who criticizes Price (1984: 10–11). Price (1999: 45) claims: "Practice not belief is the key, and to start from questions about faith or personal piety is to impose alien values on ancient Greece." Vernant (2001) argues for the inseparability of belief and practice in Greek religion. For a sophisticated and nuanced discussion, with citation of much recent work in anthropology and sociology, see Feeney 1998: 12–46.

24. Saler (2001) surveys the three basic modern theories of belief: the (classical) mental state theory, the disposition theory, and the cognitivist theory. As he points out, however, the line between

definition should suffice. By "belief" I mean both a person's conscious statements concerning religion and his or her unconscious presuppositions.[25] It is also the case that when we say that someone believes something, "we are claiming that that person has a tendency or readiness to act, feel, or think in a certain way under appropriate circumstances."[26] Finally, most of us would surely agree with John Locke that there are degrees of assent: in other words, we hold some beliefs much more strongly than we do others.[27] Yet no matter the precise definition of "belief" that one prefers, it is clear that the Greeks and Romans had strong convictions about the nature and value of divination, and indeed those thinkers who questioned divination's efficacy attempted to demonstrate that what most people "believed" was foolish.

It is important to be explicit about one's methodology, and the methodological stance taken in this study is one common in the anthropology of religion: that is to describe religious beliefs and practices with the minimum of bias and to determine their meaning and social significance.[28] Most important, it is vital to attempt to understand the role of the seer in Greek divination through the culturally determined perceptual filters of the Greeks themselves, especially the filters of those who lived during the fifth and fourth centuries B.C.[29]

Ideally, one should endeavor to enter imaginatively into the socioreligious worldview of the Greeks to the extent that the evidence allows. Anthropologists call this approach to the study of religion one of "neutrality." In this wise, "one approaches religious belief and practice without a specific dogmatic perspective or a concern with the necessary truth of specific manifestations."[30] Yet it must be admitted that the reality invariably falls short of the ideal. Even the observations of

---

these theories is far from sharp. Hahn 1973 is a good introduction to the problem of how to analyze a "belief system."

25. I have borrowed this definition from Harrison (2000: 20).

26. Saler 2001: 54, summarizing the disposition theory of belief.

27. Sperber, in what have proven to be highly influential studies (1996, 1997), argues that there are two fundamental kinds of beliefs: "intuitive beliefs," which are implicitly and rigidly held; and "reflective beliefs," which are explicitly held but with varying degrees of commitment.

28. See, for instance, Evans-Pritchard 1965: 17 and Sharpe 1987: 220–50. Evans-Pritchard 1937 and 1956 and Lienhardt 1961 are justly famous examples of this approach. Bloch (1998) stresses the importance of the anthropologist being a participant observer and of providing an ethnographic account of the conceptualization of a society that makes sense to one's native informants.

29. Sourvinou-Inwood (2003) successfully uses this method to read Greek tragedy. Some of the problems involved in the study of Greek divination are isolated by Karp (1998).

30. Collins 1978: 8–9.

trained anthropologists who study contemporary societies are by no means free from preconceptions, and that holds true not only for Evans-Pritchard, but also for his successors, even if their cultural and professional biases are different from his.[31]

MODERN ATTITUDES
TOWARD GREEK DIVINATION

Although there are some notable exceptions, modern scholars have generally been skeptical of the role of divination in ancient Greece, and various strategies have evolved aimed at devaluing its importance. One such strategy has been to claim that the status and authority of the seer was greater in archaic than in classical Greece, assuming that the emergence of the sophistic movement and of Hippocratic medicine led, of necessity, to the devaluation of divination and its practitioners. It is certainly true that Hippocratic doctors generally attempted to distance themselves from the seers, but it is not so evident that they did so successfully. For instance, in *Regimen in Acute Diseases* (8) the difference between medicine and divination is stressed; yet the author admits that the art of medicine has a bad reputation among laypeople for the very reason that it might appear to them to resemble divination. Indeed, some of the practices and techniques of the Hippocratic doctors were similar to those used in divination, especially in regard to prognosis.[32]

Texts, inscriptions, and images simply do not support the claim that the importance and influence of divination waned in the classical period. Even Plato, who is generally hostile to nonecstatic forms of divination, must admit that "the bearing of the priests and seers is indeed full of pride, and they win a fine reputation because of the magnitude of their undertakings" (*Statesman* 290d). And Aristophanes, although viciously ridiculing the *chrēsmologoi* (the professional collectors and purveyors of oracles), whom his plays depict as being charlatans and frauds, never questions the validity of divination itself. He mocks the oracle books of these men, but he never criticizes oracle centers such as Dodona and Delphi.[33]

Divinatory modes of discourse and ways of thinking existed alongside competing ways of viewing the world. Nonetheless, the evidence is overwhelming that the seers retained their traditional authority throughout the fifth and fourth centuries B.C. Skepticism and doubt existed, and are expressed in both tragedy and comedy, but this

31. See Peek 1991b and Fernandez 1991.
32. See Lloyd 2002: 36–38.
33. Smith 1989 is excellent on this point.

is characteristic of all societies that rely on seers. In other words, many Greeks may have questioned the ability or honesty of individual seers, but very few indeed doubted the validity of divination itself. As Evans-Pritchard notes of the Azande, although many of them say that the majority of witch doctors are liars whose sole concern is to acquire wealth, there is no one who does not believe in witchdoctorhood.[34] This type of doubt acts as a kind of escape valve. If a particular diviner was proven wrong, it was because he did not practice his art well: the failure of the individual practitioner does not undermine or disprove the system as a whole.

It is pretty clear that modern attempts to devalue the importance both of divination and of seers are bound up with a teleological view of the development of religion, that somehow divination is a primitive, prerational practice that continued to exist alongside more sophisticated beliefs. It is not essential to my own view of the importance of divination that such a teleological view be abandoned altogether, since different modes of thought, which may correspond to different stages of cognitive development, can coexist both within the same culture and even within the same individual.[35] Nonetheless, I believe that it is misleading to see divination as primitive.[36] Both its operation and its theoretical underpinning can be very sophisticated, and it can be as successful in helping both states and individuals to make decisions as allegedly more sophisticated methods (such as scientific and economic models that often prove wrong, or the various political ideologies of the last century). Far from being irrational, divination is actually an attempt to extend the range of the rational, to encompass things within our range of knowledge that cannot otherwise be known.[37] Thus there is no contradiction or disjunction here between so-called rational and irrational ways of understanding the world.[38] Rather, in the context of divination, they are sympathetic and supplementary ways of viewing the workings of the world and the place of human experience within it.[39]

34. 1976: 112–13.

35. See esp. Barnes 2000.

36. Nor do I believe that one can draw a distinction between so-called world religions (e.g., Judaism, Christianity, and Islam) and primitive or primal religions. For salient objections to such a categorization, see Bowie 2000: 25–28. In any case, divination is present in almost every religious tradition known to us.

37. As Vernant (1991: 308) points out, divination is a technique claiming to apply human reason to the interpretation of signs sent by the gods.

38. See Beattie 1966 and 1967 and especially the seminal study of Horton 1967 (repr. in Horton 1993). Note also Fortes 1987: 15.

39. Burkert 2005.

Furthermore, even if one is not convinced by this line of argument and insists that it is irrational to resort to divination when faced with uncertainty, it is still the case that the interpretation of oracles and signs is an eminently rational exercise. The interpretation of oracles in particular depends on the application of human intelligence, and the Greeks were in the habit of applying careful and logical arguments in their analysis of an oracle's meaning.[40] Since many Delphic oracles were ambiguous and expressed in metaphorical language, interpretation was difficult and intellectually demanding. An important feature of the Croesus story in Herodotus is that this Lydian king accepted oracles at face value (with disastrous results); the implication is that a Greek inquirer would have, or at least should have, known better. Even the most apparently straightforward oracular predictions require interpretation by the inquirer. In sum, even though divination may seem irrational, the interpretation of signs, omens, and oracles is a rational activity.

SOURCES

When it comes to sources, the natural temptation is to turn to the historians first, and then to the tragedians. But as we shall see, it is only by making all of the various genres of Greek literature work together, including inscriptions and material evidence, that real progress can be made. The end result should be a symphony in which each instrument makes its own contribution to the overall effect. In most cases there is a complex interplay between the logic of divination and the story logic of our texts. Homer, Herodotus, the tragedians, all manipulate divination so as to make it conform to their own authorial voice and the needs of their story. And so they are not a mirror that exactly reflects the practices of divination and the personae of seers; yet they do refract attitudes and methods that must have had resonance for their audiences. This interplay between representation and reality is subtle and not always easy for us to analyze.

It will cause no surprise that Herodotus's *Histories* is one of the most important sources for the role and function of the Greek seer. Herodotus names six different seers in book 9 alone, as opposed to only four in our other most informative source, Xenophon's *Anabasis*. Herodotus, moreover, tells us a great deal about three of them: Tisamenus of Elis, Hegesistratus (the Greek seer hired by the Persians) also from Elis, and Euenius of Apollonia. Although legendary seers such as Melampus

---

40. See Price 1985: 184. See further chapter 8.

and Teiresias were more famous, Tisamenus of Elis was arguably the most successful seer of historical times.[41]

Despite the importance of Herodotus, I would place him second to another author. When anthropologists study an alien culture, apart from themselves participating in and observing firsthand various rituals and activities, they consult native informants, individuals who are inside the system and who can at least attempt to explain that system in its own terms. This luxury is obviously denied to those who study cultures that exist only in the past. The closest that we can come to a native informant is the Athenian Xenophon, who describes his own experience of many varieties of divination in his *Anabasis*. In 401 B.C. he accompanied the younger Cyrus in his attempt to become King of Persia, and when he and his fellow mercenaries were stranded in the heart of the Persian Empire, Xenophon became one of the leaders who conducted them back to Asia Minor.

To all appearances Xenophon was a man of conventional, but deep, piety. In his narrative of these events, his *Anabasis*, he recounts his own personal experience of each of the major forms of Greek divination: his consultation of the Delphic oracle, a dream that was sent to him by Zeus, his use of sacrificial divination (extispicy) and of bird signs (augury), and the occurrence of chance omens. No one can report their own experiences without some degree and type of bias, and Xenophon was certainly concerned to justify both the decisions that he made and the actions that he took during the course of the expedition. To be sure, some modern scholars have suspected that Xenophon self-consciously uses divination in order to justify actions that either at the time or later exposed him to various accusations of wrongful conduct.[42] However that may be, for our purposes doubts about Xenophon's motives, or even about what he actually did at the time, do not undermine one central fact— he thought that divination would be a sufficient explanation and justification for his actions in the eyes of his intended audiences.[43]

Nonetheless, Xenophon's piety seems genuine enough, and his experience of the divinatory acts that he reports is firsthand.[44] This is in contrast to the reports of div-

41. A succinct treatment of seers and oracles in Herodotus is given by Lévy (1997). For seers in Herodotus book 9 see Flower and Marincola 2002; and for Tisamenus see further Flower 2008a.

42. So, most emphatically, Dürrbach 1893.

43. As Parker (2004: 137) well observes: "According to Dürrbach, large tracts of the work are little better than self-serving fiction. But to secure whatever apologetic aims he may have had, Xenophon must surely have needed to be at least plausible."

44. On religion in Xenophon, see Nilsson 1967: vol. 1, 787–91; Anderson 1974: 34–40; Dillery 1995: 179–94; Bowden 2004; and Parker 2004.

ination in most of our other historical sources, including Herodotus. All of them surely had personal experience of divination, but they were not always eyewitnesses of the examples that they mention in their texts. By reading and analyzing Xenophon's narrative of his own divinatory experiences we come as close as is now possible to observing a native informant. It is obviously not the same sort of experience as observing a rite of divination for ourselves; nonetheless, we would be much the poorer without Xenophon's vivid testimony.

Sometimes even a chance remark that Xenophon makes can open up a whole vista of possibilities for the imagination. Such is the case when he mentions in the *Anabasis* that when he was traveling from Ephesus to Sardis in 401 to meet up with Cyrus the Younger, he was being escorted by a seer who interpreted for him the omen of an eagle sitting on his right (6.1.23). One wonders, How usual was it for a wealthy Greek to travel with a seer? Was this an idiosyncrasy of the pious Xenophon, or was a seer a regular, if for us usually invisible, member of an aristocrat's entourage? Above all, Xenophon provides confirmation that seers did not merely provide moral support and strengthen a person's resolve to do what he had already decided upon doing. He also confirms for us that through their advice and predictions, seers could significantly influence what people, both collectively and individually, determined to do in the first place.

By contrast with his predecessor Herodotus and his continuator Xenophon, Thucydides had little interest in divination and mentions seers (with the exception of 6.69.2) only when their advice leads to disaster.[45] Thucydides' skepticism comes out most clearly in his statement that the only oracle to have proven true about the Peloponnesian War was that it would last for "thrice nine years" (5.26.3).[46] In the three places where Thucydides uses the word *manteis* (seers), he never deigns to mention a seer by name; they are anonymous and referred to in the plural. This omission is deliberate, since we know from Plutarch that individual seers played prominent roles in the Peloponnesian War. Thucydides, it is essential to realize, and not Herodotus or Xenophon, is the exception that proves the rule.

From later citations, it is apparent that the lost historians, Ephorus of Cyme,

45. At 6.69.2, when describing a hoplite battle between the Syracusans and Athenians in 415, he merely says: "The seers brought forward the customary *sphagia* [the pre-battle sacrifice]." Thucydides' neglect of religious matters is well discussed by Hornblower (1992). On the controversial question of Thucydides' belief, or lack thereof, in oracles, see Marinatos 1981; Jordan 1986; Dover 1988; Hornblower 1991: 206, 270, 307; and Bowden 2005: 73–77.

46. Cf. 2.47.4; 2.54.1–3; 5.103.2.

Theopompus of Chios, Callisthenes of Olynthus (all writing in the fourth century B.C.), and Timaeus of Tauromenium (late fourth–early third century B.C.) gave prominence to omens and portents, especially at critical moments. As Polybius (12.23.4) said of Timaeus, "his history is full of dreams, portents, and incredible tales."[47] The same also seems to have been true of the other "fragmentary" historians listed above.[48] It does not follow that these historians simply made up portents and omens as the fancy struck them. Rather, it was the case that they (unlike Thucydides) reflect the tendency to perceive omens in times of crisis that was so pervasive in Greek culture. Yet even if some stories of seers and portents are fictitious embellishments designed to add drama to the events, they still throw light, in the same way that Greek tragedy does, on the image of the seer in Greek thought and imagination. Thus no piece of evidence can be lightly dismissed. These historians are known primarily through paraphrase by later authors, among whom Plutarch and Diodorus Siculus are the ones most often used in this study. Plutarch seems to have taken a particular interest in manifestations of the divine via oracles, omens, portents, dreams, and apparitions.[49] Although Plutarch creatively adapted his source material according to his own interests and purposes, he did not add incidents of his own invention.[50]

Tragedy, by its very nature, is a genre in which calamities befall individuals, and the gods and their oracles play a role in the narrative logic of the play. It should not, therefore, be surprising that the dark, unpredictable, and dangerous side of divination is central in these plays. But this in no way demonstrates that most, or even any, members of a play's audience felt a significant level of anxiety about the reliance of Greek society on divination. In other words, even though Greek tragedy consciously problematizes Greek divinatory rituals, in every play the seers and oracles are validated, and those who ridicule them are destroyed.

Nonetheless, it is striking that, despite their infallibility, the rituals of divination

---

47. Or as Pearson (1987: 211–12) has written of Timaeus, he "does not usually let an expedition set out without an omen of success or disaster." For his religious beliefs, see Schepens 1994.

48. See, for instance, Plut. *Dion* 54.5–7, deriving from Theopompus (*FGrH* 115, F 331) on the signs that appeared to Dion and Dionyius II. For Callisthenes, see Pearson 1960: 33–38; and for Theopompus, Flower 1994: 70–71.

49. A standard treatment of religious themes in Plutarch is Brenk 1977. Plutarch's attitude toward divination is examined by Opsomer (1996).

50. Pelling 2002 is fundamental for an understanding of Plutarch's historical method. Bosworth (2003) argues that secondary sources did not add bogus "facts" to the primary sources that they employed in writing their own histories. That is, they did not engage in self-conscious fiction.

are consistently depicted as sinister and destructive. In the *Oedipus Tyrannus*, Apollo directs Laius, Oedipus, and Jocasta to their deaths.[51] Although it may be true that Thebes, where the action of this play takes place, is represented as a kind of "anti-Athens" in Athenian tragedy,[52] Apollo's oracle plays no less a dubious role in Aeschylus's *Libation Bearers*, where Orestes claims (269–84) that Apollo directed him to kill his mother. But to what degree does this reflect popular attitudes toward divination? Does the divination of Greek tragedy bear any relation to the practices and beliefs of real life?

The interpretative difficulty here lies in the fact that one function of tragedy is to destabilize and problematize popular religious beliefs.[53] Indeed, religious exploration is one of the main characteristics of tragedy. If the tragedians' view of the destructiveness of divination were the dominant one, no one would have had recourse to divination in real life. Greeks would not have gone to Delphi if they thought that there was a realistic chance of being told that they would kill their fathers and bed their mothers. Yet they still could believe, however remote the possibility, that Apollo was capable of delivering that sort of prophecy. The playwrights exploit this anxiety about the supernatural for their own dramatic purposes. This is far from saying that the average theatergoer thought that his own life was similar to that of the characters of tragic myth; but it is to say that divinatory rites could be deemed dangerous in that they had the potential to release forces that could not always be controlled or negotiated. It is dangerous to practice divination because, even though it can extend the range of one's knowledge, it can also lead one to ruin. There are some things that are better left unknown because once known they cannot be controlled. As paradoxical as it may seem, it is their becoming known that gives them their efficacy. Tisamenus of Elis went to Delphi to ask about having children; he was told that he would win the five greatest "contests" (i.e., "victories"); the first of those victories was over the Persians at Plataea. Would history have been different if Tisamenus had not consulted Delphi in the first place?

Tragedy is cathartic in that one sees one's worst fears being played out on the stage. In a society in which divination was an integral part of religious experience, the invalidation of divine signs would undermine one's entire belief in the divine order. It is difficult for us to imagine this because divination in Western society lies

---

51. On Apollo's role in bringing destruction to the Theban royal household through his oracles, see Bowden 2005: 53–54.

52. So Zeitlin 1986 and Bowden 2005: 53–54; but note the reservations of Easterling (1989: 11–14).

53. See Sourvinou-Inwood 2003: esp. 1–14.

on the fringe of religious experience; its validity or lack of validity does not affect our view of the relations between the human and the divine. The practice of divination can have unforeseen consequences, but even the fear of such consequences was not as unsettling for the Greeks as the fear of discovering that the whole system was fallacious. That explains the outburst of the chorus in the *Oedipus Tyrannus* when it is faced with the possibility that the oracles given to Laius will prove false (898–910). The chorus is so psychologically invested in its system of religious beliefs and practices that it would rather that Laius had been killed by his own son, as Apollo had long ago predicted that he would be, than by a stranger.

Nevertheless, it is significant that the seers of high literature (epic and tragedy), such as Amphiaraus and Teiresias are always proven right, while the seers of comedy are always wrong.[54] At one level of explanation, this reflects a difference in genre. Comedy takes aim at contemporary seers; it seeks to make fun of them just as it makes fun of prominent orators and generals. Such criticism should not be taken too seriously. On the other hand, the fact that the seers of tragedy always prove their detractors wrong and emerge as skilled, knowledgeable, and accurate must also be put into context. Teiresias is attacked by Oedipus in the *Oedipus Tyrannus*, by Creon in the *Antigone*, and by Pentheus in the *Bacchae*. The advice of Amphiaraus is ignored, to their loss, by Adrastus in the *Suppliants* and by Tydeus in the *Seven against Thebes*. Yet it has been well observed that criticisms of seers in tragedy "reveal considerably more about how we are to judge the critics than the seers."[55] Or to put it the other way around, Teiresias and Amphiaraus, by the conventions of Greek myth, were beyond reproach, and any who would doubt them were marked for failure.

Yet the situation is more complicated than this, because literature does not only reflect life in various ways; it can also influence it. The real-life seers of the fifth and fourth centuries, who knew of the seers of high literature, might be expected to model their behavior accordingly. I am suggesting that historical seers modeled themselves on those of epic and tragic poetry, in what we might call a self-characterizing construction of their own personae. Thus at the battle of Plataea Tisamenus of Elis played the part of Calchas, and, a generation earlier, Euenius of Apollonia became a second Teiresias. I think that it would be wrong to assert that it was Herodotus himself who forced them into that mold, because this tendency is confirmed by other types of evidence. And as for the employers of seers, they might not have expected

54. Parker 1983: 15.
55. Mikalson 1991: 100.

to hire someone with the precise skills of Amphiaraus or Melampus, but they might well have believed that somewhere individuals existed who had similar mantic abilities. Indeed, one point in a seer claiming to be a descendant of Iamus or Melampus was that he somehow shared in the abilities of his family's progenitor.

The way that cultural norms are depicted in any given work of literature depends on the conventions of a particular genre as well as on the literary aims and personal beliefs of an individual author.[56] A work of literature, no matter if the genre is poetic or historical, can never give a direct window onto reality. Historical reality is always mediated through, and so necessarily distorted by, the work that represents it. The direct access that Evans-Pritchard had to Zande rituals and attitudes is denied us (and he was not an impartial observer); rather, we must make inferences and draw conclusions from texts that themselves problematize Greek divinatory rituals. Literary texts may reflect social reality in a more or less indirect way, but they also scrutinize it, whether to confirm, challenge, or deconstruct social norms. Even so, it may be asked whether, as a general rule, the relation between representation and actual experience is the same for prose texts as for poetic texts. It is here assumed that the depiction of divination and seers in epic and tragedy is not mere literary convention, and that the seers of poetry were recognizable types to their contemporary audiences. So too for comedy: although comic representation distorts and exaggerates social roles, the exaggeration and distortion must be of a type that has a resonance for the audience. Comedy ridicules seers for characteristics and propensities that most of the audience would have recognized; in other words, the irony, satire, and ridicule require a recognizable type for their target.

In sum, as far as source material is concerned, the greatest challenge facing a study of this kind is that the evidence is to be found in every genre and species of Greek literature: epic, tragedy, comedy, lyric, philosophy, oratory, and history, as well as in inscriptions. Material evidence, in the form of vase painting and sculpted image, also has something important to contribute. Each of these media has its own rules and conventions, each speaks different languages (semantically/linguistically, rhetorically, and visually), and each has different concerns and audiences.[57] It is the

56. See the brief, but excellent, discussion by Parker (1983: 12–17), who notes "the crucial influence of a literary work's genre in determining the religious emphasis it contains" (15).

57. Mikalson (1991: 88–95) draws a sharp dichotomy between the religion of tragedy and that of "real life" (which is reflected in prose authors), whereas, at the other extreme, Bowden (2003) indiscriminately combines evidence from tragedy and prose authors. Struck (2003: 172) sensibly takes a middle ground, pointing out that even legendary incidents "are reliable evidence for how divination operated in the thought world of the Greeks."

task of the scholar to engage these genres both individually and collectively, and to tease them into a dialogue with each other. Yet as difficult and problematic as this may seem, there are indeed places where the testimony of tragedy, epic, historical writing, oratory, and inscriptions does coalesce. This is not to say that this agreement necessarily can tell us what the seer was like in real life; but, as we shall see, it does tell us that there were important aspects of the image of the seer that were not genre-specific and that reflect a broad cultural stereotype.

The topic of the Greek *mantis* rests at the cusp of literature and history. This is true for two reasons, one of which is obvious and the other, being more profound, is not. It should be obvious that one must use both verse texts and prose texts in conjunction: that is, tragedies, comedies, and epic poems, as well as histories, orations, and inscriptions. But the more profound reason has to do with the symbiotic relationship between literature on the one hand and real life on the other. The poets who depicted Teiresias and Calchas on stage or in epic had before them the seers of real life; and those seers, in turn, were surely influenced in how they acted and presented themselves by the famous seers of Greek myth. So art imitated life, and life art, and for that reason one can draw no easy distinction between the religious activity of literature and that of everyday life, between literary religion and practiced religion.

TWO · Who Is a Seer?

> So you have chosen to study Divination, the most diffi-
> cult of all magical arts. I must warn you at the outset that
> if you do not have the Sight, there is very little I will be
> able to teach you. Books can take you only so far in this
> field. It is a Gift granted to few.
>
> PROFESSOR TRELAWNEY in J. K. Rowling,
> *Harry Potter and the Prisoner of Azkaban*

A seer (*mantis*) was a professional diviner, an expert in the art of divination. There
is no exact modern equivalent, since he or she combined the role of confidant and
personal adviser with that of psychic, fortune-teller, and homeopathic healer. Yet
this comparison is rather misleading, for seers, as we shall see, did not presume to
"tell the future," nor did they claim to possess a "paranormal" power that was independent of a god's inspiration or dispensation. Since Greek religious terminology
is inexact, the person called a *mantis* dealt with a broad range of religious activities—anything that a freelance religious expert might be expected to handle. The
term also embraces an array of prophetic types, ranging from the upper-class professionals who accompanied generals on campaign to the possessed mediums at
oracular sites to street-corner purifiers and dream interpreters. Despite the fact that
both might lay claim to divine inspiration, there was no stage in Greek society in
which the poet (*aoidos*) and the seer (*mantis*) were undifferentiated.[1] They always
performed different functions and had very different social roles.

The Greek word *mantis* is variously translated as "prophet," "diviner," "sooth-
sayer," and, as I prefer, "seer." Terminology is important, even if assigning names

---

1. The claim of Nagy (1990) that the word *mantis* had once been an appropriate designation for
an undifferentiated poet-prophet is unsupported by linguistic usage and runs counter to the historical circumstances of the transmission of divination from the ancient Near East to Greece.
Already in Homer, as Nagy himself points out, poet and prophet are distinct occupations.

is not a neutral activity. By choosing the English word "seer" I am giving preference to one set of cultural images over another. Nonetheless, consistency is vital, since to the Greekless reader the pervasiveness of the Greek *mantis* in texts of every genre is concealed by the variety of terms used in English to translate this single Greek word. There are, however, two exceptions to my use of "seer." Anthropologists, as well as biblical scholars and Assyriologists, employ the term "diviner" when referring to the practitioners of technical, noninspirational divination (in contradistinction to figures whom they call "prophets"). Thus I have used the word "diviner" when discussing studies in those fields. Also, at the end of this chapter, when I contrast the seer with other "religious" types, I need to resort to the Greek word *mantis* in order to explicate the distinctions in our sources.

What does the word *mantis* actually mean? Etymologically, *mantis* derives from the Indo-European root *men and means "one who is in a special mental state" or "one who speaks from an altered state."[2] Plato was probably correct in connecting *mantis* with *mania* (madness), which also comes from the root *men and means "a special mental state." Thus the *mantis* is one who is in a special state of inspiration. To judge from the etymology, therefore, a *mantis* was originally a person who prophesied in an altered state of consciousness. Although there are other words in Greek that denote a seer (Homer, for instance, also uses *theopropos* and *thuoskoos*), *mantis* is by far the dominant term. Those other words, moreover, seem to be nearly synonymous with *mantis*. In the same sentence Aeschylus (*Sept.* 609–11) calls Amphiaraus both *prophētēs* and *mantis*, and these titles are likewise used by Pindar (*Nem.* 1.61–62) of Teiresias.

By the classical period, the seer was also said to practice what the Greeks called a *technē*, the general word for "art," "craft," or "skill." This art was called "the art of divination" (*mantikē technē*).[3] Yet the notion that the seer was the practitioner of a specialized craft emerges as early as Homer. In a list of *dēmioergoi* (literally, "workers for the community") at *Odyssey* 17.381–85, we find seer, doctor, carpenter, and inspired singer. These *dēmioergoi* are socially mobile "public workers" who travel from one *dēmos* (village) to another, and are sought after because of their specialized skills. Yet seercraft (*mantikē*) was not, like carpentry, a skill that just anyone could acquire and then hope to find gainful employment. Rather, like the singer who takes his inspiration from the Muses, a seer is the specialist to whom a god has

2. So Nagy 1990 and Maurizio 1995: 70. See also Chantraine 1974: vol. 3, 665, s.v. μάντις; Casevitz 1992; and Dillery 2005: 168–69. Roth (1982: 9–18) surveys the scholarship on this question.
3. For the term, see Aes. *PV* 484; Soph. *OT* 709; Hdt. 2.49, 83.

granted prophetic insight. And thus Solon, when writing of the different professions of mankind, observes "another has been made a seer by lord Apollo."[4]

In the Greek world a seer, who operated by a combination of skill and charismatic inspiration, was the most authoritative expert on religious matters. Seers were religious specialists, or "agents of control within their religion's symbolic universe."[5] Their competence was exceptionally broad, encompassing all of the various forms of divination that are found in our literary sources. These methods include the interpretation of the movements, behavior, and cries of birds (augury) and the interpretation of dreams and of portents (such as lightning, thunder, earthquakes, eclipses, and any unusual occurrences). The seer also examined the entrails of a sacrificial animal for marks and abnormalities of various kinds (extispicy), as well as interpreting the results of burning the entrails (empyromancy). As will be discussed more fully later on, in warfare two types of sacrifical divination were of immense importance: one was the campground sacrifice (called *hiera*), and the other was the battle-line sacrifice (called *sphagia*). Performing *hiera* entailed examining the victim's entrails, especially the liver (the "victim" was usually a sheep), whereas performing *sphagia* consisted of slitting the victim's throat (often a young she-goat) while observing its movements and the flow of blood. Ecstatic utterance was less common, but we shall see some examples of it.

And finally, there was spirit possession. This was chiefly, but not exclusively, associated with oracular centers, such as Delphi. Although the Pythia was the preeminent practitioner of so-called natural divination in the Greek world, there were other men and women who prophesied while being possessed by a god. All of them were "seers," for the term *mantis* is applied by the poet Aeschylus to the Pythia as well as to Cassandra.[6] The Sibyls too were *manteis*.[7] Herodotus (2.55) calls the priestesses of the oracle of Zeus at Dodona in northern Greece *promanties*. Elsewhere Herodotus (8.135) uses the terms *promantis* and *prophētēs* synonymously to refer to the male prophet of the oracle of Apollo Ptous in Thebes.

Modern scholars are well aware that all of the various types of divination practiced in Greece, including extispicy, had originated in the ancient Near East and

---

4. *IEG²* vol. 2, Solon 13.53.

5. Rüpke 1996.

6. *Eum.* 29 and *Ag.* 1275.

7. Suda, s.v. Sibyla Chaldaia: "*Sibylla* is a Roman word, interpreted as "prophetess," or rather "seer" (*mantis*); hence female seers (*mantides*) were called by this one name."

probably arrived in Greece between the eighth and sixth century B.C.[8] Yet this is completely unknown to classical authors. In Aeschylus, it is the culture hero, Prometheus, who "was the originator of every skill (*technē*)" and "who set in order the many ways of the art of divination (*mantikē*)."[9] The poet Hesiod, in his lost epics *Melampodia* and *Greater Ehoiai*, told how Melampus, the most famous of all mythical seers, had learned the language of birds when two snakes licked his ears,[10] and also perhaps that he obtained from Apollo the art of divination from sacrifices.[11] Herodotus, for his part, seems to have rationalized such stories: he says (2.49) that Melampus was a wise man who "acquired the art of divination for himself" and that he introduced the Egyptian cult of Dionysus into Greece, having learned of it from Cadmus the Phoenician. Elsewhere Herodotus claims that the oracle of Zeus at Dodona was founded by a priestess from Egyptian Thebes, and he claims that divination from sacrifices (e.g., extispicy) came to Greece from Egypt (2.57). No Greek source mentions a Near Eastern origin or source for any method of Greek divination. They conceived of their divinatory rites as either being homegrown or else, if mythological versions had to be rationalized, as being an Egyptian import.

It is a striking feature of fifth- and fourth-century seers that they do not primarily perform the type of divination that is found in the Homeric epics. In the *Iliad* (1.69), Calchas is "by far the best of bird interpreters"; yet bird signs play only a minor role in historical texts, and sacrificial divination does not appear in Homer at all.[12] From at least the last quarter of the sixth century onward, the primary expertise of the Greek seer was hepatoscopy, or divination by inspection of the liver, this being the most common form of extispicy, which is divination by inspection of an animal's entrails.

Extispicy probably was the last of the major types of divination to reach Greece from the Near East. I am careful to say "probably," because it is possible that Homer does not mention this form of divination for literary reasons; looking at a liver is certainly not as dramatic or vivid as the unusual actions of eagles or serpents that often portend important outcomes in the *Iliad* and *Odyssey*. On the other hand, it should cause no surprise that every variety of divination did not arrive at once.

8. West 1997: 46–51.

9. *PV* 477, 484.

10. Hes. F 261 MW.

11. Apollodorus (1.9.11) alone mentions the agency of Apollo.

12. On bird augury, see esp. Bouché-Leclercq 1879–82: vol. 1, 127–45; Stengel 1920: 57–59; Dillon 1996; and Baumbach and Trampedach 2004.

Indeed, the cross-cultural study of divination demonstrates that systems of divination are particularly permeable to external influences.[13] Images on vases confirm what the study of Homer suggests. Depictions of a warrior examining entrails appear on nineteen black-figure and on three red-figure Attic vases dating from the last quarter of the sixth century and the first quarter of the fifth century B.C. (that is, from c. 525 to 475 B.C.).[14]

Most scholars have underestimated the role of "divine inspiration" (whether feigned, real, or imagined) in the seer's performance of divinatory rituals. They do so by considering it a literary conceit or by drawing too sharp a distinction between so-called natural divination (such as ecstatic prophecy and spirit possession) and technical, artificial divination (such as extispicy and augury).[15] Also, far too much emphasis has been placed on the story of Thrasyllus, a Siphnian, who was bequeathed books on divination by his guest-friend the seer Polemaenetus. With those books in hand, he became an itinerant seer and acquired a huge fortune, eventually becoming the wealthiest of the Siphnians. All of this is reported thirdhand some fifty years later by the speaker of Isocrates' forensic speech *Aegineticus* (5–7). This narrative, of course, does not tell us how Thrasyllus might have represented himself to potential clients. He certainly would not have admitted to having learned everything he knew about divination from books that he had acquired essentially by chance.

Isocrates' *Aegineticus*, moreover, is not as good evidence as scholars are inclined to think. The story of Thrasyllus supports the speaker's own case and, in any event, would have been completely unverifiable on the island of Aegina, where the trial took place.[16] The story provides a precedent for the very type of transfer of property that the speaker is defending, and for that reason alone it should not be accepted uncritically. Indeed, near the end of the speech we are given a slightly different version of the relationship between the two men, when the speaker says that Thrasyllus "learned his art from Polemaenetus the seer" (45). This detail perhaps suggests that Polemaenetus had actually adopted Thrasyllus, treated him as his apprentice, and *personally* taught him the art of divination. Thrasyllus, for his part, could then have represented himself as Polemaenetus's biological son and thus as the

---

13. See Shaw 1998.

14. See van Straten 1995: 156–57, and the fuller discussion in chapter 3.

15. For example, Nock 1972: 539; Pritchett 1979: 73; and Parker 2005: 120.

16. Dickie (2001: 68–71), for instance, takes the narrative at face value, apart from his suggestion that Thrasyllus actually had been Polemaenetus's apprentice.

inheritor of his special mantic insight (the importance of heredity will be discussed below). He may even have been his illegitimate son—a fact that the speaker of *Aegineticus* would have wished to suppress. This would not be surprising, since we are told that Thrasyllus himself was a womanizer who had a number of illegitimate children in different Greek cities, and it is conceivable that seers were in a unique position to have families in more than one community. In any case, given his extraordinary success as a seer for hire, this Thrasyllus must have been an individual of tremendous personal charisma who was able to convince others that he possessed unique knowledge and abilities.

The expertise of the Greek seer extended beyond divination and included healing and purification. In effect, a seer could deal with any situation that fell under the broad rubric of things sent or caused by a supernatural power. The archetypal seer was the legendary Melampus, who acted as diviner, healer, and purifier. He obtained part of the kingdom of Argos as his price for curing the Argive women of their madness (see fig. 1).[17] The tradition about the philosopher Empedocles and the wonder-worker Epimenides is too unreliable for us to determine if they called themselves seers, but it seems certain that they practiced rites of purification and healing.

That seers had such a wide sphere of competence, including healing and purification, was certainly the case in the archaic age,[18] and was still true (although perhaps to a lesser degree) in the fifth and fourth centuries.[19] In Aeschylus's *Eumenides*, which was produced in 458 B.C., the Pythia refers (61–63) to Apollo as "healer-seer (ἰατρόμαντις), interpreter of omens (τερασκόπος), and purifier (καθάρσιος)," mirroring in a sense what mortal seers could do; for these titles encompass their three primary functions as healers, diviners, and purifiers. In Xenophon's *Anabasis*, we find the seers, with Xenophon's approval, recommending a purification of the army after a period of internal dissension.[20]

By the late fifth century those who attempted to heal with "purifications and

---

17. See Hes. *Catalogue of Women* F 37, 131 MW; Pherecydes, *FGrH* 3, F 114 = *EGM* F, 114; Acusilaus, *FGrH* 2, F 28 = *EGM* F, 28; Hdt. 9.34; Bacchyl. 10.44–56; Apollod. 2.2.2; Diod. 2.68.4; and Paus. 2.18.4.

18. Burkert 1992: 42–73.

19. See Pl. *Rep.* 364b–e and Hippoc. *Diseases of Women* 1; *pace* Parker 1983: 207–34.

20. 5.7.35. In Macedonia there seems to have been an annual rite of military purification (Curt. 10.9.11; Livy 40.6). There is no such evidence for Greece, and the purification of an army probably took place in connection with a serious incident, such as plague or mutiny. For discussion and evidence, see Pritchett (1979: 196–202), who, however, pushes the slight evidence for Boeotia (Plut. *Mor.* 290d) and Crete too far.

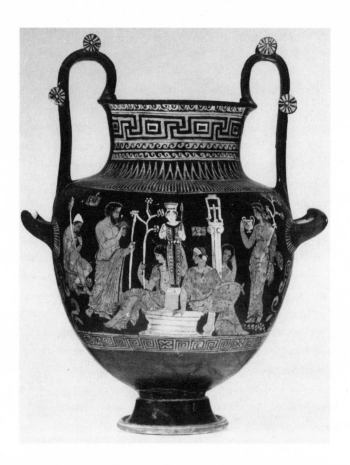

FIGURE 1.

Melampus is curing the daughters of Proteus, king of Argos, of their
madness. Even in historical times some seers claimed that they could
cure both mental and physical illnesses through drugs, sacrifices,
and incantations. For this story, see especially Apollodorus 2.2.2.
Red-figure nestoris, 380 B.C. Museo Archeologico Nazionale di
Napoli, 82125 (H 1760), Naples. See further *LIMC* vol. VI: 407–8,
sc. Melampous C. 4.

incantations" (and they surely included the traditional seers) were harshly attacked
by the practitioners of rational medicine, as seen in *The Sacred Disease* 1–4. In a
famous and often quoted passage, Plato lumps together beggar priests and seers who
wander from city to city ripping off the rich by offering both to cure them of inherited blood guilt and to harm their enemies (*Rep.* 364b–e):

Beggar priests (*agurtai*) and seers (*manteis*) frequent the doors of the rich and persuade them that they have obtained from the gods, through sacrifices and incantations, the power to heal them through pleasant rituals if some wrong was committed either by them or by their ancestors. And if someone wishes to bring ruin upon an enemy, with small expense he will be able to harm the just and unjust alike, since they have the ability through certain enchantments and binding spells to persuade the gods, as they say, to serve them.

Although Plato, here as elsewhere, is attempting to disparage the seer by association with less reputable religious experts, it seems nonetheless to be the case that a seer was competent to deal with any situation that fell under the broad rubric of things sent or caused by supernatural powers. In his *Laws* (913a), Plato implies that if someone found a buried treasure, a seer would be the natural person to ask about removing it. The underlying assumption may be that taking the treasure might anger some god or hero. Thus a seer could be consulted on a whole range of issues and problems the potential consequences of which were uncertain.

The most successful seers in Greek history were what Walter Burkert has called "migrant charismatic specialists."[21] One can explain this characterization in the following terms. They were "migrant" because they traveled throughout the Greek world from South Italy to Asia Minor, "specialists" because of their claim to arcane knowledge, and "charismatic" because of their ability to inspire confidence in their extraordinary talents and because of their self-conscious awareness of their special relationship with supernatural powers. By a combination of charisma, technical knowledge, and luck, they plied their trade for high (sometimes extremely high) wages, and they could have a tangible effect on the course of events.

Although it is usually doubted, there is actually compelling evidence for female seers who were comparable to male ones. That is to say, quite apart from the priestesses at the fixed oracular shrines, such as the Pythia at Delphi, there were also women who were wandering charismatic specialists and who practiced "artificial" or "technical" divination. Greek myth tells the story of Manto, the daughter of Teiresias and the mother of Mopsus, who moved from Thebes to Delphi to Asia Minor. Plato's Diotima, if not a historical person, at least demonstrates that the idea of a wandering female *mantis*, who had diverted the plague from Athens for ten years, was not inconceivable to an early fourth-century audience. Artistic remains

---

21. 1992: 42. On the "magnetic aura" of wanderers, see Montiglio 2005: esp. 116–17.

and epigraphical evidence (*SEG* 35.626: the epitaph of the third-century B.C. seer Satyra from Larissa) can also be brought to bear on this important topic.[22]

We will return to the topic of the female seer in a later chapter. For now it is worth considering the question of the seer's charisma more closely. The personal charisma of the typical male Greek seer is similar to the charisma of the prophets depicted in the Hebrew Bible (whatever the historicity of that depiction), even if in other respects they represent rather different types of religious figures.[23] The Greek seer, who legitimizes his religious authority through his personal charisma, is not capable of holding political authority as well. He is not like Samuel, who is simultaneously judge, priest, prophet, and general; but rather like Nathan, whose role is limited to declaring the will of God to King David. The legendary seer Teiresias resembles Elijah and Elisha as a religious authority who can stand up to and critique the impiety of kings, even if his supernatural powers are far more limited than theirs. Yet Teiresias is a "seer" and not a "prophet" because, even if he may lay claim to some variety of divine inspiration in his interpretation of signs, he generally does not communicate directly with the gods without physical techniques.[24] God speaks directly to the prophets in the Hebrew Bible, and they repeat his words verbatim. He also chooses them to be his prophets, as in the commissioning of Moses, Gideon, Samuel, Jeremiah, and Amos.[25] With the exception of those ecstatic prophets, at Delphi and elsewhere, who act as a mouthpiece for a god while in an altered state of consciousness, the experience of the Hebrew prophet is far removed from that of the Greek seer. The Greek seer is not the messenger of the gods, but rather an interpreter, even if a potentially inspired one, of signs.

His independence of employment, and the subsequent need to project an aura of charisma in order to procure clients, is one of the primary features that distinguishes the Greek seer from his Near Eastern counterparts in Babylonia and Assyria. The knowledge and practice of hepatoscopy most probably came to Greece from the Near East during the time of the Neo-Assyrian Empire. The Assyrian seer (called a *bārû*), as divinatory specialists generally did in the Near East, served kings who

22. See the discussion in chapter 8.

23. The bibliography on the social, political, and religious role of the Hebrew prophet is vast, and the relationship between historical reality and the depiction of the prophets' role in the Hebrew Bible is extremely controversial (and probably not recoverable): a good place to begin is with Grabbe 1995 and Blenkinsopp 1996.

24. On the differences and similarities between prophets and diviners and between prophecy and divination, see Overholt 1989: 117–47, and chapter 3.

25. See Exodus 3:1–4:17; Judges 6:11–14; 1 Samuel 3; Jeremiah 1; and Amos 7:12–15, respectively.

attempted to exercise a tight control over all forms of divination.[26] When the art of the seer was transferred from Assyria to Greece, whether this transferal took place directly or indirectly, the circumstances of employment and the projected image of the expert were transformed in relation to new cultural conditions. Seercraft was no longer inextricably bound to palace, archive, and king.[27] The seer became an itinerant specialist, whose body of knowledge was oral, not written, and who was not required to serve a single employer whose fortunes were bound to his own.

In the Near East, divination and diviners were largely, but not exclusively, under the control of and under the service of kings. In Greece, seers had greater freedom of movement and a more varied clientele. That may explain why some migrant charismatics probably left the Near East for the relative freedom of employment in Greece. Although some of the Greek seer's functions in the archaic age were later absorbed by other specialists, such as doctors and philosophers, they retained their importance in society. Polycrates of Samos, the Athenians Tolmides, Cimon, Pericles, Nicias, and Alcibiades, the Spartans Lysander and Agesilaus, Dion of Syracuse, Timoleon of Corinth, and the Macedonians Philip II and his son Alexander, to name but a few of the most famous Greeks, retained private seers, undoubtedly at great personal expense. Yet the seers who served the great and the powerful, or who were hired by a particular city, were not bound to them; they could leave their employ whenever they wished.

There are some striking differences between Near Eastern and Greek divinatory practices, as is only to be expected in such cases of cultural transmission.[28] There were many different categories of divinatory specialists in Mesopotamia, each with a particular expertise, and purifiers belonged to a separate category altogether. The Greek seer, by contrast, combined those various types and functions into one skilled, but versatile, professional. The actual practice of divination in the Near East was also far more complex. Although there were books on divination in classical Greece, they could not compare in complexity and size to the comprehensive omen collections in Ashurbanipal's library at Nineveh in seventh-century Assyria. All together, his library contained over three hundred clay tablets devoted to divination,

26. See, in particular, Pongratz-Leisten 1999 for the Neo-Assyrian period. For the role of the *bārû* in the Old Babylonian period, see Jeyes 1989: esp. 1–37.

27. Sweek (2002: 49) summarizes the situation: "In first millennium Assyria we may find the situation of the diviner strengthened by increasingly formal ties to the state, although also probably constricted by these ties. The mantic is required to communicate his activities to the state. He is required to give allegiance to the state."

28. These are succinctly expressed by Trampedach (2003b: 266–80).

the equivalent of many thousands of pages in a modern printed text. These tablets comprised compendia of omens of various types and categories (covering every unusual occurrence in the heavens or on the earth), including those relating to the entrails and liver of sacrificed animals. Some thirty thousand ominous signs were listed along with what they signified (in the form "If x, then y").[29] For instance, in reference to a sheep's liver: "If the base of the Presence is long and descends to the *right* Seat of the Path: The enemy will carry off the land of the prince, in battle the enemy will rout me and stand in my camp." On the other hand, "If the base of the Presence is long and descends to the *left* Seat of the Path: The prince will carry off the land of his enemy, in battle I will rout the enemy and stand in his camp."[30] There were even texts that recorded the reports of actual queries and extispicies.[31]

Diviners learned their craft from the study of such texts, even if they could not consult them while on campaign. While performing extispicies in their own communities they seem to have quoted the omen lists from memory.[32] Whether the result of the extispicy was yes or no to a particular query, however, was arrived at by calculating the sum of positive and negative, favorable and unfavorable, omens from the various organs.[33] Thus the protasis (the "if" clause) was actually of greater significance than the specific apodosis (the "result" clause). Or, to put it differently, the specific prediction in the apodosis was not as important as whether it was in itself favorable or unfavorable.

Divination as practiced by Greek seers was not as sophisticated, either in terms of the classification of omens or in the technical aspects of interpretation. Given that the itinerant Greek seer was unable either to consult archived divinatory texts (such as omen lists) or to rely on an education based on such texts, he necessarily was far less constrained by fixed rules of interpretation than his Near Eastern counterparts. There is, however, an interesting exception; but its very uniqueness actually proves my general observation to be true. An early fifth-century inscription from Ephesus

29. On the complex subject of Mesopotamian divination, a good place to start is Oppenheim 1977: 206–27. Less detailed introductory discussions are Bottéro 1992: 125–37 and 2001: 170–202. Rochburg 2004: 1–43, 287–99, is essential on the question of whether Mesopotamian divination was a "science."

30. These examples are from Koch-Westenholz 2000: 98.

31. The corpus of queries and extispicy reports, all of which date from the reigns of Esarhaddon and Ashurbanipal, has been republished by Starr (1990).

32. See Koch-Westenholz 2000: 37.

33. See Oppenheim 1977: 206–27.

contains a series of four interpretations for the flight of a bird that are set out in the style of a Babylonian omen text. Each sentence begin with the protasis "If (the bird does so and so)" and is followed by the apodosis "(it is) favorable" or "unfavorable."[34] This is a much-simplified version of the Babylonian omen lists, given that in this inscription the apodosis does not indicate a specific consequence. It is necessary to stress both that this text is unique and that it comes from a city, located on the edge of the Greek world, that was particularly open to Eastern cultural influences.[35]

There is indeed a superficial resemblance between the Greek and Assyrian systems of hepatoscopy in that Greek terminology is similar to that employed in Akkadian, even if it is much less fully developed. It looks as if the Greek terms for the parts of the liver were translated from the Akkadian. In each case the liver has a "gate," a "head," a "path," and a "river."[36] But whereas in Assyrian practice there was a strict order of examination of ten parts of the liver, the Greeks seem to have put greater emphasis on visual associations, with special emphasis on the liver's overall shape, color, and texture. Etruscan hepatoscopy, on the other hand, preserves more of the complexity of Near Eastern techniques than does Greek divination.[37]

One visually striking aspect of Near Eastern divination is the existence of liver models in clay, which first appeared in the Bronze Age (see figs. 2, 3, and 4). Such models served a variety of purposes. The simplest ones may represent a particular liver and have served to report an actual omen. More elaborate models were probably used for instruction and teaching, as well as for recording information for future reference. In any case, these models visibly demonstrate just how much less technically detailed and elaborate Greek mantic practice generally was than that of the Near East. Although liver models have been discovered in Mesopotamia, Asia

34. *SIG* 1167 (= Sokolowski 1955: 84–86, no. 30). See Pritchett 1979: 102–3; Dillon 1996: 104–7; and West 1997: 47 n. 198. Wilamowitz (1931: 145–48) considered this inscription to be "hardly Greek," and it is true no other Greek text mentions the raising of a bird's wing as being of divinatory significance. The precise translation is disputed, but the sense is as follows (omitting brackets and interpuncts): "If (the bird) flying from the right to the left disappears, it is favorable; but if it raises its left wing, and flies away and disappears, it is unfavorable. If flying from the left to the right it disappears on a straight course, it is unfavorable; but if after raising its right wing it flies away and disappears, it is favorable."

35. The purpose of this inscription is unclear; most probably it was part of a law code that regulated the actions of some official body, since another fragment of this same text mentions the taking of oaths before judges (*dikastai*) on boar's flesh.

36. See Burkert 1992: 49–50, and 183 nn. 21 and 23 for the evidence. For Assyrian terminology, see Jeyes 1978.

37. See Nougayrol 1955 and 1966.

FIGURE 2.

Clay model of a sheep's liver from Mesopotamia, eighteenth century B.C. On this model each box has a cuneiform inscription that describes the implications of a blemish appearing at that position. 14.6 × 14.6 cm. © The Trustees of The British Museum.

Minor, Syria, Palestine, and Etruria (from the Hellenistic period), none have been found in any Greek community.[38]

In sum, what we find in the Greek world is a stripped-down and simplified version of the much more sophisticated and technical Babylonian and Assyrian system of divination. This is not surprising given that Greek society of the archaic age had different needs and was less bureaucratically complex than that of the Near East.

38. See Oppenheim 1977: 213, 216; Burkert 1992: 46–48; West 1997: 48. A small votive bronze model of a liver or kidney, found on Cyprus and dating from the Mycenaean period, is probably not (*pace* Burkert) an analogous example.

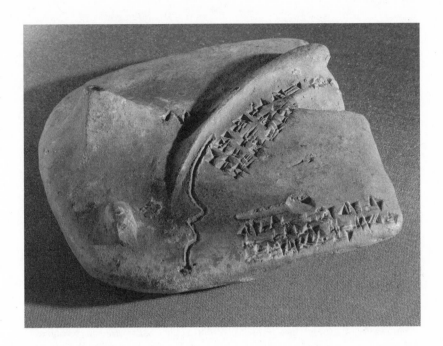

FIGURE 3.
Terra-cotta model of a sheep's liver from Emar (Mascana), late middle Syrian period (late fourteenth to early twelfth century B.C.). 10.8 × 11 × 4.1 cm. National Museum, Aleppo, Syria. Photo Erich Lessing / Art Resource, NY.

The Greeks borrowed and adapted what was useful for the particular needs of their society.

Aristander of Telmessus, who accompanied Alexander to Asia in 334 B.C., is the outstanding example of a seer whose competence covered the interpretation of entrails, bird signs, and dreams, as well as natural phenomena. But we have indications that other seers of the classical period were equally adept at reading all types of divine signs. A famous passage in the *Iliad* should not be taken to indicate that specialization, of the sort that we find in the Near East, was also characteristic of early archaic Greece. When the Achaeans are being afflicted with the plague sent by Apollo, Achilles summons them to an assembly and makes this proposal (1.62–64):

FIGURE 4.

Bronze model of a sheep's liver from Decima di Gossolengo; Etruscan, late second to early first century B.C. This life-sized model is divided into forty-two sections, each of which contains the names of one or more gods (several of whom are mentioned more than once). There are fifty-one names altogether, representing about twenty-eight different names of gods (see van der Meer 1987 and Bonfante 2006: 10–11). Museo Civico, Piacenza, Italy. Photo Scala / Art Resource, NY.

"But come, let us ask some seer (*mantis*) or priest (*hiereus*), or even an interpreter of dreams, for a dream is also from Zeus, who might be able to say why Phoebus Apollo is so greatly angry." These lines might be taken to imply a difference in function between the *mantis* (who, in Homer, was primarily an interpreter of bird signs and portents), a priest (who theoretically might inspect the burnt or extracted entrails of an animal during a sacrifice), and a dream interpreter. Yet in Homer neither priest nor seer ever looks for omens during a sacrifice. Achilles is surely engaging here in rhetorical amplification, and he is alluding to the fact that a priest, as a ritual expert, might be able to pinpoint any ritual offence committed by the Greeks that could have angered Apollo. So Homer, in this passage, is not reflecting the strict separation of divinatory functions that one finds in Babylonia and Assyria.

Perhaps the difference between the situation in Greece and the Near East can partly be explained in terms of the relationship between center and periphery. As stated above, knowledge of divination was brought to Greece either by migrant specialists from the Near East or by Greeks who had traveled abroad. Perhaps, as with "country doctors" in more modern times, the Greek seer needed to perform a whole range of specialist activities on his own. It may also be significant that divinatory rituals in the Near East were under greater state control, and that may also have contributed to greater specialization.

MANTIC FAMILIES

Although books on divination were available by the end of the fifth century B.C.,[39] the most respected and sought-after seers belonged to families that had practiced seercraft for many generations, reaching back to an eponymous ancestor who had acquired prophetic power either as the gift of a god (usually Apollo) or by some other supernatural means. Herodotus (9.92–94) tells the story of how Zeus and Apollo gave to Euenius of Apollonia "the innate faculty of divination" as a gift in exchange for his blindness.[40] The seer Deiphonus, who accompanied the Hellenic fleet to Mycale, was, or at least pretended to be, Euenius's son (9.95). The "innate faculty of divination" is a hereditary trait that is distinct from that seercraft that is acquired by study.[41] The gods, in effect, have given Euenius the gift of inner vision (or second sight) because he has lost his outer vision. This story pattern is familiar enough.[42] It begins with the legendary Theban seer Teiresias, who was blinded by Athena or Hera but then given the gift of prophecy in compensation.[43] Teiresias also was the model for Phineus, the seer of the Argonauts, who also lost his physical vision as a punishment from the gods.[44]

In the eyes of his clients, a seer's authority and credibility depended on belonging to an established family of seers. This family connection, we may presume, had

---

39. See Pritchett 1979: 73.

40. For this episode, see Kindt 2001: 34–37; Griffiths 1999; Flower and Marincola 2002: 266–70; and Grottanelli (2003), who argues that the story of Euenius serves as the foundation myth for a line of seers.

41. For innate divination, see Hom. *Il.* 1.71–72; Soph. *OT* 299; for acquired, see Hdt. 2.49; Isoc. *Aeginet.* 5–7.

42. Carp (1983) argues that the acquisition of prophetic powers by the blind is not a process of compensation, but of transcendence. But the sources themselves certainly understand the gift in terms of compensation, even if the gift endows its possessor with a type of transcendent knowledge. See also Grottanelli 2003: 215.

43. Apollod. 3.6.7. For the various versions, see Ugolini 1995.

44. Ap. Rhod. *Argon.* 2.179–84; cf. Apollod. 1.9.21.

a double purpose. On the one hand, it was proof that the craft of divination had been acquired in apprenticeship to a master who was a member of one's own family. In the Hippocratic oath, we also see this emphasis on keeping arcane knowledge and expertise within a family, whether that family is biological or adoptive. The oath specifies: "I swear to impart the rules, oral teachings, and all other instruction to my sons and to those of the man who taught me, and to those students who have accepted the covenant and sworn the oath by the physician's law, but to no one else." The emphasis on adoption of student by teacher is an old one, going back to conventions that developed in the ancient Near East. In the case of seers, however, adoption could not have been as acceptable a substitute for biological descent. This was because mantic knowledge was inherently different from medical knowledge; like medical knowledge it was technical and teachable, but unlike medical knowledge it was also an innate gift. Since written credentials did not exist, a physician had to be able to substantiate his training by naming his teachers.[45] A seer named his teachers by the very act of naming his family.

It must have been common for seers to represent themselves as having inherited an innate capacity for divination, which entailed a supranormal understanding of nature and a susceptibility to divine inspiration. The four most distinguished clans of seers were the Melampodidae, Iamidae, Clytiadae, and Telliadae. These families claimed descent from legendary seers of the heroic age: Melampus, Iamus (the son of Apollo), Clytius (a descendant of Melampus), and Tellias, respectively. The ending -*idae* in ancient Greek means "descendants/sons of": thus the Iamidae are the descendants of Iamus and so on. All but the Melampodidae came from Elis in the northwestern Peloponnese.

It is a sure indication of their prominence that members of all these families figure in the pages of Herodotus. Megistias, an Acarnanian and a descendant of Melampus, served and died with the Spartans at Thermopylae in 480 B.C. (7.219, 221, 228). The Elean seer Tellias (surely one of the Telliadae) by devising a clever stratagem helped the Phocians to annihilate a Thessalian army that had invaded Phocis (8.27). The most renowned of the Telliadae, however, was Hegesistratus, who served Mardonius at Plataea (9.37.1). Callias, one of the Iamidae, assisted Croton in its war with Sybaris and was richly rewarded with grants of land (5.44–45). And the Iamid Tisamenus won five brilliant victories for Sparta, beginning with Plataea in 479 B.C. (9.33–35).

Who were these "mythical seers" whom later practitioners claimed as the pro-

45. Dean-Jones 2003: 106–8, citing Xen. *Mem.* 4.2.5.

genitors of their families? The Iamidae is the mantic family that we know the most about.[46] Their foundation myth is told by Pindar in his sixth *Olympian*.[47] This poem was written for Hagesias of Syracuse, an Iamid who served as seer to the tyrant Hieron and who was victorious in the mule-cart race at Olympia in 472 or 468 B.C. As Pindar tells the tale (57–74):

And when Iamus had plucked the fruit of delightful golden-crowned Youth, he went down into the middle of the Alpheus River, and called upon wide-ruling Poseidon, his grandfather, and upon the bow-carrying watcher [Apollo] over god-built Delos, and under the nighttime sky he asked for himself some office that would serve the people. The clear-speaking voice of his father [Apollo] responded, and sought him out: "Arise, my son, and follow my voice here to a land that is common to all." They came to the steep rock of the lofty hill of Cronus. There the god gave him a twofold treasury of divination: at that time to hear the voice that is unknowing of lies; and later, when bold-plotting Heracles should come, the sacred offspring of the Alcidae, and should found for his father a festival crowded by people and the greatest institution of contests [the Olympic games], then in turn he bid him to establish an oracle on the summit of Zeus's altar. Since then the clan of the Iamidae has been much renowned among Hellenes. Prosperity attended them; and by honoring excellence, they walk along a conspicuous path. Each thing they do shows this.

Let me reiterate just what Iamus is said to have been given. Apollo bestowed upon his son "a twofold treasury of divination" and "from that time the clan of the Iamidae has been much renowned among Hellenes." That twofold treasury was "to hear the voice that is unknowing of lies" (most probably the voice of Apollo)[48] and "to establish an oracle on the summit of Zeus's altar" at Olympia. Although other mantic families could claim a miraculous origin for their clan's prophetic abilities, this gift is unique in that it simultaneously endows a mobile clan of seers with prophetic power and establishes a fixed oracular center.

46. The main treatments of the Iamidae are Bouché–Leclercq 1879–82: vol. 2, 59–69; Weniger 1915: 66–76; Hepding 1914; Löffler 1963: 27–28; Kett 1966: 84–93; Parke 1967: 174–78; Roth 1982: 222–31; and Flower 2008a. Note also Dillery 2005: 206–9 on Tisamenus.

47. For the substantial bibliography on this poem, see Hutchinson 2001: 371 n. 16. Carne-Ross 1979 and Goldhill 1991: 146–66 are particularly noteworthy as literary analyses.

48. Scholion 113a says of this line: "to hear the voice of the gods or of birds." Löffler (1963: 28) rightly interprets the phrase as referring to the unerring voice of Apollo: so also Hutchinson 2001: 404–5.

Art historians have speculated that the old man on the east pediment of the temple of Zeus at Olympia (constructed c. 470–457 B.C.), which depicts the preparation for the chariot race between Pelops and Oenomaus, is the seer Iamus (see fig. 5).[49] This figure well may be a seer, but the identification with Iamus is made solely by reference to Pindar's sixth *Olympian*. Whether an Iamid actually established the oracle is beyond historical recovery, but during the imperial period, and probably as far back as the fifth century B.C., the Iamidae shared the stewardship of Zeus's oracle with the Clytiadae, a post that they jointly held through the third century A.D.[50]

And so it was that at least one Iamid and one Clytiad in each generation had fixed employment at Olympia, where later sources tell us that they practiced divination atop Zeus's altar by examining the cracks in the burnt skins of sacrificial animals.[51] We should not view this as a somehow inferior or less authoritative method of divination than the extispicy that was practiced by most seers; for empyromancy, of one sort or another, is cross-culturally a widespread and respected means of divination. The reading of stress cracks caused by the catastrophic heating of turtle shells (called plastromancy) was the preeminent method of divination in Shang China (1700–1027 B.C.), and it was still important in the Han period (206 B.C.–A.D. 220).[52]

Since only one seer was chosen from each of the two families to work the oracle, other members might seek employment as itinerant diviners throughout the Greek world. On occasion a seer might settle in the community that he had successfully served, and there may have been branches of the Iamidae not only in Syracuse and Sparta, but also in Messenia, in Croton in South Italy, and in Stymphalus in Arcadia.[53] As for the Clytiadae, several fourth-century B.C. inscriptions from Chios may indicate that a branch of the family was located there.[54]

The most famous by far of the Iamidae was Tisamenus of Elis, who was launched on what is arguably the most successful mantic career of all time when the Pythia at

49. See *LIMC* V.1: 614–15.

50. Inscriptions from Olympia (for which see Weniger 1915) list only the officiating seers from 36 B.C. to A.D. 265, but Pindar calls Hagesias "steward of the mantic altar of Zeus in Pisa." Schachter (2000) argues that the Clytiadae came into prominence only at a relatively late date, but this seems unlikely given the epigram of Eperastus discussed in chapter 3.

51. See Parke 1967: 184–85.

52. For an evocative reconstruction of its use in Shang China, see Keightley 1978: 1–2. For Han China, see Loewe 1994: 160–90.

53. The evidence for a Messenian branch of the Iamidae is highly suspect, since it is found in Pausanias's account of the Second Messenian War (4.16–23).

54. An inscription from the 330s (*GHI* 87) shows a group called "the Clytidae" using sacrificial divination in order to decide whether to construct a sacred building in which they would permanently

FIGURE 5.
Marble statue of an elderly man, perhaps the seer Iamus, from the east pediment of
the temple of Zeus at Olympia, c. 460 B.C. Archaeological Museum, Olympia, Greece.
Hirmer Fotoarchiv 561.0655.

Delphi, in response to his query about having children, prophesied that he "would
win the five greatest contests" (Hdt. 9.33). The story then takes an unusual twist.
Tisamenus misunderstood the oracle as referring to "athletic contests," began to
train for the pentathlon, and almost won an Olympic victory. The Spartans, however, realized that the oracle actually referred to the "contests of war," and determined to hire him. In exchange for his services as a seer, he demanded Spartan citizenship for both himself and his brother, a price that the Spartans were forced by
circumstances to pay. Indeed, Herodotus claims that Tisamenus and his brother were

store "the common sacred things" that were hitherto kept in private houses. It is unfortunately
unclear whether these Clytidae were members of a tribe (as is usually maintained) or of some sort
of gentilitial group. The fact that they use sacrificial divination, rather than the more usual consultation of an oracle, in order to resolve a matter relating to cult might suggest a connection with the
mantic family from Olympia. See further Sokolowski 1969: no. 118 (= $Syll.^3$ 987), with Roth 1982:
231, 258–59. Any connection, however, between the Elean "Clytiadae" and the Chian "Clytidae"
is denied by Bouché–Leclercq 1879–82: vol. 2, 336; Weniger 1915: 59 n. 3; and Kett 1966: 96 n. 34.

the only foreigners ever to be given Spartan citizenship, and we know from other sources (both literary and epigraphic) that their actual descendants, as well as those who later claimed to be, practiced seercraft at Sparta for more than six hundred years.[55] Given that Herodotus simply did not make up the tale of Tisamenus's consultation, is it possible to guess its origin and purpose? One possibility is that the story was part of Tisamenus's own self-advertisement as a seer with an appropriately high price tag; another is that it was part of an attempt by his descendants at Sparta to capitalize on the memory of his successes. Just as lord Apollo speaking through his priestess at Delphi had validated Tisamenus's status as a divinely sanctioned seer, so the story of that consultation validated the status of his descendants. Implicit in Herodotus's story is the subtext that not just any seer trained in the craft of divination could have "won" those five victories, but only a divinely selected Iamid in whom the prophetic gift given to Iamus by Apollo himself was particularly potent.[56]

If Tisamenus was the most illustrious and successful of "historical" seers, Melampus was arguably the most famous of all legendary ones. A list of his mythical/legendary descendants is given in Homer's *Odyssey*, when the poet is introducing the seer Theoclymenus, who accompanied Telemachus from Pylos to Ithaca.[57] Here we are told that among Melampus's distinguished descendants were the seers Amphiaraus (one of the Seven who attacked Thebes and perished there) and Amphilochus, as well as Theoclymenus's father Polypheides, "whom Apollo had made a seer, and far the best among mortals, after Amphiaraus had died." This passage reflects the importance of genealogies in establishing a seer's credentials. As late as the third century B.C., as we shall see, we know of seers who were claiming, and boasting of, descent from Melampus.

The importance of belonging to one of the established families of seers is manifest, but does it actually tell us anything about who seers were? Genealogies are malleable entities. Even when people sincerely believe them to be accurate, they may be false. To ask if Melampus, Iamus, Clytius, and Tellia were in fact historical persons (perhaps migrant charismatics who had emigrated from the Near East) is akin to pondering if Achilles, Agamemnon, and Helen were "real" people. The former, at least, are inventions of the Greek imagination, archetypal images of the anonymous migrant seers who proliferated during the archaic age. They became the mythical eponymous ancestors of the leading families of seers in classical Greece—

55. See Flower 2008a.

56. In Flower 2008a I treat Iamid family tradition and self-representation in more detail. See also Flower and Marincola 2002: 165. For a different view, see Vannicelli 2005.

57. 15.220—86; see also 508—46.

the Melampodidae, Iamidae, Clytiadae, and Telliadae. By a similar process the kings of Sparta claimed descent from Heracles.

As mentioned above, Herodotus tried to rationalize the various stories of how Melampus came to be a seer. But that does not mean that we should follow suit. On the one hand, stories about Melampus and other early seers obviously served to confirm and legitimate the claims to special status of those seers of archaic and classical times who identified themselves as their descendants, and it is natural enough to suspect that such stories were invented for just that purpose. It seems safe to say that myths, like oral traditions, reflect the concerns of those who tell them. Thus the myths about the famous seers Melampus, Mopsus, Amphiaraus, Teiresias, and Calchas should tell us something about how the seers who were contemporary with our versions of the myths both represented themselves and were perceived by others. Yet even so, extreme skepticism is sometimes undercut in unexpected ways.

Myth, legend, and history have been thought by some to come together in the case of one particular seer who was celebrated in archaic poetry. That is the seer Mopsus.[58] According to legend, Mopsus was the grandson of the blind seer Teiresias by his daughter Manto. He is said to have emigrated to Clarus, where he founded the famous oracle of Apollo there, and then he moved on to Cilicia, where, with the Greek hero Amphilochus, he founded the oracle at Mallus. Such legends are hardly likely to contain even a kernel of historical truth, and it is clear that this legend, as most others, evolved with the telling (in another version it was Manto who founded the oracle at Clarus). But in this case there is a singular coincidence of legend and documentary evidence. This coincidence seemingly gave support to that faction among an older generation of scholars who used early Greek poetry as a source for reconstructing the historical individuals, wars, and migrations of late Bronze Age Greece.[59] The name Mopsus appears in a Hittite document of the fifteenth century B.C. as "Muksus." This Muksus seems to have been the founder of a dynasty in Cilicia, for in 1928 a remarkable bilingual Luwian-Phoenician inscription was found at Karatepe in Cilicia, dating from the eighth century, which names a King Azitawadda from the "house of Mopsus." Or rather, the Luwian text calls him Moxus, whereas the Phoenician text has "mps." Since Phoenician is written, like Hebrew, without vowels, this can be construed as Mopsus.

What can all of this mean? Can a fifteenth-century Cilician king named Moxus/

---

58. On Mopsus, see esp. Burkert 1983: 52–53; Scheer 1993; and Baldriga 1994.
59. For instance, in the *CAH*[3] vol. 2, pt. 2: 355–56, 363–66, 678–81.

Mopsus be the same person as the Greek seer of late Bronze Age myth named Mopsus? Or was Mopsus a hereditary name among the kings of Cilicia? And if so, should we be thinking in terms of an eighth-century Cilician king having been culturally metamorphosed into a Greek seer? The earliest Greek source to mention Mopsus was Hesiod in his lost *Melampodia*. He recounted a contest between Calchas, the seer of the Greeks at Troy, and Mopsus. Strabo cites these lines from Hesiod (F 278 MW), in which Calchas set the following test:

> "Wonder holds my heart, how many figs this fig tree holds, although it is indeed small. Can you say the number?" Mopsus responded: "They are ten thousand in number, or a *medimnos* in measure; but one is left over, which you would not be able to put in." Thus he spoke, and the number of the measure was seen by them to be true. And at that time the sleep of death covered over Calchas.

It is just possible that this story reflects the historical fact that extispicy was brought, either personally or through indirect cultural contacts, to Greece by Near Eastern diviners of high social class, whose methods were preferred to those of the native bird diviners. I would not want to suggest that there was a real person, either Greek or Cilician, named Mopsus in the eighth century, but only that the story of his defeating Calchas may embody a mythic explanation of an actual historical process. If this is true, then the legend encodes the process but has inverted the direction of cultural influence. But why, one may ask, is extispicy not mentioned either in Hesiod's account of the contest or in various later versions (some of these versions derive from the mythographer Pherecydes of Syros and from the tragedian Sophocles, but there seem to have been many elaborations of the tale).[60] The contest, as it appears in every one of our sources, is not between practitioners of two different types of divination, but between two inspired seers. Mopsus intuits the number of figs, or, in some later accounts, the number of piglets in a sow's womb. Thus it is a contest of second sight, of divinely inspired intuitive vision. We would have to assume therefore that not only the direction of influence has been altered, but that the technical nature of that influence has been translated into the realm of inspired nontechnical divination.

In effect, the Mopsus of Greek myth has more in common with the Teiresias of Sophocles or the Euenius of Herodotus than with the better-documented military seers of the fifth and fourth centuries. Finally, whoever the Cilician Mopsus was,

60. See Gantz 1993: 702–3.

whether king or seer, the purpose of the Greek legends has nothing at all to do with him. Rather, the legend of the contest was intended to supply heroic credentials for the founder of the oracle at Clarus. The religious specialists who ran the oracle could claim as their founder a grandson of Teiresias who had outperformed Calchas, the greatest seer in Homer. As H. W. Parke has well expressed the situation, "the legend of Manto provided a pedigree for the prophets of Clarus, and the legend of Mopsus and Calchas vouched for their credentials."[61] In other words, regardless of whether there was a Cilician family of seers all of whom bore the name Mopsus, any such historical kernel was adapted by the Greeks of Asia Minor for their own purposes. The "historical" Greek seer Mopsus, if he ever existed, eludes us.

Herodotus, as it turns out, also gives us a cautionary tale when it comes to the reliability of claims to descent. He says that the seer Deiphonus, who was serving with the Greek fleet in 479, passed himself off as the son of the famous seer Euenius of Apollonia (9.95): "I have before now heard that trading on the name of Euenius he was contracting work throughout Greece, although he was not the son of Euenius." This single sentence tells us two important things: that a blood connection to a successful seer was helpful for gaining upscale employment, and that such claims were not accepted uncritically. Society was not a tacit accomplice in a sham, nor were seers merely the members of guilds, such as the Homeridae or Asclepiadae, among whom the adoption of an apprentice by his master was clothed in the language of kinship. It was fundamentally important that the seer was believed to be what he claimed to be, literally the blood descendant of another seer. At the same time, sincere belief in a genealogical connection, it must be stressed, does not make it true.

Likewise, in the ancient Near East descent from a seer, or even from the antediluvian King Enmeduranki, was an essential qualification. The Assyrian gods Samas and Adad had given to Enmeduranki "the Tablet of the Gods, the liver, a secret of heaven and the nether world," and he, in turn, shared this with the citizens of Nippur, Sippar, and Babylon. The Enmeduranki text, dating from the late Assyrian period (perhaps c. 900 B.C.) then describes the diviner as follows (lines 14, 19–29):[62]

The learned savant, who guards the secrets of the great gods, will bind by oath before Samas and Adad by tablet and stylus the son whom he loves and will teach him. When a diviner, an expert in oil, of abiding descent, offshoot of Enmeduranki, king of Sippar, who sets up the holy bowl, holds the cedar,

61. Parke 1985: 115.
62. Lambert 1998: 152.

benediction priest of the king, long-haired priest of Samas, a creature of Ninhursag, begotten by a reverend of pure descent, he himself, being without defect in body and limbs, may approach the presence of Samas and Adad where (liver) inspection and oracle (take place).

The qualification of descent, however, does not exclude the possibility of adoption, which was common in ancient Mesopotamia. W. G. Lambert, in his critical edition, interprets this passage as follows: "If a bārû had no children, or only daughters, he could obviously adopt a son to assist in his work and eventually to succeed him in his profession, and the 'son whom he loves' would presumably cover such a case."[63] Nonetheless, we do know of some Mesopotamian families in which being a diviner was an occupation over several generations. A boundary stone from Sippar of the Cassite period shows that one family produced sangu-priests (the highest ranking of the Mesopotamian priests) and bārûs for a period of more than two hundred years.[64] Generally, however, as in Greece, the fiction of descent for validating the system was far more important than the genetic realities.

Although most of the evidence comes from Elis, there are indications that seercraft was also hereditary in other parts of the Greek world. The Acarnanian Megistias, who, as mentioned above, claimed descent from Melampus, took his only son with him to Thermopylae, and then sent his son away before the Greeks were surrounded. Herodotus does not say so (7.221), but it is a fair inference that the boy was serving as apprentice to his father. Unfortunately, Herodotus does not tell us his name or what later became of him. At Athens we know of a father and son who were seers: a stele from an Attic peribolos tomb of the classical period bears the inscription "Here I cover a wise and just man, Calliteles, the *mantis*, son of the honored *mantis* Meidoteles."[65] And at Plataea in Boeotia it seems likely that the seer Theaenetus, the son of Tolmides (Thuc. 3.20.1), was the grandson of the seer Theaenetus who had served the Athenian general Tolmides between 466 and 457 B.C. (Paus. 1.27.5).[66] The city of Telmessus in Caria, if one can compare a community to a clan, was famous

63. 1998: 143.

64. See Starr 1974: 221 n. 119 and Cryer 1994: 201.

65. *SEG* 23 (1968) 161. See Mastrokostas 1966: 282 and Garland 1982: 168–69.

66. This is probably a case of ritualized guest friendship between the Athenian Tolmides and his seer of Plataean extraction; that is, Theaenetus named his son Tolmides after his employer, and this Plataean Tolmides named his son after his own father (see Herman [1989: 90–91], who leaves open the possibility that the Theaenetus mentioned by Thucydides is an Athenian and the son of the general Tolmides). It would be nice to know if all three were seers.

for its seers,[67] and was the homeland of that Aristander who so successfully served both Philip II and Alexander in the second half of the fourth century.

Finally, is it just a coincidence that Tisamenus and Hegesistratus, who were both from Elis, have names that are appropriate for their profession, the former meaning "avenger," and the latter "the leader of the army"? Hippomachus of Leucas (Hdt. 9.37) has a name meaning "cavalryman," and Polemaenetus (whose home city we are not told) has a name that may be rendered "praised in war." One could cite further examples of telling names, such as the Spartan Cleomantis, or "famous seer" (Plut. *Alex.* 50.5). It is possible, I suppose, that individuals who became seers changed their names in order to increase their mystique.[68] It seems more likely, however, that practicing seers gave names to their sons that would both suit and advertise their future careers, and this would be yet another indication that seercraft was an hereditary occupation.

The evidence that has been surveyed above does not merely indicate that some seers, and many of the most famous ones, came from established mantic families. It also reveals that they were members of the elite. And that is exactly what one should expect of families that traced their descent back either to a god or to a hero figure of Greek legend. When we turn to Etruria in northern Italy and to the Near East, we find a similar pattern. There too seercraft was a high-status profession that tended to be passed down in certain families.

The Etruscan seers (called *haruspices*) who were of greatest repute were members of the elite and belonged to certain clans.[69] These were the professionals who were later consulted by the Roman senate and who formed a college of sixty members. Others were lower-class itinerant diviners, called *vicani haruspices* by Cicero (*Div.* 1.132), who quotes the poet Ennius. When Cato the Elder in his essay *On Agriculture* (4.4) advises that the manager of one's farm should not consult a *haruspex*, he is certainly also referring to this itinerant type. Both aristocrat and commoner shared the title *haruspex*, even if the official college or *ordo* (of uncertain date) included only the former.[70] One Etruscan diviner (*haruspex*) of about 200 B.C., Laris Pulenas, even claimed descent from a Greek seer named Polles, who had allegedly migrated from Greece in the mid-fourth century B.C. This we know from Pulenas's rather remark-

---

67. Hdt. 1.78, 84; Ar. F 554 Kassel-Austin; Cic. *Div.* 1.91, 94; Arr. 2.3.3. There were two cities in Asia Minor called Telmessus, one in Caria and one in Lycia. Harvey (1991) convincingly demonstrates that the Carian city was the one famous for its seers.

68. Immerwahr (1966: 295 n. 164) suggests that seers may have been hired in part for their names.

69. Cic. *Div.* 1.92; Val. Max. 1.1.1.

70. On this topic, see Thulin 1905–9; Rawson 1978; North 1990; Haack 2002 and 2003; and De Grummond 2005. MacBain (1982) stresses the political influence of the *haruspices* at Rome.

FIGURE 6.

The Etruscan *haruspex* Laris Pulenas on a sarcophagus from Tarquinia in northern Italy. The scroll that he is unfolding contains his curriculum vitae, as well as his genealogy, going back to his great-grandfather, the Greek seer Polles. Museo Nazionale Etrusco di Tarquinia. By permission of the Soprintendenza per i Beni Archeologici dell'Etruria Meridionale.

able sarcophagus (see fig. 6). He is depicted semi-recumbent on its lid as he unrolls before him a papyrus roll that is labeled "this haruspicinal book"; that is, the sort of volume in which one would expect to find recorded the precepts of Etruscan divination. In fact, however, his *curriculum vitae* is inscribed on the roll, giving his religious offices at the town of Tarquinii and his ancestry going back to his great-grandfather "Laris Pule the Greek."[71] He also claims to have written books about divination.

An Etruscan mirror of the late fourth century B.C. depicts a winged Calchas examining a liver while leaning over an altar (see fig. 7). Although it is difficult to explain why he has wings, the fact that the figure is labeled Calchas must reflect on

71. See Heurgon 1957 and 1964: 235–36; Pailler 1988: 475–80; and Bonfante 2006: 13 (for additional bibliography).

FIGURE 7.
Bronze mirror from Vulci, late fourth century B.C. A winged seer examines a liver, while
other entrails are lying on the altar. The name Kalchas is inscribed next to the figure, thus
identifying him as the famous seer of the *Iliad*. Height 0.18m. Although historical seers
did not have wings, the pose over the altar is plausible enough. Vatican, Museo Gregoriano
Etrusco 12240. After E. Gerhard, *Etruskische Spiegel* (Berlin 1884–97) vol. III, pl. 223.

the social aspirations of contemporary Etruscan seers. Yet in Greece too not all seers
were members of the elite, so the Etruscan pattern appears essentially the same as the
Greek one. As in Greece, the most highly paid and sought-after seers came from certain famous clans. But just as in Greek communities anyone could call himself a seer
(*mantis*), so too anyone could call himself a *haruspex* and seek private employment.

Diviners in the Near East were certainly of high social status, as is spectacularly
demonstrated by the fact that the last great king of the Neo-Assyrian Empire, Ashur-

banipal, who reigned from 668 to 626, was trained in the craft of divination. Ashur-banipal himself boasted: "I am versed in the craft of the sage Adapa; I studied the secret lore of the entire scribal craft, I know the celestial and terrestrial portents. I discuss with competence in the circle of the masters; I argue about (the work) '(If) the liver is a correspondence of the sky' with expert diviners { . . . } I have read the intricate tablets inscribed with obscure Sumerian or Akkadian, difficult to unravel, and examined sealed, obscure and confused inscriptions on stone from before the Flood."[72]

During the Old Babylonian period, the seer Asqudum, who was married to a princess, occasionally led military expeditions, and his house, which covered more than a thousand square meters, resembled a scaled-down palace.[73] It is also noteworthy that whereas Babylonian and Assyrian seers (*bārûs*) were well-educated members of the elite, contemporary prophets and ecstatics were of lower social status.[74] This was perhaps true of Greece as well. The Delphic priestess, at least by Plutarch's time in the first century A.D., was a local peasant woman. Yet, as we shall see in chapter 8, it is possible that the Pythia was a well-educated, and perhaps upper-class, woman during the archaic and classical periods.

OTHER QUALIFICATIONS
FOR BECOMING A SEER

As we have seen, belonging to a family of hereditary seers or being the son of a successful practitioner was extremely important in establishing one's credibility as a seer. Apart from family descent, what were the necessary requirements to be a seer? Or were there any? Unlike in the ancient Near East, the seer did not need to be free from physical defects. The Enmeduranki text, quoted above, excludes any person from practicing divination as a *bārû* (diviner) who "is of impure descent, not without defect in body and limbs, with squinting eyes, chipped teeth, a cut-off finger, a ruptured(?) testicle, suffering from leprosy, a eunuch" (lines 30–33).[75] This is comparable with *Leviticus* 21: 16–23, where the Lord says to Moses:

> Say to Aaron: "For the generations to come none of your descendants who
> has a defect may come near to offer the food of his God. No man who has any

---

72. Translation is from Kuhrt 1995: 523.
73. See Charpin 1985 and Cryer 1994: 202–3.
74. On Babylonian and Assyrian prophets, see Huffmon 2000 and Nissinen 2000b.
75. Lambert 1998: 152, 147.

defect may come near: no man who is blind or lame, disfigured or deformed; no man with a crippled foot or hand, or who is hunchbacked or dwarfed, or who has any eye defect, or who has festering or running sores or damaged testicles. No descendant of Aaron the priest who has any defect is to come near to present the offerings made to the Lord by fire. He has a defect; he must not come near to offer the food of his God. He may eat the most holy food of his God, as well as the holy food; yet because of his defect, he must not go near the curtain or approach the altar, and so desecrate my sanctuary. I am the Lord, who makes them holy.

In the Greek world blindness was obviously not a disqualifying defect. Both Teiresias and Euenius, famous mythical and historical seers, respectively, were blind. In fact, physical blindness seems to have been an advantage in Greek thought, since it promoted "inner vision." Indeed, it is true of many cultures that blind people are thought to have special insight.[76]

The Greek seer could not rely on extensive written records of omens and prodigies such as were available in the Near East. He had to rely on his own judgment rather than on archival research. This may help to explain his role as a charismatic figure, whose ability to interpret divine signs properly and correctly was partly a function of his inner vision. The Babylonian or Assyrian seer, by contrast, primarily needed a good memory and access to a library. Books on divination existed in Greece by the end of the fifth century, but these were on a vastly smaller scale than their Mesopotamian counterparts and could have given only very schematic and general instructions, if such was their intent. As a matter of fact, we know very little about the nature of these books. They may have served more by way of self-advertisement or display of antiquarian knowledge than as instruction manuals. Indeed, one wonders why any successful seer would have wanted to demystify his art by laying bare all of its secrets.

The poet Hesiod is said to have written a poem on the interpretation of bird signs, called *Ornithomanteia*. This poem, however, was deemed to be inauthentic by the scholar Apollonius Rhodius, who was the librarian at Alexandria in the mid-third century B.C. Whatever its date and authorship, it probably described the significance of different kinds of birds and related mythical stories about them.[77] One could not have learned the craft of divination solely by hearing this poem any more than one could have become a farmer by studying Hesiod's *Works and Days*.

76. So Lienhardt 1961: 68.
77. West (1978: 365) suggest that fragments 355 and 312 of Hesiod may come from this poem.

The known titles of prose works are as follows. In the second half of the fifth century the Athenian sophist Antiphon wrote a work on the interpretation of dreams.[78] Demon, also an Athenian (third century B.C.), composed *On Sacrifices (Peri thusiōn)*.[79] Another Athenian, Cleidemus (fourth century B.C.) wrote an *Exegesis* (a work dealing with the explication of sacred rites).[80] A certain Autocleides (probably in the next century) also published an *Exegesis*.[81] The famous Athenian scholar and seer Philochorus (c. 340–260 B.C.) produced an epitome of an earlier work with the title *On Omens from Sacrifices (Peri hierōn)*, as well as writing two works of his own. One was *On Divination (Peri mantikēs)* in four books, and the other was *On Sacrifices (Peri thusiōn)*, probably in one book.[82] Alexander the Great's seer, Aristander of Telmessus, perhaps wrote a book on portents (if we can trust a passing reference in Pliny the Elder), and more certainly a book on dream interpretation.[83]

It is worth stressing that, despite modern assumptions to the contrary, it is quite unclear to what extent these works could have served as manuals for the practice of divination (the ancient equivalent of "Seercraft for Dummies"). When one looks at the fragments of Philochorus in particular, one is struck by the fact that they deal with famous seers and famous divinatory incidents from the past. In other words, Philochorus, in addition to whatever else he may have discussed, was providing a sort of history of divination. In the first book of his *On Divination* he claimed that the mythical singer Orpheus had been a seer, and he subsequently discussed the meaning of the lunar eclipse that had prevented the Athenians from leaving Syracuse in 413.[84]

As far as we can tell from the examples recorded by Cicero, Antiphon's dream book, which was probably the first such book of its kind, did not present a systematic theory of dream interpretation. Rather, it was a collection of individual dreams with two examples of interpretation for each dream—an inferior one by someone else and a superior one by Antiphon himself.[85] Thus this book, it seems to me, was

---

78. Pendrick 2002: FF 78–81B.

79. *FGrH* 327, F 3.

80. *FGrH* 323, F 14 (= Athen. 409f–10b).

81. Athen. 11.473b; *FGrH* 353, F 7; Plut. *Nic.* 23.9; Jacoby 1949: 252 nn. 69–72.

82. *FGrH* 328, T 1.

83. Pliny *HN* index 17.243. For the dream book, see Artem. 1.31 and 4.23, with Lieshout 1980: 192–95.

84. *FGrH* 328, F 76–77 (Orpheus), F 135 (eclipse). Note too that in F 79 he attributes the authorship of two of Epicharmus's poems to a certain Axiopistus.

85. This is the view of Pendrick 2002: 49–53 (cf. Lieshout 1980: 223). Note esp. Cic. *Div.* 2.144 (= Pendrick 2002: F 80a).

not a manual for others to use, but an advertisement of the author's abilities. Similarly Philochorus gave the "correct" interpretation of the eclipse whose significance the seers on the spot had misconstrued.

Other such books will have been for merely private use, such as those "books concerning *mantikē* (divination)" inherited by Thrasyllus from his guest-friend the seer Polemaenetus.[86] It is also worth stressing that the dates of all of these works are relatively late. Antiphon is the earliest, at the end of the fifth century, but the rest all belong to the late fourth and third centuries B.C. Since none of these books survive, it is impossible to say just how detailed they were. Philochorus's work *On Divination* was perhaps the longest at four books. One ancient "book" comprised a papyrus roll and could fill anywhere between 30 and 120 pages in a modern printed text (to give a very rough estimate).

In theory, of course, anyone can recognize and interpret signs that the gods send, just as anyone can conduct a sacrifice.[87] When conducting any sort of sacrifice it was essential to ascertain whether it was acceptable to the gods. That was an action related to, but functionally distinct from, the procedures for asking specific questions through divination. A standard way of doing this apparently was to place the base of the spine and the tail (that is, the chine) of a sacrificed ox on the altar. If the tip of the tail turned up with the whole tail forming a curve, as modern experiment shows that it invariably would have done, that was a favorable omen.[88] It obviously would not have taken an expert seer, or even a priest, to read this type of sign.

In the *Anabasis*, for instance, Xenophon interprets his own dream, which he believed to have been sent by Zeus, and he himself knew how to conduct a divinatory sacrifice, including how to interpret the entrails. But if just anyone can do this with equal effectiveness and accuracy, then why hire a seer? Why not just do it yourself, picking up the skill either by observing others or from a book?

As mentioned above, some twenty-one vases depict a scene in which a warrior examines the entrails of a sacrificed victim.[89] Unfortunately, it is unclear whether these scenes are mythical or idealized versions of "everyday life," or how they relate

---

86. Isoc. *Aeginet.* 5–6, 45, discussed above.

87. One did not need to be a priest or a seer in order to perform a private sacrifice either at home or in a sanctuary. See Sourvinou-Inwood 2000b: 39–40; Jameson 1999: 338–39.

88. See Jameson (1986: 60–61), who identifies twenty-eight examples in Attic vase painting and who experimented with placing ox tails on a fire. See further Van Straten 1995: 118–44. The scholion to Ar. *Peace* 1054–55 is of particular importance.

89. For a succinct overview, see Van Straten 1995: 156–57; and, for more detail, Van der Meer 1979; Kossatz-Deissmann 1981; Durand and Lissarrague 1979; Lissarrague 1990: 55–69.

FIGURE 8.

A boy is presenting a liver to a young warrior, who is holding part of the entrails (perhaps a gallbladder) in his right hand. To the left is a Scythian archer, and to the right a woman is holding a *phiale*. The figures are labeled, but unfortunately the inscriptions make no sense (see Immerwahr 1990: 82 and *CVA* Würzburg 2, 19). Attic red-figure amphora, Kleophrades painter, 500–475 B.C. Martin von Wagner-Museum der Universität Würzburg Photo: K. Oehrlein 507 [Van Straten 1995: V262].

to actual contemporary practices.[90] The most common type of scene depicts a warrior who is facing left and inspecting the liver that is presented to him by a small boy (who is bearded on two vases) standing opposite him. In eighteen of the vases an old man stands directly behind the boy and gestures with one of his hands. On one vase, the old man is substituted for the warrior and inspects the entrails himself (see figs. 8–11). The focus of these vases is the warrior inspecting the entrails, especially

90. Ferrari (2003) problematizes the received opinion that representational scenes on Greek vases depict either myth (including epic subjects) or "genre," whose frame of reference is contemporary everyday life.

FIGURE 9.
A boy is presenting the entrails to an old man. A Scythian archer stands to their left. To their right (not shown here) are another warrior, a woman, and a Scythian archer. Attic black-figure amphora, fragment. Copenhagen, Nationalmuseet 3241 [Van Straten 1995: V247]. Drawn by Isabel Flower.

the liver, before departing for war. It is surely the case that he is not a seer, but a soldier who, like Xenophon, has enough of a working knowledge of extispicy to judge for himself whether the signs are favorable for departure. This should not at all surprise us, since in many cultures in which divination is widely practiced most men know how to divine without the aid of an expert.[91]

But who is the old man who is gesticulating to the left of the warrior in these

91. Zeitlyn (1990: 660) writes of Mambila spider divination: "Most married men know how to divine, but have varying degrees of confidence in their own skills. Hence if a problem is serious, it is likely to be taken to one of the acknowledged experts."

FIGURE 10.

A bearded hoplite examines the liver of a victim, which a youth holds out for him. On the left an old man gestures with his left hand. Black-figure amphora, c. 525–500 B.C. Château-Musée, Boulogne-sur-Mer, France [Van Straten 1995: V243]. Photo Erich Lessing / Art Resource, NY.

FIGURE 11.

A small bearded man (perhaps a slave) is presenting a liver to a bearded warrior. To the left an old man is gesturing with his left hand. Attic black-figure neck amphora, 525–500 B.C. Bonn, Akademisches Kunstmuseum 464.39 [Van Straten 1995: V242]. Photo Jutta Schubert.

scenes? Is he his father or some other older relative or a seer?[92] The former reading is more likely for two reasons. First of all, on one vase the old man is labeled "Nestor." This label serves to elevate the familiar scene by placing it in a heroic context. At the same time, the choice of "Nestor" suggests that the painter did not expect his audience to understand the old man to represent the type of the idealized seer. Second, the figure of the old man appears on other types of scenes as well, those marking the arming, leave-taking, and return of the warrior.[93] In all such

92. According to Van Straten (1995: 157), "the gesticulating old man in most cases can be interpreted as an experienced *mantis*, expounding on the signs he observes, while in some cases he may have been given the role of the old father taking leave of the departing warrior." This seems unlikely to me, and I see him as being a father figure in each case.

93. See Lissarrague 1989 and 1990: 55–69.

scenes the old man, warrior, and women who are depicted represent an idealized family group. Insofar as these vases depict a generic scene, it may well not be a contemporary scene, but one from the mythical/legendary past, perhaps a warrior setting out for the Trojan War.[94]

Oracles delivered by ecstatic utterance were open to the interpretation of any who heard them; that is, both the inquirer himself and all with whom the oracle was shared. The Assembly of Athenian citizens debated the meaning of the famous wooden wall oracle that it had obtained from Delphi. Both the professional interpreters of oracles (the so-called *chrēsmologoi*) and Themistocles offered rival interpretations, and it was up to the citizen body to choose between them.[95] But in practice, the seer was the acknowledged expert in the interpretation of nonverbal modes of divination. The citizen body may have felt competent to subject the ambiguities of Delphic utterances to rational examination, but the analysis of the entrails of an animal or of the visions in a dream was not analogous to evaluating the words of speakers before the Assembly or of litigants in a court of law. The former entailed esoteric knowledge and inherited charismatic skill. Seers were "craftsmen of the sacred," and their skill was highly specialized.

SEERS, PRIESTS, AND ORACLE-SINGERS

It is essential to distinguish seers from priests, since they performed different functions in Greek society and are often confused. Seers tended to move from city to city and attached themselves to prominent generals and statesmen as their personal advisers. A priest (*hiereus*), whether male or female, was an appointed public official who obtained office by lot, election, birth, or sale. Priests usually had no special religious training or knowledge, and their function was principally concerned with ritual. The priest's prime responsibility as *hiereus* was to manage offerings, sacrifices, and the sanctuary itself and its property, all of which were *hiera* (sacred).[96] The difference between priest and seer has been well expressed as follows: "In contrast to the priest, whose prestige derived from the renown of the cult he administered, the seer owed his prestige to the success and reliability of his prophecies."[97]

94. Following the general line of interpretation suggested by Ferrari 2003.
95. Hdt. 7.142−43.
96. Mikalson 2004: 11.
97. Harris 1995: 27. On the relationship between priest and seer, see further Trampedach 2007.

Of course, both seer and priest could derive prestige from their membership in an aristocratic clan or lineage (*genos*); the Athenian families of the Eumolpidae and Kerykes, for example, were the hereditary priests of the Eleusinian Mysteries. But unlike a priest, a seer was not merely a performer of prescribed rituals; he had to be successful in the practice of a skill or craft that depended on expertise and experience, and that might involve considerable personal danger.

The seer was endowed with personal charisma, which was due to his *personal* qualifications, as opposed to the charisma of office (a type of institutionalized charisma) that might be possessed by a priest.[98] The priest, insofar as his authority depended on his office, had no need to possess personal charisma; for the seer, such charisma was the basis of his authority and an essential aspect of his persona.

The seer was the most authoritative expert in the Greek world on matters pertaining to religion for another reason as well. He was free from the control of civic authorities, whether that authority be the *dēmos* collectively or a board of magistrates. Most, but certainly not all, seers were hired privately. In a sense, they were religious mercenaries. They could also act as mobile priests. A very famous scene brings this point home. During the banquet of reconciliation after the mutiny at Opis, Alexander's famous prayer that Persians and Macedonians might rule together in concord and partnership (Arr. 7.11.9) was preceded by the pouring of libations that were intiated by "the Greek seers and the magi" (the priests of the Zoroastrian religion). What is striking here is that the two peoples, Macedonians and Persians, are represented by the religious specialists who are most authoritative in their respective religious traditions. It is not their "priests" (*hiereis*) who represent the Macedonians, but their seers (*manteis*).

Sometimes our sources reveal a seer engaged in activities that we might otherwise expect to be within a priest's sphere. Thus, as mentioned above, it is the seers who pour the libations at Alexander's banquet of reconciliation. There is also the unique role that the Iamidae and Clytiadae played at Olympia. In the case of these particular seers, the general distinction between seer and priest becomes blurred; for in addition to practicing divination, they were responsible for the care of the great altar of Zeus and for certain monthly sacrifices, and those were duties of a kind that usu-

98. The classic treatment of charismatic authority is Weber 1978: vol. 1, 241–54 (first published in 1922). For criticism of Weber's view, see Geertz 1983 and Bourdieu 1987, and, in general, Lindholm 1990. Despite qualifications to his detailed theory, I still believe that the distinction between these two types of charisma is valid.

ally belonged to priests, not to seers.[99] Finally, Xenophon relates (*Anab.* 4.5.3–4) an incident that took place as the Ten Thousand were marching through Armenia that is doubly revealing, for it opens a window both into the initiative that a seer might take on his own and into the system of belief that formed the context of his actions. When a harsh north wind was blasting the soldiers in their faces, "one of the seers told them to sacrifice to the wind, and the sacrifice was made, and it seemed completely clear to everyone that the harshness of the wind abated." This seer is very much acting like a mobile priest who knows how to appease the gods through sacrifice rather than as a diviner per se.

There are two other groups with whom seers are sometimes confused. One is the *chrēsmologoi*, who were professional collectors, chanters, and interpreters of oracles.[100] The other group is the *exēgētai*, or interpreters of sacred law, about whom we know very little.[101] The relationship between seers and *chrēsmologoi* is both crucial to an understanding of how seers saw themselves and highly controversial in modern scholarship. Major collections of oracles were in circulation, attributed to the legendary prophets Musaeus, Bacis, and Orpheus, or to the various Sibyls.[102] *Chrēsmologoi* might offer to interpret oracles from their own personal collections, or, as at Athens in 481, they could presume to interpret oracles that had come from Delphi.

The scholia to Aristophanes and to other poets of Old Comedy, but never contemporary sources of the fifth and fourth centuries, call some individuals (such as the Athenian seer Lampon) both a seer and a *chrēsmologos*. Classical authors, on the other hand, are careful to distinguish between the two.[103] As a point of method, however, confusion in the scholia, which were compiled at a much later date, should not lead us to believe that there was no distinction in the classical period; in short, the

---

99. See Paus. 5.13.11 and 5.15.10, with Weniger 1915: 104ff. and Roth 1982: 181–83.

100. See Fontenrose 1978: 145–58; Shapiro 1990; Baumgarten 1998: 38–48; Henrichs 2003: 52–54; Bowden 2003; Dillery 2005; and Parker 2005: 111–15. The term *chrēsmologos*, because it designates a varied range of activities, is impossible to render by a single English word. As Fontenrose (1978: 153) points out, "the *logos* suffix appears to reflect either of the two meanings of *legein*, "speak" or "gather," so that a *chrēsmologos* may be either an oracle-speaker . . . or an oracle-collector." Cf. Dillery 2005: 169–70.

101. See Oliver 1950 and Clinton 1974.

102. Herodotus, for example, quotes oracles that he attributes to Bacis at 8.20. 8.77, and 9.43.

103. Thuc. 8.1.1; Eur. *Heracl.* 401–3; and perhaps Pl. *Ap.* 22c, *Meno* 99c–d, and *Ion* 534d. Plato's distinction between χρησμῳδοί and θεομάντεις may correspond to that between χρησμολόγοι and μάντεις; but this is problematic because he sees both χρησμῳδοί and θεομάντεις (like poets) as being inspired prophetic figures.

scholia's confusion should not be ours.[104] It is not sufficient, however, merely to assert that the scholia are mistaken; one needs to explain how and why this happened. The following is an attempt to do so. Religious experts, whom other sources referred to as *manteis* (seers), were lampooned in Old Comedy as being *chrēsmologoi*. If this suggestion is correct, then Lampon, and even perhaps Hierocles, were not *chrēsmologoi*, but they were portrayed and referred to as such on the comic stage. The sources of our extant scholia, being of a different cultural milieu and not knowing the function and nature of Attic comedy, explained the discrepancy between comedy and various prose texts by assuming that such individuals were both *manteis* and *chrēsmologoi*. The distinction would have been lost even on as early a source as the great Alexandrian scholar Aristarchus of Samothrace (c. 216–144 B.C.), who wrote commentaries on the plays of Aristophanes.

When Thucydides says (8.1.1) that the Athenians in 413 B.C. "were angry both with the *chrēsmologoi* and the seers (*manteis*), and with as many others who, through the practice of divination, in some way at that time had caused them to hope that they would capture Sicily," he is clearly not treating these terms as synonymous. The difference in function and role is also made explicit in a passage of Euripides' play *The Children of Heracles*, which was perhaps performed in 430 B.C. Demophon, the king of Athens, has made preparations for battle with the invading Argives and declares (399–404):

The city is in arms, the sacrificial victims stand in readiness for the gods to whom they are to be sacrificed, and offerings are being made throughout the city by seers. I gathered all of the singers of oracles into one place and closely examined their prophecies.

The seer sacrifices, but the "singers of oracles" chant from their collections of prophecies. Seer and *chrēsmologos* practiced related, but not identical, professions.[105] They were related in that both professions dealt with divination, with making the will of the gods known to men; but they went about this task in very different ways that required a different expertise.

---

104. An overlap between seers and *chrēsmologoi* (with some individuals calling themselves by both names) is argued by Oliver 1950: 6–11; Garland 1990: 82–86; Baumgarten 1998: 47; and Bowden 2003. Those who argue for a clear distinction include Argyle 1970; Smith 1989: 142 n. 6; Olson 1998: 269; Parker in his review of Baumgarten (*BMCR* 2000.01.12); and Dillery 2005: 170.

105. This point is nicely made by Dillery 2005: 170.

The social distinction between the seer and the oracle-singer is well brought out in a passage of Aristophanes' *Peace* (1052–1119).[106] Trygaeus has been preparing a sacrifice to the goddess Peace, when Hierocles, wearing à laurel crown, approaches Trygaeus and his slave. The slave says: "Now who in the world can that be? He looks like a charlatan (ἀλαζών). Is he a *mantis*?" Then Trygaeus answers: "No, by Zeus, but it is Hierocles, the *chrēsmologos* from Oreus." It appears from this passage, as well as from others, that the role of *mantis* was more prestigious than that of *chrēsmologos*. In fact, the point of the joke may be that theo Hierocles of real life would never have called himself a *chrēsmologos*. We know from a fragmentary line of a lost comedy called *Poleis*, performed during the same dramatic festival as Aristophanes' *Peace*, that the playwright Eupolis called Hierocles a *chrēsmōidos* (a person who chants oracles).[107] The distinction between the prestige of the seer and the marginality of the *chrēsmologos* was probably true as a general rule.

Yet this same Hierocles is mentioned in an inscription of 446/5 (or, less likely, of 424/3), a decree concerning Athenian relations with the city of Chalcis on the island of Euboea. He here appears as undertaking an important commission by the *dēmos:* "Three men, chosen by the Council from among its members, in company with Hierocles, are to make the sacrifices required by the oracles concerning Euboea as quickly as possible. That it be done most speedily shall be the joint responsibility of the generals and they shall supply the money required for it."[108] I have given a literal translation in order to emphasize the fact that Hierocles is not on a par with his three colleagues in this sacrifice: he apparently is some sort of religious expert, whereas they are ordinary members of the Council of 500. Unfortunately, Hierocles is not given a title in this inscription. Yet if he is the same man as appears in Aristophanes, then his expertise as an interpreter of oracles may have recommended him for this particular religious commission. And his reward may have been significant, if he is called "from Oreus" (a city in Euboea) because he had been given an allotment of land that had been confiscated from the native Euboeans.[109] So either a *chrēsmologos* could be charged with important tasks and duly awarded for performing them (and as is discussed in chapter 3, Hierocles may have been given the

---

106. The interpretation of this passage by Bowden (2003: 263) is far-fetched.

107. F 231 Kassel and Austin: "Hierocles, best lord of oracle chanters."

108. *IG* I². 39; *ML* 52; Fornara 103, lines 65–69. On Hierocles, see Olson 1998: 268–69; Bowden 2003: 266–68; and Dillery 2005: 193–95. Olson (1998: 269) suggests that "the oracles in question may well have been pronounced by Hierocles himself." That, of course, is nothing more than an imaginative conjecture.

109. As suggested by Halliday (1913: 97), and repeated by subsequent scholars.

high honor of permanent dining in the Prytaneum), or the point of Aristophanes' joke has been lost on modern scholars who tend to take his "factual" statements at face value. In sum, Aristophanes and Eupolis may have lobbed an insult at Hierocles by calling him on the stage what he never would have called himself in real life— saying that he was not a *mantis*, but a *chrēsmologos*.

In theory as well as in practice, as we have seen, the functions of *mantis* and *chrēsmologos* were distinct. In other words, when investigating the nature of religious specialists, as Max Weber famously does in his *Sociology of Religion*, it is useful to isolate "ideal types."[110] Although such attempts at classification have largely fallen out of favor in recent scholarship, nonetheless, these types may indeed correspond to the way some religious specialists think about themselves and their role in society. In practice, as Weber himself realized, contrasted types flow into one another. The situation in ancient Greece may have been fluid because a *mantis* or *chrēsmologos*, unlike a *hiereus*, was not authorized by the state or by a sanctuary; anyone could call himself by those terms, and legitimacy depended on one's being accepted as such by one's clients. Yet those clients, it would appear, did not expect the same person to exercise both functions, and the expertise of the *mantis*, who practiced extispicy and augury, and that of the *chrēsmologos*, who interpreted written oracles, were quite different. And indeed their functions are depicted differently in our sources. Herodotus mentions both, and whereas the *mantis* is in charge of divinatory sacrifices, the *chrēsmologos* is concerned only with the recitation and interpretation of oracular verse. There is also some evidence that in addition to peddling their collections of ancient oracles, some *chrēsmologoi* wrote poems and hymns in their own names.[111] Some historical seers of the late classical and Hellenistic periods wrote prose books on divination, but not one of them appears to have written verse.

The most famous, and perhaps most influential, *chrēsmologos* was the Athenian Onomacritus. Herodotus tells us (7.6) that his services were much used by Hippar-

110. 1963 [1922] 20–31. Wach (1944: 331–73), elaborating on Weber, distinguished nine discrete types of religious authorities. His scheme is attacked by Rüpke (1996), who subsumes all religious experts under the rubric of "agents of control." Frankfurter (2002) presents a taxonomy of patterns of ritual expertise that allows for fluidity among "types" of ritual experts. See further Turner 1968b.

111. Onomacritus of Athens, who was closely connected with the Pisistratidae (Hdt. 7.6), apparently wrote a poem (in hexameters) that mentioned Heracles, and another about Dionysus (Paus. 8.31.3, 37.5), and his contemporary and rival, Lasus of Hermione, composed a *Hymn to Demeter* that famously was written without the letter sigma (Athen. 467a, 455c, 624e). See further Shapiro 1990.

chus, the son of the tyrant Pisistratus, and that he "edited" the oracles of Musaeus. He fell from favor, however, when he was "caught in the act" by Lasus of Hermione (perhaps a person of the same profession) of inserting an oracle into the verses of Musaeus.[112] He was consequently exiled by Hipparchus. After being reconciled with the family of Pisistratus, he went with them to the court of Xerxes and there recited from his collection those poems that prophesied Persian success in an expedition against Greece, carefully omitting anything that indicated failure. It is noteworthy that in Herodotus's account Onomacritus does not interpret any portents or perform any rite of divination. He was a clever and successful performer to be sure, but the tools of his trade were quite different from those of contemporary seers.

There is, however, one odd exception to the general distinction that I have tried to draw. Herodotus tells the story of the *chrēsmologos* Amphilytus (1.62), who became inspired and gave a verse prophecy to Pisistratus before the battle of Pallene in 546 B.C. (quoted in chapter 3). This passage stands alone as evidence for a "historical" itinerant religious specialist producing his own inspired prophecy in verse (as opposed to interpreting omens, dreams, portents, livers, and legendary oracles).[113] Indeed, in a striking passage, the travel writer Pausanias, when describing the oracle of Amphiaraus in Boeotia, makes this general distinction (1.34.4): "Except those whom they say were inspired by Apollo with madness in ancient times, none of the seers was a *chrēsmologos,* but they were good at explaining dreams and interpreting the flights of birds and the entrails of victims. My opinion is that Amphiaraus devoted himself most to the exposition of dreams. It is clear that, at the time when he was recognized as a god, it was a dream oracle that he set up." Here *chrēsmologos* probably means "singer of oracles," and Pausanias, writing in the first century A.D., is claiming, rightly or wrongly, that "historical seers" (including the for us "mythical" Amphiaraus) were not the inspired singers of verse prophecies.

For reasons that are not completely clear *chrēsmologoi* largely disappear from the historical record after 413 B.C. This was surely not exclusively a result of their support for the ill-fated Sicilian expedition undertaken by the Athenians in 415–413. It is likely that their social status and prestige were already in decline by the second

---

112. On this incident see the excellent discussion by Dillery (2005: 167–68, 190–92), who plausibly suggests that Onomacritus and Lasus were engaged in a competitive public performance of oracular texts.

113. The line of verse attributed by Herodotus (8.96) to an otherwise unknown Athenian *chrēsmologos* by the name Lysistratus is not analogous. Herodotus cannot date him and merely says that his prophecy was delivered "many years before" the battle of Salamis, to which it pertained.

quarter of the fifth century and that the Sicilian expedition merely accelerated a process that was well underway.[114] Already in Herodotus *chrēsmologoi* are depicted as being less competent and less trustworthy than seers. Indeed, according to Herodotus (7.143), if the Athenians had accepted the advice of the *chrēsmologoi* in 481 B.C., they would have abandoned Attica and colonized some other land without even making an attempt to resist the Persians with their fleet. They were wrong about Salamis and wrong again about Syracuse. It would be nice to know what the majority of them had counseled about undertaking the Peloponnesian War with Sparta in 431 B.C. Had they discredited themselves yet again? By the early fourth century it is hard to find a trace of them. Xenophon has repeated references to seers but only once mentions a *chrēsmologos*, and that was in Sparta, not Athens.[115]

Perhaps too they were victims of the transition from oral to written culture. By the end of the fifth century one could more easily buy collections of oracles, and thus the professional reciters of those collections were less in demand. Their function in society depended on their special access to arcane knowledge, in the form of oracle collections that could assist one in difficult situations. They also were extremely familiar with these oracles and sometimes even edited their own collections of them, which meant that they could pick out the appropriate oracle for any given situation. Once those texts were widely available, the prestige of the *chrēsmologos* could depend only on his skill at interpretation, rather than on the fact of his possessing the text. With the rise of rhetoric in the later fifth century, the other claim to exclusive or specialized knowledge was also removed. Now any literate person with a knowledge of rhetoric could interpret those texts for himself, and he might even purchase them for his own personal perusal.

THE GREEK SEER
BETWEEN MAGIC AND RELIGION

Just as controversial, and as important, is the relationship between the seer and the magician (*magos*) and sorcerer (*goēs*). Plato tends to conflate seers and magicians, and recent modern scholarship has argued that the boundary between religion and magic is a fluid one or even that there is no real difference between the two.[116]

---

114. Shapiro (1990: 344–45) argues that their status may already have been in decline by 480.
115. Xen. *Hell.* 3.3.3. This Diopeithes, who is mentioned as being in Sparta in 400 B.C., may have been an Athenian; see further chapter 4.
116. *Rep.* 364b and *Leg.* 909b.

Nonetheless, our sources suggest that the Greek seer straddled that boundary as it was perceived to exist by the Greeks themselves; that is, seers sometimes attempted, as did magicians, to manipulate and coerce the gods by supernatural means. On other occasions, particularly when practicing sacrificial divination, they merely interpreted the signs that were sent by the gods; but even then it was within their competence to avert unfavorable signs through the proper rituals. Nevertheless, one thing remains clear. The Greeks had different conceptual categories for seer, on the one hand, and for magician/sorcerer/beggar priest, on the other. And whereas *mantis* was usually a positive term and one to which a high status could be attached, *magos, goēs,* and *agurtēs* were generally terms of reproach. There is room for confusion, however, because none of these social roles or occupations were certified by the state or community. Anyone could insult a *mantis* by calling him a *magos,* and any *magos* could lay claim to higher status by calling himself a *mantis.* You could call yourself whatever you wanted; the proof of expertise lay in what *other* people were willing to call you.[117]

The fact that the same person could perform different functions under a variety of appellations does not in any way entail that the Greeks made no distinction between the social value and acceptability of those functions. Two famous texts illustrate these points. When Oedipus turns on Teiresias in the *Oedipus Tyrannus* (385–96), he asserts that Teiresias is no *mantis,* but a *magos* (wizard) and *agurtēs* (beggar priest).[118] And in Aeschylus's *Agamemnon* (1273–74), Cassandra laments how she was treated by her fellow Trojans: "Like a wandering begging priestess (*agurtria*), I endured being called 'beggar, poor wretch, and starveling.'" Far from showing that there was a single class of persons who presented themselves as simultaneously being *manteis, magoi,* and *agurtai,* these passages demonstrate quite unambiguously the opposite.[119] The harshest insult that one could pay a *mantis* was to call him or her a *magos* or *agurtēs.* The latter might claim to be *manteis,* but no

117. See Parker 2005: 118, 134.

118. Rigsby (1976), however, argues that the term *magos* has the same meaning here as in Herodotus, where the Persian magi are conspicuous for their bold and treacherous political maneuvering; he thus suggests the translation "kingmaker" (*contra* Dawe [1982: 132–33] and Bremmer [1999: 3], who argue for the meaning "quack, charlatan"). But this negative characterization of the magi is restricted to the story of the false Smerdis in book 3. Elsewhere in Herodotus, the magi are loyal advisors to the King in regard to omens and portents. For *magos* as "wizard" or "sorcerer" in Greek thought, see Graf 1997: 20–35 and Dickie 2001: 27–46.

119. For a different interpretation of these passages, see Dickie (2001: 60–74), who argues that there was no strict differentiation in role between seers and magicians and between other forms of holy men and magicians.

respectable *mantis* would employ those designations as part of his or her self-advertisement. One wonders, Did anyone ever call himself or herself an *agurtēs*, or was it always a term of reproach, like the English term "quack" (an abbreviation of "quacksalver") for someone pretending to have medical training?[120]

In his famous work on Dinka religion, the anthropologist Godfrey Lienhardt noted there were people called *tyet*, "a class of specialists that comprise individuals of widely differing reputations for occult knowledge and powers." One of the least prestigious was called an *acoor*. Lienhardt observes: "It would be unlikely that any *tyet* with a high reputation would be spoken of as *acoor*, though an *acoor* would also be referred to as *tyet* by those who thought highly of him."[121] So too, one might imagine, was the relationship between seers and other religious specialists.

The relationship between magic and religion (or even whether they should be seen as distinct phenomena) has been, and continues to be, the subject of heated debate. Both terms are also problematic in the sense that there may not be a universally applicable definition of either of them. In a very influential essay, Talal Asad has argued that "there cannot be a universal definition of religion, not only because its constituent elements and relationships are historically specific, but because that definition is itself the historical product of discursive processes."[122] If Asad is correct, or even partially so, it follows that we may need to construct a definition of "religion," and therefore also of "magic," that is uniquely appropriate to the Greek city-states. I think that one would not go far wrong in defining Greek *polis* religion as "those practices, rituals, and beliefs that constitute a culturally patterned interaction with culturally postulated supernatural beings."[123] Yet accepting so general, and so vague, a definition of Greek "religion" will not get us very far in solving the problem of how to distinguish it from "magic."

However that may be, it is easy to be seduced by the definition of James Frazer, who famously and influentially postulated that magic is coercive and religion is per-

---

120. The verb ἀγυρτάζειν (to collect by begging) has a pejorative meaning in Homer at *Od.* 19.284 (its only appearance in Greek literature).

121. 1961: 68.

122. 1993: 28.

123. I am here adapting the influential definition of Spiro (1973: 96), who defines religion as "an institution consisting of culturally patterned interaction with culturally postulated superhuman beings." There is also something useful in Horton's view (1993: 23) that religion is "an extension of the field of people's social relationships beyond the confines of purely human society," in which humans see themselves in a dependent relationship with supernatural beings. I discuss the problem of how to define Athenian religion in Flower 2008b.

suasive.[124] Magical practices seek to harness and coerce supernatural powers for self-interested ends; religious practices, by means of prayer and sacrifices, attempt to persuade specific deities to render their assistance.

Frazer's definition is attractive because of its simplicity and because it seems to be foreshadowed by Plato, who in his *Laws* (909b) prescribes imprisonment for life for those who "promise to persuade the gods by beguiling them through sacrifices and prayers and spells."[125] The proper object of piety, as Plato expresses it in the *Euthyphro* (14b–15a) and which may be taken to be the normative view of his contemporaries (although not his own view), is "to say and do things gratifying to the gods by praying and sacrificing." What the gods specifically desire from mortals via sacrifice is "honor, prerogatives, and gratitude." Thus those priests and seers who attempt to bind the gods practice a perversion of religion, and in his *Laws* Plato specifies the death penalty as the punishment for any *mantis* who attempts to harm someone through spells and incantations (*Leg.* 933d–e). Plato's formulation is problematic, however, because his religious beliefs were not necessarily those of the average Greek, or even Athenian, and his distinction between religion and magic is surely far more narrow than the popular one, insofar as most Greeks even thought about the distinction at all.

In actual experience, the distinction between magic and religion is fluid, and both can coexist within the same body of ritual acts. Both religion and magic rely on prayer, sacrifice, and incantation to achieve their ends. But whereas religious practices tend to be under the control of the *polis*, magical practices are beyond public

---

124. This is the Frazerian definition, following Graf 1997: 20–27 (cf. Graf 1995). Note also the very useful definition offered by Thomassen (1999: 65): "Magic is the appropriation of ritual power for personal ends, offsetting the balance between the individual and the collective which forms the sanctioned norm of ritual practice in societies. Magic depends on normal ritual and relates dialectically to it, by combining features which are the same as the ones performed in normal rituals—hymns, prayers, invocations, sacrifices, etc.—with features which are deliberately different from it. A kind of intertextuality thus operates between magic and the official religious ritual forms. This suggests that the most fruitful approach is neither to make an absolute distinction between religious ritual and magical practices, nor to pretend there is no difference. Historically, religious rites and magic have always existed side by side—there is never the one without the other. Theoretically, too, the mutual relationship and interdependence of the two should be more basically interesting than religion and magic studied separately." At the other extreme, Gager (1992: 24–25) argues that there is no distinction at all between "magic" and "religion" and that "magic, as a definable and consistent category of human experience, simply does not exist." Bremmer (1999: 9–12) accepts that there exists in our Greek sources a contrast "between magic and normative religious practices," but nevertheless rejects the contrast between "religion" and magic as a Victorian invention. See further Versnel (1991), who gives a full bibliography on this problem.

125. For Plato's concept of magic, see Graf 2002: 97–99.

control and therefore are perceived as being dangerous. Yet the difference between magic and religion is also one of context and social approval. Magic is activity meant to achieve the goals of prevailing religion in ways disapproved of by that religion.[126] Thus both magic and religion are goal-oriented, but the relationship of each to the supernatural, at least in Greek eyes, was different.

Seers could be employed officially by the *polis* and even officially assigned to specific generals (as at Athens).[127] The rites of public divination that seers conducted were not seen as "magical" by their contemporaries, although they might seem so to us. Rather, extispicy, hepatoscopy, and ornithomancy were considered to be normal procedures of established religion. As our texts unambiguously indicate, it was in no way extraordinary, unusual, or suspicious for either an individual or a community to use divination for guidance on difficult issues, and it was expected that one would seek the services of a professional seer in order to do so. In this respect it has been cogently pointed out that magic and divination bear an inverse relationship to each other:

> To put it simply, magic acts to affect a result directly or to influence events while divination produces signs—a text to be read. The ritual sacrifice is a gift offered to the gods which passes from the human to the divine realm. The exta of the sacrificial animal becomes the vehicle for the crossing of domains in the other direction when the gods inscribe divinatory meaning on the exta. What divination reveals, magic can resolve.[128]

Yet who was responsible in Greek society for the resolution of what divination revealed? That is, apart from simply avoiding those actions that the gods disapproved of, what sort of "ritual" action could be taken? There is some evidence (discussed in the next chapter) that seers could avert unfavorable signs through apotropaic sacrifices. Beyond that it was preeminently the secret rites of initiation and cursing, mentioned by Plato, that could be used to link the *mantis* with the practitioners of sorcery and wizardry. Seers were also wanderers, moving from city to city. Thus Plato can link them rhetorically with itinerant beggar priests who wander from city to city ripping off the rich by offering to cure them of inherited

126. See Fowler 2000, 322–23, 339–43.
127. See chapter 4, note 37.
128. Guinan 2002: 18

blood guilt through sacrifices and incantations and to harm their enemies through spells.

In the end, one is faced with a simple question. Why was an individual or a community ready to pay a great deal of money in order to hire a famous seer? Was it just because of a seer's skill and experience in correctly reading omens? Or was there some implicit idea that a good seer could make the signs turn out in a favorable way? Such a notion of casually obtaining favorable omens, it must be stressed, is never stated explicitly. Yet it is hinted at in a small number of texts. Some texts hint that the seer was expected, in some mysterious way, to work success for his client, to obtain somehow, perhaps by virtue of his abilities or special relationship to supernatural beings, favorable omens. This possibility is discussed in chapter 3.

In conclusion, if one were to ask how someone became a seer, the answer might be something as follows. It was helpful, but not absolutely essential, to be the son of a seer. Aptitude was probably just as important as genealogy. Nonetheless, it must have been important to become an apprentice to a well-respected seer. In many cultures, the diviner must be accredited by undergoing a public initiation, but evidence for this is lacking for Greece—not surprisingly so, since seers often traveled between cities.[129]

The would-be seer had to be ready and willing to interpret various kinds of signs, both solicited and unsolicited. The former was required when one's employer was about to engage in some important activity and sought divine approval. It was then that the seer needed to sacrifice an animal and examine its entrails or set up a station for examining the flight of birds. But it wasn't sufficient simply to perform by prearrangement. One also had to be ready, even on the spur of the moment, to interpret unsought signs—that is, chance utterances and natural phenomena. Lightning, thunder, the flight of birds, even an eclipse, might occur at any time, and the seer would be expected first of all to decide if the occurrence was an omen, and then, upon its being accepted as an omen, to interpret its meaning.

The prospective seer needed a quick wit and a charismatic personality. It was just not enough to be able to interpret god-sent signs correctly, whether solicited or not; one had to project an image of self-confidence, trustworthiness, and, if at all possible, of enjoying the favor of the gods. Employment might take one far from one's native city, whether serving other Greek communities or even foreign princes, such as Cyrus the Younger. Successful seers at the high end of their profession were able

129. See Fortes 1987: 10.

to make very large sums of money. It was a great advantage at the start of one's career to be able to claim descent from one of the great mantic families or at least to be a member of the aristocracy. Nevertheless, there was plenty of scope for talent to assert itself and to be recognized. Deiphonus, it is worth remarking once again, contracted work throughout Greece by claiming that he was the son of a very famous inspired seer, a sort of historical Teiresias figure. Herodotus tells us that not everyone was convinced, and, for all his contemporaries knew, Deiphonus might just as well have been a brash upstart without a pedigree who was extremely good at what he did.

THREE

The Role and Image
of the Seer

I know that what the lord Teiresias sees, is most often
what the lord Apollo sees.

THE CHORUS in Sophocles, *Oedipus Tyrannus*

In general terms divination may be defined as "the attempt to elicit from some higher power or supernatural being the answers to questions beyond the range of ordinary human understanding."[1] In other words, divination is a means of bridging the gap between gods and humans in such a way that humans may profit from the knowledge thus acquired. What one scholar of ancient Near Eastern religion has said of Neo-Assyrian prophecy holds true for Greece as well: "The legitimation of all divination was based on the idea that gods indeed communicate with humans and that the decisions of the heavenly world affect earthly circumstances. There were different channels, however, through which the divine will was brought to humans' attention, as well as different human beings who were qualified to take care of the logistics."[2]

What the Greeks called "the craft of divination" (*mantikē technē*) was the art of interpreting the meaning of signs that were sent by the gods. The god-sent sign is the instrument of mediation between the knowledge of the gods and the more limited knowledge of humans.[3] It was not only the responsibility of the seer to choose the correct interpretation amidst a range of possible interpretations; it was also essential first to recognize the sign as a sign. A chance event becomes an omen when the cir-

1. Loewe and Blacker 1981: 1.
2. Nissinen 2000b: 110.
3. On the function of the sign in Greek divination, see esp. Manetti 1993. Note also Burkert 1996: 156–76; Leszl 1996; and Reynolds 2004.

cumstances require it, "when the underlying tension of a personal situation kindles the signifying power of an omen."[4] The meaning of some omens and portents was obvious once they were recognized as such, of others less so; but in either case there could be no interpretation until the act of recognition had taken place.[5] The experienced seer, therefore, needed both to recognize the portent and then to interpret it.

The most sophisticated definition of divination to be found in an ancient source is that put forward by the third-century B.C. Stoic philosopher Chrysippus, as quoted by Cicero (*Div.* 2.130): "Divination is the power to see, understand, and explain premonitory signs given to men by the gods. Its duty is to know in advance the disposition of the gods toward men, the manner in which that disposition is shown, and by what means the gods may be propitiated and their threatened ills averted." This definition is predicated on the belief that the gods know more than humans and that they are willing to share that knowledge. Indeed, Xenophon's general observation at *Hipparchicus* 9.8–9 may be taken to apply to the whole of archaic and classical Greek culture: "In a war enemies plot against one another but seldom know whether these plots are well laid. It is impossible to find any other advisers in such matters except the gods. They know everything, and they give signs in advance to whomever they wish through sacrifices, birds of omen, voices, and dreams. And it is likely that they are more ready to give advice to those who not only ask what they should do when they happen to be in need, but even in good fortune attend to the gods in whatever way they are able." Although the notion that the gods were omniscient may have been an innovation of Xenophon's own generation, in general terms Xenophon has concisely expressed the Greek attitude toward divination from Homer onward.[6]

4. Guinan 2002: 21, which is a particularly insightful analysis of the nature and psychology of divination.

5. As Guinan (2002: 22) points out: "Therefore, a divinatory reading is a two part process. First, an observer recognizes an omen which stands out from the phenomenal background of life and then subsequently finds and resolves the prediction."

6. Xenophon represents Socrates in the *Memorabilia* as believing both that the gods know everything and that they are willing to communicate their knowledge to mortals through signs (see esp. 1.1.9 and 1.1.19; cf. *Cyr.* 1.6.46). Although Xenophon treats Socrates' belief in the efficacy of divination as being normative, he nonetheless claims that his emphasis on the gods' omniscience is in contrast to what the majority think, who "believe that the gods know some things but not other things." The whole point of this depiction is to demonstrate that Socrates' religious views were essentially mainstream and conventional, and thus that he could not possibly have been guilty of impiety. But Socrates' conventional piety also serves to sanction Xenophon's own religious actions as described in the *Anabasis* (as noted by Price [1999: 86]). On the religious beliefs of Xenophon himself, see Dillery 1995: 179–94.

THE SOCIAL FUNCTION
OF DIVINATION

It is possible, however, to go beyond the definitions given by our sources to uncover the social function of divination. That is to say, the Greeks resorted to divination because they believed that the gods were willing to communicate with mortals; at the same time, the various rites of divination were socially useful. We must not think that any seer who attached himself to a particular client was a type of primitive therapist, whose primary function was to relieve his client of doubt and indecision. Rather, as has been well expressed in a seminal article by the anthropologist George Park, "divination normally provides more than the 'psychological release that comes from the conviction that subsequent action is in tune with the wishes of supernatural forces' (Herskovits 1938, II, p. 217); the association of divination with situations of problematical action is best explained, after all, by the fact that it lends to a client's subsequent act a peculiar but effective type of legitimation."[7]

In general terms, divination not only provides answers to perplexing and difficult questions; it also facilitates decisive action in cases where individuals might otherwise be at a loss to act. When faced with a number of alternative courses of action, divination allows one to bypass indecision and to proceed with confidence with a specific course of action. Such was the case when Xenophon could not decide whether to accept the sole command of the Ten Thousand (6.1.22–24): because he could not decide, he sacrificed to Zeus the King, who unambiguously indicated to him (through extispicy) that he should neither seek it nor accept it. This example, however, is not completely transparent because Xenophon realized that accepting the sole command would have been very risky (as discussed below).

A less ambiguous incident comes near the end of the *Anabasis* (7.6.43–44). Xenophon was again faced with a critical personal decision, and this time, unlike in the previous example, both alternatives were fraught with danger. Xenophon had to choose whether to remain in Thrace as the possessor of fortified positions on the coast that the Thracian king Seuthes has promised to give him or to accompany the remainder of the Ten Thousand as they undertook military service for Sparta. On the one hand, Seuthes had failed to keep any of his promises in the past, and there was no good reason to trust him now. On the other hand, Xenophon had heard rumors, both from Seuthes himself and from other sources, that the new Spartan

7. Park 1963: 196. Note also Fortes 1987: 11. Among works of classical scholarship, see esp. Morgan 1990: 153–55.

commander Thibron intended to execute him as soon as he got him in his power. Faced with two uncertain futures, each fraught with danger and each impossible to evaluate by human reason and knowledge alone, Xenophon naturally turned to the gods for assistance. Accordingly, he "took two victims and sacrificed to Zeus the King whether it would be better and preferable for him to remain with Seuthes on the conditions that Seuthes says, or to go away with the army. He [Zeus?] declares to him to go away."

On some occasions, and especially in connection with oracles, divination serves to define the parameters of the problem and to isolate for the inquirer just what his alternatives are. For example, the famous wooden wall oracle of 481 B.C. set out for the Athenians their options with the likely consequences for each option: they could emigrate to a new land, fight a land battle and surely be defeated, or fight at sea and possibly win.[8] In either case, when divination indicates a specific course of action or defines the range of possible actions, it serves as an aid to decision making and requires the exercise of reason to interpret the oracular response. And finally, divination brings objectivity into human conflicts and can arbitrate between opposing and mutually exclusive points of view. In sum, divination provides answers when answers are not otherwise available. In some societies those answers may be socially useful answers as well, providing a means of avoiding potential conflict among members of a community or forcing individuals to deviate from habitual modes of behavior that might prove harmful.[9] In the specific case of warfare, divination also served as a mechanism of reassurance, which helped amateur soldiers to face the terrors of hoplite battle.[10] It was only natural for commanders to advertise good omens as a means of boosting the morale of their troops before battle.[11]

What use did knowledge of the future provide? First of all, it is necessary to point out that the function of divination is normally to provide a guide to action. Knowledge of the future was not sought for its own sake, as a matter of idle curios-

8. Parker 1985: 301–2.

9. See Park 1963 and Collins 1978: 237–39. Among the Yoruba of Africa, divination is used by young men to select a house site when they get married, thus eliminating the potential social friction involved in choosing which kinship unit to join. Scapulimancy (divination by means of heating an animal's shoulder blade over a fire) was employed by the Naskapi of Labrador in Canada to choose the direction in which to hunt; in practice it acted as a chancelike instrument that kept them from overhunting the game in a particular area (something that habit, based on success, might otherwise have led them to do).

10. So Wees 1996: 11–12 and Parker 2000: 303–4.

11. See Pritchett 1979: 58–60.

ity.[12] Divination, in the words of Xenophon (*Mem.* 1.4.15; *Symp.* 4.47), tells us "what we ought to do and what not." Likewise, the primary function of an oracle was to provide advice about present problems, not necessarily to predict the future.[13] This is already made explicit in our earliest source for Delphic prophecy, the *Homeric Hymn to Pythian Apollo* (287–93), where Apollo says that he intends to establish an oracular center where he will give "unerring advice" to all who consult it.

Nevertheless, the distinction thus made between "present" and "future" is somewhat slippery. By asking "Should I do x or y?" it is true that the inquirer seeks advice about a problem in the present, but his subsequent action, or lack of action, must by definition take place in the future. So all oracles, it would be more accurate to say, deal with present problems, which have a future frame of reference (or future consequences). The gods act as advisers (as both Herodotus and Xenophon make clear), and that implies that individuals have real choices.[14] The future is not inexorably fixed in all of its details.

The Greeks of the archaic and classical periods had no sense of "fate" in the strong sense of the word; that is, in terms of an unchangeable and all-encompassing predetermination.[15] In fact, they had no single word that corresponds to fate in that sense. The closest equivalent is *moira*, which is one's allotted share or portion, used often in reference to the length of one's life. But even one's *moira* was alterable. It could be extended by divine intervention. And so Apollo, as a favor to Croesus, persuaded the fates, the *moirai*, to delay the capture of Sardis by three years (Hdt. 1.91), and Athena persuaded Zeus to grant the protection of the "wooden wall" to the Athenians (Hdt. 7.141). One's *moira* could be shortened by one's own foolish acts. At the beginning of the *Odyssey* (1.32–41) Zeus explains that Aegisthus brought about his own destruction "beyond his fate" by marrying Clytemnestra and murdering Agamemnon, even though the gods had warned him of the consequences. One could even choose between fates. In Euripides' tragedy *Phoenissae* (930–59), the seer Teiresias tells Creon that the death of his son can save Thebes, but that this

---

12. Bremmer 1999: 33; Parker 2000: 77.

13. Dodds 1973: 177 n. 3.

14. Hdt.1.157.3; Xen. *Cyr.* 1.6.46 and *Hipparch.* 9.9.

15. Vernant (1991: 314–15) claims that the Greeks conceived of the future as irrevocable and irremediable, and as inexorably fixed; and that is his explanation for why oracles must be obscure and ambiguous. Otherwise, if humans had the same clear knowledge of the future as do gods, the distinction between the human and the divine would disappear. Yet the texts cited above belie his view of their conceptions.

outcome is contingent (951–52): "Choose one or the other of these two fates [here the word is *potmos*]. Save either your son or the city." The Croesus example is especially significant: if Apollo unsuccessfully attempted to persuade the Fates on Croesus's behalf to delay the fall of Sardis for a whole generation, it was because in principle they were open to persuasion.

The concept of fate, when evoked, may have served the function of explaining why the gods do not always prevent bad things from happening to the pious and innocent. In that sense, it serves a similar explanatory purpose to the justice of Zeus, which might wait several generations before punishing the descendant of a transgressor. Both of these explanations for the seeming injustice in the world come together in the story of Croesus. Despite Croesus's lavish dedications to Apollo at Delphi, he lost his kingdom. When he complained about this, the Pythia gave a threefold justification: that he paid for the crime of his ancestor Gyges who had unlawfully seized the throne; that Apollo saved him from being burned alive; and that he had misunderstood the oracles given to him (Hdt. 1.91). In the time of Gyges a Delphic oracle had declared "that retribution will come to the Heracleidae [the line of the previous kings] in the time of the fifth descendant of Gyges" (Hdt. 1.13.2). The Pythia later explains (Hdt. 1.91.3) that "Apollo delayed the capture of Sardis by three years; and let Croesus know this, that he was captured three years later than what was allotted."

This passage, and the last sentence in particular, have been consistently misunderstood by modern scholars.[16] The Pythia is not saying that the manner of Croesus's fall was predetermined in detail, that he had to be captured in the precise way that he was.[17] Rather, it was the *moira* (portion) of Croesus, who had reigned for a fixed number of years, to pay retribution for the crime of Gyges by losing his kingdom: but the manner whereby he lost it and the circumstances under which he would fall from power were completely open. It was his own hubris that caused him to take the offensive against Cyrus and to end up on the pyre. Other possible scenarios, other endings, were possible (such as surrender or flight, as recommended by the Pythia at 1.53.2). Cyrus can even imagine Croesus having sought his friendship rather than attacking him (1.87.3). Insofar as Greek thought took a consistent line on such matters, it is evident that causation took place on two levels, the divine and the human, and that divination was the link between them. If all human action

16. Most recently by Harrison (2000: 227).
17. *Pace* Harrison. For a more nuanced treatment of Croesus, see H. Flower 1991.

were predetermined, then divination would have had no value; for it profits one naught to be forewarned if no evasive actions can be taken. Within the general framework of one's "portion" or "share" in life, one could fare well or badly. Divination helped one to make the appropriate choices.

Rites of divination were concerned with obtaining information and guidance from the gods, but the reference point of that information was not confined by space and time. Apollo can see all past, present, and future as one, since the gods stand outside of mortal time.[18] Knowledge of the past is necessary for correct action in the present, and decisions made in the present have consequences for the future. The seer must have knowledge of the past, present, and future, for the three are inextricably linked and the boundaries between them are fluid. Just as divine knowledge transcends the boundaries of time and space, so necessarily must divination transcend those boundaries. Calchas in the *Iliad* is said by Homer (1.70) "to know the things that are, the things that will be, and the things that have been." The implicit point is that such knowledge is fundamental to the successful exercise of his position in society. This expression, however, is strikingly similar to Hesiod's description of his own poetic inspiration in the *Theogony* (32), where he tells us that he shall sing "of the things that shall be and of the things that were."[19] Yet seer and poet, though both inspired and in possession of superior knowledge, always exercised vastly different functions in society. They were among the specialists who migrated from community to community, but one could not do the work of the other. In archaic Greece the well-equipped aristocratic household needed both.

There were occasions, most notably in epic and tragedy, where a seer might directly prophesy a future event. At *Iliad* 7.44–53, Priam's son Helenus somehow intuits or overhears the deliberations of the gods. And in the *Odyssey* the seer Theoclymenus has a surreal vision of the future. Speaking to the suitors in Odysseus's house he says (20.351–62):

Ah, wretched men, what evil is this that you are suffering?
Your heads and faces and the knees underneath are shrouded in night;
the sound of wailing has been kindled, your cheeks are covered

18. So Manetti 1993: 15: "Gods rule time by means of a simultaneous 'sight' of past, present, and future; divine omniscience stems precisely from the possession of panoptic vision."

19. For the vast bibliography on Hesiod's self-representation as a poet, see the insightful study of Katz and Volk (2000) and note in particular Murray 1981. I agree with Katz and Volk that "v. 32 implies that Hesiod is inspired specifically with the truth" (2000: 123). For the connection between poetry and prophecy, see esp. Chadwick 1942 and Leavitt 1997.

with tears, and the walls and fair panels are sprinkled with blood.
The porch is full of ghosts, full also is the court,
as they hasten down to the underworld beneath the darkness.
The sun has perished out of the sky, and a foul mist covers all.

Quite obviously this is an image of the suitors being slain and descending into the netherworld. Theoclymenus does not himself interpret this vision, as, for instance, he had earlier interpreted a bird omen for Telemachus (15.525–34). The seer, when in a state of altered consciousness never interprets his or her own vision—that is left to his audience, whether the audience in the text or the audience of readers outside of the text.

There is some evidence that seers sometimes did deliver prophecies in real life, and like the Pythia, they perhaps did so in a state of altered consciousness. Herodotus reports that before the battle of Pallene, in 546 B.C., Amphilytus, an Acarnanian *chrēsmologos*, was inspired to utter a hexameter prophecy to Pisistratus (Hdt. 1.62.4–63.1). The Athenians from the city and the army of Pisistratus were encamped opposite each other: "Then, under divine guidance, Amphilytus the Acarnanian, a *chrēsmologos*, stood next to Pisistratus, and approaching him he declared a prophecy in hexameter verse: 'The throw has been cast, the net has been spread out, the tunny fish shall dart along through the moon-lit night.' He prophesied these things under divine inspiration (*entheazōn*), but Pisistratus, who understood the oracle and declared that he accepted the prophecy, began to lead out his army."[20] What happened next fulfilled the oracle very nicely: the Athenians from the city, who were occupied with their midday meal, dicing, and sleeping, were taken completely by surprise and routed. In effect, Amphilytus had counseled a surprise attack, and Pisistratus acted upon the suggestion.

It is essential to realize, however, that the obtaining of favorable signs or omens, according to how the Greeks perceived their significance, did not necessarily guarantee victory or success. The divinatory act merely ascertained the will of the gods in relation to the question at issue. Nor, as argued above, did the Greeks believe that the will of the gods was fixed or that future events were somehow fated or predetermined to take place in a specific, unalterable way. As will be discussed below, by means of ritual the seer could attempt to divert those evils that unfavorable omens might predict. Now if it were merely the case that the gods knew more than men and

20. The importance of this scene for Herodotus's account of Pisistratus's tyranny is analyzed by Lavelle (1991).

were willing to share some of what they knew, that would be reason enough to engage in divinatory rites. But it was also the case that the gods were thought to intervene directly in human affairs, often by punishing the wicked and the impious and by helping the just and the pious, or sometimes by striking down those who had become too proud or too powerful. It was, therefore, doubly important and doubly relevant to consult the gods concerning any important issue or proposed course of action.

AVERTING BAD OMENS

Divination is the means whereby one can ascertain the will of the gods. This may mean no more than simply learning whether the gods give their consent to a human enterprise, whether they are willing that the individuals concerned should proceed with that enterprise. But divination may do more than that—it may also vouchsafe a prediction about the future, whether a general one (disaster will strike) or a quite specific one (the king will die). The seer should be able not only to read the signs that the gods send, but also, by employing the correct sacrificial rites, to avert bad omens whenever possible.

Alexander the Great and his seer Aristander of Telmessus spent the night before the battle of Gaugamela sacrificing to Fear and performing secret sacred rites (Plut. *Alex*. 31.4). These were not magical rites, but rather apotropaic ones, which were meant to divert fear from the Macedonians and strike it into the heart of the Persians. (This passage probably derives from Callisthenes of Olynthus, Alexander's court historian, who mentioned the presence of Aristander during the battle.) A few years later, in 328, Alexander ordered the two seers, Aristander and Cleomantis the Lacedaemonian, to sacrifice on behalf of Cleitus in response to an unfavorable omen (Plut. *Alex*. 50.5). This time, of course, Aristander's sacrifices were unsuccessful, and Cleitus was soon dead by Alexander's own hand.

The potential, and probably ill-defined, power of the seer to procure good omens and to divert bad ones explains the famous reproach of Agamemnon to Calchas in the first book of the *Iliad* (1.106–120): "Seer of evil things: never yet have you told me anything good. Always the evil things are dear to your heart to prophesy, but no excellent word have you yet spoken or accomplished." It also explains Herodotus's assertion that the Spartans wanted to kill the Elean seer Hegesistratus "on the grounds that they had suffered at his hands many dreadful things." The sense of agency in the phrase "at his hands" (ὑπ' αὐτοῦ) suggests that Hegesistratus not only successfully predicted the outcome of events, but in some sense also caused them to turn out in the way that they did. This should not, however, be pressed to mean that a *mantis* was expected to work success for his clients by overtly magical means,[21] if by "magic" we mean the nonnormative appropriation of ritual power for personal ends.[22]

Just as the seer transcended and crossed civic boundaries, so he also negotiated the space between religious and magical activities. He was a crosser and negotiator of the boundaries between magic and religion, civic ritual and private ritual, and the human and the divine, even as he simultaneously played a role in setting them. To be sure, there are societies in which certain individuals, whether they be called witch doctors or shamans, are thought not only to be able to discover the source of misfortunes and evils, but also, by virtue of their supernormal powers, to cause them. The Greeks may have believed that some seers could divert evil by appeasing the gods through sacrifice, but seers were not Hellenic versions of Siberian shamans.[23]

The passage in the *Iliad*, in which Agamemnon taunts Calchas, actually has a nice counterpart in the Hebrew Bible (1 Kings 22). When Jehoshaphat, the king of Judah, asked of King Ahab of Israel if there was another prophet of the Lord of whom they could inquire before attacking the Syrians, Ahab responded: "There is still one other by whom we may inquire of the Lord, Micaiah son of Imlah; but I hate him, for he never prophesies anything favorable about me, but only disaster." After he predicts a military defeat, Ahab again says: "Did I not tell you that he would not prophesy anything favorable about me, but only disaster?" Jehoshaphat and Ahab fail to listen to Micaiah, and both are killed in battle. There is no suggestion, however, that Micaiah acts out of spite or contrivance. Although his method of divination is completely different from that of Calchas (Micaiah saw the Lord sitting on his throne and overhead Him discussing events with his supernatural advisers, whereas Calchas appears to make a calculated inference based on the facts of the case), both claim to report the intentions of the deity in question. There is no hint that they themselves can somehow influence supernatural powers to act against the kings who consult them.

---

21. *Contra* Halliday 1913: 95–98; Roth 1982: 124–70.

22. See the discussion in chapter 2.

23. "Shamanism," which is itself a contested concept, is nicely discussed by Bowie (2000: 190–218). Note also Morris 2006: 1–43. Kingsley (1995: 40, 225–27) sees the influence of north-Asiatic shamanism in the fragments of Empedocles, especially in his claim that his disciple will learn how to retrieve the life force of a dead man from Hades. However that may be, it is highly unlikely that Empedocles called himself a *mantis*, despite the inference that later writers made from his poetry (see Diog. Laert. 8.61–62 = Diels-Kranz F 112). See further Dodds 1951: 135–78.

The fullest, most authoritative, and most explicit account of a seer being expected to procure good omens and avert bad ones took place in 400 B.C. and is reported by Xenophon in his *Hellenica* (3.3.4).[24] Although Xenophon was not a participant in this incident, he shortly thereafter became a confidant of a person who was, King Agesilaus of Sparta. When Agesilaus was still in the first year of his reign, as he was making one of the regular sacrifices on behalf of the city, "the seer said to him that the gods were revealing a conspiracy involving the most terrible things. When Agesilaus sacrificed a second time, the seer said that the victims revealed things still more terrible. And when he sacrificed a third time, the seer said: 'Oh Agesilaus, the signs appear to me just as if we were in the very presence of our enemies.' After this they sacrificed both to the gods who avert evils and to those who bring safety, and when with difficulty they had obtained good omens, they ceased. Within five days of the end of the sacrifice someone brought information to the ephors [the executive officers of the Spartan assembly] about a conspiracy and denounced Cinadon as the leader."

It is slightly puzzling why Xenophon thinks that the apotropaic sacrifices were successful when they did not, strictly speaking, avert the coming into being of a major conspiracy against the whole Spartan social and political system. I suppose that Xenophon took the favorable signs as indicating not that the plot would fail to materialize, but that the threat to the state would be overcome. Were the gods then simply warning Agesilaus in advance so that he could prepare himself, or were they also giving him the opportunity, by using apotopaic and saving sacrifices, to gain their assistance in averting the danger? Perhaps neither Xenophon nor Agesilaus nor the unnamed seer gave much thought to fine theological distinctions. It only made sense to try to win the favor of the gods in the way that Greek religion deemed appropriate and efficacious—that is, through prayer and sacrifice. The gods both warned mortals of impending dangers and could be persuaded to alter the outcome of those dangers.

Nonetheless, it was clearly recognized in Greek culture that there were strict limits on a seer's ability to divert disaster through ritual appeasement of divine powers. As Solon wrote, "another man lord Apollo, who works from afar, has made a seer, and if the gods are with him, he sees a distant evil coming upon a man. But assuredly neither a bird of omen nor sacrifices will ward off what is destined."[25] Whereas in the ancient Near East or in Republican Rome such failures to divert

24. See Jehne 1995 on this incident.
25. *IEG*² vol. 2, Solon 13.53–56.

calamity were attributed to "ritual error," the Greeks recognized that there were inherent limits to the power of religious specialists.

Apart from such apotropaic rituals, it might be possible to "earn" favorable omens in quite another way, insofar as the gods might grant favorable signs to the pious, which is still not the same as an absolute guarantee of success. Xenophon claims that Spartan kings while on campaign always sacrifice while it is still dark "in order to seize in advance the goodwill of the gods" (*Lac. Pol.* 13.3), and he is quite certain that the gods give favorable omens in a crisis to those who reverenced them when things were going well (*Hipparch.* 9.8–9 and *Cyr.* 1.6.3). This was not exclusively a Socratic view. Pindar implies much the same thing at the beginning of his eighth *Olympian* (1–8). Nonetheless, even the pious might find it difficult to interpret a particular omen, and it must have been the norm that both armies received favorable omens before an engagement. The gods gave advice and indicated their will; they did not guarantee success or victory.

Most methods of divination leave some room for negotiation on the part of the interpreter. One can decide what type of question to ask and when to ask it. And when consulting an oracle, one can, in principle at least, ask for explication if the oracular response is unclear, and, in addition, one may need to interpret the response. In the case of extispicy (which is the examination of the victim's entrails), a seer could perform a sacrifice, it would seem, up to three times on a single day,[26] and he could attempt to divert unfavorable signs, as mentioned above, by rites of expiation. So if the omens were unfavorable, one at least had the option of telling one's seer to try again or to attempt to stop some portended evil from taking place. The scope for these types of negotiation will have varied with circumstances. The Athenian ambassadors at Delphi in 481 threatened that they would not leave the temple but would stay until they perished, unless Apollo gave them a more favorable response. Not everyone was in a position to be so bold, but the episode indicates that, if beseeched in the right way, even the gods might make concessions to mortals. The response of the Pythia to Croesus, when he complained that he had been misled by Apollo, reveals another strategy for negotiation. When he was told

26. Xenophon (*Anab.* 6.4.16, 19) implies that one could sacrifice only up to three times each day, and this seems to have been standard for Babylonian and Assyrian diviners (see Szymanski 1908: 76–77 and Pritchett 1979: 77). This is doubted by Parker (2000: 311 n. 31), who suspects that there may not have been a limit; but Parker does not discuss the Babylonian evidence. It is a striking coincidence that in Han China neither turtle shells nor yarrow stalks (two major forms of divination) could be consulted more than three times in connection with the same question: see Loewe 1994: 175.

that he would destroy a great empire, he should have inquired which empire was meant, his own or that of Cyrus. Even if this story was invented at a later time, it nevertheless indicates what the Greeks thought to be possible in terms of the etiquette of consultation. Or, to put it another way, if one function of this story is to defend Delphi against a charge of misleading Croesus, the defense is a weak one if in fact it was not permissible, at least in theory, to ask the oracle for clarification regarding an ambiguous answer. Most individuals, of course, were not in a position to consult Delphi repeatedly, and few indeed would have reproached Apollo as boldly as Croesus is depicted as having done.

TOWARD A TYPOLOGY
OF GREEK DIVINATION

Although it seems possible to give a universally valid definition of what divination is, it is, at the same time, highly doubtful if any single typology of divination will account for its manifestations in every society. So what I propose to give is a typology that fits the evidence for Greece, but that might not fit other societies at other times without considerable modification. In other words, although divination is a feature of nearly every culture, not all cultures practice the same forms or have the same understanding of how divination works. Nor do all societies assign the same value to divination and its practitioners. Anthropological and ethnographical studies provide important comparative material that can help us to understand how systems of divination work in practice, but the greatest emphasis must be given to what our Greek texts tells us about Greek attitudes and beliefs.

Beginning with Plato and continuing to this day in the work of modern anthropologists, there has been an attempt to differentiate between two types of divinatory acts. In a famous passage in his *Phaedrus* (244), Plato derives *mantis* from *mania* (madness). He claims that the art of the seer was originally called the *manic* art, but that the Greek letter tau was added later, thus giving *mantic*. According to Plato, the Delphic priestess, the priestesses at Dodona, and the Sibyl all prophesy in a state of madness, using "inspired prophecy" (*mantikē entheos*). He contrasts this with divination by the observation of birds and other signs, which is conducted by individuals who are "in their right mind." This dichotomy is found again in the first surviving ancient work devoted specifically to divination, Cicero's essay *On Divination*, which was published in 44 B.C.[27]

27. 1.6.11–12; 1.18.34; 2.11.26–27; 2.100.

In that dialogue, Cicero's brother Quintus distinguishes between two types of divination, one dependent on art, which is artificial, and another dependent on nature, which is natural. Artificial divination (which one might also call "inductive" or "technical") is based on conjecture and long-term observation of like occurrences and includes predictions made from the examination of entrails, portents, the flights of birds, and signs of various kinds. Natural divination, on the other hand, is a function of prophetic inspiration. Anthropologists have attempted to construct typologies along similar lines. So too scholars of the Hebrew Bible typically stress the difference between "prophecy" and "divination," the prophet being an inspired individual who takes the initiative in speaking the word of God to a third party, whereas the diviner is consulted by clients and relies on technical learning and interpretative skill.

It is indeed tempting to separate inspirational divination (possession) from non-inspirational divination (the interpretation of both fortuitous and deliberate events).[28] One could then categorize the whole category of prophets/diviners either as "messengers" (a mediumistic process) or as "interpreters" (an intellectual process).[29] This gains support from another passage of Plato. In the *Timaeus* (71e–72b), he argues that those *manteis* who operate by what we have called artificial divination are strictly speaking "interpreters."

It may be doubted, however, whether any such rigid typology corresponds to actual experience in the Greek world, or indeed elsewhere.[30] In these passages and in many others, Plato is determined to represent the practitioners of nonecstatic divination as the practitioners of a mere *technē*, and a faulty one at that, and this is part of his attempt to devalue the importance of technical divination in Greek society. Plato was being consciously provocative in challenging the prevalent concept of divination in Greek culture. By limiting the validity of divination to the small group of female prophets who underwent mediumistic/spirit possession, he thereby undermined the self-representation and claim to authority of those seers who did not enter into ecstatic states of altered consciousness. In effect, what Plato says about the function of seers in Greek society is both descriptive and proscriptive.

Plato's dichotomy between natural (inspirational) and artificial (noninspirational) divination can be refuted on several grounds, by appealing both to compar-

28. Lessa and Vogt 1979: 33.

29. Zahan 1979: 86.

30. See Trampedach 2003a. Manetti (1993: esp. 22) mistakenly assumes that Plato's opinions represent the general view of ancient Greek culture with regard to natural divination.

ative anthropology and to the statements of other Greek authors. First of all, in many systems of divination ecstatic states and inductive methods can be combined in a way that is difficult to categorize. There are cultures in which a diviner will both become possessed and at the same time practice an empirical form of divination such as ornithomancy (augury) or cleromancy (divination by drawing lots).[31] On occasion, even the Delphic Pythia, the primary example of spirit possession in the Greek world, may have used cleromancy. Strange as it may sound, the Greeks even considered the practice of ecstatic divination to be a *technē* (craft or skill). The chorus in Aeschylus's *Agamemnon* refers (1209) to Cassandra as "seized by the inspired arts *(technai entheoi)*," and they express (1132-35) fear of the "wordy *technai*" of prophets *(thespiōidoi)*. In his *Eumenides* the Pythia says (17-19) of Apollo: "Zeus made his mind inspired *(entheon)* with the *technē* and places him as the fourth seer on this throne. Loxias [Apollo] is the spokesman *(prophētēs)* of his father Zeus." The implication is that just as Apollo acts as his father's spokesman by means of an inspired *technē*, so too the Pythia is able to function as Apollo's mouthpiece through a kind of *technē*. She is indeed called "the spokesperson *(prophētis)* of Apollo" by Euripides *(Ion* 321, 1322) and Plato *(Phdr.* 244b).

Second, if looked at from the point of view of their social function, both the inspired prophet and the learned diviner fulfill the same role in society as intermediaries in the process of communication between the human and divine spheres. Both diviner and prophet are recognized by others in their community as individuals who are qualified to perform this particular social function.[32] And third, as the anthropologist Philip Peek has pointed out, "all analyses try to distinguish those forms involving ecstatic states from those performed in normal states of consciousness, yet the only real difference between them is that in ecstatic states the occult powers 'speak' through the diviner rather than the divinatory apparatus. All divination forms involve a non-normal state of inquiry which then requires a "rational" interpretation of the revealed information by the client if not by the diviner."[33]

---

31. See Maurizio 1995: 79–80 and Zeusse 1987. Overholt (1989: 139–40) gives a number of interesting examples, including that of the Ugandan Kigaanira, who in the mid-twentieth century simultaneously had a career as a diviner and functioned as the possessed prophet of the god Kibuuka.

32. See Overholt 1989: 140–41.

33. 1991b: 12.

It strikes me, however, that there is a fundamental difficulty with these ways of viewing the divinatory session, in that they conflate the point of view of the diviner with that of the client. From the seer's point of view there is a very real difference whether he or she perceives himself or herself as being possessed or as engaging in a purely interpretative act, whereas from the point of view of the inquirer it may or may not make an empirical difference whether supernatural powers are communicating directly through the mouth of the seer or are encoding a message on some physical object, such as the liver of a sheep. Seer and client, even given the social construction of methods of divination, may not necessarily agree on which form of divination is most authoritative. What is at issue for the study of the Greek evidence is whether seers, even when engaged in artificial, deductive divination, still felt themselves to be making their interpretations with the help of divine inspiration.

Even though we do not have the evidence to ascertain how seers personally conceived of their abilities, we can hope to reconstruct the image that they projected to their clients and to society at large. Plato is not particularly good evidence because he is biased against those seers who practiced seercraft as a craft (*technē*) and makes repeated attempts to diminish their authority. For instance, in the *Statesman* (290c–d) he has the stranger say: "There are men who have a portion of a certain menial knowledge that has to do with divination; for they are, I suppose, considered to be interpreters from gods to men." A few sentences later he adds: "The bearing of the priests and seers is indeed full of pride, and they win a fine reputation because of the magnitude of their undertakings."

Plato should not be seen as representing the cultural world of the Greek as it existed in everyday experience, but as he thought that it should exist. For instance, he claims (*Leg.* 720) that there were two types of doctors: slave doctors who treated other slaves, and free doctors who treated citizens; yet all of our other evidence fails to support this claim. Like so much in Plato, this claim represents what he thought should be the case. Thus Plato's dichotomy between ecstatic and technical divination is too schematic and elides Greek experience. Indeed, there is a third type of divination that appears in our sources and that Plato does not recognize: this is the innate faculty of divination (*emphutikos mantikē*). We might call it intuitive divination or "second sight," in which the diviner spontaneously "sees" or "knows" reality or the future. This type of intuition is the one-time gift of a god and can be passed down to the recipient's descendants. It does not depend on the seer's being possessed (*entheos*) at the very moment of the act of divining. It is rather an innate intuitive ability to see things that others cannot see, or a supernormal understanding of past, present, and future. Thus the evidence indicates that, as in many other cultures, there were actually three basic types of divination in Greece, which we might call possession divination, intuitive divination, and technical divination.[34]

The possibility that I want to raise is this. Did all seers in the Greek world attempt to represent themselves as being in some sense "inspired"? Even Plato talks about different kinds of inspired madness, one of which is the madness of the poet inspired by the Muses. It is once again worth pointing out that Calchas, the seer of the Greeks at Troy, was "by far the best of the bird interpreters, who knew the things that are, the things that will be, and the things that have been, who led the ships of the Achaeans into the land of Ilium through that seercraft that Phoebus Apollo had given him" (*Il.* 1.71–72). Although only an interpreter of bird signs, and thus a mere practitioner of artificial divination, Calchas had a special intuitive insight that Apollo had vouchsafed him. We would not call this "possession," for Calchas is not in an ecstatic state; rather, he operates by prophetic intuition.

The same holds when in Aeschylus's *Agamemnon* (104–204) the chorus tells how Calchas had "interpreted" (οὕτω δ' εἶπε τεράιζων: 125) the portent of the two eagles devouring the pregnant hare. His interpretation was that Troy would eventually be captured, but that Artemis, being angered, would send adverse winds and could be appeased only by an unlawful sacrifice. This too is not an example of "ecstatic prophecy" but of intuitive prophecy. It has been pointed out that Aeschylus's audience would not have had any trouble in recognizing the mantic reasoning behind Calchas's interpretation: to wit, this event has an ominous character that is distasteful to Artemis; therefore, if any deity tries to hinder our expedition, it will be Artemis.[35] But there is also much in his interpretation that goes far beyond the sort of simple inference that any reasoning person might make. Only a special insight could have revealed Artemis's plea (apparently to Zeus) that the ominous part of the portent be fulfilled, and knowledge of the "child-avenging Wrath" that dwells in Agamemnon's palace.

But the picture is more complex still, because divinatory possession is itself of two types. One type is prophetic inspiration. During the act of prophesying, the medium's general awareness of the world and of the self is preserved, although the

---

34. This is a variation of Zeusse 1987: 376. Zeusse proposes three general types of divination: intuitive divination, possession divination, and wisdom divination; but the scheme here differs in that I include extispicy under possession of nonhuman agents rather than under wisdom divination (where the diviner decodes impersonal patterns in reality), since the latter does not seem to be a category in Greek divination.

35. Dover 1973: 62.

degree of self-awareness and lucidity may vary greatly. An example of inspired prophetic possession is Cassandra in Aeschylus's *Agamemnon*. She has a terrible vision of past and future, and she is in a state of psychological agitation, but she still retains a strong sense of self and place. The chorus says of her (1083–84): "She is going to prophesy, it seems, about her own miseries. The divine gift (*to theion*) abides in her mind, even though her mind is enslaved."

The other type of possession is spirit possession. This is when both self-awareness and world awareness are said to be lost, since the god takes over the medium completely and speaks directly through the mouth of the medium to the audience. Obviously, the most famous example in Greek culture of someone experiencing spirit possession is the Pythia at Delphi, who served as the mouthpiece of the god Apollo. The same individual, as we will see later, might practice all three basic types of divination, though the last two—intuitive and technical—were practiced together by the male seers of greatest fame and highest status. It is sometimes claimed that spirit possession, being wholly passive in character, was principally the realm of women, not of men.[36] As a general rule, the inspired mediums of Apollo were women, but there are notable exceptions, such as the male prophets of Apollo at Clarus and at the Theban sanctuary of Apollo Ptous (Hdt. 8.135).

The means by which the various types of possession occurred was less important to most Greeks than the fact that they did occur. In Plato's *Symposium* (202d–3a), the character Diotima puts forward the intriguing suggestion that daemons (who are intermediate in status between gods and mortals) act as interpreters and messengers between gods and men in matters relating to divination, sacrifice, and sorcery. But most Greeks would hardly have conceived of the process in those terms. For them the gods intervened directly, and Apollo in particular was the seer who directly possessed his priestesses. Dionysus too, though more rarely, possessed male and female seers at oracular sites. In the case of technical divination, it was the gods who directed the flight of birds or implanted markings on the entrails of sacrificial victims.

The general belief is stated by Xenophon in his *Memorabilia* (1.1.3) in terms that probably represent the theological understanding of most Greeks: "Socrates did not introduce anything stranger than other people, all those who believe in divination (*mantikē*) and employ birds and voices and portents and sacrifices. They do not suppose that it is the birds or the people whom they chance to meet who know what is advantageous for those using divination, but the gods are indicating those things

36. So Roth 1982: 46–49; *contra* Parke and Wormell 1956: vol. 1, 10.

through them [i.e., birds and chance encounters]; and he also believed this." In modern anthropological terms, these birds, voices, and portents are randomizing devices, which during divination are directed by, or possessed by, supernatural forces. It is claimed that the purpose of randomizing devices is to establish resistance and to insure "that the human diviner or client cannot control the outcome of divination, which appears as the spirit's message."[37] Yet it would be difficult to imagine divination as taking place at all if no such devices were used, for the gods need some means of transmitting their messages to mortals.

In the end, the distinction between inspired and technical divination, although seemingly helpful, is in fact misleading. Rather than accepting this type of strict dichotomy under the spell of Plato and Cicero, we should rather think in terms of a spectrum or range of activities. The military *mantis* was not "inspired" in the same way or to the same degree as the possessed Pythia, nor was conducting a sacrifice with a specific question in mind the same as interpreting a chance occurrence. Nonetheless, the seer serving on a military campaign might claim divine inspiration or "second sight." No Greek before Plato thought in terms of his distinctions, and his view passed to the Stoics and then on to Cicero. Plato was concerned to demonstrate that only the possessed prophetess could have any claim to knowledge, whereas the *mantis* could not be allowed to compete with the philosopher.

The various types of divination employed in classical Greece are summarized in a passage of Aeschylus's *Prometheus Bound*. Prometheus claims to have taught humankind the art or craft of divination and details the five significant media that have mantic significance; these are dreams, chance utterances, unexpected signs or omens, the flight of birds, the shape and color of entrails, and the flames from burnt sacrifice (484–99):

> I set in order the many ways of the art of divination, and I first of all distinguished from dreams the things that are necessary to come about during waking hours, and I explained to mortals chance utterances that are difficult to interpret and signs that one encounters on the road, and I defined the flight of crooked-taloned birds, which ones are favorable and which sinister, and the habitat that each one possesses, and what enmities and affections and gatherings they have in relation to each other; and I defined the smoothness of entrails, the color of bile that is pleasing to the gods, and the many-colored

37. Maurizio 1995: 81. See also Ahern 1981: 53.

symmetry of the lobe. Having burned thigh bones and the long chine wrapped in fat, I set mortals on the road of a skill difficult to judge, and I opened the eyes of fiery signs that were previously covered with cataract.

It is interesting that Aeschylus does not mention mediumistic possession. Obviously, it was not perceived as being (despite the Pythia's implicit claim in the *Eumenides*) a *technē* in the same sense that these other forms of divination were. The seers who prophesied in a state of spirit possession were not thought to employ any skills or knowledge of their own; they were simply the mouthpieces of the god who spoke through them. This does not mean, however, that the types of divination detailed by Aeschylus were exclusively technical, even though they are presented as being such in the dramatic context of Prometheus's speech. Again to turn to Calchas, he practices divination by the inspection of birds, which is one of the skills bequeathed to humankind by Prometheus, but he does so through the gift of Apollo. The chorus in Aeschylus's *Agamemnon* concludes its account of Calchas's interpretation of the eagle-and-hare portent and of Iphigenia's consequent sacrifice with these words (248): "The *technai* of Calchas were not unfulfilled."[38]

In conclusion, just as possession divination was dependent on an inspired *technē*, so technical divination, to be practiced most successfully, was in need of an innate prophetic gift. I have called this intuitive divination. Apollo was not thought to be inspiring Calchas every time he divined from the flight of birds, but rather Apollo's gift consisted of a particular grant of prophetic insight that remained operative within Calchas; and, what is more, that insight could be passed on from parent to child. This type of insight enabled one to see things that others could not, such as when the seer Mopsus counted the 10,001 figs on a fig tree and predicted how many piglets were in a pregnant sow and when she would give birth to them (Strabo 14.1.27). This type of knowledge is similar to divine knowledge. So Apollo tells the representatives of Croesus that he knows how many are the grains of sand on the beach and the measure of the sea (Hdt. 1.47.3). In effect, Apollo, through his gift of seercraft, enables a mortal to share, albeit on a smaller scale and to a lesser degree, in the type of knowledge that the gods themselves possess. That is why the chorus in the *Oedipus Tyrannus* (298–99) can refer to Teiresias as "the divine seer, in whom alone of mortals truth is implanted."

38. On the possible implications of these words, see Dover 1973: 62.

THE SELF-IMAGE OF THE SEER

Of these various types of seers, although all of them can be considered charismatic specialists, which type was the most common? It has often been argued that the oracles and seers of epic and tragedy have little relation to those of "real" life. It is claimed that the "authentic" oracles of Delphi, like those of Dodona, give advice about present problems but do not predict the future in the way that purely literary oracles, such as those given by Apollo in Sophocles' *Oedipus Tyrannus* or in Herodotus's *Histories*, sometimes do. Cassandra as well, it has been asserted, is a purely literary figure.[39]

So too the military seers of real life, it is often asserted, simply report whether the omens are favorable or unfavorable for an engagement; whereas the seers of tragedy, such as Calchas and Teiresias, sometimes offer detailed descriptions of present and future events. For instance, when we first meet Teiresias in the *Oedipus Tyrannus*, Oedipus introduces him by saying (300–301); "Teiresias, you who observe all things, both things that can be taught and things that are unspeakable, things in heaven and things that tread upon the earth." And in the *Antigone* (1064–90), Teiresias can predict in precise terms what evils are to befall Creon as a result of his intransigence, including the imminent death of his son. Teiresias's methods of divination are observing the behavior of birds (ornithoscopy/ornithomancy) and observing burnt offerings (empyromancy), methods that by themselves should not be able to produce such specific information. At the beginning of Aeschylus's *Seven against Thebes* (21–29) the audience is told that the seer Amphiaraus, "the herdsman of birds, considering in his ears and mind, apart from fire [i.e., without burnt sacrifice], his bird oracles with unerring skill," foretold that the Argives in night council were planning a massive attack on Thebes.

This dichotomy may sound reasonable on the surface. After all, how many Athenian women of the fifth century were empowered to act like Antigone or

---

39. Mikalson 1991: 88–95 and 2003: 152–53; cf. Nock 1972. Mikalson draws a false and artificial dichotomy between the religion of tragedy and that of "real life." He constructs the latter, which he calls "popular religion," on the basis of prose authors (principally Xenophon and the orators) and inscriptions (this methodology is set out in his earlier book: 1983: 3–12). It is not the case, however, that poetic texts (or the historian Herodotus for that matter) can tell us little about popular beliefs and practices, nor are Mikalson's preferred texts transparent windows into "popular religion." Literary convention in the context of tragedy undoubtedly stresses certain aspects of divinatory ritual, whereas orators and historians are interested in different aspects. For a critique of Mikalson's method, see Sourvinou-Inwood 1997.

Clytemnestra? But there is a problem. In the pages of Herodotus there are seers and oracles that resemble all too closely those of poetry, and it would be a transparently circular argument to dismiss Herodotus's examples for the very reason that they give divination a function that must have been foreign to that of real life. For the evidence must determine the theory, not the theory the evidence. In the *Histories* of Herodotus, Euenius of Apollonia is the counterpart of Teiresias, the Pythia that of Cassandra, and Tisamenus of Elis that of Calchas.

Confirmation that historical military seers were capable of reporting more than just whether the *hiera* and *sphagia* were favorable or not is also found in the activities of the greatest seer of his day, Aristander of Telmessus, who served first Philip II and then Alexander the Great between c. 356 and 327 B.C. The Delphic oracle too was thought capable of predicting the future, as when the Pythia foretold that Tisamenus would win the five greatest victories. He had come to Delphi to ask about having a child, and this was what he was gratuitously told instead. The whole story of his consultation may be a folk story about a famous individual (a sort of Robin Hood or Davy Crockett figure), but the important point is that the story was believable. It was the sort of prediction that Delphi was thought capable of giving both in the theater and in real life. Amphiaraus had predicted his own death before he set out for Thebes with the Seven. Cassandra, although no one understood her, also foresaw her own death. If we had no other evidence, that would sound like a purely literary *topos*—the seer who vainly foretells his or her own demise. Yet this sometimes happened in real life. The seer who took the omens for the Athenian democrats who fought the Thirty at Munychia in 404 predicted that they would be victorious if they did not attack until one of their own number was wounded or killed, and that he himself would die in the battle (Xen. *Hell.* 2.4.18). He then seems to have self-consciously fulfilled his own prophecy in an act of self-sacrifice, for Xenophon comments: "And he did not speak falsely; but when they took up their arms, just as if he was being led on by a certain fate, he was the first to spring forward and, falling upon the enemy, he was killed."

There is a factor, however, that problematizes the study of historical seers in relation to literary ones. Xenophon's unnamed seer at Munychia undoubtedly has some affinities with Amphiaraus. Even so, Tisamenus of Elis much more clearly plays the role of Calchas in the text of Herodotus. Just as Plataea was the greatest victory of historical times, so the Trojan War was the greatest conflict of mythical times. Has Herodotus consciously molded his portrayal of Tisamenus upon that of Calchas, and thus is the narrative of Herodotus just as "literary" and nonhistorical as the text of Homer? Or did the historical Tisamenus deliberately act out the role of his

Homeric predecessor, just as Alexander would later act out the role of Achilles? We cannot underestimate the extent to which both of these phenomena are occurring simultaneously. That is to say, both the recording of history and the real-life actions of individuals were fashioned upon the template of Homeric epic, especially the *Iliad*. Nor should we underestimate the influence of epic poems now lost to us, such as the *Thebaid*, in which the seer Amphiaraus played a prominent part. The story in Xenophon that was discussed above seems to be an unambiguous case of a seer acting out a mythical prototype. I am not saying that Xenophon's text is a completely transparent lens into the past, for no text can function as such. Nonetheless, in so much as he was a contemporary witness with personal experience of military divination, he confirms the impression of how seers comported themselves that one gets from Herodotus's account of Tisamenus.

On at least one occasion, however, Herodotus adds a piece of external evidence that confirms his own portrayal of the self-image of the seer. The poet Simonides, he tells us, wrote this epigram for his guest-friend Megistias, the seer who served the Spartans at Thermopylae (7.228.3):

This is the memorial of famous Megistias, whom once the Medes
slew after they had crossed the river Spercheius,
a seer who, although at that time he knew clearly that the Karae
[spirits of death] were coming, did not endure to abandon Sparta's leaders.

Here we have the seer who boasts both his special knowledge and his unassailable loyalty. This is not exactly the seer of the *Iliad*, who quarrels with King Agamemnon, but an improved version, someone with Calchas's mantic powers, but also a person in complete harmony of purpose with his employers. The seer, in his public role as interpreter of the divine will, was a self-conscious performer in a tradition of seercraft reaching back to epic and including its representation in Attic tragedy. Life and art influence each other and coexist in a symbiotic relationship.

The interrelationship of life and art comes clearly into play when one looks at the language used to convey the nature of the seer's contribution to success in war. It is quite at odds with those modern scholars who downplay the influence of seers and make them mere morale boosters in the service of others that both poetic and prose texts speak of seers as "winning" battles. According to Herodotus (9.33–35), when the Spartans were attempting to hire him before the battle of Plataea, they wished "to make Tisamenus the leader (*hegemōn*) in their wars, together with those of the Heracleidae who were kings." Since it was the prerogative of the kings at Sparta to command the army, the Spartan offer comes as something of a surprise. Indeed, the language here suggests a position tantamount to "joint commander with their kings," and this notion is reinforced by the verbs "shall win" and "helped them to win," which Herodotus uses of Tisamenus's activities. Yet Herodotus does not depict Tisamenus as having any active role in the actual battle, either in marshaling the troops or in the fighting. Herodotus must therefore mean that Tisamenus was the leader in the same way as was Calchas, the seer of the Greeks at Troy. Homer speaks of Calchas as the one who "led the ships of the Achaeans into the land of Ilium through that seercraft (*mantosunē*) that Phoebus Apollo had given him" (*Il.* 1.71–72). Like Calchas, then, Tisamenus "leads" the army and practices the art of divination as Apollo's gift.

As it happened, Tisamenus's grandson was seer to the Spartan admiral Lysander, who brought the Peloponnesian War between Athens and Sparta to an end when he captured the entire Athenian fleet at Aegospotami in 405 B.C. Although Lysander achieved great fame as a result of that stunning victory, it may come as a surprise that he was not given full credit for it. Pausanias, the travel writer of the first century A.D., tells us something that our other sources leave out (3.11.5): "They say that Agias while acting as seer to Lysander captured the Athenian fleet at Aegospotami except for ten ships." This is not a case where we must trust a late source for an otherwise unattested and peculiar detail. Pausanias's opinion that it was Lysander's seer who captured the Athenian fleet is partly confirmed by a monument that was erected at Delphi and has been partially recovered (Paus. 10.9.7). On the so-called Navarchs monument Lysander dedicated a statue both of himself and of his seer Agias. There was also a bronze statue of Agias in the marketplace at Sparta (Paus. 3.11.5). This Agias was obviously a famous person at Sparta and perhaps throughout the whole of Greece.

Here again poetry and prose confirm each other. In Euripides' *Phoenissae* (854–57), the seer Teiresias claims the credit for securing Athens' victory over Eleusis: "I made the sons of Cecrops victorious, and, as you can see, I possess this golden crown, which I received as the firstfruits of the enemy spoils." In poetry and in prose, in myth and in history, seers can win battles.

As we move into the fourth century B.C. the same pattern still holds. The Athenian orator Aeschines (*On the Embassy* 78) says that his uncle Cleobulus, whom we know from his grave epigram was a *mantis*, "along with Demaenetus, won the naval victory over Cheilon the Lacedaemonian admiral."[40] One strongly suspects that seers depicted

40. On this passage, see Harris 1995: 23–27. For the inscription, see below.

themselves not just as advisers to kings and generals, but even as individuals who literally could "win" battles for their clients. This conception of the seer "leading" an
army may go back to the Near East, for an analogous expression was used of the
Babylonian seer, who was said to "walk in front of the army."[41] And as mentioned
before, the Babylonian seer Asqudum occasionally led military expeditions.

Seers must have advertised themselves in the search for clients and in the quest
to establish a reputation. How did they go about doing that? Charismatics author-
ize their activities and establish confidence in themselves by projecting an image, and
one can recover that image by looking closely at a range of texts. On rare, but valuable, occasions it is possible to observe this dialogue between poetry and real life in
a context that is independent of literary texts such as Herodotus. In 387 B.C. the
maternal uncle of the Athenian orator Aeschines participated, it would seem, in a
naval action in which he greatly distinguished himself, perhaps being formally
awarded the *aristeia*, or prize for valor. Aeschines (*On the Embassy* 78), as mentioned above, claims that his uncle, "along with Demaenetus, won the naval victory
over Cheilon the Lacedaemonian admiral." His grave stele was found near the Attic
deme of Acharnae.[42] It has a relief depicting an eagle carrying a serpent in its talons
(an obvious reference to the portent that appears to Hector at Hom. *Il.* 12.195–229;
see fig. 12). The name and occupation of the deceased is inscribed above the relief:
"Cleobulus, from Acharnae, seer."[43] An epigram is inscribed below the relief in
smaller letters and consists of four hexameters:

Cleobulus, son of Glaucus, the earth covers you in death,
being good both as a seer and as a fighter with the spear,
you whom once the *dēmos* (people) of great-hearted Erechtheus [crowned]
having been the best throughout Greece [to win glory].

Whether or not Cleobulus was officially awarded a prize for valor is unclear from
the language;[44] what is clear and highly significant for our understanding of man-

41. In the Old Babylonian period, there are references to the diviner as "the one who walks in front
of the army." See Jeyes 1989: 22–23; note also West 1997: 349.

42. For the inscription, see *SEG* 16.193; Papademetriou 1957; Daux 1958; Pritchett 1979: 57; and
Clairmont 1970: 145, no. 68. Hansen (*CEG* vol. 2, no. 519) restores the last two words of the fourth
line as "having glory," on the mistaken assumption that a seer does not "win glory."

43. Κλεόβολος Ἀχάρνευς μάντις.

44. It is very difficult to distinguish in our sources between official awards and unofficial claims
to excellence. On this problem, see Flower and Marincola 2002: 232.

tic self-representation is his claim to excellence both as a fighter and as a *mantis*. Pindar, for instance, in his sixth *Olympian* (472 or 468 B.C.) emphatically stresses that the seer Hagesias was due the same praise that Adrastus had given to the seer Amphiaraus (16–17): "I long for the eye of my army, one who was good both as a seer and to fight with the spear." The association of mantic and warlike abilities was fairly common, and the phrase "good both as a seer and to fight with the spear" had a long history both before and after Pindar. Pindar had borrowed this sentence from an epic poem called the *Thebaid*,[45] and a roughly similar description of Amphiaraus appears in Aeschylus's *Seven against Thebes* (568–69), performed in 467 B.C. The messenger who is describing the seven heroes refers to him thus: "I would say that the sixth warrior is a man most prudent, the best seer in valor, the might of Amphiaraus." There are very few cases in which the evidence of different genres can be brought into perfect harmony, and thus it is highly significant that in this particular instance epic (the *Thebaid*), lyric (Pindar), tragedy (Aeschylus), prose (Aeschines), and an inscription (on Cleobulus's stele) all convey the very same image of the seer.

It should not cause surprise that seers frequently used the language of epic as part of their self-projection. In the early fourth century B.C. an otherwise unknown seer by the name of Symmachus composed a poem for an honorary inscription that was set up by the Lycian dynast Arbinas.[46] This inscription was inscribed on the base of a statue of Arbinas himself, and it praises the ruler's exploits and personal qualities. We are even told that Apollo's oracle at Delphi sanctioned the dedication of the monument. But for our purposes what comes at the end of this remarkable document is particularly noteworthy. The author reveals himself with the boast "Symmachus, son of Eumedes, of Pellana, a blameless seer, with good intelligence made these elegies as a gift for Arbinas." It is the Homeric tag "blameless seer" as much as the literary pretension that catches one's attention.[47]

Apart from allusions to the seers of myth and legend, seers might also advertise themselves in novel ways. In the Hellenistic period, we find Thrasybulus, who was an Elean from the family of the Iamidae, serving with the Mantineans against the Lacedaemonians under King Agis IV (244–241 B.C.). He "both foretold victory to

---

45. According to scholion 26 on Pindar's sixth *Olympian*.

46. *SEG* 28.1245. For discussion, see Bousquet 1975 and 1992. For text and commentary in English, see *GHI* no. 13. Arbinas ruled in Lycia c. 390–380 B.C.

47. But note that the epithet "blameless" has been restored on the basis of *Il.* 1.92, where it is used of Calchas: the inscription reads μάντις ἀ[μύμων]. See Bousquet 1975: 139.

FIGURE 12.
Grave stele of the seer Cleobulus, discovered
near Acharnae in Attica, early to mid-fourth
century B.C. An eagle holds a snake in its
talons, with a hexameter inscription below.
National Archaeological Museum, inv.
no. 4473. Hellenic Ministry of Culture/
Archaeological Receipts Fund.

the Mantineans and himself took part in the fighting" (Paus. 8.10.5). He must have been a person of great wealth and influence, since he dedicated a statue of King Pyrrhus of Epirus at Olympia (Paus. 6.14.9). If Pyrrhus was another of his employers, as seems likely enough, then the dedication of this statue was a means of advertising the success of that employment.

Thrasybulus, however, had an even more conspicuous means for showing off his talents. Pausanias (6.2.4–5) saw a remarkable and iconographically unique statue of Thrasybulus himself at Olympia. A gecko lizard was crawling toward his right shoulder, and a dog was lying beside him, cut in two with its liver exposed. The divinatory significance of both animals is uncertain. Pausanias thought that Thrasybulus had established his own personal method of divination in which he uniquely examined the entrails of dogs; he does not discuss the lizard, but it is a reasonable inference that Thrasybulus claimed to understand the language of animals, or at least of lizards.[48] It has been suggested, however, that the description "cut in two" refers to the rite, as practiced in Macedonia and Boeotia, of purification of an army, whereby the troops passed between the parts of a severed dog.[49] Since some seers still performed rites of healing and purification in classical times,[50] it is not impossible that Pausanias has misinterpreted the iconography of the statue. Or it may be that Thrasybulus used the dog both for purposes of divination (and thus the depiction of the exposed liver) and for purification. What is clear is that even within an extended mantic family, individual members might represent themselves quite differently. Indeed we should expect that a seer would want to emphasize that although he belonged to a particular clan, all of whose members shared inherited and proven abilities, he nevertheless was exceptional in some way. The dog and the lizard mark Thrasybulus as different from other seers and even from other Iamidae; they are emblematic of his claim to be someone with a special access to the supernatural world.

Another statue at Olympia bears comparison with this one, even if it is of a Clytiad rather than of an Iamid. In the late fourth or early third century B.C. an Elean seer by the name of Eperastus, who won at Olympia in the race in armor, emphasized his claim to belong to two distinct, if related, mantic families. Pausanias records the inscription on his statue at Olympia as follows (6.17.5–6): "I boast to be a seer of the clan of the prophetic-tongued Clytidae, blood from the godlike

<hr />

48. See Pritchett 1979: 54, 196–202; and Parke 1967: 168.

49. So Pritchett 1979: 54, following Nilsson 1955–67: vol. 2, 230 n. 1. The main texts are Plut. *Mor.* 290d, for Boeotia; and, for Macedonia, Livy 40.6 and Curt. 10.9.11.

50. Xen. *Anab.* 5.7.35; Pl. *Rep.* 364b–e; and Hippoc. *Diseases of Women* 1.

Melampodidae." This may not be elegant poetry (and Clytiadae seems to be spelled Clytidae in order to fit the meter), but Eperastus has managed in a single couplet to attribute to himself the qualities of being "prophetic-tongued" (*hieroglōssos*) and "godlike" (*isotheos*), as well as belonging to two illustrious families of seers (since Clytius, the progenitor of the Clytiadae, was in turn a descendant of Melampus). If Eperastus was intending to attract clients (as I presume that he was), then this statue with its inscription would have served as a very effective and conspicuous advertisement of his martial abilities and prophetic credentials.

WHAT CAN ONE ASK A SEER?

When a god, such as Apollo or Zeus, speaks directly through the mouth of his priest or priestess, we have considerable evidence as to both how the question might be phrased and what form the response might take. Our sources, however, generally do not specify the form of question and answer that takes place in sacrificial divination, other than to say that the omens were favorable or unfavorable. When unfavorable, we are sometimes told that the liver lacked a lobe, but no further description is usually given. One exception is in Euripides' *Electra* (826–32). When Aegisthus, as reported in the messenger's speech, examined the entrails of a calf, he discovered that "there was no lobe in the viscera, and the portal vein and gallbladder showed onsets of harm near at hand for the one examining them." Orestes then asked Aegisthus why he looked so upset, and he responded: "Oh stranger, I fear some deceit at my door." His interpretation was correct, since Orestes slew him moments later when he was in the very act of examining the remaining entrails one by one; yet the signs were not so specific that they portended imminent death. So we might well wonder what kinds of questions a seer might pose while examining the entrails and what kinds of answers he might get. The best evidence comes from two passages in Xenophon's *Anabasis*. Although Xenophon was not himself a seer, he claims that he sacrificed frequently and knew a great deal about how to interpret signs and omens (5.6.29).

When Seuthes, the king of Thrace, offered that Xenophon remain with him, Xenophon (7.6.44) "took two victims and sacrificed to Zeus the King whether it would be better and preferable for him to remain with Seuthes on the conditions that Seuthes says, or to go away with the army. He [Zeus?] declares to him to go away." Xenophon apparently believes that Zeus communicates his answer by implanting some mark on the entrails of the victim, the nature of which mark he does not specify. It is also left unspecified what deity gives the answer, although the context indicates that it is Zeus. The same procedure, but with more detail, is reported earlier in the *Anabasis,* when Xenophon was trying to decide whether to accept the sole command of the Greek army (6.1.22): "Since he was at a loss what to decide, it seemed best to him to consult the gods; and having placed two victims next to himself, he sacrificed them to Zeus the King. . . . When he sacrificed the god quite clearly indicated to him neither to ask for the command in addition nor, if they should elect him, to accept it." When the troops would not accede to Xenophon's arguments as to why he was not the best choice, he addressed them again (6.1.31): "Well, soldiers, in order that you may understand the matter fully, I swear to you by all the gods and goddesses, that when I perceived your opinion, I sacrificed if it would be better for you to entrust this command to me and if it would be better for me to undertake it. And the gods gave me such signs in the sacrifices that even a private person could recognize that it is necessary for me to keep away from this sole command." This apparently put an end to the debate; for Xenophon next says: "And so indeed they chose Cheirisophus."

Several things in this passage are revealing. First, Xenophon depicts the evidence of the sacrifices as decisively settling the issue of the command in the eyes of the troops. For the average Greek hoplite the evidence of divination was far more authoritative than so-called rational arguments, insofar as Xenophon had already explained at length why it was not a good idea for the command to be given to an Athenian in preference to a Lacedaemonian. Second, in Xenophon's speech to the troops Zeus has become "the gods." And third, in this episode and in the one concerning Seuthes, Xenophon sacrifices two victims. It is not the case that one of them is merely held in reserve in case the answer is not clear during the first sacrifice, for the grammar makes it clear (especially in the second case, where *ta hiereia* is the object of both verbs) that Xenophon has sacrificed both victims. It is legitimate, therefore, to infer that Xenophon asked different questions of each victim as a type of checking: while sacrificing one victim he asked: "Is it better for the army to entrust the command to me?" and while sacrificing the other: "Is it better for me to turn down the command?" Only the sequence "yes-no" or "no-yes" would count as a reliable answer.[51]

This type of question—that is, one that expects a yes or no answer to the query "Is it better to do x?"—seems to be the only type that could be asked during a sacrifice. One could follow this up with a second sacrifice in which one asked the question "Is it better to do y?" But one could not ask in regard to the same sacrificial victim "Is it better to do x or y?" for it was not possible to choose between two alter-

51. As is pointed out by Parker (2004: 150–51), who cites the Zande poison oracle as a parallel.

natives by examining the markings on a single liver. In military divination, the campground sacrifice must usually have taken the form "Is it better to advance against the enemy?" and "Is it better to remain on the defensive?" This, at any rate, certainly seems to be the form of the question that lies behind Herodotus's report of the omens taken by the Greeks at Plataea (9.36): "The omens proved to be good for the Greeks if they remained on the defensive, but not good if they cross the Asopus River and begin battle."

Finally, it is striking that this formulation is very similar to a common form of question put to oracles.[52] Over 1,400 lead oracular tablets have been discovered at the site of the oracle of Zeus at Dodona in northern Greece.[53] The following is a typical form of question: "X enquires of Zeus Naios and Dione whether it would be better and more good to do y." That is also the form of the question that Socrates thought that Xenophon should have asked at Delphi. "Socrates," Xenophon writes (*Anab.* 3.1.7), "censured Xenophon because he had not first of all asked this, whether it was better for him to go on the expedition or to stay at home." (Instead, Xenophon had asked to which of the gods he should sacrifice and pray in order to have a successful trip and return home safely). In this case, however, one can put a more nuanced question to the Pythia and expect to get a more sophisticated and articulated reply. Whereas the mute liver can indicate only yes or no to a single proposition ("Should I go on the expedition?"), the voice of the Pythia can declare between two alternatives. This is one reason among many why divination through mediumistic possession was more authoritative than sacrificial divination and why the Pythia had more prestige as a seer than any migrant diviner. Yet if one was unable or unwilling to travel to an oracular shrine, then a seer for hire could conceivably consult a sheep's liver on a whole host of private domestic issues (the very same questions that we know were asked at Dodona as well as at Delphi):[54] Should I marry? Will I have children? Should I go on a voyage? Should I enter a business agreement? Should I buy this house? Did my neighbor steal from me? Is my spouse faithful? Will my child recover from illness? He or she could ask these questions in the privacy, and secrecy, of his or her own home.[55]

---

52. This observation is well made by Parker (2004: 150): "The hotline to Zeus is always open; the commander has his mobile as long as he can find a sheep to sacrifice."

53. See Parke 1967 and Christidis, Dakaris, and Vokotopoulou 1999: 67–68.

54. Plutarch (*Mor.* 386c) implies that inquirers at Delphi typically asked "if they shall be victorious, if they shall marry, if it is advantageous for them to sail, to farm, to go abroad."

55. See Parker 2005: 118–19.

A passage in Aristophanes' *Birds* (593–97) plays off the fact that private individuals asked seers about mining operations and commercial voyages. Indeed, the Athenian general Nicias is said to have kept a seer at his house whom he consulted about his private affairs and especially about his silver mines.[56] And Plato, in the *Laches* (195e), has this same Nicias say: "It is necessary for a seer to recognize the signs of what will take place, whether a person is to meet with death or disease or loss of property, or with victory or defeat in war or some other contest."

Yet there were certainly occasions, how many we cannot say, when a seer ventured something more than simply saying that the omens were or were not favorable in relation to a particular question. Here too a comparison with Dodona may be revealing. Although most of the questions put to the oracle there require a simple answer (either yes or no, or the name of the appropriate god or gods to sacrifice to), some demand a more sophisticated response. We have two examples of an inquirer asking what occupation he should undertake; no alternatives are given, and the question is essentially open-ended.[57] Seers too might be asked questions that gave them some scope for a creative response.

The Ambraciot seer Silanus predicted while sacrificing that the King of Persia would not fight with his employer, the Persian prince Cyrus the Younger, within ten days.[58] And Sthorys of Thasos was given the rare and high honor of Athenian citizenship for a prediction that he made from the sacrifices that he performed before the battle of Cnidus in 394.[59] Just what that prediction was, or indeed what form it took, is left unspecified in the inscription that grants him citizenship. The text, as restored, might be translated as follows: "He prophesied on the basis of the prebattle sacrifices the things that took place in the sea battle."[60] But he must have done more than merely indicate that the omens from sacrifice were favorable for battle. An eclipse of the sun may have preceded the battle, and one scholar has suggested that Sthorys interpreted this as indicating the eclipse of Spartan power.[61] One thing is for certain: the Athenian people were very grateful to Sthorys, and they showed their gratitude in the most conspicuous way that was available to them.

56. Plut. *Nic.* 4.
57. Parke 1967: 268, no. 16; and 271, no. 25.
58. Xen. *Anab.* 1.7.18; see further chapter 6.
59. Osborne 1981: no. D8, lines 26–29. See further chapter 4, note 35.
60. προ[εῖπε ... τὰ γενόμ]ενα περὶ τῆς ναυμαχίας [μαντευσάμενος ἐκ τῶν ἱερῶν τῶν εἰσιτητηρίων ὧ[νπερ ἔθυσεν].
61. Xen. *Hell.* 4.3.10, with Dillery 2005: 203.

FOUR

· Divination as a System
of Knowledge and Belief

There is to my knowledge no nation, no matter how
cultivated and learned or rude and barbaric, that does
not believe that future events are discernable and that
they can be understood and predicted by certain people. .

CICERO, *On Divination*

It would be easy enough for the modern student of antiquity, to the extent that divination is not part of his or her worldview, to be skeptical about its role in Greek
society. On the one hand, one might imagine that practitioner and client, as
allegedly in so many other areas of ritual activity, simply went through the motions
of conducting divinatory rites, and especially so on the field of battle. Such rites, as
when crossing borders, leaving camp, or beginning battle, could be exploited from
time to time by general or seer to suit the strategic or personal interests of either;
but one might speculate that for the most part such rites were routine and mundane.
Alternatively, such rites might seem to be a calculated means whereby leaders could
control followers. Weren't the results of divinatory sacrifices arranged in advance?
Weren't seers the willing agents of their employers, who in this role consciously
manipulated the sacrifices in order to validate what the generals and statesmen had
already decided to do?

It is absolutely essential to come to terms with such questions, since one's reading of a significant amount of Greek literature, as well as one's understanding of
critical events in Greek history, very much depends on the answer. The testimony
of Greek authors, across genres and across time, paints a very different picture from
what was imagined above. The rites of divination were not only ubiquitous in
Greek society; they were also uniquely authoritative. This was true not only for the
uneducated masses, but also for the elite, and not just in the archaic period, but even

during the classical and Hellenistic periods. How can we explain the vast gulf in outlook between "them" and "us"?

The answer may be found by employing the concept of a belief system. What may seem incredible to those who subscribe to one system of belief can seem perfectly natural to the members of another. This is also where anthropological studies are most helpful. It can be dangerous to use comparative anthropology to fill out the details of our evidence for ancient Greece; for instance, by arguing that if shamans in a particular African society use magic to make the omens turn out right, then Greek seers must have done likewise.[1] Where anthropology is useful is in providing models for how and why people believe things. As Evans-Pritchard discovered by living among the Azande of the southern Sudan, consulting the poison oracle on a daily basis was a very satisfactory way of conducting his own life. So too Greek generals found it both natural and convenient to rely on seers for guidance. As I proposed in chapter 1, we should attempt to view both Greek divination and the role of the seer in the divinatory system through the perceptual filters of the Greeks themselves.

The emotional intensity that could be involved in undergoing a divinatory ritual is graphically documented by the experience of Pausanias (9.39) when he visited and consulted the oracle of Trophonius at Lebadeia in the second century A.D. He tells us that after the inquirer emerges from the oracular cave, where he encountered the god either in sight or in sound, he is "overcome with terror and unconscious both of himself and of his surroundings. Later, however, he will recover his senses no less than before, and the ability to laugh will return to him." Although this description is strictly speaking beyond the chronological limits of this book, it is extremely valuable as an eyewitness testimony. Pausanias was willing to subject himself to this disorienting experience not because he had to or because it was expected of him, but because the experience was useful and meaningful for him.

The various rites of divination, taken together, constituted a rational and coherent, as well as a socially useful, system of knowledge and belief for the Greeks. It was socially useful in that it aided decision making, circumvented indecision, and arbitrated disputes. It was logical in that it was predicated on an implicit set of beliefs that made sense for the Greeks: that the gods are concerned for the welfare of humankind, that they know more than humans, and that they are willing to share some of that knowledge by way of advice. This set of interlocking suppositions is implicitly

1. This is the approach of Halliday 1913.

expressed by Socrates in Xenophon's *Memorabilia* (1.4.2–9), and explicitly made a basis for divination by Xenophon in his *Cyropaedia*. He puts into the mouth of Cyrus's father this advice for his son (1.6.46): "Human wisdom does not know how to choose what is best any more than if someone were to draw lots and do as the lot fell. But the gods, my son, who always exist, know all things, both the things that have taken place, the things that are, and whatever shall come to pass as a result of each past and present event. And when men consult them, they indicate in advance to those whom they favor both what they ought to do and what they ought not to do. But if the gods do not wish to advise everyone, that is not surprising. For there is no necessity for them to care for those whom they do not wish to." In his *Symposium* (4.47–49) Xenophon provides an example of the type of person that the gods wish to help. The conventionally pious Hermogenes is so dear to the gods that they are constantly sending him signs through sounds, dreams, and birds—signs that indicate to him "the things that he ought to do and the things that he must not do."

The same set of beliefs was used as a proof for the validity of divination in the famous syllogism of the third-century B.C. Stoic philosopher Chrysippus, who asserted (to paraphrase Cic. *Div.* 1.82–83) that if the gods exist, they must be concerned for us, and if they are concerned for us, then they must give us some indication of future events (since they know what they plan to do and such knowledge would make us more prudent) as well as giving us the means to understand those indications; thus, there is such a thing as divination.[2] The chief difference between Xenophon and Chrysippus seems to be the latter's assumption that the gods are concerned for all mortals. By contrast, Xenophon's statement is typical of the conception of the gods found in Homer and the tragedians that they support their favorites among mortals but that this support is fickle. Or to put it in more theoretical terms, the Greeks' understanding of how and why the gods communicated with humans fitted the conceptual framework within which they located all of their religious activities. The relationship between gods and humans was conceived of in terms of reciprocity (an ongoing exchange of voluntary, if socially prescribed, favors).[3] The gods' willingness to communicate with mortals through the rites of divination was one aspect of that reciprocity.

---

2. On the Stoic philosophical background to Cicero's *On Divination*, see Hankinson 1988 and Struck 2004: 187–92. For Chrysippus's writings on divination, see Gourinat 2005. Cicero's own views and their cultural context are examined in Linderski 1982; Denyer 1985; Beard 1986; and Schofield 1986.

3. See Parker 1998. Note also Yunis 1988: 50–56, 100–111.

Although the Stoics had their own peculiar views about how the world works, Chrysippus's syllogism, with the qualification noted above, works well as a summary of what most Greeks of archaic and classical times thought about the relationship between gods and humans. And given their view of that relationship, it was perfectly rational for them to turn to the gods for advice. The normative Greek view of divination in the classical period is surely that attributed to Socrates by Xenophon in his *Memorabilia* (1.1.6–9), since it is a key part of his demonstration that Socrates' religious attitudes were traditional. There we are told that Socrates advised his close friends "that if an action was unavoidable, to carry it out as they thought best, but where the result of an action was uncertain, he sent them to use divination to see if the action should be taken. He said that anyone who proposed to run a household or a city efficiently needed the help of divination."

Socrates qualified this advice, however, with the proviso that it was not appropriate to employ divination with respect to issues that were within the realm of human intelligence. It was wrong, for instance, to ask the gods whether to hire a qualified or unqualified driver for a carriage or helmsman for a ship. "But what is hidden from human beings," he continues, "we should try to find out from the gods by divination; for the gods give signs to those whom they favor." It is noteworthy that when it comes to these sorts of everyday questions, Socrates does not explicitly recommend consulting an oracular center such as Delphi or Dodona. His use of the word meaning "use divination" is ambiguous, since it is usually used in connection with oracles.[4] But Xenophon uses this same verb at the beginning of the *Memorabilia* to mean "those who inquire by divination" by the use of birds, voices, portents, and sacrifices, and the word surely has the same broad sense in this passage too. It was the seer who gave the Athenian, whatever his social standing or economic wealth, immediate and even daily access to divine knowledge.

Because Greek divination comprised an eminently coherent and logically interconnected set of beliefs and practices it was able to accommodate and explain any apparent contradictions between prediction and actual experience. If the omens proved favorable for a particular action, and the action then failed, in the minds of the participants this did not prove the system to be false. And even if some contemporaries did not believe in the truth of divination, it would have been difficult for them, as indeed it would be even for us, to falsify the system in the minds of those who did believe. For one could appeal to a whole range of secondary elabo-

---

4. He uses the participle μαντευσομένους from the Greek verb μαντεύεσθαι. At Ar. *Birds* 593, 596, this verb can mean either "to practice divination" or "to consult seers."

rations of belief that explained the apparent failure. For instance, the failure was due to the fact that the seer had misinterpreted the omen or the recipient had misconstrued the meaning of the oracular response or the gods had merely given their approval (as they must almost always have given it to both armies at the start of an engagement) but were not guaranteeing victory. In effect, an individual or a community could easily explain any failure of divination in terms of its own beliefs.[5] As the anthropologist Meyer Fortes has observed, "diviners, however, are but human and known to be not infallible. Thus, there are always loopholes in a system of divination which enable the mistakes of its practitioners to be explained away and confidence in the system to be maintained."[6]

A substantial number of case studies among twentieth-century religious groups show that failed prophecies do not necessarily lead to serious problems for such groups or bring about their disintegration. On the contrary, if the believer is part of a community of individuals who share the same beliefs and who support each other when their beliefs are challenged, then even when presented with unequivocal and undeniable evidence that his belief is false, "the individual will frequently emerge, not only unshaken, but even more convinced of the truth of his beliefs than ever before."[7] If this situation holds for a fringe group (that is, for a religious movement that represents a minority within a larger community), it will certainly be the case when the entire community adheres to the same set of beliefs, especially when the community is as small and heterogeneous as a Greek *polis*.

For most Greeks there was no such thing as "coincidence." Every uncanny or untoward event, such as an earthquake or storm, a strange light at sea, an unusually high tide, or even the swarming of bees, was a sign sent by some supernatural power.[8] It was the task of the seer to interpret precisely what the sign portended. Yet in a society in which even fairly banal occurrences had a meaning that transcended

5. See Evans-Pritchard 1976: 146–75 for the concepts expressed here. But also note Overholt (1989: 133–34), who isolates three factors militating against disbelief: the belief that the gods stand behind the system of divination; the nature of the problems dealt with that may make accurate assessments of results difficult; and the existence of procedural safeguards that may serve to inhibit the diviner from manipulating a result.

6. Fortes 1987: 11.

7. The quotation is from the seminal study of Festinger, Riecken, and Schachter (1956). See also Melton 1985 and Dein 1997.

8. Gould 2003 is a brief but incisive discussion of this aspect of Greek thought. Gould draws on the study of Dinka religion in Lienhardt 1961, which is one of the seminal works in the anthropology of religion.

surface appearances, there was undoubtedly a tendency to look for signs at times of particular stress or uncertainty. To be sure, omens and portents are sometimes recognized, or indeed invented, only after the fact in order to explain an unfortunate event that could have been avoided, if only the omen had been recognized. Thus divination provides both a way of knowing about events that are about to take place and an explanation for those events that have already occurred.

It should come as no surprise, therefore, that in our sources portents tend to cluster around important events.[9] It is impossible for us to be sure when such signs are after the fact retrojections or were actually observed in advance of the events that they portended. This is not a problem that we need worry about, however. It is not important for assessing the reliability of our sources whether signs were in fact noted before the events that they signified. In the aftermath of trauma, individuals often look back and see omens that would have warned them had they noticed them at the time. Psychologically, omen formation represents an attempt to regain a sense of control over events that proved disastrous or chaotic.[10] Moreover, individuals can also experience "time skew," which is "a disordered perception of temporal sequence in which events that occurred after the trauma were seen as coming before."[11] And surely it must be the case, not only for the Greeks but cross-culturally, that some of these events are "imagined" retrojections. "I remember seeing x (a black cat)" can become "I remember seeing xy (a black cat giving me an evil eye)."

In any case, all of the portents and omens in our sources cannot be literary fabrications on any commonsense reading of the texts.[12] Even well-educated Greeks, such as Herodotus or Xenophon, saw portentous happenings as proof of the workings of some supernatural power. Herodotus was not saying anything controversial in terms of Greek religious belief when he commented (6.27): "There is

---

9. So Pritchett 1979: 39–41, 151. Portents in Greek texts are collected and discussed by Steinhauser 1911; Popp 1957: chap. 1; and Pritchett 1979: 91–153.

10. See Guinan 2002: 24–26. She is here discussing a particular incident that occurred in 1976 in Chowchilla, California, when a school bus carrying twenty-six children (ages 5–14) was hijacked at gunpoint. Omen formation was one of the most common posttraumatic manifestations, affecting nineteen of the twenty-six children, who "looked back and saw 'omens' that would have warned them if only they had been alert." It strikes me as an eminently reasonable inference that adults, especially given a cultural context in which the perception of omens was common, would react in much the same way.

11. See Guinan 2002: 25.

12. This point is thoroughly discussed by Pritchett (1979: 140–53), although much more could still be said in support of this view.

usually some sign given in advance when great misfortunes are about to befall a city or nation."[13] And given how even today in Western societies stories of miracles, prodigies, and portents are widespread, historians such as Timaeus and Theopompus, both of whom recorded portents with frequency, did not necessarily need to engage in fictitious embellishment in order to enliven their histories. Whatever their personal beliefs may have been, they need only have reported popular stories and traditions without attempting to rationalize them.

It is again worth stressing that both in literature and in real life, portents and omens cluster around momentous events and times of crisis. One example that will be looked at several times in this book has to do with Dion's expedition to Sicily in 357 B.C. in order to depose Dionysius II, tyrant of Syracuse. Portents, as narrated by Plutarch in his *Dion* (24), were thick on both sides. Dion and his mercenary forces experienced a lunar eclipse and the swarming of bees at the sterns of their ships. Meanwhile many portentous signs were given to Dionysius. An eagle seized the spear of a member of his bodyguard and dropped it into the sea; the seawater that washes against the acropolis of Syracuse was sweet and drinkable for one day; and pigs were born that were normal in other respects but lacked ears. Once the seers recognized these happenings as omens they then needed to interpret them. Miltas, Dion's seer, interpreted the eclipse as a favorable omen, predicting that they would extinguish the tyranny of Dionysius as soon as they reached Sicily; but the swarming of bees indicated that their successes would flower only for a short time and would then wither away.

On the other hand, if the seers who served Dionysius II really gave the interpretations that Plutarch attributes to them, they could not have curried much favor. "The seers declared the missing ears to be a sign of rebellion and disobedience, on the grounds that the citizens would no longer listen to the tyranny; but the sweetness of the sea indicated for the Syracusans a change from distressing and oppressive times to excellent circumstances. An eagle is a servant of Zeus, and a spear is an emblem of authority and power. Therefore, the greatest of the gods desires the obliteration and dissolution of the tyranny." All of this may sound far-fetched to us, given our own culturally determined perceptual filters; but Plutarch ends by citing the fourth-century historian Theopompus of Chios as his source, who, as I have

---

13. Context is always important: here Herodotus is commenting on two disasters that happened shortly before the battle of Lade in 494 B.C. and the subsequent conquest of Chios by Lesbos. One was a plague that killed 98 Chian youths who had been sent as a chorus to Delphi, and the other was the collapse of a schoolhouse on Chios that killed 119 boys.

attempted to show elsewhere, was not a historian who invented material whole cloth.[14]

An extraordinary set of portents surrounded Timoleon's mission to Sicily in 344 B.C., which was also directed against Dionysius II. And in this case there are empirical reasons for believing that the portents have been reported accurately, since they seem to have been recorded by at least two different primary sources.[15] The two secondary accounts that have come down to us, in Plutarch and Diodorus, differ only in minor details. Plutarch gives the fuller version of the two in his *Life of Timoleon* (8). When the expedition was ready, "the priestesses of Persephone at Corinth had a dream in which they saw the goddesses getting ready for a journey and heard them say that they were intending to sail with Timoleon to Sicily. Consequently, the Corinthians equipped a sacred trireme and named it after the two goddesses." When Timoleon had set sail and had reached the open sea during the night, "the heavens seemed to break open over his ship and to pour forth a great and conspicuous fire. Then a torch, like those used in the celebration of the Eleusinian Mysteries, rose up and, running along beside his ship, descended upon the very part of Italy that the helmsmen were aiming for." It was up to the seers who were part of the expedition to interpret this series of portents, and they did so, not surprisingly, in a way completely favorable to the success of the expedition: "The seers declared that the apparition confirmed the dreams of the priestesses, that the goddesses were taking part in the expedition and were displaying the light from heaven. For, they said, Sicily was sacred to Persephone, since her seizure [by Hades] is said to have taken place there, and the island was given to her as a wedding gift."

Given that the decision whether to send Timoleon to Sicily in order to intervene at Syracuse was so stressful and so full of uncertainties for the Corinthians, it is likely enough that the priestesses of Persephone actually had this dream. As E. R. Dodds pointed out long ago, the content of dreams is culturally determined.[16] So

14. *FGrH* 115, F 331. It is unclear, however, whether Plutarch means that he found the material about both sets of portents in Theopompus, or only about those that occurred at Syracuse. For Theopompus's historical method, see Flower 1994, esp. 184–210. His view of Dion, however, cannot be ascertained from the extant fragments (on this problem see Sanders [1997], who fails to perceive the significance of this passage).

15. Pearson (1987: 211–12 [cf. 149–50, 196–97]) argues that Plutarch (*Tim.* 8) and Diodorus (16.66.3–5) found the account of these portents in different sources. Talbert (1974: 32 n. 2) had already reached the same conclusion. According to Pearson, Plutarch was using Timaeus, and Diodorus found the story in Ephorus or Dyillus.

16. 1951: 102–34.

would not the priestesses of Persephone expect the goddess to appear to them in such circumstances? It is unclear from our sources whether the dream appeared to them sequentially or on the same night to each of them. If the former, then the power of suggestion can easily be invoked in order to provide a rationalizing explanation for the phenomenon. The light at sea is also possible for us to explain, for it corresponds to the natural phenomenon of a meteor shower.

A famous example of a self-evident omen is reported in the *Anabasis* (3.2.8–9): when Xenophon was first addressing the Ten Thousand and while uttering the phrase "With the gods we have many fair hopes of safety," someone sneezed. The soldiers with one accord then prostrated themselves before the god. Both they and Xenophon immediately recognized this to be an omen sent by "Zeus the savior" without any seer needing to point it out for them.[17]

It was important that the Greek soldiers who were listening to Xenophon should react as they did, because there is an implicit assumption in Greek thought that verbally accepting an omen makes it irrevocable in the sense desired by the person who accepts it.[18] Herodotus records (8.114) that the Spartans received a Delphic oracle after the battle of Salamis to the effect that "they should seek restitution from Xerxes for the murder of Leonidas and should accept whatever was given by him." They dispatched a herald to Xerxes, who was still in Thessaly with Mardonius, and when the herald made this demand, Xerxes laughed and pointed to Mardonius, saying that the latter would pay back whatever was fitting. This story is not as likely to be true as Xenophon's (since Herodotus was not an eyewitness). Nonetheless, the acceptance by the herald of Xerxes' response that Mardonius would pay restitution for the death of Leonidas is a sure indication to Herodotus's readers that Mardonius's fate was sealed.

Finally, in a society that had this degree of openness to supernatural manifestations, it might be all too easy to see signs everywhere when one is under extreme psychological pressure. And even without such stress a sort of obsessiveness is all too likely to arise. Theophrastus's superstitious man (*Characters* 16) is a purely literary example of this kind of person. An actual example might be the Hermogenes in Xenophon's *Symposium* (4.47–48), who was mentioned above. Xenophon depicts him as claiming that day and night the gods were constantly sending him signs as

17. Lossau (1990) and Tuplin (2003: 128–29) argue that this sneeze is modeled on the sneeze of Telemachus in the *Odyssey* (17.541), which follows Penelope's implied wish for the return of Odysseus and the destruction of the suitors. The Homeric resonance may be a reason why Xenophon has included the sneeze, but I do not think that he has invented it whole cloth for the sake of a literary allusion. For a sneeze as an omen, see Pease 1911.

18. Halliday 1913: 46–49.

guides to action. Hermogenes, we are told, believed that things went well for him whenever he obeyed the signs, but when he distrusted them he was punished. This same frame of mind seems to have characterized Alexander the Great by the last year of his life; for he became so excessively superstitious during his final sojourn at Babylon that he filled his palace with sacrificers, purifiers, and seers (Plut. *Alex.* 75).

The Greeks and Romans themselves, despite their reliance on divination in all aspects of political and social life, were aware that there were few fixed rules of interpretation. In the Hippocratic treatise *Regimen in Acute Diseases* (8), the author complains about the differences of opinion among physicians over the proper choice of remedies in acute diseases, and then makes the telling observation that "laypeople are likely to object that their art resembles divination; for seers too think that the same bird that they hold to be a good omen on the left is an unlucky one when on the right, while other seers maintain the opposite. The inspection of entrails (*hieroskopia*) shows similar differences in its various aspects." Yet here again one could negotiate the apparent contradiction by asserting that just as one doctor is better than another, so one seer excels another. Or perhaps there were certain contingencies that could explain why on one occasion the left is lucky, but on another the right. For instance, in the augury inscription from Ephesus, discussed in chapter 2, the lifting of a wing reverses the usual left/right dichotomy. The author of this treatise does not realize that what may be a weakness in medical practice is actually a strength of divinatory practice.

Cicero (*Div.* 2.28) thought that he had scored a decisive point against the validity of divination when he asserted that there was no agreement in the interpretation of entrails by the seers (*haruspices*) of Etruria, Elis, Egypt, and Carthage, and thus no universal system (*nec esse unam omnium disciplinam*). He also makes the same argument in regard to the interpretation of bird omens and of thunder, pointing out that the left side is favorable for Romans, whereas the right is favorable for Greeks (2.76, 82). Here, as often, Cicero is not as clever as he thinks he is, for one could make the counterassertion that the gods communicate to different peoples in different ways. When devising their coded messages the gods take local customs into account. In any case, as we shall see, uniformity of interpretation was far less important to the Greeks than the ability to give a successful reading of a particular sign on any given occasion.

Despite how difficult it is to understand the meaning of an omen or portent, it can be even more difficult to recognize one in the first place. In a brilliant article with the unlikely title "A Severed Head Laughed," Ann Guinan observes: "The reason omens stand out from the background resides in the cognitive model of the observer.

An individual sees many birds during the course of a journey, or two people pass the same black cat, or observe extraordinary events. But a cat, a crow, a flash of light in the sky only becomes an omen when the circumstances demand it. The underlying tension of a personal situation kindles the signifying power of an omen."[19]

Now it may be true that some omens are recognized as such only under certain conditions. But it also true that others, regardless of the psychological state of the observer, are manifestly signs that cannot be ignored within a given cultural context. I think that if I ever were to observe a severed head laughing (and I sincerely hope that I do not), I would immediately and without hesitation understand it to be an omen, and a rather bad one. And that judgment would be independent of any particular personal problems I might have at the time. Although not as arresting as a severed head, earthquakes and eclipses of the sun or moon were always taken to be ominous by the Greeks and had the potential to disrupt the movements of armies. Whether any particular occurrence was a positive or negative sign, however, was open to interpretation. And in each case interpretation was surely colored by the concerns of the moment.

For instance, in 400 B.C. an earthquake caused King Agis of Sparta to abort his invasion of Elis, whereas in 388 King Agesipolis interpreted an earthquake that occurred after he had entered Argive territory to be a propitious omen. The partial solar eclipse of October 2, 480, prevented the Spartan commander Cleombrotus from advancing beyond the Isthmus of Corinth against the invading Persians, whereas Alexander the Great took the lunar eclipse before the battle of Gaugamela to be a positive sign.[20] As a paradigmatic example, let us take a close look at the episode that is best attested in our sources, the lunar eclipse of 413 B.C. that prevented the Athenians from leaving Syracuse while they still could.[21]

A CASE STUDY: THE ATHENIANS AT SYRACUSE

In 415 B.C. the Athenians and their allies set sail for Sicily with a huge armada, eventually comprising 207 warships (triremes) and some 50,000–60,000 men, only a

19. Guinan 2002: 21.

20. For earthquakes stopping Spartan armies, see Thuc. 3.89.1, 6.95.1; Xen. *Hell.* 3.2.24; with Parker 1988: 156. For Agesipolis, see Xen. *Hell.* 4.7.4; for Cleombrotus, Hdt. 9.10.3; and for Alexander, Arr. 3.7.6.

21. The main treatments are Jacoby 1949: 252 n. 72; Gomme, *HCT* vol. 4: 428; Pritchett 1979: 109–10; Powell 1979; and Trampedach 2003b: 31–42.

very few of whom returned home alive. When the siege of Syracuse was going badly, the Athenian generals Nicias and Demosthenes finally decided to return home. Their plan was to do so as secretly as possible and at a given signal, obviously in order to escape the notice of the Syracusans. But just as the Athenians were on the point of embarking on their ships, there was a total eclipse of the moon. The date was August 27, 413 B.C. The historian Thucydides, in his terse account, primarily lays the blame for the Athenian reaction on the Athenian general Nicias (7.50.4):

> When everything was ready and they were on the point of sailing away, the moon, which happened to be full, was eclipsed. Most of the Athenians, taking it to heart, urged the generals to wait, and Nicias (who indeed was somewhat too much given to divination and the like) said that he would not even still discuss how the move should be made until they had waited thrice nine days, as the seers were prescribing. For this reason the delay came about for the Athenians who had been about to depart.

This famous passage in Thucydides, perhaps more than any other, shows the influence that seers could have, for good or ill, on the course of events. This passage is particularly revealing because it is evidently not an after-the-fact explanation for why the Athenians failed at Syracuse, in the way that some portents might appear to be invented later in order to provide an explanation at a religious level for unfortunate events. One might think of the ominous incidents surrounding the departure of the Athenian general Cimon for his last campaign in 451 B.C., as recorded by Plutarch (*Cim.* 18). Cimon was forewarned of his death by a dream in which a bitch spoke to him in a human voice, by the portent of ants pasting his big toe with the blood of a sacrificial victim, and by the that fact that the victim's liver lacked a lobe. Yet in Thucydides' account, unlike in the case of Cimon's expedition, the purpose of recalling the portent is not to impose a divinely sanctioned explanation for failure. Rather, the eclipse occurred, and if it had not been interpreted in the way that it was by the seers, the Athenians would have escaped. Did those seers have to interpret the eclipse in the way that they did, in the sense that their system of divinatory knowledge imposed that particular reading upon them?

First of all, it might be helpful to imagine the impression that the eclipse would have made on the Athenian army. Modern studies of the Earth's past rotation both confirm Thucydides' account and can help us to understand why the rank and file would have been so alarmed. A recent investigation describes this particular eclipse as follows: "This would start at 8:15 p.m. (about 1½ hours after sunset) and end towards midnight (11:40 p.m.). Totality would last for about 45 minutes (between 9:35 and 10:20 p.m.) and during that time the sky would be considerably darkened. Following the characteristic pattern of total lunar eclipses, the Moon would probably turn blood red in colour, or may possibly have even disappeared from sight for a while."[22] If this were not alarming enough, something happened that Thucydides does not mention, but that may well have added to the Athenians' unease. A large partial lunar eclipse had occurred in the early spring of the same year, 413 B.C., on March 4. This earlier eclipse was also visible at Syracuse. What were the gods trying to tell them?

Thucydides implies that it was in Nicias's power, had he been less susceptible to divination, to overrule the sentiments of his troops and the recommendation of his seers. If we had only Thucydides' account, it would appear that the choice was a simple one: either to ignore the seers' interpretation (perhaps in favor of some rational and scientific explanation of the eclipse) or else to remain for the prescribed twenty-seven days. As mentioned above, the various rituals of divination ideally provided a socially useful means of aiding decision making, circumventing indecision, and arbitrating disputes. If one reads the incident in that fashion, then this does look like a case in which both these specific seers and divination as a system of knowledge failed to be socially useful. Plutarch, however, provides a rather different perspective on this event (*Nic.* 23.5–6):

> It befell Nicias at that time not even to have an experienced seer. For Stilbides, who was his intimate and who removed most of his superstition, had died a little before. And indeed the sign, as Philochorus says [*FGrH* 328, F 135], was not obnoxious to fugitives, but indeed very favorable: for deeds done in fear are in need of concealment, whereas light is an enemy to such deeds. And besides, as Autocleides has written in his *Exegesis* [*FGrH* 353, F 7], men used to be on their guard for three days in the case of portents of the sun and moon. But Nicias persuaded them to wait for another full period of the moon.

This is valuable information because Philochorus (c. 340–260 B.C.) was himself a seer and Autocleides (third century B.C.?) was an expert on the interpretation of omens. It is unclear who suggested that if Stilbides, who was Nicias's personal seer, had still been alive, then Nicias would have acted differently. Is that Plutarch's own

---

22. Stephenson and Fatoohi 2001: 249.

inference, or did he find it in Philochorus or in another of his sources for this particular life? It is often difficult to tell where a citation of a "fragmentary" author begins and ends; but we know from a scholiast's comment on line 1031 of Aristophanes' *Peace* that Philochorus mentioned the participation of Stilbides in the Sicilian expedition.[23] That makes it very likely that Philochorus himself asserted that Stilbides would surely have correctly interpreted the eclipse as a favorable omen. However that may be, one thing is completely clear. Philochorus and Autocleides, who were writing during the third century B.C., had the advantage of hindsight. They also needed, perhaps subconsciously, to come up with an explanation that would save the validity of divination as a source of knowledge. So even if in 413 there could have been only one explanation for the meaning of the eclipse, in later years it was necessary to provide others.

The fundamental questions, however, are these: Did the seers serving Nicias really have a choice between alternative recommendations? Or were they constrained by fixed rules of interpretation? Or was it just a matter of guessing both the meaning and the appropriate action to be taken when it came to a natural occurrence such as an eclipse? If there is a basic principle at work in the practice of divination, I would say that it is this. A seer needs to tailor his interpretation to the social context of a particular consultation.[24] In this case, they needed to take into account both the military situation and the inclinations of those who held military command: in other words, context informs interpretation. As it unfortunately turned out, Nicias's seers made a mistake; but religious specialists in any tradition sometimes do.[25] Of course, it is possible that the Athenians could still have defeated the Syracusans, as they almost did in the second sea battle in the harbor (Thuc. 7.71), in which case the seers would have been vindicated; it is only from the vantage of hindsight that the Athenian cause seems irremediably doomed after their decision to stay. The important thing, however, is that a "mistake" can be accommodated within the system itself. The complete destruction of the Athenian force was not taken as proof that an eclipse has no significance as an omen, but rather that the seers on the spot had misinterpreted its significance. If they had understood the omen properly, as Philochorus realized, then they would have departed immediately and thus been

23. Philochorus, *FGrH* 328, F 135a.
24. This topic is fully discussed in chapter 7.
25. Green (1970: 297–98) makes the implausible suggestion that the Athenian seers had been bribed by the Syracusans to make the interpretation that they did.

saved. By hiding the light of the moon the gods were both indicating to the Athenians their approval for their plan to flee and were tangibly aiding their escape.

Two important points emerge from Plutarch's account. First, the seers on the spot did not have to interpret the omen of the eclipse in the way that they did. They were surely influenced, even if only subconsciously, both by the mood of the troops and by their knowledge that Nicias himself was extremely reluctant to leave Syracuse without having captured the city. For Nicias knew, according to Thucydides (7.48), that if he returned unsuccessful, he was liable to stand trial in Athens and face execution. In other words, if neither the soldiers nor Nicias wanted to depart, there must have been tremendous psychological pressure to recommend a delay. Second, it was possible to interpret the eclipse as a negative omen, and yet to delay their departure for only three days. So why did they prescribe twenty-seven days, which was another full period of the moon? Plutarch lays the blame on Nicias, asserting that it was he who determined the length of the delay, as does also Diodorus (13.12.5) in his somewhat garbled account. But surely Thucydides' version is to be preferred, and it was the seers who specified the number of days. As it turned out, the length of the delay was important, since the Athenians still had plenty of time in which to leave. It was only after a subsequent major naval battle in the harbor that the Syracusans were bold enough to block up the entrance. Again, the seers must have felt pressured to advise the longer period.

As indicated earlier, this incident brings out a general principle in systems of divination. Apart from a liver that lacks a lobe, most phenomena could be read in more than one way. Indeed, in 357, when Plato's friend Dion was about to set out from Zacynthus for an expedition against Dionysius II, tyrant of Syracuse, there was a lunar eclipse. As with the Athenians in 413, the soldiers were greatly disturbed. But this time his seer, the Thessalian Miltas, interpreted it as a positive sign, to wit, that the gods were indicating the eclipse of something resplendent and that there was nothing more resplendent than the tyranny of Dionysius, the brightness of which they would extinguish as soon as they reached Sicily.[26] Miltas, one suspects, had the example of Nicias before his mind and was well aware that Dion's chances depended on the element of surprise, that any delay would be disadvantageous, and that he needed to boost the morale of Dion's rather small band of mercenaries. Here was a seer who had a good understanding of the military situation and who could think

---

26. As narrated by Plutarch in his *Life of Dion* (24), where he is perhaps drawing on Theopompus of Chios (see note 14 above). I am not persuaded by the conjecture of Thiel (1994: 91) that Dion's soldiers compelled him to wait a month before sailing.

on his feet. In effect, the significance of this eclipse for the future was constructed in relation to the concerns of the present and the knowledge of the past.

There is one other aspect of this incident at Syracuse in 413 that is relevant to questions of belief. Although it might seem to be obvious to some moderns that divination and natural science provide mutually exclusive means of understanding how the world works, the Greeks did not feel that to be the case. Although he leaves it implicit, it is pretty clear that Plutarch did not see a scientific explanation for a lunar eclipse (which he claims had been discovered by the natural philosopher Anaxagoras of Clazomenae) as being mutually exclusive with a religious explanation (such as that correctly offered by the seer Philochorus). Indeed, in his *Life of Pericles* (6) he tells a famous story about how the head of a one-horned ram was brought to Pericles from his country estate. The seer Lampon interpreted this as a sign that Pericles would become the leading statesman in Athens, whereas the natural philosopher Anaxagoras dissected the head and gave a physiological explanation for the deformity. As Plutarch points out, nothing prevented both seer and philosopher from being correct in their interpretation: for the philosopher gave the cause of the phenomenon, but the seer gave its meaning. As we might say, divine powers work within the laws of nature in order to give signs to humans; it is the task of the seer to explain the meaning of the sign, and that task is not at all incompatible with scientific inquiry. It makes no difference whether this particular story is a complete fabrication or contains a kernel of historical truth;[27] for the attitude that it conveys is at least as old as the fourth century B.C.

DISREGARDING THE OMENS

Belief in the efficacy of divination was maintained not only by the ability of those who believed in it to explain failures and contradictions in terms of the system itself, but also by the apparent disaster that befell those who flagrantly or contemptuously disregarded the omens. In three of the most prestigious genres of Greek literature (epic, tragedy, and history) ill-fortune befalls those who mock seers or ridicule their advice. Indeed, one theme that spans the whole of Greek poetry from Homer to Sophocles is plainly this—those who ignore omens and belittle seers pay for their impiety and arrogance in the end, either with their own lives or with the lives of those most dear to them.

27. Yunis (1988: 69) is skeptical.

This idea was probably much older than the earliest Greek literature. Like divination itself, it probably originated in the Near East and is a subset of the notion that the gods punish those who disobey them. The belief that disaster falls upon those who ignore omens goes back at least to the Babylonian epic *Naram-Sin and the Enemy Hordes* (standard Babylonian recension, eighth–seventh century, lines 72– 87), in which Naram-Sin, king of Akkade, decides to attack the enemy hordes that are ravaging the Near East. He inquires of seven gods by means of extispicy, but when the omens continue to be unfavorable, he arrogantly decides to ignore them and attacks; his armies are wiped out to a man three years in a row.[28] This legend "was the classic propagator of extispicy, which it presented as an infallible means of studying the divine will, and as a necessary prerequisite for any important undertaking."[29] In the Hebrew Bible, King Saul is defeated and killed because he joins battle with the Philistines without favorable omens, being unable to obtain them through any of the means available to him: dreams, the Urim (a type of dice), prophets, or even necromancy (1 Samuel 28–31).

The same pattern is found in Greek literature, beginning with Homer. In the *Iliad*, there are two exemplary scenes between Hector and Poulydamas. Although Poulydamas evidently is not a professional seer and indeed is never called one in the poem, these scenes had a lasting resonance in the way subsequent Greeks thought about the relationship between seer and commander.[30] In the earlier scene, Hector disregards Poulydamas's counsel not to attack the Achaean ships because of the portent of an eagle being bitten by a snake and then dropping it amidst the Trojans (12.200–250).[31] In a later debate, Hector ignores Poulydamas's advice to withdraw within their walls and not fight in the plain with the Achaeans (18.243–314). This theme also finds expression in tragedy. In Aeschylus's *Seven against Thebes,* there is a verbally vivid description of Tydeus growing impatient with his seer Amphiaraus (377–83):

Tydeus now rages at the Proetid Gate, but the seer does not allow him to cross the river Ismenus. For the *sphagia* are not favorable. But Tydeus, raging and eager for battle, shouts as a snake hissing at midday, and he strikes at the wise

---

28. Westenholz 1997: 316–19.

29. Parpola in Tadmor, Landsberger, and Parpola 1989: 46–47.

30. *Contra* Dillery 2005: 172–73, *Iliad* 13.730–32 does not imply that Poulydamas was a seer.

31. On the consequences of Hector's decision to ignore the bird omen, see Redfield 1975: 143–52 and Taplin 1992: 156–60.

seer, the son of Oecles, with reproaches, saying that he shrinks from death and battle through cowardice.

Although the audience is meant to understand that the omens never prove favorable, Amphiaraus eventually lifts the ban on crossing the river, in full knowledge that this would bring about his own death (587–89). Nonetheless, Aeschylus's audience would not have considered Tydeus as thereby exonerated from crossing the river in the face of adverse omens.

In the *Oedipus Tyrannus*, Oedipus ridicules the advice of Teiresias only to suffer for it, and the same applies to Creon in the *Antigone*. In both the *Oedipus Tyrannus* and the *Antigone* the authority of Teiresias on matters concerning the will of the gods is absolute. Oedipus and Creon challenge his wisdom, knowledge, and integrity at their own peril. In the *Antigone* the issue at the heart of the play, whether human law or divine law should take precedence in matters of state, is decisively settled by Teiresias. At first Creon will not follow his advice and accuses him of accepting bribes, just as Oedipus had done in the *Oedipus Tyrannus*. But after Teiresias, provoked to anger by Creon, delivers his prophecy, Creon backs down and reverses his order to bury Antigone alive. All others had failed to convince Creon of his error, yet the terrible prophecy of the unerring seer was alone necessary and sufficient to undo Creon's stubborn resolve and bring him to his senses.

What we would call "historical" incidents, mostly taken from the works of Xenophon, are discussed in the next chapter, but one example is worth mentioning here. During the battle of Plataea in 479 B.C., by ignoring the recommendation of his Greek seer not to cross the Asopus River, Mardonius put himself in the wrong and brought about the destruction of his entire army. Although the particulars differ, both Mardonius and Hector are too headstrong and stubborn to listen to sound counsel, and their eagerness for a pitched battle proves their undoing.[32] As ironic as it may seem, such tales of disaster serve to validate the entire system and to prove its infallibility. The fact that disaster inevitably befalls those who disregard divinatory rites demonstrates the efficacy of those rites and provides a warning. And this warning is articulated both in the mythical past and in the historical present. There is, moreover, a mutual cooperation between divination and the other aspects of

32. See Flower and Marincola 2002: 181. I disagree with the interpretation of Struck (2003: 175–78), who concludes: "Doubtless, the strongest message from the Hector episode, in its intricate construction, is the superior nature of Hector's bravery and leadership." I would rather see this episode as demonstrating his headstrong obstinacy.

Greek religion, because falsification of divination would undermine faith in religion generally. That is why the chorus in the *Oedipus Tyrannus* is so concerned that the oracles of Apollo about Laius, no matter the immediate consequences, should prove true (lines 898–910, also discussed in chapter 5).

There is, moreover, an additional way to read the role of the seer in tragedy. Calchas, Amphiaraus, and Teiresias have knowledge that is superior to that of the leaders whom they serve (Agamemnon, Tydeus, Oedipus and Creon, respectively). They are seers who know better than anyone else the secret causes of events, and thus their wisdom is superior to that of any other mortal. Only on rare occasions and in specific contexts might a seer in historical times function as they did. Certainly, these examples of disaster were the negative mythical paradigms that might have inspired historical commanders not to disregard or disparage what their seers told them. And so Leonidas did not question the prediction of Megistias at Thermopylae that death would come with the dawn, nor did Pausanias, the commander of the Greek forces at Plataea, fail to head Tisamenus's advice to remain on the defensive and not cross the Asopus River.[33]

DIVINATION AND ATHENIAN DEMOCRACY

It has often been assumed that seers declined in influence at Athens due to the rise of democracy.[34] Even if we did not know that in 394/3 Sthorys of Thasos was awarded Athenian citizenship as a reward for the divinatory sacrifices that he offered before the naval battle of Cnidus, there would be good grounds for doubting this modern hypothesis.[35] Seers were present during every meeting of the Athenian Assembly.[36] In the second century B.C., and perhaps earlier, at least one seer was annually designated to serve each board of Athenian generals. The most eminent generals of the fifth century (Tolmides, Cimon, Nicias, Alcibiades, and perhaps Pericles) were accustomed to employ private seers, and it is possible that the state provided their pay while on campaign.[37] Another phenomenon is even more telling

---

33. Hdt. 7.219 and 9.36.

34. E.g., Bremmer 1993: 157–59; Bremmer 1996. Bowden 2005 (esp. 152–59) demonstrates the continuing importance of Delphi to the Athenian democracy throughout the fifth and fourth centuries.

35. *IG* II² 17 + *SEG* 15.84 + *SEG* 16.42 (= Osborne 1981: no. D8), lines 26–29. For discussion, see Osborne 1970 and 1981: 43–45; 1982: 45–48.

36. Cic. *Div.* 1.43, 95.

37. This is a controversial topic. See Pritchett 1979: 62–63 and Parker 2005: 117–18. We know from two Athenian catalogues of magistrates (*IG* II² 1708 and *AthMitt* 67 [1942]: no. 25.19), dating to the

and is worth exploring in depth—the active engagement of seers and *chrēsmologoi* in politics.[38]

The mid-fifth-century Athenian seer Lampon is particularly interesting.[39] He assisted in founding the Panhellenic colony of Thurium in 443/3,[40] he was the first Athenian signatory of the Peace of Nicias in 421 and of the alliance with Sparta that followed, he moved a rider about the olive harvest to the decree that regulated the offering of first fruits at Eleusis (ML 73), and he apparently was a close associate of Pericles.[41]

It is a significant mark of their perceived importance in classical Athens that the seers Sthorys and Lampon, as well as the *chrēsmologos* Hierocles, were all apparently granted free meals in the Prytaneum, the building that housed the city's sacred hearth. Sthorys was invited on two different occasions for a single meal.[42] Hierocles and Lampon, if we can trust Aristophanes and the scholia to his plays, were given permanent dining privileges (such public maintenance was called *sitēsis*).[43] That was an honor usually reserved for the most important benefactors of the state. In the case of Lampon the right to dine there might have been granted to him ex officio because

---

first half of the second century B.C., that there eventually existed an official post of "seer to the Athenian generals." It is not known, however, when this post became regularized. Already in 395 B.C. Sthorys was receiving an official payment, but the implications of this are unclear (see Osborne 1970: 166 n. 81).

38. On the intellectual background of these seers, see Roth 1984. Cf. Nilsson 1940: 133 and Dodds 1951: 189–90.

39. On Lampon, see Yunis 1988: 69–70 and Stadter 1989 on Plut. *Per.* 6.2; and Dillery 2005: 193–97.

40. Diodorus (12.10.3) claims that Lampon and Xenocritus were cofounders. Ehrenberg (1948: 164–65) assumes that Lampon's primary role in the foundation was to act as a *mantis*. While Aristophanes' reference to *Thouriomanteis* at *Clouds* 332 surely does refer to him, it by no means demonstrates that Lampon was chosen as founder *because* he was a *mantis*. The scholia (332a–b) on that passage, however, claim that Lampon was chosen "to act as exegete for the foundation of the city." See further Malkin 1987: 97–101.

41. The First Fruits decree (ML 73 = Fornara 140) probably dates from the late 420s: Cavanaugh (1996: 73–95) argues strongly for c. 435, but see the cogent objections of Rosivach (1997). Dillery (2005: 196) suggests that Lampon stood to gain personally (in a financial sense) from his role in the foundation of Thurium and possibly also from his rider to the First Fruits decree; but this is far from certain.

42. See Osborne 1982: 46–47.

43. See Olson 1998: 277. The evidence for Hierocles (from Ar. *Peace* 1084–85) and for Lampon (from the scholia on Ar. *Birds* 521b and *Peace* 1084) is actually not as secure as it is assumed to be (see Parker 2005: 117 n. 4). When Trygaeus says to Hierocles, "Nevermore shall you be dining in the Prytaneum in the future nor fashion any more prophecies after the event," should this neces- sarily be taken literally?

he had been appointed an "exegete," one of the official interpreters of sacred laws.[44] But whatever the precise terms and tenure of these invitations, it was still the highest civic honor that the city could bestow.

Another Athenian active in politics was Diopeithes. He, however, was not a seer, but a *chrēsmologos*, as all of our sources make clear. But what makes him particularly interesting is his role in publicly opposing the teaching of the sophists. Plutarch (*Per.* 32.2) ascribes to his initiative a decree against impiety that he allegedly had proposed shortly before the outbreak of the Peloponnesian War.[45] The authenticity of this decree is problematic. But even if, as some scholars think, it has been constructed by some late source on the basis of a joke about Diopeithes in a now lost comedy, it still shows that Athenian *chrēsmologoi* were thought capable of taking an active role in the political-religious affairs of the community.

The Athenian *chrēsmologos* Diopeithes may well be the same person who proposed a decree regulating the payment of tribute by Methone in c. 429 B.C.[46] That would not be too surprising. But was he also the *chrēsmologos* named Diopeithes who just over thirty years later played an unsuccessful role in the contention over the royal succession at Sparta?[47] Plutarch describes this latter Diopeithes as "a man who was a *chrēsmologos* in Sparta, full of ancient oracles and seeming to be wise and experienced in matters relating to the divine."[48] The phrase "in Sparta" is unfortunately ambiguous.[49] Does Plutarch mean to say that he was a Spartan citizen, or someone who happened to be in Sparta at that time? There is no way for us to tell.

The situation in Sparta was as follows. Upon the death of King Agis in 400 B.C., both his son Leotychidas (who was suspected of being a bastard) and his younger brother Agesilaus claimed the kingship. Diopeithes intervened on behalf of the son by producing an oracle of Apollo to the effect that Sparta should "guard against a

---

44. Olson (1998: 277) thinks that both Hierocles and Lampon were entitled to permanent dining privileges in the Prytaneum in their capacity as official functionaries of the city. For the right of some officials to eat in the Prytaneum, see Osborne 1981.

45. See Connor 1963; Dover 1988: 146–47; Yunis 1988: 68–70; Ostwald 1986: 528–32.

46. *IG* I³ 61.4–5 = ML 65 = Fornara 128. Note, however, that his name has been restored as D[iopeith]es.

47. Connor (1963) and Bowden (2003: 268–69) think they are the same; Yunis (1988: 70 n. 33), however, suggests that "Diopeithes" may have been a common name for men of this profession. Dunbar (1995: 550) doubts the connection on chronological grounds.

48. *Ages.* 3.3.

49. See Shipley 1997: 86–87.

lame kingship."[50] Since Agesilaus was physically lame, this was a shrewd gambit. Lysander, however, had a better interpretation: the oracle referred not to physical lameness but to a king who was not a legitimate descendant of Heracles.[51] The whole affair illustrates quite vividly the importance that oracles and their providers could play in political debates. But one aspect of this whole affair remains perplexing. How did an Athenian citizen, who was not only a purveyor of oracles but also a passer of decrees, find himself playing an active role in the selection of one of Sparta's two kings? There is reason to believe that *chrēsmologoi*, like seers, moved from city to city. But Diopeithes, like Lampon, was not your typical migrant religious specialist. Had Diopeithes been one of the *chrēsmologoi* who had used his oracles to foretell an Athenian victory in Sicily, and did he then find it prudent to ply his trade elsewhere rather than face the anger of the Athenian people?[52]

The practice of seercraft, therefore, was not irreconcilable with the ideology of the radical democracy at Athens, nor, for that matter, with the oligarchic ideology of Sparta. What was its relationship with sophistic teaching? Another tenet of modern studies is that the two were incompatible. It is seldom noticed, however, that Antiphon the sophist wrote a book on the interpretation of dreams.[53] Aristotle called him a *teratoskopos*—that is, "an observer of portents," "a diviner."[54] The fact that this sophist was also a seer should not be explained away either by positing that he was a different Antiphon or by claiming that his book actually was a rationalization of dreams. The ancient sources are clear that seer and sophist were the same person and that he interpreted dreams in the manner of a traditional seer.[55] If this

50. Only Xenophon labels it an oracle of Apollo. Plutarch quotes all four lines of the oracle, but they are likely to be the invention of one of his Hellenistic sources, such as Duris of Samos, whom he cites at *Ages.* 3.

51. Xen. *Hell.* 3.3.3; Plut. *Lys.* 22.5–6, *Ages.* 3.3; with Bowden 2003: 268–69. Bowden, however, fails to realize the consequences of identifying this Diopeithes with the Athenian of the same name. If he were merely a speaker who had "associated himself with oracles and other religious issues," he could hardly have advertised himself in Sparta as an expert in the interpretation of oracles.

52. Connor (1963) connects Diopeithes' departure from Athens to Sparta with an anecdote recorded in the Suda: an Athenian named Diopeithes proposed a law establishing a curfew in the Piraeus, and then was prosecuted for breaking it himself.

53. In general, see Lieshout 1980: 217–29 and Pendrick 2002: 49–53.

54. Diog. Laert. 2.46. See Pendrick 2002: T 5.

55. See Pendrick 2002: 49–53; but I am not convinced that it is a mere narrative device that has Antiphon appear as a dream interpreter in the examples reported by Cicero (*Div.* 2.144) and Diogenes (F 80A and 80B).

Antiphon was also the Athenian speechwriter and oligarch of the same name, it would have important implications for our understanding of religious attitudes during the fifth century. It does seem remarkable that the same person could have composed speeches for the law courts, written sophistic treatises, practiced as an interpreter of dreams and portents, and also been the mastermind behind the short-lived oligarchic coup that toppled the Athenian democracy in 411 B.C. But it is certainly not impossible.[56]

THE SEER IN THE HELLENISTIC WORLD

Seers were highly influential in the aristocratic culture of archaic Greece, they gained political influence during the height of Athenian democracy, they were trusted advisers to the Macedonian kings Philip and Alexander, and they continued to play an important role in the wars of the Hellenistic kings. It has been argued, however, that the so-called Xenophontic system of military sacrificial divination (*hiera* and *sphagia* performed in the context of pitched battle) operated in its fully developed form only from about 700 to 350, a period that corresponds to the fighting of hoplite battles between amateur armies led by generals appointed by the community. But by the reign of Alexander the Great this system either was greatly curtailed or fell out of use completely, since its social function had been undermined by changes in the social and political structures of society. Professional armies no longer needed the morale boost of divination, and autocratic generals could countenance no limits on their authority. In other words, one could argue that prebattle divination declined in importance outside of the context of the *polis*, because "the civic general, obedient both to the gods and the city, gave way to the charismatic king, guarantor of success and divine favour in his own person."[57]

This conclusion should be resisted. It is a misconception due to the particular biases of our sources for Hellenistic history. Because Polybius and Hieronymus of Cardia (who was Diodorus's main source in book 19 of his *Historical Library*) were not interested in the rites of divination and mostly excluded mention of them in their histories, modern scholars have posited an actual decline in those rites. Yet even our

---

56. Two important studies of Antiphon appeared in 2002: Pendrick argues against the identification of sophist and speechwriter as the same person, whereas Gagarin argues for it. Woodruff (2004) discusses both books.

57. Parker 2000: 302–5; but to be fair one must point out that he only tentatively suggests that prebattle divination did in fact decline, since he is sensitive to the limitations of our evidence.

limited sources for Hellenistic history can be used to paint a very different picture, and from them it is clear that military divination was still being performed by both Alexander and his successors right to the end of the independent Hellenistic monarchies. If we had other sources, such as Timaeus of Tauromenium, who is criticized by Polybius for including portents and omens in his history, the pattern would seem very different. Individual sources can be a poor guide to religious activity.

It is remarkable, for instance, that Thucydides mentions battlefield divination only twice. In describing the first battle between the Syracusans and Athenians in 415 he says (6.69.2) that "the seers brought forward the customary *sphagia*." And before the battle of Delium in 424 he has the Theban general Pagondas attempt to persuade the Boeotians to fight the Athenians by mentioning that the omens (*hiera*) from sacrifice were favorable (4.92.7). Yet the frequent mention of prebattle sacrifice in Xenophon demonstrates conclusively that Thucydides simply chooses not to mention a practice that was ubiquitous, either because he thought military divination unimportant to an understanding of tactics or because he disapproved of it in principle.

All of the evidence indicates that if traditional seercraft declined in Hellenistic times it was not a direct consequence of the political eclipse of the *polis* in the Greek world, nor was it due to a fading of traditional religious beliefs and practices. Rather, it was related to a development of an altogether different kind, the new interest in astrology and in personal horoscopes (which were then being made for the first time).[58] Yet there is significant evidence for the continuing importance of traditional forms of divination, including extispicy and augury.

Although the literary sources for the career of King Pyrrhus of Epirus are fairly meager, they indicate that he relied on seers in a way that was typical of fifth- and fourth- century generals. We know the names of two seers who were employed by him. One was the Thrasybulus who dedicated a statue of him at Olympia (Paus. 6.14.9), and the other was the seer Theodotus who is mentioned by Plutarch as not allowing Pyrrhus to participate in a peace agreement when one of the victims for sacrifice, a ram, fell dead. Before Pyrrhus's attack on Sparta in 273 B.C., a seer, who unfortunately is not named, told him that a victim without a lobe indicated that he would lose one of his relatives (who turned out to be his son).[59] Plutarch leaves the

---

58. On Babylonian horoscopy, Rochberg 2004 supersedes previous studies. The two earliest Babylonian horoscopes date to 410 B.C.; the remainder come from the period 298 to 69 B.C. The first extant horoscope written in Greek dates to 62 B.C. and was made for the coronation of Antiochus I of Commagene (see Neugebauer and van Hoesen 1959: text 1). For astrology in Hellenistic Greece, see Barton 1994: 21–37.

59. Plut. *Pyrrh.* 6.5, 30.3

context vague, which is not surprising given that his interests are more biographical than historical. It would not be unreasonable to infer that in Plutarch's source the seer discovered that the victim's liver lacked a lobe while conducting a prebattle sacrifice.

One unimpeachable example of the importance of military divination comes at the very end of the Hellenistic period—unimpeachable because it derives from the testimony of a king who himself put his faith in divination. In book 1 of his treatise *On Divination* (1.15.26–27), Cicero has his brother Quintus declare that their guest-friend Deiotarus, when tetrarch of Gallograecia and king of Lesser Armenia, never undertook any business or travel without first taking the auspices (divination from bird signs) and often turned back from a journey even after traveling for many days if the auspices were unfavorable. His faith in this type of divination was caused, it seems, or at least reinforced, by what we would call a lucky escape: he was once induced by the flight of an eagle to abandon a journey, and the room in which he was to stay collapsed on the very next night. We are then told that although the auspices were favorable for his joining Pompey in the civil war, he did not regret that decision despite the fact that Caesar deprived him of his tetrarchy and kingdom.

Deiotarus represents the type of the true believer, whose trust in the system cannot be shaken and who is able to rationalize any apparent inconsistencies. As he told Quintus, "the birds had counseled him well because glory was more important to him than his possessions." This is an extremely good example of how belief in the validity of divination is immune to defeat or failure. Cicero's own rejoinder to this example in book 2 of this same work (2.37), that "the birds certainly deceived him, if they indicated that the outcome would be successful," would not have convinced someone who believed that birds were merely the unconscious conveyors of the divine will and that the gods desired Deiotarus to follow the more honorable course.

Quite apart from the question of sources and their biases, there is a consideration of another kind. This has to do with the nature of divination itself and whether it was seen as threat or embarrassment to the power of the king. The intention of military divination, as we know it from Xenophon, was not so that the community might exercise a control, even if indirectly and unconsciously, over the general.[60] The purpose and rationale was that the general, through the offices of his seer, might obtain the consent and advice of the gods. The general chose his own seer as far as we can tell, and that seer often was an outsider not answerable to the com-

<hr />

60. *Pace* Parker 2000: 303–4.

munity. It was the gods who were putting a check on the power of the general. Any commander or king who believed himself a god might in theory not need the counsel of other gods; yet even Alexander, who uniquely may have come actually to believe in his own godhead, relied on the advice of his seers until the very end of his life. Indeed, his dependence on divination seems to have increased, rather than diminished, in proportion to his own superhuman achievements. Plutarch (*Alex.* 75) says that "Alexander became so superstitious at the end of his life, turning every unusual and strange occurrence, no matter how trivial, into a prodigy and portent, that his palace at Babylon was filled with sacrificers, purifiers, and seers."

According to Onasander (10), who wrote a treatise on generalship in the first century A.D., the general should neither lead out his army on a journey nor marshal it for battle without first having sacrificed with his seers, and he should not begin any undertaking until the omens are favorable. Good omens, moreover, should be reported to the troops, since soldiers are much more courageous when they believe that they are facing dangers with the approval of the gods. But under no circumstances must he change his position if the omens are unfavorable, and no matter how inconvenient the delay might be. All of this reminds one of the practices described by Xenophon in his *Anabasis*, but there are subtle differences (such as the claim that it is easy to learn how to examine entrails, *hiera*), and the belief that the motions of the heavenly bodies are indicated through extispicy). So Onasander is not presenting an anachronistic system that no general of his time would actually have practiced; rather, he means for his advice to be useful.

As books dealing with various aspects of divination began to circulate during the late fifth and fourth centuries, and then into the Hellenistic age, it is possible that the art of the seer began to be demystified. It is certainly true that Xenophon knew quite a lot about how to read the entrails of a sacrificial victim, and in his *Cyropaedia* (1.6.2) he has Cyrus's father say to the young prince that he had him instructed in the art of divination in order that he should not be dependent on seers, who might wish to deceive him, and in order that he should not be at a loss how to read the divine signs if he ever found himself without a seer. The father concludes by saying to Cyrus: "Understanding through divination what the gods are advising, you should obey them." Xenophon clearly believes that divination is a teachable craft, and that any intelligent person can learn it. Nonetheless, he is not saying that professional seers are unnecessary. Rather, he is asserting that a commander needs to be able, if the circumstances should require it, to get along without one.

In this respect, however, Xenophon may be at one end of a cultural norm. That is, military commanders at all periods may have found it useful and prudent to know something about divinatory techniques (if for no other reason than to protect them-selves against fraudulent practitioners), yet Xenophon may have known more than most. And he may have used his philosophical treatment of Cyrus the Great, an ide-alized monarch, to suggest to his readership that such knowledge was very impor-tant for a successful leader. Furthermore, Xenophon seems to displace the efficacy of divination from the skill of the seer who must read the signs to the piety of the person requesting that signs be given; thus Cyrus says to his father (6.1.3): "I always take care, as you have instructed me, that the gods should be gracious to us and should wish to give us advice." This does not necessarily mean, however, that by Xenophon's time *mantikē* had become a mere *technē*, one that any intelligent per-son could learn with precision; and, provided that they were pious, the gods would tell them what to do. There must still have been a lively market for the "inspired" seer, the son of a seer in a family of seers who practiced seercraft by divine gift. Indeed, the self-advertising statues at Olympia of the seers Thrasybulus and Eper-astus, descendants of Iamus and Melampus, respectively, virtually prove as much.[61]

Techniques of divination, however, were not static in the Hellenistic period any more than they had been in archaic Greece. Although seers who employed tradi-tional methods of divination played a very conspicuous role in the campaigns of Alexander, there is an incident that took place near the end of his life that reveals a novel use of extispicy. Arrian tells a very interesting story that he found in Aristo-bulus, one of his two principal sources. Moreover, Arrian claims that Aristobulus had himself heard the story from one of the two principal actors, the seer Peitha-goras.[62] Apollodorus, the brother of this Peithagoras, was the garrison commander at Babylon and was summoned by Alexander upon his return from India in 325. When he saw that Alexander was punishing various satraps, he wrote to his brother "who was a seer who divined from entrails" and asked him "to read the entrails about his own welfare." When Peithagoras learned the cause of Apollodorus's fears, he "sacrificed first with regard to Hephaestion," who was Alexander's closest friend. Since the lobe could not be seen on the victim's liver, Peithagoras predicted that

---

61. See the discussion in chapter 3.

62. Arr. 7.18. A much shorter, and slightly different, version of the same story is told by Plutarch at *Alex.* 73.3–5. For the historical context, see Bosworth 1996: 23–24. Other discrepancies aside, there is one suspicious detail in Arrian. In his version, when Alexander reaches Babylon he asks Peithagoras what this sign (a liver without a lobe) portended, whereas in Plutarch's version Alexander is well aware that the sign is a serious one. Surely Alexander, who consulted seers on a regular basis and who was well versed in Greek literature, knew that this was an especially bad omen. Was he testing Peithagoras?

Hephaestion would soon be dead, and sure enough the letter conveying this information arrived one day before Hephaestion died. "Peithagoras then sacrificed with regard to Alexander, and also in the case of Alexander the liver of the victim proved to be without a lobe." This time, instead of keeping the information to himself, Apollodorus shared it with Alexander in an attempt to demonstrate his goodwill for the king.

What is so unusual about this story is not that a lobeless liver should portend death, which had always been the standard interpretation, but that a seer could employ extispicy to discover the well-being of a person who was not actually present. This type of divination from a distance concerning the health or safety of an individual is without parallel in earlier Greek sources. Where did Peithagoras learn to do this? The answer is not far to seek. The Babylonian seer might perform extispicy for the health of the reigning king, and Peithagoras surely added this to his repertoire during his sojourn at Babylon. It is characteristic of systems of divination across cultures and across time that they are highly permeable by external influences.[63] Aristobulus added that this Peithagoras later acted as a seer for Perdiccas and Antigonus, two of the most powerful of Alexander's successors. After the same sign (i.e., the lobeless liver) had appeared for each of them, they both died in battle, Perdiccas during his invasion of Egypt in 321 and Antigonus at the battle of Ipsus in 301. This Peithagoras is a good example of the seer who is successful because he can adapt his techniques to new situations and even to a new cultural setting. His patrons were two of the most powerful men of his time, and he must have been paid well. If only we knew what befell him after he had accurately predicted their demise!

63. See Shaw 1998 for a modern case study.

FIVE · Disbelief and Skepticism
about Seers

Is the Best Seer the One Who Guesses Well?

A serious prophet upon predicting a flood should be
the first man to climb a tree. This would demonstrate
that he was indeed a seer.

STEPHEN CRANE, *The Red Badge of Courage*

The Greeks indeed had an answer to Stephen Crane's implied criticism that seers
are unable to make reliable predictions in matters that affect themselves. Xenophon's
Socrates gives expression to what appears to be a commonplace belief when he
observes (*Symp.* 4.5): "Even seers are said, of course, to predict what is about to
happen to others, but not to foresee the thing that is going to befall themselves."

That formulation, however, expresses only part of the reservation that many
Greeks must have felt about their society's dependence on seers. Even someone who
sincerely believes in the validity of divination may not necessarily believe that the
particular seer under his employ is especially good at his craft. A spatial or temporal divide may be imagined as separating the potential client from the true seer. But
there is always the hope that the unerring seer, one similar to those of legend, might
be located in the next village or town.[1] Moreover, if it is one of the salient characteristics of Greek civilization to question traditional or normative ideas, should one
not expect to see doubts about seercraft expressed in our sources? We are entitled,
therefore, to ask questions such as the following: How serious and how common
were doubts about the validity of divination as a system of knowledge? How widespread was skepticism about the competence and honesty of seers? And were these
sentiments ever of such a magnitude as to undermine the efficacy of the entire
system?

1. For this phenomenon, see Evans-Pritchard 1937: 195–201.

There are three things to consider: statements of disbelief in divination generally, statements of disbelief in seers or in particular seers, and statements of disbelief in oracles. There are differences in the kind and intensity of doubt among these categories. First of all, it is necessary to stress that expressions of doubt did not suddenly emerge in the later half of the fifth century B.C., either because of a supposed general crisis in traditional religious beliefs or, more specifically, as a reaction to the support of seers for the disastrous Sicilian expedition of 415–413 B.C. Already in Homer, we find the same types of criticisms that occur in fifth-century texts.[2] Skepticism toward signs and their interpreters is expressed in the *Iliad* by Hector (12.237–43) and Priam (24.219–22) and in the *Odyssey* by Telemachus (1.413–16) and the suitor Eurymachus (2.180–86). Hector's criticism is the strongest, since it challenges the very basis of divination from signs.

In book 1 of the *Iliad*, when Calchas tells Agamemnon that Apollo will not stop the plague until he sends back without ransom the daughter of the priest Chryses, Agamemnon attacks the seer (1.106–8): "Seer of evil things: never yet have you told me anything good. Always the evil things are dear to your heart to prophesy, but no excellent word have you yet spoken or accomplished." Nonetheless, Agamemnon proceeds to do exactly what Calchas has prescribed. He has attacked the seer's disposition toward him (you like to give me bad news, don't you?) but neither questions his abilities nor the value of divination. An attack on the mantic craft per se comes later in the poem, in book 12 (195–250).

Hector and Poulydamas are on the point of crossing the ditch that protected the Achaean camp and are eager to press their attack against the Achaean ships, when a bird sign (*oiōnos*) appears. An eagle appears on their left, carrying in its talons a gigantic snake. When the snake bites the eagle, the eagle drops it in the midst of the Trojan forces. Poulydamas reasonably takes this to be a bad omen and urges that the Trojans turn back. Hector, however, ignores the advice of Poulydamas (who, as noted earlier, is not a seer) and accuses him of cowardice (12.231–43):

Poulydamas, these things that you are saying please me no longer.
You know how to contrive another speech better than this one.
But if indeed you are truly saying this in all seriousness,
then surely the gods themselves have destroyed your senses,
you who are telling me to forget the counsels of loud-thundering

2. On seers in Homer, see Chirassi Colombo 1985; Karp 1998; Di Sacco Franco 2000; Piepenbrink 2001; and esp. Trampedach 2008.

Zeus, that he himself promised to me and nodded assent.
But you tell me to put my trust in birds, who spread
wide their wings. I care nothing for them, I think nothing of them,
whether they go to the right toward the dawn and the sun,
or whether they go to the left toward the murky darkness.
No, let us put our trust in the counsel of great Zeus,
he who is lord over all mortals and all the immortals.
One bird sign is best, to fight in defense of one's country.

Hector considers bird signs to be worthless, but he still believes that the gods communicate their wishes to mortals. He believes, wrongly as it happens, that Zeus has communicated to him directly that he will defeat the Achaeans. So, strictly speaking, this passage does not deny the existence of lines of communication between gods and men. Rather, it calls into question the validity of a particularly subjective means of ascertaining the divine will, especially when that means runs counter to what one otherwise deems to be the better course of action. It is also important to note that this passage does not quite have the same resonance as Agamemnon's attack on Calchas at the beginning of the poem, since Poulydamas is not himself a professional seer. He gives a commonsense interpretation of the eagle-and-snake portent (one that any Trojan or Greek might take to be obvious, especially since the left side was considered unlucky): to wit, that after initial success, they would be beaten back by the Achaeans with heavy losses. He then comments (12.228–29): "So an interpreter of the gods (a *theopropos*) would answer, one who in his mind had clear knowledge of portents, and whom the people believed in." Thus it is precisely because he is a layman, and not someone who "had clear knowledge," that Hector can dismiss his opinion so readily. Hector is not morally the equivalent of Eurymachus, the suitor in the *Odyssey*, who threatens the seer Halitherses.

In that scene Telemachus had just finished rebuking the suitor Antinoös when two eagles appeared over the assembled men of Ithaca (*Od.* 2.146–193). To everyone's astonishment the eagles swooped over their heads, began to tear at each other with their talons, and then sped away to the right. The old warrior Halitherses, who is described as "surpassing the men of his generation in understanding the meaning of birds and explaining their portents" (158–59), interpreted this as portending the return of Odysseus and destruction for the suitors. He further claims to have foretold to Odysseus when he was setting off for Troy that he would come home in the twentieth year, with all of his companions lost, and recognized by no one. To this speech the suitor Eurymachus arrogantly responds (177–93) that Halitherses should go home and prophesy to his children, and he asserts that he can give a better interpretation: "Many are the birds who under the sun's rays wander the sky; not all of them are ominous; Odysseus has perished far away, and would that you also had died with him." Moreover, he accuses Halitherses of stirring up Telemachus's anger, "looking for a gift for your own household, which he might provide." Finally, he threatens to lay a penalty upon him if he continues to stir up Telemachus. This scene is a more sinister version of the disagreement between Hector and Poulydamas, but not quite as nasty as that between Oedipus and Teiresias in Sophocles' famous play.

Despite the fact that Hector made the wrong decision and failed to understand the significance of the portent, his declaration that "only one bird sign is best" was considered by Aristotle, writing in the fourth century, to be a common maxim.[3] And indeed, by the time we reach the fifth century the attack on the practitioners of divination has become more sophisticated. In a somewhat different form than in Homer, skepticism about the validity of seercraft emerges in Attic comedy and tragedy of the last third of the fifth century. A fragment of Euripides (F 973 Kannicht) captures its spirit: "The best seer is the one who guesses well." Or as the chorus proclaims in Sophocles' Oedipus Tyrannus (499–501): "Zeus and Apollo are wise and know the affairs of mortals; but when it comes to men there is no sure test that a seer carries more weight than I." Teiresias has just revealed Oedipus to be the murderer of Laius, but the chorus, who are deeply grateful to Oedipus for delivering them from the Sphinx, cannot accept this. An even stronger statement is made by the old servant in Euripides' Helen (at 744–57, discussed below).

Accusations of greed are commonly leveled against seers in Greek literature.[4] They begin with Homer's Odyssey (2.186) and continue in prose, tragedy, and comedy. Creon surely expresses a common-enough sentiment when he exclaims to Teiresias in Sophocles' Antigone of 441 B.C. (1055): "The entire race of seers is fond of silver." In a famous and much-quoted passage of Sophocles' Oedipus Tyrannus (produced in c. 430 B.C.), Oedipus begins by attacking Teiresias personally (380–403), calling him a "wizard hatcher of plots" and a "deceitful beggar priest" who "only has sight for profit, but in his art is blind."

Euripides has his characters express a similar sentiment to that in Sophocles in

---

3. Arist. *Rh.* 1395a10–14. Plutarch (*Pyrrh.* 29.4) claims that before his attack on Sparta in 273 B.C. Pyrrhus quoted this line but changed "country" to "Pyrrhus."

4. See Morrison 1981: 106–7 and Smith 1989.

two plays that were written between 408 and 406 B.C. In Euripides' *Bacchae*, Pentheus says of Teiresias (255–57): "By introducing this new divinity [Dionysus] to humankind you wish to watch the birds and to take payment for burnt offerings." And Agamemnon, prompted by the mention of Calchas, exclaims in *Iphigenia at Aulis* (520): "The whole race of seers is basely fond of honor." To this Menelaus replies: "Yes, unpleasing and useless—when it is present."[5] So too in the same play Achilles says in regard to Calchas (956–58): "What kind of man is a seer? He is a man who tells a few truths and many lies, and that is when he hits the mark; when he misses it, he is finished." Finally, there is the dismay of Orestes in *Iphigenia among the Taurians* of c. 413 B.C. (570–75): "One thing alone brings grief to a man, and that is when someone who is no fool is influenced by the words of seers and meets the death he meets, as only those who have experienced it know." The suggestion in all of these passages, whether it is made explicitly or implicitly, is that seers are liars who seek to make money at the expense of their clients.

It is worthwhile to look a little more closely at the most extended of these passages, that in the *Oedipus Tyrannus*. The attack there on Teiresias's credentials is motivated by Oedipus's belief that Creon has enlisted Teiresias in a plot to remove him from his rule over Thebes. He then poses the question how it was that Teiresias, if he really was a true seer, could not help the Thebans with the riddle of the Sphinx, a task that required mantic art. Oedipus concludes by suggesting that bird divination is useless (397–98): "I put a stop to her [the Sphinx], having hit upon the truth through intelligence (*gnōmē*), not by what I learned from birds." This is similar to the sentiment of Hector in that both disavow that knowledge can be gained from the observation of birds. The difference is that Oedipus thinks that human intelligence is alone sufficient for successful human actions.

Later in the play, Jocasta too delivers an attack on divination (707–25). She begins with the general point that "nothing mortal is possessed of the art of divination (*mantikē technē*)," and then proceeds to attack Delphi. As mentioned previously, this is a unique passage in Greek literature, because however strongly some Greeks may have doubted the efficacy of "deductive/technical" divination as practiced mostly by male seers, no one dared to question the truthfulness of Apollo's oracle at Delphi. For that would have been tantamount to doubting the existence or power of Apollo himself. Thus Jocasta cannot quite attack the validity

---

5. This line is corrupt. I am here translating the text in the Teubner edition of Euripides edited by A. Nauck (3rd ed., Leipzig, 1892–95).

of Delphic prophecy. She says: "An oracle once came to Laius, I shall not say from Apollo himself, but from his servants, that it was his lot to die at the hand of his son, a son to be born of me and of him." It would be quite wrong to take this as evidence that the Pythia herself, in most instances, did not deliver her own oracles. Rather, Jocasta is pulling her punch by suggesting that, in this particular instance, the oracle about Laius being killed by his own son was not a true oracle, in the sense that it did not come from the mouth of the Pythia. At this point she just cannot bring herself to utter what she really thinks about the nature of divination as a whole.

The depth of her skepticism, however, is revealed by something that she says a little later. After Oedipus becomes concerned that he may have been Laius's murderer, Jocasta reiterates her disbelief in Delphic prophecy on the grounds that Laius could not have been killed by his own son because that son had predeceased him (849–58). Her concluding statement goes far beyond a disbelief that is restricted to this one particular oracle: "So far as divination (*manteia*) is concerned, in the future I would look neither to this side nor to that."

The reaction of Sophocles' audience to the doubts expressed by Jocasta can be inferred, I believe, from the reaction of the chorus (898–910):

> No longer shall I go in reverence to the sacred navel of the earth, nor into the temple at Abae, nor to Olympia, unless these oracles shall fit together so that all mortals may point to them. But, oh ruler, if indeed you are rightly called Zeus, lord of all things, let this not escape your notice or that of your deathless everlasting rule. For already they are annulling the old oracles of Laius, which are fading away, and nowhere is Apollo manifest in honor, but all that pertains to the gods is perishing.

It is one thing to doubt the integrity of a particular seer or even of bird divination as a legitimate skill, but quite another to doubt the validity of oracles. If the gods do not have the power either to deliver true oracles or to ensure that those oracles come to pass, then the whole belief structure of Greek religion would collapse. In effect, from the chorus's point of view, the whole system of religious belief hinges on the oracle to Laius being fulfilled, and that explains the chorus's intense anxiety. Sophocles has brought the whole system of communication between gods and humans to the brink of dissolution, and then reaffirms it in the starkest terms. The transgressive skepticism of Oedipus and Jocasta serves as a vehicle for reaffirming the validity of divination as an unimpeachable access to knowledge. Human intelligence on its own pales by comparison.

When we turn from Sophocles to Euripides, the attacks are similar, but the defense is not quite as compelling or seemingly sincere. Two fragments of Euripides seem to express doubts in the craft of seers, but the context is missing for both of them. One is the famous line, already quoted (F 972 Kannicht), "The best seer is the one who guesses well." It is not really surprising that a character in a play might say this: the sentiment is already latent in Hector's rebuttal to Poulydamas that "one bird sign is best, to fight in defense of one's country." We should like to know why a character expressed this opinion and what happened to him or her in the play in which these lines appear.

The other fragment comes from Euripides' lost *Philoctetes* (F 795 Kannicht): "Why do you swear, while sitting on your mantic chairs, that you know clearly the things of the gods? Humans are not the craftsmen of divine words. Whoever boasts that he has knowledge about the gods knows nothing more than how to persuade using words." To make a guess, these lines may be delivered by Philoctetes himself in regard to Helenus's oracle that Troy would be captured when he returned to the Achaean army with Heracles' bow. If that is right, then Philoctetes, like all others who express such doubts in Greek tragedy, will have been proven wrong by the action of the play itself. As noted previously, in Euripides' *Iphigenia at Aulis*, Achilles declares that he will not let Iphigenia be sacrificed, and alleges that seercraft is mere guesswork (955–58): "If Calchas begins the sacrifice with the barley and the purifying water, he will regret it. What kind of man is a seer? He is a man who tells a few truths and many lies, and that is when he hits the mark; when he misses it, he is finished." In the end, of course, Achilles is persuaded by Iphigenia herself that he should let her be sacrificed.

It is probably not a coincidence, however, that the passage that both contains the most general attack on seercraft and, unlike those in Sophocles' plays, where Teiresias is proven right in the end, remains unanswered appeared in the year after the annihilation of the Sicilian expedition.[6] The play in question is Euripides' *Helen*, produced in 412. Thucydides says at the beginning of book 8: 'When the Athenians had recognized the facts [about the destruction of their forces in Sicily], they were harsh to those of the orators who had shared in their enthusiasm for the expedition, and they were angry both with the oracle-collectors (*chrēsmologoi*) and with the seers (*manteis*), and with as many others who, through the practice of divination, in some way at that time had caused them to hope that they would capture Sicily."

6. See Radermacher 1898; Kannicht 1969 on *Helen* 744–60; and Mikalson 1991: 96–100.

Thucydides, in a striking analepsis, has transposed the role of the seers and *chrēs-mologoi* in these events until after the failure of the expedition. Plutarch, however, gives us a hint of what that role had been, implying (*Nic.* 13) that both Nicias and Alcibiades employed seers who supported their respective positions. Alcibiades was in favor of the expedition, whereas Nicias was against it. The Peloponnesian War, like the Persian Wars before it, provided abundant opportunity for freelance religious specialists to display their wares in Athens and throughout the Greek world. At the outbreak of the war, Thucydides (2.8.2) says that "many prophecies (*logia*) were uttered and many things chanted by the *chrēsmologoi* both in the cities that were about to fight and in the other cities as well." When the Athenians were debating whether to fight or not during the Peloponnesian invasion of 431, "*chrēsmologoi* were chanting oracles of every kind, as each man was inclined to hear them" (2.21.3).[7] The political influence of these oracles and of the *chrēsmologoi* who traded in them is demonstrated by Aristophanes' penchant for spoofing them in his comedies.

Partially as a result of the debacle in Sicily the influence of the *chrēsmologoi* at Athens seems to have suffered a setback from which it never recovered. Three of Aristophanes' plays produced before the destruction of the expedition in 413 contain extended scenes in which *chrēsmologoi* are attacked. These are his *Knights* (425 B.C.), *Peace* (421 B.C.), and *Birds* (414 B.C.). Yet not a single one of his later plays so much as mentions them. Either the chresmological profession had been so thoroughly discredited that it virtually disappeared from Athens, or their political influence, given its horrific consequences, was no longer considered a fit subject for comedy.[8] Similarly, one might argue, Aristophanes never mentions the plague that broke out in 430: some things were just too sensitive to poke fun at. The seers, however, even if they suffered immediate recriminations, retained their influence and importance over time. This was perhaps due to the fact that their expertise in performing certain civic sacrifices and in interpreting divine signs was not replaceable. Or to put it differently, seercraft played an essential role in maintaining a proper relationship between the human and divine spheres.[9] The *chrēsmologoi*, however, were dispensable. They and their collections of oracles had been useful tools in the hands of politicians, but the normative religious life of individual and community

---

7. Bowden (2003: 270–71) plausibly suggests that such oracles were discussed in the Athenian Assembly.

8. For the former view, see Oliver 1950: 30 and Mikalson 1983: 40; for the latter, Smith 1989: 155.

9. Thus Plato preserves an official role for seers, along with priests, priestesses, and exegetes, in the ideal community described in his *Laws* (828b, 871d).

did not depend on their expertise. Nonetheless, in a society that often looked for scapegoats, there was bound to be a backlash.

In Euripides' *Helen,* Menelaus's servant delivers a comprehensive attack on the craft of the seer and, what is more, suggests a different procedure for obtaining the goodwill and support of the gods (744–60):

> But, to be sure, I now realize how worthless and full of lies are the things of seers. There is nothing sound in the sacrificial flame, nor are the cries of winged creatures sound. Surely it is simpleminded even to think that birds profit mortals. For Calchas did not say nor did he indicate these things [i.e., that Helen was not at Troy] to the army, while watching his friends die on behalf of a cloud; nor did Helenus say anything, but the city was plundered in vain. You might say that it was because the gods were not willing [i.e., to indicate that the real Helen was not at Troy]. Why do we seek divinations? It is necessary, sacrificing to the gods, to ask for good things, but to let divination alone. For divination was invented merely as bait for making a living. No idle man has become rich through sacrificial flames. But intelligence (*gnōmē*) and good planning are the best seer.

To this the chorus responds approvingly: "My opinion about divination coincides with that of the old man. Someone who has the gods as friends would possess the best art of divination in his home."

Euripides' authorship either of some or indeed of all of these lines has been questioned. But if there has been interpolation by actors, then this will have occurred in the fourth century B.C., and thus we are still dealing with attitudes to divination that were current in the classical period.[10] However that may be, this speech recalls several of the assertions of Oedipus in his attack on Teiresias: that seers are out for profit; that they cannot solve the problems that face the community; and that human intelligence (*gnōmē*) is the best guide to action. Oedipus challenged Teiresias on the grounds that he could not solve the riddle of the Sphinx; the messenger here charges Calchas and Helenus with the failure to inform their respective comrades that they were fighting over a mere shadow. In this passage Euripides anticipates and answers the counterargument that a seer might make, and surely did make on the actual bat-

---

10. Kovacs (2003: 40–41) suggests deleting the entire passage as an interpolation (which is completely unwarranted). Diggle (in the Oxford Classical Text) more reasonably brackets lines 746–48 and 752–57; so too Dale 1967: 117–19. I agree with Wright (2005: 366–67) that the whole passage should stand.

tlefields of ancient Greece: to wit, "I can only report what the gods are willing to make known." The response—"Then why do we use divination at all?"—is not strictly logical, but it does have an emotional appeal. Seers, it might be thought, can tell us something useful, if not everything that we need to know; for who could deny that Tisamenus helped the Spartans win the battle of Plataea, even if the sum total of his advice was not to cross the Asopus River?

The speaker's other recommendation is equally suspect, for who could offer prayer and sacrifice, and then remove the entrails of the animal without noticing the appearance of those entrails, or offer burnt sacrifice without observing the nature of the smoke and flame? On purely *prima facie* grounds, this is a rather specious attack. And yet the action of the play neither confirms nor refutes this criticism of the mantic art as practiced by the sort of seers that were involved in the Sicilian expedition.[11] Divination itself is vindicated in the person of the exotic Egyptian prophetess Theonoë, who seems to "know" the plans and intentions of the gods.[12] But the relationship of Theonoë to prophetic figures of the type familiar in the Greek world is never made clear. Euripides' religious attitudes, whatever precisely they may have been, do not seem to reflect popular piety.[13]

Although authorial intent is a notoriously slippery business, if Euripides actually believed that "the best seer is the one who guesses well" (in the words of the much-quoted fragment), his contemporaries continued to act as if they believed otherwise. Throughout the fourth century, seers were still held in high esteem in Athens. As Plato in the *Statesman* (290d) has the stranger say, "the bearing of the priests and seers is indeed full of pride, and they win a fine reputation because of the magnitude of their undertakings."[14] In 394/3 B.C. the seer Sthorys of Thasos was awarded Athenian citizenship for his assistance during the battle of Cnidus.[15] We may confidently infer that the strong reaction against seers in the aftermath of the Sicilian expedition was short-lived.

Near the beginning of the tragedy *Rhesus*, Hector gives a speech that on a superficial reading might seem to imply that the author of this play was hostile to the influence of seers. *Rhesus* is either an early work by Euripides, datable to c. 450 B.C., or, more probably, a work of the early fourth century that was later attributed to

---

11. So Mikalson 1991: 98, 100.

12. See Zuntz 1960.

13. For Euripides' rationalism, see Reinhardt 1957 and Mastronarde 1986.

14. As Garland (1984: 82) notes, "Plato has no reason to be complimentary."

15. See *IG* II² 17, lines 26–29 (= Osborne 1981: no. D8), with Osborne 1970.

Euripides.[16] This play depicts a Hector who is angry with his seers for convincing him not to launch a night attack upon the Achaeans, an attack in which he was convinced that he could have destroyed them. In the belief that the Achaeans have run away, he laments (63–69): "I was eager to make a night attack and take advantage of the stroke of luck sent by god; but those wise seers, who indeed know the divine will, persuaded me to wait for the light of day, and then to leave not one Achaean in the land. But the enemy is not waiting for the counsels of my soothsayers [*thuoskooi*]. In the darkness of night a runaway gathers strength." But a few lines later Aeneas gives the same opinion as the seers, chiding Hector for his poor grasp of strategy, and persuades him not to launch a night attack. Nonetheless, Hector's outburst in lines 63–69 may reflect the frustration that some real-life generals felt about the interference of seers in their strategy, even if the play in no way vindicates that frustration.[17]

Outside of tragedy and comedy, there is only one passage in prose where a seer is laughed at. This occurs in Plato's *Euthyphro*. After Socrates explains the charges against him, Euthyphro says that he too has been the object of misrepresentation (3c): "For whenever I speak in the Assembly about things pertaining to the gods [literally, "divine things," *ta theia*], foretelling to them the things that will take place, they laugh at me on the grounds that I am mad. And yet of the things that I have predicted I have said nothing that is not true; but, all the same, they envy all such as us." Shortly thereafter Socrates calls Euthyphro a *mantis*.[18] Should we infer from this passage that all seers were laughed at, or at least those who had the audacity to foretell the future? Is Euthyphro an example of a new type of *mantis* that arose in Athens in the late fifth century?[19] Or are we meant to realize that Euthyphro, like Socrates himself, was an unusual character. Not every seer so audaciously gave unsolicited predictions to the public, and thus not every seer was laughed at. Euthyphro, if indeed he was a real person, was surely atypical.

Throughout this book I have stressed that it is possible to relate the representa-

---

16. For the latter view, see Jouan 2004: XV, LXIII–LXX.

17. So Dover 1973: 64: "Hector in Eur. *Rhesus* 63–69, describing wryly and with a touch of sarcasm how he yielded to his seers against his own sound military judgment, is modeled equally on the Hector of *Il.* xii 195–250, who scorns Poulydamas's scruples over a strange omen, and on scores of commanders in the Classical period."

18. Parker (2005: 114) mistakenly calls him a *chrēsmologos*.

19. So Roth (1984), who sees him as a "theological sophist," who possesses a distinctive theology, a talent for eristic, and a keen interest in etymology, and that he falls into a category that included the Athenians Lampon, Antiphon, and Philochorus. See also Mastronarde 1986.

tion of religion in Greek tragedy and epic (so-called high literature) to what people actually experienced in everyday life. One method is to compare, wherever possible, the attitudes contained in the plays to those expressed in other genres, while recognizing that each genre has its own conventions and that no particular genre can give us an unmediated view of real life. Here again, I want to turn to Xenophon's *Anabasis*. Xenophon, as mentioned before, is concerned to represent both his own actions and those of his comrades in a particular way; nevertheless, he had to do so in a way that was credible to his intended audience. In other words, the representation of religious beliefs and attitudes that is found in the *Anabasis* should correspond more precisely to those of Xenophon's audience than is the case in Greek tragedy. Again, we are best informed about the actual beliefs of real people in those cases where the various genres combine to create the same image.

In a famous episode Xenophon represents the Ten Thousand as being restricted to their camp at Calpe for three days without provisions and in great hardship because the omens were not favorable for marching out. Xenophon describes a rather tense situation in which he himself was the target of the soldiers' frustrations (*Anab.* 6.4.13–16):

> The generals were sacrificing, and the seer was Arexion the Arcadian (for Silanus the Ambraciot had already run away, having hired a boat from Heracleia). When they sacrificed with a view to marching out the omens were not favorable. Therefore, they rested for this day. Certain men were daring to say that Xenophon, since he wished to colonize the place, had persuaded the seer to say that the omens were not favorable for marching out. Then, on the next day, he had it proclaimed by herald that anyone who wished could be present at the sacrifice, and, if someone were a seer, he sent round a message for him to be present for the purpose of participating in the examination of the victims; after that, he sacrificed. And many were present. But even though he sacrificed three times with a view to marching out, the omens were not favorable. As a result the soldiers were angry, for the provisions that they had brought with them had run out and there was as yet no market.

This is an important passage in that it confirms a sentiment that we found elsewhere and one that we might have inferred as being probable in certain situations. The soldiers, or at least some of them, thought it a real possibility that the seer Arexion could be bribed to give a false report of the omens. Xenophon's method of disproving this was to invite any seer who happened to be in the army to join in inspecting the entrails. Unfortunately, Xenophon does not say how many seers, or indeed *if any*, took up his offer. His statement that "many were present" includes common soldiers as well as any seers. Yet the terms of the invitation verify what we might otherwise have guessed—that some individuals might attempt to pass themselves off as seers, even if no one was willing to employ them.[20]

When the omens again proved to be unfavorable for marching out, the army, despite its hardship, accepted the will of the gods. The rituals of divination overrode all other considerations and proved decisive, just as they had earlier when Xenophon had turned down the offer of sole command over the army, allegedly against the wishes of the troops. So in the *Anabasis*, as in Greek tragedy, we have doubt in particular seers expressed and then refuted. Xenophon does not permit any skepticism about divination as a system to enter into his narrative, but that cannot be taken as proof that none of his compatriots felt it. After all, one group led by the general Neon of Asine did disregard the omens and marched out, only to suffer significant losses; five hundred of them were killed. Just like the disbelievers in epic and tragedy, they paid highly for their disregard of seercraft.

I think that we can now return to the questions posed at the beginning of this chapter. And the answer to those questions, to my mind at least, is clear. The skeptical utterances that appear in our texts should not be taken to indicate a general and deeply held disbelief. For one thing, it may be misleading to quote them out of their literary context. Teiresias, after all, was right about Oedipus, and Euripides' famous barb may be an ironic echo of a similar, but less pejorative, remark by the sophist Antiphon. When Antiphon was allegedly asked "What is the art of divination?" he responded: "The conjecture of an intelligent man."[21] This is very close to Euripides' comment "The best seer is the one who guesses well." Although the context, as well as the date, of both remarks is unknown, the tone and point of each may have been rather different. We do not know what character spoke Euripides' line or indeed what befell him in the course of the play. Perhaps he learned, like Oedipus or Creon, that there was more to divination than "guesswork." Antiphon, however, was probably making a serious point. An essential aspect of divination is "the discovery of

---

20. This passage is misinterpreted by Bowden (2003: 259), who claims: "The implication is that any soldier might have learned the skills of a *mantis*." It may be true that anyone could learn something about how to read the signs in a divinatory ritual, but it is not legitimate to conclude that anyone could be called a *mantis* from the fact that anyone could learn something about divination.

21. Pendrick 2002: T 9.

analogies or resemblances between the divination-sign and the real-life situation signified."[22]

On the other hand, some of these skeptical passages (the *Helen* was performed in 412) are likely to reflect the disastrous role that seers had played in encouraging the Athenians to sail to Sicily in 415 and in keeping them from leaving in 413 while they had the chance (Thucydides 7.50.4; 8.1). But over and above any specific, and ephemeral, historical explanation, a general consideration is relevant. One of the salient features of divination as a cross-cultural phenomenon is the tendency to abuse individual seers while maintaining faith in the system itself.[23]

As Robert Parker has astutely pointed out, "professional seers were always exposed to ridicule and accusations of charlatanism, but anthropology teaches that societies which depend on seers also regularly deride them."[24] That explains why Aristophanes liked to make fun of them; it was because at least some of them were so influential. But it is also the case that there was a hierarchy of methods of divination. What Evans-Pritchard says about the status of witch doctors in Zandeland well captures the attitude to seers among the Greeks: "Thus we again find scepticism about witch-doctors expressed in this gradation of oracles. The Zande shows his suspicions of the human element in oracles by placing greater reliance on the poison oracle and the termites oracle, which work through natural agencies, than on the rubbing-board oracle or witch-doctors, the one manipulated by human direction, the other in itself a human agency."[25] This distinction equally explains the greater authority among the Greeks of oracle centers, especially those based upon mediumistic possession, than of the interpretation of signs by seers. And even among the class of individuals whom we might call charismatics, the seer, or *mantis*, had a far more respected position in society than the *chrēsmologos*, or expounder of oracles. Thus, as we have seen, a common way of slandering a *mantis* was by calling him something else, such as a magician, wizard, or begging priest, all of whom were charismatic figures on the margins of society.

The study of the Azande, moreover, may reveal yet another reason why seers were held in lower prestige than oracular centers and why we find attacks on them in Greek literature. Evans-Pritchard observed that as witch doctors built up a clientele for themselves, from which they derived both wealth and reputation, they grew envious of the

22. Pendrick 2002: 243.
23. See Parker in Buxton 2000: 80–81. Note also Lloyd 2002: 36.
24. *Oxford Classical Dictionary*[3], s.v. "divination: Greek."
25. 1979: 114.

encroachment of competitors and tried to defeat their rivals by slander and denigration. He concludes: "Thus, the jealousies which lead witch-doctors to cast aspersions on one another must also lessen their prestige among laymen."[26] We do not have much evidence for such rivalries among Greek seers, but surely they must have existed, since competition for employment at all levels would have been lively enough. One can easily imagine that there was also rivalry and competition among the leading mantic families as well as among individual seers. There is indeed a trace of such competition in the contest of divinatory skill between Calchas and Mopsus.

The seer's value to society as the practitioner of a socially useful craft in turn depended on his human audience's faith in his ability properly to interpret the signs sent by the gods.[27] Thus the worst accusation that one could level against a seer was that he was influenced by greed to give knowingly false interpretations. Such accusations, which are fairly common in Greek literature, reveal both the high value that society placed on divination and an attendant anxiety about its proper performance. Such accusations of greed and ambition should not surprise us; or rather, it would be more surprising if they were absent altogether. One did not become a seer out of altruism or from a sense of piety or out of a desire to serve the gods. Even Melampus, the archetypal seer, demanded first one-half and then two-thirds of the kingdom of Argos in exchange for curing the Argive women of their madness.

A seer had an expert skill that was in high demand, and accordingly he was in a position to command a high price. As long as the employer got the desired results, complaints were probably few. There is no hint in Herodotus, for instance, that the Spartans ever regretted giving citizenship to Tisamenus and his brother. And considering the five victories that he vouchsafed for them, why should they have complained? But if one predicted an outcome that was not to the best interests of one's employers, one could incur their displeasure. So Teiresias laments in Euripides' *Phoenissae* (954–59):

> Anyone who practices the art of interpreting burnt offerings is foolish. If he indicates that the signs are adverse, he makes himself an enemy to those for whom he observes the flight of birds; but if out of pity he tells falsehoods to those consulting him, he commits an injustice against the gods. Phoebus [Apollo] alone should prophesy to men, for he fears no one.

26. 1979: 114.

27. For the social function of divination, see Park 1963 and the important collection of articles in Peek 1991a. For the performative aspects, see also LaGamma 2000 and Pemberton 2000.

A good seer was indeed the one who got it right. But the greed and ambition even of successful seers was impugned, because getting it right entailed making enormous sums of money. The stakes, in military divination at least, could be very high. A miscalculation might lead not merely to loss of future employment, but even to death on the battlefield. Seers must have defended themselves against the charges of greed and charlatanism. Can we infer how they might have done so? The same charge that was brought against the seers, of wandering from city to city for the sake of profit, was also applied to the sophists. And perhaps too the seer defended himself in somewhat similar terms. The sophists could claim that their itinerant lifestyle was a means of communicating their special knowledge.[28] So too the seer could claim that his expertise was profitable to those who employed him rather than to himself. The seer, like his fellow learned wanderers—the sophist, bard, and physician—wandered in order to display knowledge rather than to acquire it, ostensibly for the benefit of others.

HOW DOES ONE TEST A SEER?

Outside of the world of Greek poetry, how often was it that someone would actually put an oracle or a seer to the test? Skepticism, and even downright disbelief, are one thing; putting one's skepticism into practice is quite another. The most famous example of testing oracular knowledge appears in Herodotus. King Croesus of Lydia set out to test seven of the most famous oracles by dispatching messengers to each of them simultaneously (Hdt. 1.46–49). These were the oracles at Delphi, Abae in Phocis, Dodona, and Didyma, of Amphiaraus and Trophonius in Boeotia, and of Ammon in Libya. On the hundredth day from their departure from Sardis, these messengers were to ask the oracles what Croesus happened to be doing. No sooner did the Lydians enter the inner sanctuary of the temple of Apollo at Delphi than the Pythia, without even hearing the question, uttered one of the most extraordinary of extant oracles:

I know the number of grains of sand and the measure of the sea,
I understand the mute, and I hear the one who does not speak.
The odor of a hard-shelled tortoise has come into my mind,
being boiled in bronze at the same time with lamb's flesh;
bronze is spread under it, and with bronze it is covered over.

28. For itinerant sages and sophists in archaic and classical Greece, see Montiglio 2005: 91–117.

Apollo knew that Croesus was making tortoise and lamb soup in a bronze caul-dron. What are we to make of this story? Was this particular Pythia a clairvoyant?[29] Was the story made up later, or did it happen as recorded? An apparent incon-sistency in the story itself may raise suspicion. At one point we are told that only Delphi passed the test and that Croesus considered Delphi alone to be a true oracle (1.48), but a few sentences later (1.49) we learn that he also considered the oracle of Amphiaraus at Thebes to be true. And at the very end of his account of Croesus, Herodotus informs us that he had made dedications to the oracle of Apollo at Didyma that were equal in weight and similar to those at Delphi (1.92). It should be obvious that Herodotus's Delphic sources stressed that Delphi had uniquely passed the tortoise and lamb soup test, but that Croesus himself must also have trusted in the veracity of other oracles apart from Delphi.[30] Modern scholars, not surprisingly, have seen this story as a Delphic invention. Nonetheless, it is highly probable that Croesus did test Delphi, as well as other oracles, even if he did not use the precise test recorded by Herodotus.

I say "highly probable" not without recourse to evidence external to Herodotus's account. We know from other sources that Near Eastern kings sometimes tested ora-cles, and thus Croesus would not have lavished an immense amount of gold dedi-cations upon Delphi if he had not been convinced of the oracle's truthfulness in the modern positivist sense of truth.[31] The most famous Near Eastern example is per-haps the Akkadian literary text known as the "Sin of Sargon," in which Sargon's son, the Assyrian king Sennacherib, seeks to discover the cause of his father's death by means of divination from the examination of entrails.[32] He does so by dividing his diviners into three or four groups that were not allowed to approach or to speak to each other, and then posing the same question to each group. As it turned out, each group gave the same answer. Sennacherib's ghost proposes the same procedure to his own son, Esarhaddon, and it appears from one of Esarhaddon's inscriptions,

29. As Dodds (1973: 166) well points out, "neither he [Croesus] nor Herodotus knew that it was a telepathic experiment: they thought he was testing the alleged omniscience of various foreign gods or heroes." As Dodds observes, this now would be called an experiment in "long-distance telepathy." Myers (1921: 39–42) suggested that this response was a product of true second sight, but the vast majority of scholars see it as invented after the fact (or that it is legendary rather than historical). Dobson (1979: 353) claims that "it is too perfect an exemplar of oracular style."

30. On all of this, see H. Flower 1991.

31. See Klees 1965: 65–98.

32. For text and discussion, see Tadmor, Landsberger, and Parpola 1989.

dated to c. 670 B.C., that he followed this procedure with his own diviners.[33] In stark contrast to Greek attitudes, the Assyrians and Babylonians considered the examination of entrails to be a far more authoritative means of ascertaining the will of the gods than ecstatic prophecy.

In any case, Delphi had passed an empirically verifiable test. Yet the idea of testing an oracle was foreign to the Greek mentality. The Lydian Croesus, despite the fact that there were Greek communities within his kingdom, seems to have been completely unaware of the impiety involved in his act from the Greek point of view. Xenophon makes it clear that he strongly disapproved of Croesus's attempt to see if Apollo "was able to speak the truth" (*Cyr.* 7.2.17). Plato considered Delphic Apollo to be the highest authority on matters of religion (*Rep.* 427b), and Euripides has Orestes proclaim (*El.* 399–400): "The oracles of Loxias [i.e., Apollo] are steadfast, but I dismiss the seercraft (*mantikē*) of mortals." The oracle of Apollo at Delphi was on a higher plane than the activities of seers and was beyond the scope of rational doubt. Similarly no Zande doubted or tested the poison oracle, just as no Tibetan tested the Chief State Oracle. A seer, however, was primarily the interpreter of divine signs, and there was no impiety involved in showing him up as an incompetent interpreter.

It has been claimed that "the precise enquiry about the present by which king Croesus 'tested' the oracles would seem as irregular to an African as it did to Greeks."[34] Although, as mentioned above, witch doctors were held in less esteem than either the poison oracle or the termite oracle, there is an almost exact parallel for Croesus's test in the unabridged 1937 edition of Evans-Pritchard's classic study *Witchcraft, Oracles, and Magic among the Azande.*[35] This book is almost always cited in its abridged 1979 edition, but the passage that I am interested in did not make the editors' cut. The Azande, a people of the southern Sudan, are most famous for the poison oracle that is administered to chickens, but witch doctors were also essential actors in their religious system.

Evans-Pritchard had a Zande friend named Mbira, who placed a knife in a covered pot and summoned witch doctors to tell him what the pot contained. The first three made a number of wildly incorrect guesses. The fourth secretly followed Mbira into a hut and begged him to divulge what was in the pot so that he could save

33. Borger 1956: AsBbA, no. 53, pp. 82–83.
34. Parker 2000: 78.
35. 1937: 183–86.

his reputation. Mbira, however, refused his request, called him a knave, and sent him away without payment. Evans-Pritchard then comments: "Yet Mbira believed firmly in every kind of magic, was, in fact, himself a magician of standing, and believed, moreover, in the particular kind of magic which gives prophetic powers to witch-doctors. When he was in trouble he summoned practitioners to his home-stead and listened with respect to their words. He was convinced that some witch-doctors were genuine and could tell you their names. These genuine practitioners might make mistakes, but they possessed excellent medicines which gave them real prophetic powers, and, above all, they possessed *mangu* (witchcraft-substance)."[36] It is clear that skepticism is included in the pattern of belief about witch doctors; indeed, one might say that the function of skepticism in systems of divination is to explain failures in such a way as to allow the general belief to remain intact.

Evans-Pritchard's student Godfrey Lienhardt made the same observation while studying another African people, the Dinka.[37] On one occasion he purposefully mis-led an itinerant Dinka diviner (a class of individuals called *tyet*) by expressing false concerns about imaginary problems in his personal life (something that no anthro-pologist would now do), problems about which the diviner gave him reassurances. The reaction of his Dinka companions is surely typical cross-culturally: "The Dinka, who then knew what was happening, lost faith in his statements about them, saying that after all there were many fraudulent *tiit*, diviners, or people who 'are not real *tiit*'; but of course the experience of one false diviner, far from calling into doubt the abilities of all, reminded them of many others who really had the insight which this man claimed."

One question, however, remains. In these three tests, those of Mbira, Senna-cherib, and Croesus, exactly who or what is being tested? Is it the omniscience of supernatural powers, or the competence of religious specialists? In the first two cases, it is surely the latter: it is not a god who is being put to the test, but rather the ability of a mortal to display magical powers in the Zande case, or to act as the god's interpreter in the Assyrian example. With Croesus it is not exactly clear whether he is testing the Pythia's ability to channel Apollo or the Greek god's omniscience. Nonetheless, this distinction would have been lost on the Greeks themselves. Inasmuch as the Pythia was the god's mouthpiece, testing the oracle was tantamount to testing the god himself. If a particular Pythia gave a manifestly false answer, it

36. 1937: 186–87.
37. 1961: 68–69.

was because she had been bribed to speak in her own voice—the god himself never erred.[38]

In terms of religious sensibilities, however, it may have been permissible to ask the same question of more than one oracle. The people of Apollonia asked both Delphi and Dodona about a dearth (Hdt. 9.93). Both Delphi and the oracle of Amphiaraus gave the same reply to Croesus when he applied his aforementioned test (Hdt. 1.153), and there is no hint anywhere in Herodotus's history that it was unacceptable to petition more than one oracle at a time, as the Persian Mardonius later did in 479 B.C. (Hdt. 8.133). Although Thucydides neglects to tell us, there is a tradition that before their expedition to Syracuse in 415 B.C. the Athenians consulted the oracle of Zeus Ammon at Siwah oasis in Libya (Plut. *Nic.* 13 and 14), the oracle of Zeus at Dodona (Paus. 8.11.12), and the oracle of Apollo at Delphi (Plut. *Mor.* 403b; *Nic.* 13).[39] There is only one incident that even vaguely approaches the testing of an oracle by a Greek. This took place in 388 B.C., when the Spartan king Agesipolis consulted the oracles at both Olympia and Delphi about breaking a specious religious truce that was being offered by the Argives (Xen. *Hell.* 4.7.2). When he received the answer that he wanted at Olympia, that it was all right to break it, he asked Apollo if he agreed with his father. Agesipolis's tactic came very close to being a trick, if not a test, and other Greeks did not follow his example.

Although testing oracles was considered out of bounds, it would be nice to know if Greeks ever staged contests between seers, or indeed if seers would even have consented to participate in some kind of competition between themselves. Testing a seer, or even staging a competition between seers, was simply not the same as testing an oracle, and therefore was not in itself unacceptable in religious terms. The contest between Mopsus and Calchas was intended to show who was the better seer, and is analogous to contests between poets, sophists, and doctors that were part of the agonistic milieu of the fifth century, in which public displays of learning were judged and appreciated by a larger public.[40] The imaginary contest between Aeschylus and Euripides in Aristophanes' *Frogs* mirrored the wisdom contests of everyday experience.

In the last analysis, although both belief in divination generally and confidence in the efficacy of particular types of divination are likely enough to have waxed and waned in relation to particular circumstances and fashions, we really do not have the

38. For examples of bribery, see Hdt. 5.63, 90–91; 6.75, 122; and the discussion in chapter 6.
39. I argue that these consultations are historical in Flower 2008b.
40. On this milieu see Lloyd 1987: 83–108 and Thomas 2000: 249–69.

evidence to trace these variations in any detail. What we can say, what the evidence unequivocally shows, is that most people throughout antiquity had a belief in the validity and importance of divination. As in all societies that practice divination, the figure of the seer was both respected and ridiculed, but he or she was never wholly dismissed. And even if a particular seer was shown up as a charlatan or a failure, a person could and did take comfort in the conviction that other seers were competent and trustworthy. One really had no choice if one wanted to take advantage of such knowledge and advice as the gods were willing to share.

SIX · A Dangerous Profession

The Seer in Warfare

> Cleobulus, son of Glaucus, the earth covers you in
> death, being good both as a seer and as a fighter with
> the spear.
>
> From an Attic grave stele

The most important role of the seer in Greek society was arguably on the field of battle.[1] Until quite recently, most scholars viewed seers as the willing agents of their generals and as consciously manipulating the sacrifices in order to confirm what the generals had decided to do.[2] Thus they were seen as tools in the building of morale and not as important players in their own right. This rationalizing view has begun to give way to more nuanced explanations and models. It is now common to read of the symbiotic relationship between general and seer.[3] There must have been tremendous pressures on both men to perform successfully when under stress or scrutiny. Given the high stakes involved, it would not be surprising if seers, to one degree or another, subconsciously interpreted the sacrifices in accordance with what the situation demanded. Nonetheless, in order to be successful over a long career a seer needed to project an image of objectivity.

The way in which divination is practiced depends on its usefulness in a particular culture. If a form of divinatory ritual habitually hinders individuals from doing

---

1. Important studies of the seer in warfare are Popp 1957; Lonis 1979; Pritchett 1979; Jameson 1991; and Parker 2000.

2. Anderson 1970: 69–70 is typical.

3. Parker (2000 and 2004: 144) takes what he calls "a middle way": "It can be argued that enough flexibility was built into the sacrificial system to allow one both to be a more or less sincere believer, and to act most of the time more or less as one felt to be sensible in secular terms: the only projects which a general really abandoned because of bad omens were ones which he genuinely suspected might not be advisable." For a similar position, see Zucker 1900.

what they need or want to do, then that form would be abandoned or modified. On the other hand, divination must appear to be objectively valid and not a mere rubber stamp.[4] Objectivity depends on resistance to manipulation and on a general belief that bad things happen to people who ignore or despise the advice of seers. The function of military or prebattle divination is an issue of great importance for our understanding both of Greek warfare and of Greek religious attitudes in general. Was the function of prebattle divination merely to boost morale and to legitimate strategy, or did it actually influence strategy and tactics?

In what has become the standard work on Greek warfare, W. K. Pritchett has stated that seers might report sacrifices as being unfavorable contrary both to the plans put forth by the general and to the exigencies of the tactical situation. But not all of Pritchett's examples are persuasive, and a more subtle exposition of the evidence is necessary. Nevertheless, as Pritchett points out, "the *mantis* practices seer-craft, as a doctor practices medicine." It is important to realize that both in the Near East and in Greece the interpretation of entrails, and especially of the liver, was a very complex skill that tended to be passed down in certain families. Seercraft, by its very nature, is liable to subconscious manipulation; but that is far from saying that seers merely saw what they wanted to see.[5] There were some objective criteria that could not be explained away. If a victim's liver lacked a lobe, that was an unequivocally bad sign.[6] So too the fighting of birds unequivocally portended a coming disaster.[7]

Nonetheless, there was considerable scope for interpretation in reading the signs. All "scientific" observations are theory laden and subjective by nature, and this is as true for a modern doctor as it was for a Greek seer. Even when books on divination were in circulation, they cannot possibly have described every possible combination of markings, color, and shape that any particular organ (spleen, stomach, kidneys, heart, lungs, liver) might display. No two livers, in fact, are exactly alike.[8] So a seer had to have an understanding of the strategic situation as well as

---

4. So Fortes 1987: 11: "Thus it is an essential aspect of divination that its revelations should be objectively verifiable as objectivity is understood in a given society."

5. See Overholt 1989: 136–39 for examples from many cultures.

6. Xen. *Hell.* 3.4.15 and 4.7.7; Eur. *El.* 826–32; Plut. *Ages.* 9.5, *Alex.* 73.4, *Pyrrh.* 30.5; Arr. 7.18.2–4; Cic. *Div.* 2.32. Note also Plut. *Cim.* 18, where "the lobe does not have a head." When the sources say that a victim's liver was missing a lobe, this does not refer to one of the main lobes (of which a sheep's liver has two), but rather to an appendix of the upper lobe (the *lobus pyramidalis*). This appendix is what the Greeks called the λοβός and the Romans the *caput* and is now called the *processus pyramidalis*. See Pritchett 1979: 74–76 for discussion and bibliography; and note esp. Körte 1905 and Thulin 1906: vol. 2, 24–44.

7. Hom. *Od.* 2.146–76; Aes. *PV* 488–92; Soph. *Ant.* 998–1004; Plut. *Alex.* 73.2.

8. Pritchett 1979: 77.

confidence in his own divinatory skill and training. There doubtless were charlatans, but many seers were apparently reluctant to force the signs to be favorable when they clearly and apparently "objectively" were not.

Nevertheless, although a general might turn to his seer for advice, it was up to him to decide when and how often his seer would sacrifice. And no matter what the results of those sacrifices were, the ultimate decision of when and where to attack resided with the general. In the words of Plato (*Lach.* 199a), "the law enjoins that the general rules the seer and not the seer the general." Yet the Greeks believed that the gods had good strategic sense and that they communicated with men by means of signs. So any general who disregarded the omens and the advice of his seer did so at his own peril.[9] Furthermore, the relationship between seer and general (despite Plato) was not cut-and-dried, and this ambiguity may have been necessary and helpful.

Seers, for their part, were also subject to tremendous pressures. When a seer performed a sacrifice before battle, it was a public act with serious implications for the morale of the army, the authority of the general, the outcome of the battle, and the seer's own future employment. The act of sacrificing and then of interpreting the omens was, in other words, a public performance before an audience of mortals and of gods. We have examples of when the omens, after continual daily sacrifices, were not favorable for an attack. What was a seer to do in such circumstances?

Herodotus provides one of our most graphic examples of divining under pressure. In the final moments before the battle of Plataea in 479 B.C., the engagement that would decide once and for all the success or failure of Xerxes' attempt to conquer Greece, with a hail of Persian arrows falling upon the Spartans, a desperate Pausanias praying to Hera, and the Tegeans already beginning to advance against the enemy, what choice did Tisamenus have but to see a favorable sign in the battle-line sacrifices, called *sphagia*?[10] The exigencies of this critical situation must have affected interpretation, even if only subconsciously. At the end of the same century,

9. As Dover (1973: 63–64) observes, when faced with unusual events or ominous occurrences (such as an eclipse or an earthquake) that appear to be communications from a supernatural being, "the commander may be no better equipped to decide on the action appropriate to these intimations than he is to set a fracture or paint a shield. He must go to his experts, the seers, and when he has listened to their interpretations he must decide whether to trust them and act on their advice, risking disaster if they turn out to be mistaken, or to defy and overrule them, trusting in his own judgment and risking punishment from gods and men if the seers prove to have understood the divine intention correctly."

10. Although Herodotus does not mention Tisamenus by name in this passage (9.63), it was surely he, and not Pausanias, who performed the *sphagia* (as at Plut. *Arist.* 18).

the Arcadian seer Arexion, who had succeeded the Ambraciot Silanus as the chief seer to the Ten Thousand (Xen. *Anab.* 6.4.13), was put in a somewhat similar position. The enemy appeared at a distance of about a mile and a half (fifteen stades), and Xenophon says (*Anab.* 6.5.8) that "Arexion, the seer for the Greeks, immediately sacrificed, and the *sphagia* were favorable on the first try."

It seems to be an implicit assumption in modern studies that the best interests of seer and general were precisely identical. To be sure, both would have desired to win the battle or campaign in which they were currently participating. But if things seemed to be going badly or if the odds for success did not look particularly good, then their interests might well have diverged. The seer, for his part, needed to think in terms of finding a substitute employer.

Herodotus gives a graphic instance of this as well. He tells how the Elean seer Callias, who was of the family of the Iamidae, assisted Croton in southern Italy in its war with Sybaris in 510 and was richly rewarded with select estates (5.44–45). Herodotus claims that Callias's descendants still possessed that land in his own day. But this Callias must have needed to explain something that was especially awkward and embarrassing: that is, how did he end up serving the Crotoniates when he had been hired by the tyrant of Sybaris? His justification may be embedded in Herodotus's narrative: "The people of Croton say that Callias ran away from Telys the tyrant of the Sybarites and came to them, since the sacrifices (*hiera*) were not turning out favorable for him when he was sacrificing against Croton." One is tempted to rationalize this explanation by conjecturing that the Crotoniates had offered Callias more money or that he calculated that Sybaris would lose the war, even if Herodotus himself seems to take this explanation at face value and apparently expects his readers to do the same. Within the Greek divinatory system of knowledge and belief, in which system Callias was a specialist, unfavorable omens from sacrificial divination were a necessary and sufficient explanation for human action. The imperfect tense in the phrase "were not turning out favorable" indicates that Callias tried many times to get good omens, but that the gods were unwilling to grant them. He thus represented himself as having fully discharged his duties to his original employer; the will of the gods was clear, and there was no need to perish in a doomed cause.

TAKING THE INITIATIVE

On a few occasions we can see seers taking the initiative in an even bolder fashion. Herodotus gives two examples. There were peaceful relations between the Argives and their former slaves living at Tiryns until the seer Cleander, who was from

Phigalea in Arcadia, arrived on the spot and persuaded the slaves to attack their former masters. After a long and bitter struggle, the Argives prevailed (Hdt. 6.83). This particular seer must have seen an opportunity for personal profit in this situation; he then tried to exploit it by using his mantic authority to initiate a war. Tellias, an Elean seer, took the initiative rather more successfully, but this was at a moment of peril. When the Phocians, whom he was serving, were cooped up on Mount Parnassus by the invading Thessalians, he contrived a most clever stratagem. He chalked over the best six hundred Phocians and launched them on a night attack upon the Thessalian camp, telling them to kill anyone they saw who had not been whitened. So effective was this trick that the Phocians collected the corpses of four thousand Thessalians (Hdt. 8.27; cf. Paus. 10.1.3—9).

For those who distrust Herodotus, especially when he is narrating events from before the time of the Persian Wars, confirmation that seers might take the initiative can be found in Thucydides. During the siege of Plataea by the Peloponnesians and Boeotians in 428 B.C., 212 of the Plataeans managed a daring escape by night. Thucydides claims (3.20.1) that "the attempt was suggested to them by Theaenetus, the son of Tolmides, a seer, and by Eupompidas, the son of Daïmachus, who was a general."

In addition to formulating strategy, seers might also play a major role in conspiracies. In fact, it might have seemed inconceivable to undertake a coup d'état without having a seer as an accomplice. The great-grandson (or perhaps great-nephew) of the Tisamenus of Elis who fought at Plataea was also named Tisamenus. This second Tisamenus, for reasons that we can only guess, was involved in the conspiracy of Cinadon at Sparta in 399.[11] He was executed along with Cinadon and the other conspirators after being paraded through the streets of Sparta in a dog collar, while being whipped and goaded (Xen. *Hell.* 3.3.11). It is an ironic testament to the family's fame that "Tisamenus the seer" is the only one of Cinadon's fellow conspirators who is named by Xenophon.

The seer Theocritus played a major role in the conspiracy led by Pelopidas that put down the oligarchy in Thebes and resulted in the expulsion of the Spartan garrison in 379 B.C. Although the role of Theocritus is only known from Plutarch's *Moralia* (in the fictional dialogue *On the Nature of Socrates* (575b—598f) and is not mentioned in his *Life of Pelopidas*, it is confirmed in a spectacular way on a remarkable late fourth-century B.C. gold amphora found in Bulgaria in 1949 (see fig. 13). It has been argued, with extreme plausibility, that the figures on this amphora repre-

---

11. Figueira (1986: 193 n. 70) suggests that he may have been an "inferior" (*hypomeiōn*), one of those Spartiates who had lost their citizen status due to an inability to pay their monthly mess dues.

FIGURE 13.
It is very likely that this scene depicts a historical event. The seer Theocritus holds a
liver that he shows to a youth standing next to him, while Pelopidas and his fellow conspirators assault the house of the Theban oligarch Leontiades. A scene on the Panagjurischte gold amphora, late fourth century B.C. Adapted from *JHS* 94 (1974): pl. V.

sent Pelopidas and his fellow conspirators, including the seer Theocritus, attacking
the house of the oligarch Leontiades (unfortunately, none of the figures are labeled).[12] Four men armed with swords assault the house door, which is held ajar by
a small, startled bearded figure. A trumpeter stands to their left. Two other figures
form a pair: an elderly man holds a liver that he shows to a youth standing next to
him. If this elderly man, with liver in hand, represents the seer Theocritus, this part
of the scene corresponds to the place in Plutarch's story where Theocritus advised
his accomplices that the sacrifices were favorable for immediate action (595f): "The
seer also urged us on, since his sacrifices (*ta hiera*) indicated deliverance and proved
favorable and assured our safety."

This Theocritus makes a further appearance in Plutarch's *Life of Pelopidas* (21–
22), where just before the battle of Leuctra he convinces Pelopidas to sacrifice to the
daughters of Scedasus a filly with a red mane that has run into the Theban camp,
rather than a red-haired virgin, as Pelopidas seemingly had been told to do in a
dream.[13] The details in both affairs involving Theocritus have surely been embroi-
dered in the telling, but one need not doubt that the seer was a close associate and
adviser of Pelopidas in events of great moment.

Despite these striking and not historically insignificant examples, it was probably

12. Borthwick 1976. For plates and drawings, see Roux 1964 and Griffith 1974.
13. On this passage, see Georgiadou 1997: 163–72.

the case that for the most part the seer acted as a consultant rather than as the insti-
gator of policy. Yet if a seer desired or felt compelled to take charge or suggest strategy, he had the charisma and influence to command a following. Some generals
might feel threatened, but others, such as the Theban Eupompidas, might well have
welcomed the assistance in difficult situations.

When, and under what circumstances, seer and general might publicly and openly
clash is unclear. Our historical sources do not report heated confrontations, but in epic
and tragedy political-military leaders and seers often come into conflict. Those genres, of course, focus on confrontation, and so it is only to be expected that Oedipus,
Creon, and Pentheus will disregard the counsel of Teiresias or that Agamemnon will
turn on Calchas, when the latter appears to undermine his authority.[14] Insofar as historical seers modeled themselves on mythical prototypes, they might have wanted to
imitate their claims to special knowledge, and in the poetic confrontations mentioned
above, it is the seer who knows best and who is proved right. But surely no seer with
a concern for his reputation and prospects for future employment would have
wanted to go head to head with his employer. The adaptation of mythical exemplars
must necessarily have been selective and have concentrated on the display of
prophetic knowledge rather than on the circumstances attending that display. At the
same time, no general or statesman would have desired life to imitate art in respect of
his being responsible for a disaster because a seer's advice had been neglected. The
relationship between art and life was subject to constant negotiation, for the Greeks
took mythical paradigms seriously, and they influenced behavior in the present.

PERFORMING THE SACRIFICE: *HIERA* AND *SPHAGIA*

Although seers practiced divination through various means, sacrificial divination
was the principal art of the seer who assisted generals on campaign and who won
battles in partnership with them. The military seer was responsible for two types of
divination that necessarily preceded an engagement: the campground sacrifice
called *hiera* and the battle-line sacrifice called *sphagia*. The former (*hiera*) was usually performed by examining the victim's liver (the "victim" was usually a sheep),
and the latter (*sphagia*) by slitting the victim's throat (often a young she-goat) while
observing the animal's movements and the flow of blood. The seer was the one who
sacrificed the victim during the campground sacrifice and then examined the entrails
while the commander looked on.

14. Soph. *OT* 316–462 and *Ant.* 988–1090; Eur. *Bacch.* 215–369; Hom. *Il.* 1.1–120.

A possible exception might be that a Spartan king, in his capacity as priest, might himself conduct the sacrifice and interpret the entrails without a seer to assist him. When Xenophon decribes the king's predawn sacrifice in the military camp, a seer is conspicuously absent from the list of onlookers (*Lac. Pol.* 13). It is also possible that the king performed the *sphagia* himself, or at least was competent to do so (as Plutarch implies at *Lyc.* 22.4). It seems rather more likely, however, that here as elsewhere our sources have elided the procedure and that the kings of Sparta, although they had priestly functions, were attended by seers who assisted them. For instance in the Persian Wars, the kings Leonidas and Leotychidas, as well as the regent Pausanias, were served not just by seers, but by famous ones who were very well paid.

Since the words *hiera* and *sphagia* form the fundamental vocabulary of Greek military divination, it is worthwhile to look at them more closely. *Hiera* (τὰ ἱερά) are "signs" or "omens." In a sacrificial context the words may mean (1) "rites" (broadly speaking), (2) the particular parts of the sacrificial victim that are examined for signs, or (3) the signs themselves that emerge from examination.[15] The difference between 2 and 3 is often blurred. *Hiera* were performed in camp before setting out and were consultative in nature. Although the purpose behind the sacrifice was specifically to obtain omens, the meat could be eaten later. The *hiera* differ in both nature and purpose from the battle-line *sphagia*, which was a slaughter sacrifice in which the meat was not eaten.

Sphagia (τὰ σφάγια) are technically the battle-line sacrifices that were performed only when the two opposing armies were on the point of engaging. The sacrifice, which was both propitiatory and divinatory in purpose, entailed slitting the throat (σφάζειν = "to cut the throat") of the sacrificial victim (for the Lacedaemonians a young she-goat) and observing the way in which the blood flowed and the animal fell; if the omens were favorable, the phalanx then advanced against the enemy.[16] In addition to *sphagia* being divinatory, this rite was propitiatory in a double sense, for the animal stands for two distinct kinds of human victim. At one and the same time the death of the animal was a harbinger of the death of the enemy, and it served as a substitute for the death of one's own comrades.[17] Since most Greeks believed that the gods communicated with men through divinatory sacrifices, no Greek general

---

15. I have borrowed this set of definitions from Jameson 1991: 200–201.

16. Xen. *Lac. Pol.* 13.8; Plut. *Lyc.* 22; Xen. *Hell.* 4.2.20; Thuc. 6.69.2. Studies include Stengel 1886 and 1896; Eitrem 1938; Pritchett 1971: 109–15 and 1979: 83–90; Jameson 1991; and Parker 2000. Pritchett argues that *sphagia* were exclusively propitiatory in nature, but Jameson has persuasively shown that they were also divinatory.

17. See the superb discussions by Jameson (1991) and Parker (2000: 307–9).

would advance until the *sphagia* proved favorable, and they were not always successful on the first try.[18]

We are seldom told who perfomed the *sphagia*, but in most cases it must have been a seer. Xenophon may have performed the *sphagia* himself in an emergency situation, as *Anabasis* 6.4.25 seems to imply, but it is also possible that he has simply used that type of narrative shorthand that omits the presence of a seer. In another passage (*Anab.* 6.5.8), he specifically tells us that the *sphagia* were performed by the seer Arexion. In the case of *hiera*, there is one example in Greek tragedy of someone other than a seer examining the entrails. That is Aegisthus in Euripides' *Electra* (826–39); but Aegisthus was king of Mycenae and as such, like the historical kings of Sparta, was perceived as having priestly functions. The sacrifice would have taken place at a makeshift altar, and both seer and general would have been garlanded (as at Xen. *Anab.* 7.1.40).

As it happens, we know much more about the precise details of Near Eastern practice than of Greek. In the Neo-Assyrian period the extispicy took place at dawn. The diviner would begin with a prayer addressed to "Samas, lord of judgment, and Adad, lord of the extispicy ritual and divination." The diviner then whispered the words of the query, which were addressed to "Samas, great lord," into the ears of the sacrificial victim (almost always a sheep). Beginning with the liver, which received special attention, the entire exta of the sheep came under scrutiny according to a fixed sequence.[19] The answer to the query was a binary yes or no verdict. The result of the extispicy, whether the god's answer was yes or no, was arrived at by calculating the sum of positive and negative, favorable and unfavorable, omens from the various organs.[20] The preparations for the extispicy ritual seem to have been quite extensive, and that may explain why they took place only once a day by the Neo-Assyrian period.

Did the Greek seer begin with a prayer of invocation, as in the ancient Near East, or was the Greek rite a much simpler and quicker ritual, as among the Azande, who without much ceremony merely put a simple question to the poison oracle? To judge from our literary sources, which may abridge the procedure, the ritual was quite simple and could be repeated up to three times in one day. Xenophon, as mentioned before, even sacrificed two victims at once. We have no evidence that elaborate prayers or extensive preliminary rituals of any kind were carried out, or that the seer needed to examine any part of the exta other than the liver.

The technical aspects of sacrificial divination have been the topic of several stud-

18. This is the implication of Xen. *Anab.* 6.5.8.
19. See Starr 1983: 30–106; Jeyes 1980; Starr 1990: Cryer 1994: 168–80.
20. See Oppenheim 1977: 206–27.

ies.[21] Yet the distinction between the various forms of sacrifice is all too often a matter of confusion in modern commentaries and military histories. The specialist literature on these technical, yet fundamentally important, aspects of divination has simply not reached a wide-enough audience. One misleading feature of our literary texts is their shorthand of saying that "someone sacrificed," whether that someone be Xenophon or a Spartan king. One might take this to mean that the person made the sacrifice himself without a seer in attendance, but in most cases what the text really means is that a seer conducted the sacrifice on behalf of the named individual, who stood by and watched. There is an unambiguous example of this situation in Xenophon's *Anabasis* (2.1.9), where one of the attendants of the Spartan general Clearchus summons him from a meeting to examine the entrails that had been removed from a sacrificed animal, "for he [Clearchus] happened to be conducting a sacrifice." Clearchus obviously was sacrificing through a proxy, who summoned him after the entrails had been removed.

This type of shorthand is analogous to having individuals speak without interpreters when one party does not know Greek. (In Xenophon's *Anabasis* Cyrus sometimes uses an interpreter when speaking to Greeks, and sometimes no interpreter is mentioned. The obvious conclusion is that Cyrus does not know Greek and that Xenophon does not wish to encumber his narrative by mentioning an interpreter in each instance). Whenever the narrative calls for precision of expression, Xenophon makes it explicit that a seer is sacrificing for him.[22] So too Spartan kings, we may imagine, were accompanied by seers who performed the actual divinatory sacrifice. When it was a matter of purely private concern, there was nothing to keep an individual, if he felt competent in his own skill, to sacrifice by himself (as perhaps was done on occasion by Xenophon), but this would never be the case when omens were taken on behalf of the entire army or in any official capacity.[23]

Yet even when client and seer conducted the sacrifice together, it may have been the case that neither of them actually killed the animal with his own hands. Just as in nondivinatory sacrifices the priest (*hiereus*) had the option of delegating the actual killing of the animal to one or more expert attendants, so perhaps also the seer had this choice before him.[24] Here there may be a distinction between *hiera* and *sphagia*,

21. For example, by Szymanski (1908), Eitrem (1938), Rudhardt (1958: 249–300), Pritchett (1971 and 1979), and Jameson (1991).

22. As in the incident at Calpe, recorded at *Anab.* 5.6.13–37.

23. This may be the case at *Anab.* 6.5.8.

24. See Zaidman and Schmitt Pantel 1992: 50 and Jameson 1999: 325, 338.

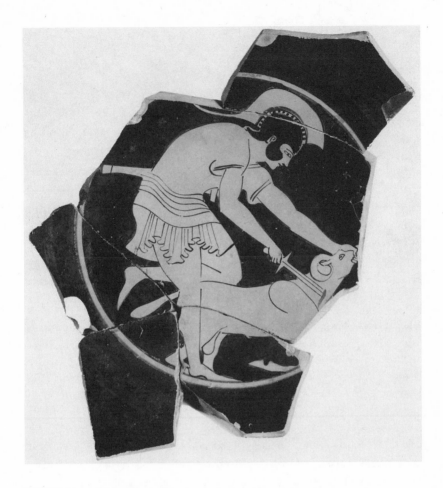

FIGURE 14.

This scene in the tondo of a red-figure cup apparently depicts a seer performing the battle-line sacrifice (called *sphagia*) by piercing the throat of a ram. It is surely emblematic of heroic status that this figure (like the sacrificer in fig. 15) is beardless and wears no body armor apart from a helmet. Fragment of a Kylix (Greece, Attic, c. 490–480 B.C.). Red-figure terracotta; D: 10.1 cm. © The Cleveland Museum of Art, 2004. Dudley P. Allen Fund 1926.242.

since in the latter the nature of the ritual may have necessitated that the seer slit the animal's throat with his own hands, as is depicted on a red-figure cup of 490–480 B.C. that shows a helmeted, but otherwise unarmed, beardless man in the act of piercing the throat of a ram (see fig. 14). This scene possibly depicts a seer in the moment of performing *sphagia* before battle. A frieze in a Lycian tomb of the first

FIGURE 15.
A seer is about to perform the prebattle sacrifice called *sphagia* by driving a sword into a ram's neck, while his commander stands next to him and raises his right hand in prayer. Meanwhile, their city is under siege. From a Lycian tomb of the fourth century B.C. Heroon von Trysa: Stadtbelagerung (ANSA I 462, 463, 464). Kunsthistorisches Museum, Vienna.

half of the fourth century similarly shows a beardless and helmeted man, again without body armor, about to drive a sword into a ram's neck, while his commander, wearing breastplate and helmet, looks on with his right arm raised in a gesture of prayer (see fig. 15).[25]

If these sacrificers are indeed seers, their clothing may be emblematic of their particular status within the army. Insofar as they are soldiers, they wear a helmet and carry a sword; but as craftsmen of the sacred, they do not wear the breastplate or greaves of the regular soldier. There may, of course, be a concomitant practical explanation, in that it may not have been very easy to wrestle with a ram while wearing stiff body armor. Perhaps after the *sphagia* proved favorable, the seer had time to don the rest of his panoply in the moments before the fighting began. Yet another oddity of these scenes is that the sacrificer is beardless, showing that he is a young

25. See Eichler 1950: 62 and pl. 19 (upper left) and Jameson 1991: 217–19 and n. 49.

man. Perhaps this is the youthful hero of myth, and these works of art show not the seer of contemporary life, but that of the mythic past. Whether these works of art are read as representing contemporary life or the mythic past, it is noteworthy that the image of the helmeted, beardless, and unarmored seer should remain the same over such a span of time and space.

However that may be, when performing the *hiera* the seer very likely wore different attire and acted in a different manner than when conducting the *sphagia*. The seer set himself apart from others in society by his distinctive dress and costume, which seems to have resembled that of a priest. It included long hair (on occasion), a garland or crown, a white tunic, a staff, and a laurel branch.[26] He also may have spoken in a high-pitched voice; for in the *Agamemnon*, Aeschylus says that Chalcas "shrieked out" his interpretation of the portent of the eagles devouring the pregnant hare, as well as his remedy for Artemis's wrath.[27] One cannot put too much weight on a single passage; yet an unusual tone to the voice would in itself have served as a randomizing device.

CAN A SEER PROMISE YOU VICTORY?

A fundamental distinction that is often obscured in modern studies has already been discussed, but it is important enough to revisit. Indeed, it would not be an exaggeration to say that the function of Greek divination as a system of knowledge and the role of the seer within that system cannot be understood without appreciating this single point. When a seer proclaimed that "the omens were favorable," this did not mean that success or victory was guaranteed. Such sacrifices "were intended to find out whether the movement towards an engagement with the enemy should proceed."[28] In other words, the gods were indicating their will but were not promising victory if their will was followed. Even if a general followed his seer's advice, it was still possible for him to lose the battle if he made some strategic or tactical blunder.

Xenophon claims (*Anab.* 1.8.15) that at the battle of Cunaxa in 401 B.C. he was told by Cyrus himself that "both the campground sacrifice (*hiera*) and the battle-line sacrifice (*sphagia*) were favorable." Yet, despite the fact that Cyrus was killed (due to the disobedience of Clearchus and Cyrus's own impetuosity), Xenophon still

26. The evidence for the seer's appearance is piecemeal; see Kett 1966: 103–4; Roth 1982: 141–42, 166–69; and Mantis 1990.

27. Lines 156 and 201 (ἀπέκλαγξεν/ἔκλαγξεν).

28. Jameson 1991: 205; see also Nock 1972: 542.

remained an unquestioning believer in the validity of sacrificial divination (*Anab.* 6.4.13–27; *Hipparch.* 9.8–9). It was perhaps easy enough for him to remain so, because both the Greeks and Cyrus's native troops were victorious over the forces that faced them. Indeed, only one of the ten thousand Greek mercenaries was killed in the battle, and Cyrus's six hundred cavalry routed the six thousand that were stationed in front of the King. If Cyrus fell, it was not because the gods had deceived him, but because he had "lost control of himself" and rashly charged against his brother King Artaxerxes (*Anab.* 1.8.19–27).

Again, it is important to stress that in Herodotus and Xenophon, the omens from sacrifice are either "good" (*kala*) or "favorable" (*chrēsta*), or the reverse, "not good" or "not favorable"; they never say that omens indicate "victory" (*nikē*). Later writers, such as Diodorus and Plutarch, mistakenly believed that favorable omens indicated victory in the literal sense, and the distinction between *hiera* and *sphagia* is lost on them. Thus Plutarch (*Arist.* 15.1 and 18.2) completely misunderstands the nature of Tisamenus's prediction in the text of Herodotus, and he gives an impossible account of the sacrifices that preceded the battle of Plataea.[29] Plutarch, it seems, simply misunderstands.

With Diodorus, who wrote during the first century B.C., the problem is rather more complex. Since he was drawing on the fourth-century historian Ephorus of Cyme, it is surprising that he can be so inaccurate.[30] If only we knew more about Ephorus than we do, much would be clearer.[31] Before the battle of Mantinea in 362 B.C., Diodorus says (15.85.1) that "the seers on both sides performed the *sphagia* and proclaimed that victory was foreshown by the gods." Since the battle was in fact indecisive, with both sides claiming victory (Diod. 15.89.1; Xen. *Hell.* 7.5.26–27), this sounds like a sensationalized piece of literary fiction, and it is just the sort of fiction that one might expect from Ephorus. It is worth pointing out that this is the only

---

29. Plut. (*Arist.* 18) makes explicit what Herodotus leaves unsaid, that it was the seer Tisamenus who actually conducted the *sphagia* while Pausanias looked on. Otherwise, as Jameson (1991: 207–8) demonstrates, Plutarch's elaboration of this scene at *Arist.* 17–18 has no independent value.

30. It is generally agreed that Ephorus was Diodorus's source for books 11–16 of his *Bibliothēkē.* See Hornblower 1994: 36–38; Flower 1998: 365; Stylianou 1998: 49–50. Ephorus's history covered events from the return of the Heracleidae in 1069 B.C. to the siege of Perinthus by Philip of Macedon in 341 B.C.

31. Most modern scholars regard Ephorus as a thoroughly second-rate historian, but that may be too harsh a judgment, given that his work has not survived to be judged on its own merits. Recent treatments of Ephorus's historical method are Stylianou 1998: 49–139, esp. 124–28; and Flower 1998.

time that we are explicitly told by any source that the sacrifices for opposing armies were favorable for both of them.

If Diodorus were not the source for an incident of great importance, we could let the matter of his reliability lie here. But the seers on each side play an important supporting role in his account of the battle of Arginusae, which was fought between the Athenian and Peloponnesian fleets in 406 B.C.[32] In this passage too one suspects that divination is being given a special emphasis for purely literary reasons. And here as well, if we knew more about Diodorus's working methods and the methods of his sources, we would be in a much stronger position in evaluating the evidentiary value of this narrative.

Unfortunately, Xenophon's account of this battle is fundamentally different from that of Diodorus, and he does not mention divination at all.[33] Xenophon begins his account of the year 406 with the statement that the moon suffered an eclipse and that the old temple of Athena Polias at Athens was burnt; though he does not say so, he surely intends his reader to see these as ominous portents of what was to come.[34] But, unlike Diodorus, why does he not mention the portents that took place during the battle of Arginusae itself? Did he omit them because he had not heard about them or because he did not believe in the veracity of what he had heard?

Whatever we choose to make of Xenophon's personal, political, and religious biases, he at least either witnessed or lived at the time of the events he reports. It is far more difficult a task to evaluate Diodorus. The link between Diodorus's narrative and "what actually happened" at Arginusae is particularly complex because it is distorted by Diodorus's adaptation of Ephorus as well as by Ephorus's reworking of his own source, the fragmentary history now known as the *Hellenica Oxyrhynchia*. Since the latter two treatments of Arginusae are no longer extant, it is really impossible to filter out the later literary and rhetorical accretions from the eyewitness testimony of the original participants in the battle. Furthermore, modern scholars are not in agreement about the relative merits of Ephorus and the *Hellenica Oxyrhynchia* in relation to Xenophon, and, even if they were, their conclusions could never rise above a fairly low level of probability. In other words, the chain of transmission from Arginusae to us is particularly long and tenuous.

Having said that, it is still worthwhile to look at Diodorus's account of Arginusae for what it tells us about attitudes toward divination and the Greek *mentalité*. The

---

32. 13.97—103.
33. *Hell.* 1.6.24—1.7.35. See Andrewes 1974 for an attempt to reconstruct the battle.
34. *Hell.* 1.6.1.

battle of Arginusae was notorious because the Spartan admiral, who was known for his Panhellenic sentiments, was killed in the action, and particularly because the Athenian generals were subsequently tried and executed for failing to pick up the dead for burial. With that background in mind, let us consider the function that divination plays in Diodorus's narrative.

Diodorus says that the Spartans and Athenians put off the battle due to bad weather but were planning to fight on the next day, "although the seers on both sides were forbidding it." In the case of the Lacedaemonians, the head of the sacrificial victim, which was lying on the beach, was lost when a wave broke over it. The seer proclaimed this to mean that the admiral would die in the sea battle (a pretty obvious interpretation one might think). Callicratidas, however, was undeterred and announced that his death would not make Sparta less famous.

A portent also occurred in the Athenian camp. The general Thrasyllus (mistakenly called Thrasybulus by Diodorus) saw a vision in the night. He dreamed that he and the six other generals were acting in the *Phoenician Women* of Euripides before a full theater, while their competitors were performing the *Suppliants*. He dreamed that this resulted in a "Cadmean victory" for them and they all died in imitation of those who made the expedition against Thebes. When the seer heard this, he disclosed that seven of the generals would be slain. This too, we might say, is pretty obvious, since both plays were on the theme of the Seven against Thebes, in which expedition six of the seven leaders were killed. Yet either the seer made a minor mistake or Diodorus has slightly muddled the story, since just as six of the seven heroes who attacked Thebes were killed, so six, not seven, of the Athenian generals at Arginusae were executed upon their return to Athens. Nevertheless, the sacrificial victims foretold victory, and so the generals forbade any report to be given of their own death, but announced to the whole force the victory revealed in the sacrifices. Callicratidas, for his part, "having heard from the seer about his coming end, was eager to make his death especially splendid."

It is impossible for us to say whether any of these portents actually occurred, but given the historiographical problems mentioned above and the silence of Xenophon, it is highly probable that they were invented after the fact. But why were they invented, and what can the act of invention teach us? The portents serve to explain in theological terms the unusual fact that the commanders on both sides, and especially the victorious Athenian commanders, lost their lives, thus helping to impose a kind of moral order on a disturbingly chaotic event. Divination also serves to heighten the heroism, as well as the irony, of their fate. The generals knew what was to befall them, but they still decided to press on with the attack. So too Cimon knew that his expedition to Cyprus in 451 would lead to his death (as discussed in chapter 4). So even if either a particular historian or Greek oral tradition has invented the role of divination at Arginusae, this narrative still opens a window into divinatory ways of thinking. The fact that divination can be used to frame, structure, and explain the narrative of one of the most notorious battles in Greek history shows just how important signs, omens, and portents were in the Greek worldview.

The seers in Diodorus's narrative take a back seat to the portents themselves. Diodorus does not bother to name them, and their interpretation of the headless victim and Thrasyllus's dream is all too obvious and easy. This narrative could have been composed differently, shifting at least some of the emphasis from the signs themselves to the skill and person of the interpreter. The partnership between seer and general, with its attendant tensions and mutual supports, comes more clearly in view when we turn to the reign of Alexander the Great later on in this chapter.

WHEN SEER AND GENERAL DISAGREE

When the seer was on campaign, was he in any way constrained by the explicit orders and desires of his employer? We have already discussed the subjective elements in divination; but there must have been cases, indeed the law of averages demands as much, when the omens simply would not turn out favorable for a desired course of action. There are many seemingly unambiguous examples of bad omens keeping a Greek general from doing what he really wanted to do and of disregard of a seer's advice leading to disaster. The following examples are illustrative. They cover a two-hundred-year period and come from a variety of sources.

At the battle of Plataea in 479 B.C. the seer Tisamenus of Elis declared that "the omens were favorable for the Greeks if they remained on the defensive, but not favorable if they should cross the Asopus River and begin battle."[35] The Medizing Greeks had their own seer, Hippomachus of Leucas, and he too was unable to obtain omens that were favorable for an offensive. Herodotus claims (9.37, 41, 45) that Mardonius, the Persian commander, was eager to engage the Greeks because he was running short of supplies and the Greek army was increasing in size every day. He

---

35. I have elsewhere discussed the possibility that Simonides of Ceos gave a fuller and much more elaborate version of Tisamenus's prophecy in F 14 (*IEG*²) of his recently restored elegiac poem on the battle of Plataea, but the fragments are so lacunose that it is impossible to tell whether it is some god or a mortal who is speaking, or indeed exactly what is being said (M. Flower 2000: 67 n. 9; Flower and Marincola 2002: 318).

was, nevertheless, restrained from attacking for ten days because his Greek seer, Hegesistratus of Elis, claimed that the omens were unfavorable for an offensive. We know both from Babylonian texts and from Xenophon that a seer could sacrifice up to three victims each day in regard to a particular query, so there was nothing to prevent Hegesistratus from repeatedly trying to get a favorable outcome. But he never obtained good omens, and Mardonius eventually attacked without them, losing both the battle and his own life.

Modern scholars are suspicious of Herodotus's account because it made strategic sense for both the Persians and the Greeks to lure the other side across the Asopus River, and thus the seers were actually recommending what common sense dictated. It also stretches the imagination that Hegesistratus could fail to get favorable omens over so long a period, especially if he was sacrificing three times each day. It is certainly possible that Mardonius decided to attack only when his shortage of provisions forced his hand.[36] Since Herodotus was writing forty to fifty years after these events, one may entertain doubts that he actually knew what Mardonius was planning, even if his account is important for understanding the role and image of the seer.

The testimony of Xenophon is particularly important here because he was an eyewitness to the events he records and because he claims to know something of divination himself. Xenophon and the Ten Thousand were detained at Calpe for three days without sufficient provisions because the sacrifices were unfavorable (*Anab.* 6.4.13–27). In this incident we see various attempts to explain why the omens were unfavorable either for departure or for a foraging expedition. On the first day Xenophon was accused of bribing the seer; on the second day someone said that he had heard that Cleander, the Spartan harmost (governor) of Byzantium, was about to appear with ships (i.e., to take them away by sea); and on the third day Xenophon himself speculated that an enemy force had assembled in the vicinity (which the sequel showed was in fact the case). Although the troops were suffering greatly from hunger, they still wanted to see some correlation between their present circumstances and the belief that the gods were looking out for them. To the question "Why aren't the omens favorable for us to do something that will get us food" the answer is "Either the seer is dishonest or the gods know something that we do not know (such as boats are on the way, or a large enemy force is waiting to attack us)."

Yet there is an even more remarkable example in the *Anabasis* (5.5.1–4). Xeno-

---

36. See Flower and Marincola 2002: 22–25 and Cawkwell 2005: 112–16.

phon tells us that the generals (which must include himself) desired to attack the fortresses of the Tibarenians, which were less strong than those of the people whose territory they had just passed through. Nonetheless, "after many victims had been sacrificed, all of the seers finally declared the opinion that the gods in no way permitted war." The generals, consequently, accepted gifts of hospitality, and the army proceeded through the territory of the Tibarenians without plundering it. If there is some "rational" explanation for this reading of the victims, it is not at all obvious.[37] Perhaps Xenophon is attempting to suggest to the reader that he and his troops were not the brigands that some made them out to be, because even when they wanted to do something bad, the gods would not let them.

Also difficult for us to rationalize or comprehend is the behavior of the Spartan Cleander, who was the harmost (governor) of the important city of Byzantium. Xenophon claims in the *Anabasis* (6.6.33–36) that he desired to take over command of the Ten Thousand when it was offered to him, and was indeed still more eager to do so when he saw the good discipline of the soldiers, but was unable to obtain good omens after three days of sacrificing. Should we think that he was never seriously interested and was looking for an excuse to back out,[38] or that he very much wanted this command but was forced completely against his will to refuse it? Or is there a middle ground, that he found the offer attractive, but not irresistibly so in the face of negative omens?[39] Or perhaps the explanation lies in Xenophon's own desire to depict the Ten Thousand as the kind of well-disciplined force that a high-ranking Spartan would want to command and would indeed have commanded if only the gods had been willing. However one reads this incident, one thing at least seems certain: Xenophon expected his audience to accept at face value the motivation and intentions that he attributes to Cleander. There is no hint in the text of duplicity or hesitation.

There are also cases where disregard of a seer's advice leads to disaster, quite apart from the purely literary examples that were discussed in the last chapter. Xenophon provides several apparently unambiguous examples of this phenomenon. In his *Hellenica*, Xenophon reports (3.1.17–19) that in 399 B.C. the Spartan Dercylidas was forced to delay his assault on the city of Cebren for four days due to unfavorable sacrifices (*hiera*), despite the fact that he was in a great hurry. Nevertheless, one of his subordinate officers, thinking that the delay was stupid, rushed

37. For various explanations, see Parker 2004: 145–46.
38. So Zucker 1900: 39–41.
39. The view of Parker (2004: 146 n. 43).

into action and found his company defeated and himself wounded. Later in the *Hellenica* (4.8.35–39) the Spartan Anaxibius contemptuously ignores unfavorable sacrifices (*hiera*), and then falls into an ambush in which he and many of his men are killed.

Xenophon is not the only author to emphasize the disaster that can befall a commander who ignores the recommendations of his seer. In 329 B.C. Alexander was eager to cross the river Tanais in order to attack the Scythian nomads who were mocking him, yet his trusted seer Aristander of Telmessus insisted that the sacrifices were not favorable even after two attempts.[40] Indeed, the omens specifically indicated that there would be "danger for Alexander." Alexander, however, was not inclined to accept this result, asserting, so we are told, that it was better to be exposed to extreme danger than to be an object of laughter to Scythians. Arrian (4.4.3) then comments: "Aristander refused to interpret the sacrifices in any way contrary to the signs from the divinity merely because Alexander wished to hear other things." Alexander crossed nonetheless, and although he defeated the Scythians, he almost died as a result of drinking tainted water. Arrian concludes his account with a statement of his own belief in divination, and one that is typical of Greek thought generally: "If Alexander had not taken ill, all of the Scythians would have perished in their flight. And Alexander himself fell into extreme danger and was carried back into the camp. In this way Aristander's act of divination (*manteia*) was fulfilled."[41]

I have called such examples "seemingly unambiguous" for a reason. For they are not as transparent as some have claimed.[42] A very subtle, perhaps largely subconscious, manipulation lies beneath these texts. Most obviously, it is very tempting to attribute military disaster, the death or wounding of a leader, or an unpopular need for delay to divine causes. This is an area where a sensitivity to literary and historiographical criticism can contribute to a more complex interpretation of Greek attitudes toward divination. Nonetheless, it is striking that there is not even the slightest hint in the *Histories* of Herodotus or in the entire corpus of Xenophon that sacrificial divination was not a valid method of ascertaining the divine will. Here again sentiments expressed in Xenophon's works, such as at *Hipparchicus* 9.8–9, are

---

40. Arr. 4.4.

41. Curtius (7.9.29) has a very different version, according to which Aristander changed his prediction on sacrificing a second time and declared "that he had never seen more favorable entrails," but this whole account is an invention of Curtius himself and reflects his own skepticism about the validity of sacrificial divination (cf. 7.7.8; 7.7.23). For Curtius's attitude toward divination in general, see Baynham 1998: 114–15, 162–63.

42. Esp. Popp 1957 and Pritchett 1979.

surely normative: "In a war, enemies plot against one another but seldom know whether these plots are well laid. It is impossible to find any other advisers in such matters except the gods. They know everything, and they give signs in advance to whomever they wish through sacrifices, birds of omen, voices, and dreams." This same notion appears also in Xenophon's *Cyropaedia*, when Cyrus's father gives this advice to him (1.6.44–46): "Learn this too from me, my son, which is the greatest thing. Never endanger either yourself or your army contrary to the sacrificial omens and the bird signs, knowing that men choose their actions by conjecture, although they have no idea at all from which of them good things will come."

Nonetheless, when one takes all of these examples together, one thing does seem to emerge. Many seers, it would seem, chose to stick to their interpretations and not be pressured either by over-eager commanders or by the situation at hand, calculating perhaps that their reputation for objective knowledge would be enhanced in the long term. Examples in Xenophon in fact show that seercraft, as in the Near East, had aspects of an exact science. As we will see in the next chapter, Xenophon makes sure that the seer Silanus does not misrepresent the omens from sacrifice. This proves that one did not simply subjectively see what one wanted to see. Xenophon did not trust this man and thus made sure that he did not purposefully give a false interpretation of the signs; for Xenophon himself knew enough about sacrificial divination to verify the results.

It was perfectly possible, however, to conduct the rites of divination in such a way as to obtain a desired result without compromising religious belief or engaging in what we would call self-conscious manipulation. This may seem counterintuitive, but a few examples will illustrate the general principle clearly enough. In 396 B.C. King Agesilaus of Sparta aborted his campaign into Phrygia when the victim lacked a lobe (Xen. *Hell.* 3.4.15).[43] Not coincidentally, on the previous day his Greek cavalry had been beaten by an equal number of Persian horse. Xenophon then says: "The day after the cavalry battle, when Agesilaus was sacrificing with a view to advancing further, the liver of the victim proved to be lacking a lobe.[44] Nevertheless,

---

43. Note also Plut. *Ages.* 9.3, with Shipley 1997: 150–51.

44. For the Greek phrase ἄλοβα γίγνεται τὰ ἱερά, both the Loeb and the Penguin translations use the plural: "the livers of the victims" lacked a lobe. This could be correct, since the word for "sacrifice/parts of the victim" (*ta hiera*) is a neuter plural and can refer either to one or to several sacrifices (note Xen. *Anab.* 6.5.2, where we are told that "the *hiera* were favorable with the first victim"). But it strikes me as much more probable that Agesilaus, inasmuch as he realized that an advance was highly problematic, sacrificed only once. When he had been given an unfavorable sign on the first attempt, he sensibly enough would have stopped there.

when this sign appeared, he turned and proceeded to the sea. Realizing that unless he acquired a cavalry force he would not be able to campaign in the plains, he decided that such a force needed to be prepared, so that it would not be necessary to fight while running away." Xenophon did not see either the procedure or the rationale as being unusual. The logic of the narrative is left implicit in the text, but the explanation would have been obvious enough to anyone who shared in the belief system of Xenophon's contemporaries: to wit, the gods did not give Agesilaus favorable omens precisely because his cavalry force was insufficient for an advance.

This attitude of Agesilaus toward divination is, in fact, similar to Alexander's reaction when his troops mutinied in 326 and refused to cross the Hyphasis River in the Punjab. According to Arrian (5.28), Alexander told his men that he would go on alone if he had to, and then spent three days sulking in his tent. This ploy, which had been successful before and would be so again, failed.[45] When the troops would not recant, "Ptolemy, the son of Lagus, tells us that he then nonetheless offered sacrifices with a view to crossing the river, but that as he sacrificed the victims proved unfavorable." Alexander then decided to turn back.

These two incidents should not be taken as evidence that either Agesilaus or Alexander was constrained by the omens from proceeding with his advance;[46] nor, at the other extreme, should we conclude that each was consciously manipulating the omens in order to save face. First of all, on both occasions, professional seers were the ones who read the entrails, even if they are invisible in our accounts. Second, there was nothing to have prevented them from sacrificing twice more on that particular day, and then, if the omens remained unfavorable, to try again on subsequent days. My point is that it was both permissible in terms of divinatory practice and convenient under the circumstances at hand to stop sacrificing and to accept the negative omens. Agesilaus knew that he could not march inland in the face of the superior Persian cavalry, and Alexander knew even better that he could not cross the Hyphasis and advance to the Ganges by himself; and thus they stopped with a negative sign. Indeed, Agesilaus received the most unfavorable sign that extispicy could reveal. It was this flexibility that makes the rites of divination so efficacious in all areas of life—social, political, and military. There is no need to posit self-conscious manipulation. The gods were not stupid; they had good strategic sense. At the same time, negative omens could be a convenient means for a commander to save face.

Nevertheless, even if belief was widespread, manipulation of omens did occur.

---

45. Arr. 5.25.3; Curt. 9.3.18–19; Plut. *Alex.* 62.3. Carney 2000 is an insightful discussion.
46. As do Popp (1957: 57 n. 62) and Pritchett (1979: 81).

Or perhaps one could say, because belief was widespread, there was something to be gained, especially at times of crisis, by fabricating or exaggerating propitious omens. Before the battle of Leuctra, according to Xenophon (*Hell.* 6.4.7), "a report came from the city to the Thebans that all of the temples had opened spontaneously and that the priestesses were saying that the gods were indicating victory. They said also that the weapons from the temple of Heracles had disappeared, indicating that Heracles had set out for the battle." But then Xenophon adds: "Some say that all of these things were contrivances of the leading men." Diodorus (15.53) says explicitly that it was the Theban general Epaminondas, a name completely missing from Xenophon's account of these events, who was responsible for this manipulation of popular belief.[47]

It is significant, I believe, that neither Diodorus nor Xenophon attributes this manipulation of religious sentiment to a seer, but rather to a general and statesman. Yet Epaminondas may not have been the only culprit. The historian Callisthenes of Olynthus recorded various prebattle omens that appeared at Sparta, Thebes, Delphi, and Dodona.[48] And Plutarch ends his account of Pelopidas's dream and the sacrifice of the filly (discussed above) by saying that Pelopidas and the seer Theocritus disclosed an account of the dream and the sacrifice throughout the camp. The animal sacrifice, the supernatural dream, the public announcement of good omens, were all part and parcel of the way in which the Greeks managed moments of crisis. I would be very hesitant to attribute all of these omens either to the invention of the historians Callisthenes and Ephorus or to the machinations of Epaminondas and Pelopidas. Given that the Theban victory over Sparta at Leuctra was both universally unexpected and epoch making in that it permanently changed the balance of power in the Greek world, it should not in the least surprise us if omens were perceived retrospectively by the parties concerned. In fact, a lack of portents and ominous signs in the tradition about the events leading up to the battle would be far more surprising than their presence.

There is, however, a famous anecdote about a seer who, obviously acting in concert with his general, did self-consciously fabricate an omen as a means to boost morale. One measure of the clever scholar is his facility in explaining away and dismissing examples that run counter to his theories. Nothing, however, should arouse

47. On this passage, see Stylianou 1998: 393. For the function of divination in the Leuctra campaign, see Trampedach 2003b: 218–34.
48. Cic. *Div.* 1.74 and 2.54 = *FGrH* 124, F 22a. Callisthenes narrated the battle of Leuctra in his *Hellenica*.

greater suspicion than the floating anecdote, especially when it is found only in late sources; for the following story is told of Agesilaus, Alexander the Great, Eumenes of Cardia, and Attalus of Pergamum.[49] In the fullest version (Polyaenus 4.20), a Chaldean seer (note that he is not a Greek, but a Babylonian) by the name of Soudinus, who was in the service of King Attalus of Pergamum, wrote the words "victory of the king" in reverse on the palm of his hand and then pressed his palm on the smooth side of the liver of the sacrificial victim.[50] This was then shown to the troops, who were greatly encouraged. Such a ploy should be taken as the exception and not the rule.

It is striking that classical sources, although they contain numerous castigations of the greed and dishonesty of seers, provide no concrete examples of this kind. But it is also striking that the troops had no trouble believing that the gods would want to write in Greek on the victim's liver, something that is also completely anomalous. Perhaps what emerges most clearly and most credibly from this story is the ability of the seer to affect the morale of the army. This story is emblematic of the seer's ability to influence morale—it should not be taken as evidence for what seers literally did to their victims.

Although no seer is mentioned as being involved, a ruse of Agathocles, the tyrant of Syracuse, bears comparison with Soudinus's alleged trick. Agathocles encouraged his army before a pitched battle with the Carthaginians in 310 B.C. by releasing a number of owls that settled on the shields and helmets of his men. According to Diodorus (20.11), the soldiers took this to be an omen of victory because the owl was considered sacred to Athena. This ploy too is without parallel. As with the story of the inscribed liver, it reveals far more about the readiness of common people to believe in the gods' willingness to send signs than it does about elite manipulation of that belief.

PARTNERSHIPS

Although the evidence is piecemeal, it does strongly suggest that generals and seers formed partnerships that might last many years. In such cases, the association between them was potentially one of intimacy. The seer served as a close adviser to the general whom he served, and their fortunes might be intimately linked. A successful partnership between seer and general is illustrated in Herodotus's account of

49. Plut. *Mor.* 214f; Frontin. *Str.* 1.11.14–15; and Polyaenus 4.20, respectively.
50. For Soudinus (or Sudines) see Barton 1994: 23.

arguably the most important battle in Greek history. As mentioned before, Tisamenus came from the Elean family of the Iamidae and won five great victories while serving Sparta.[51] Tisamenus's first and most splendid victory was the battle of Plataea in 479 B.C. If we are to believe Herodotus's account, which may well depend on Iamid family tradition, he had not previously acted as seer. If that is true, his was a most extraordinary debut. At the time of Plataea both Tisamenus and Pausanias, the Spartan commander in chief, were young and untried. The relationship between them must have resembled that of many seers and generals in archaic and classical Greece. In education, background, and interests, they can have differed but little. Both were aristocrats from two of Greece's most distinguished families, Tisamenus claiming descent from Apollo, and Pausanias, as a Heraclid, from Zeus.

The Athenian general Tolmides worked with the seer Theaenetus between 466 and 457 (Paus. 1.27.5), and their close friendship is marked by the apparent fact that Theaenetus's son was named Tolmides (Thuc. 3.20.1). Pausanias saw their statues on the Athenian acropolis, and though he does not say so explicitly, his narrative implies that Theaenetus was present on all of Tolmides' campaigns. There also seems to have been an intimate association between the Athenian Cimon and his seer Astyphilus of Poseidonia (Plut. *Cim.* 18), who accompanied Cimon on his last campaign in 451 B.C. Nicias, Plutarch tells us (*Nic.* 23.5), relied heavily on his seer Stilbides. Plutarch cites a lost dialogue by the third-century B.C. writer Pasiphon of Eretria (*Nic.* 4.2). According to this source, Nicias kept a seer at his house, whom he consulted about both public and private matters, and particularly about his silver mines at Laurium. A late source claims that Diopeithes, the well-known *chrēsmologos*, was an associate (*hetairos*) of Nicias.[52] Alcibiades seems to have employed seers in his attempt to persuade the Athenians to launch the expedition to Sicily in 415 (Plut. *Nic.* 13.1–4). And one can cautiously infer from Plutarch (*Nic.* 13.1) that during the debate in 415 concerning the Sicilian expedition both Nicias and Alcibiades used the seers in their private service to support their competing positions. Thus both for the believer in traditional religion (Nicias) and for the skeptic (Alcibiades), the testimony of oracles and religious experts was important ammunition in making their respective cases to the Athenian people.

---

51. Apart from Plataea in 479, his other victories were at Tegea in c. 473–470, at Dipaea (or Dipaeis) in c. 470–465, either at Mount Ithome or the Isthmus of Corinth (the text of Herodotus is corrupt) in the 460s, and at Tanagra in 457. See Hdt. 9.35.2 with Flower and Marincola 2002: 172–73.

52. The scholion at Ar. *Eq.* 1085.

We are not told whom Pericles took on campaign with him, but Lampon is a good candidate, given the evidence for their close association on other matters. The Spartan Lysander, as mentioned before, erected a statue at Delphi of himself standing next to Agias, his seer at the battle of Aegospotami. As also discussed earlier, Dion of Syracuse was associated with the Thessalian seer Miltas at least from 357 to 354 B.C. (Plut. *Dion* 22–27). When Timoleon undertook in the mid-360s to assassinate his brother Timophanes, who had made himself tyrant of Corinth, he chose two accomplices: one a relation, Timophanes' brother-in-law, and the other a friend, the seer Orthagoras.[53]

The evidence on this topic is fuller when we turn to Alexander the Great. One of the most persistent problems in modern scholarship on Alexander has to do with his attitude toward his own status as mortal, hero, or god. It seems beyond reasonable doubt that after his consultation of the oracle of Zeus Ammon at Siwah oasis in Egypt, or perhaps even earlier, Alexander was convinced that he was the biological son of Zeus. But being the son of a god (such as were Achilles, Sarpedon, and Perseus) did not make one a god oneself in Greek thought. The exception that proves the rule is Heracles, but even he became a god only after his death. It is likely enough, but unprovable, that Alexander believed himself to have become a god before his untimely death in 323. At any rate, certain of the Greek cities in Asia Minor had granted him divine honors in his lifetime, and there apparently was a debate in Athens over whether to recognize his godhead.[54]

Whatever Alexander felt about his own status, he depended heavily on seers throughout his entire career, and that dependency continued right up until his death. In fact, he seems to have become ever more obsessed with divination and omens of various kinds. In his *Life of Alexander* (75), Plutarch gives a vivid description of the king's disposition during his last days in Babylon: "And so Alexander, since at that time he had given in to divine signs and was confused and fearful in his mind, turned every unusual and strange occurrence, no matter how insignificant, into a portent and omen, and his palace was full of sacrificers, purifiers, and seers."

If Alexander did consider himself to be a god, this was unusual behavior. For there is not a single example in all of Greek literature of a god resorting to divination or being moved by superstitious fear. It is not our purpose, however, to spec-

53. Plut. *Tim.* 4. This incident is collaborated by three different sources, since Plutarch claims that Theopompus gave the seer's name as Satyrus, but Ephorus and Timaeus as Orthagoras.
54. The bibliography is vast, but see esp. Badian 1981; Bosworth 1988: 278–90; and Flower 1997: 258–61.

ulate about Alexander's state of mind, but merely to investigate the important role that seers played throughout his campaign. By far the most influential of those seers was Aristander of Telmessus.[55]

Aristander is, in fact, the outstanding example of the seer who can interpret any portent and has mastered every means of nonmediumistic divination. He interpreted a dream for Philip about Alexander's birth,[56] and then he served Alexander from the start of his expedition until he disappears from the historical record after 328/7 B.C. When a sweating wooden statue of Orpheus was a cause of alarm, he claimed that it was an indication that poets would have to labor hard to commemorate Alexander's achievements.[57] He interpreted a dream of Alexander's relating to the capture of Tyre, and he successfully predicted the taking of that city during the current month (Alexander wanted to assist him by adding a few days to the month, but this proved unnecessary since Tyre was indeed captured on that very day).[58] During the siege of Gaza, when a bird dropped a clod of earth on Alexander's head, he predicted that Alexander would capture the city but be wounded in the process.[59] He predicted the future prosperity of Alexandria,[60] and had no difficulty interpreting a lunar eclipse as a favorable sign.[61] Like his predecessors in the pages of Xenophon, he performed extispicy before battle—or, to be more precise, before crossing the Jaxartes River in order to engage the Scythians.[62] Not even a spring of oil at the Oxus confounded him: it portended tribulations followed by victory.[63]

After Alexander killed his friend Cleitus in a drunken rage, Aristander tried to comfort him by pointing out that the incident had been preordained.[64] In an earlier age, Aristander would have purified Alexander after the murder of Cleitus. But his role has partly been usurped by the philosophers who employ philosophical arguments as the medicine for Alexander's psychological distress, whereas Aristander would have employed rites of purification. Or did Aristander indeed do this, but our

55. See Greenwalt 1982, and for a full treatment, King 2004.
56. Plut. *Alex.* 2.3.
57. Arr. 1.11.2; Plut. *Alex.* 14.5.
58. Arr. 2.18.1 and Plut. *Alex.* 25.1–2, respectively.
59. Plut. *Alex.* 25.3–4; Arr. 2.26.4, 2.27.2; cf. Curt. 4.6.11–24 for a much elaborated version.
60. Arr. 3.2.2; Plut. *Alex.* 26.6; Curt. 4.8.6.
61. Arr. 3.7.6, 3.15.7.
62. Arr. 4.4.3–9.
63. Arr. 4.15.7–8; cf. Plut. *Alex.* 57.5.
64. Plut. *Alex.* 52.1.

sources, with their emphasis on the rival sophists Callisthenes of Olynthus and Anaxagoras of Abdera, simply do not mention it?

Our most vivid picture of Aristander and his crowning moment of glory comes at the battle of Gaugamela. Aristander and Alexander spent the night before the battle of Gaugamela sacrificing to Fear and performing secret sacred rites (Plut. *Alex.* 31.4). And then the two, king and seer together, made a striking appearance before the army (Plut. *Alex.* 33.1–2): "Alexander made a very long speech to the Thessalians and the other Greeks, and when they encouraged him with shouts to lead them against the barbarians, he shifted his spear into his left hand and with his right he called upon the gods, as Callisthenes says, praying to them, if indeed he was truly sprung from Zeus, to defend and strengthen the Greeks. The seer Aristander, wearing a white mantle (χλανίς) and a golden crown, rode along the ranks and pointed out an eagle soaring over the head of Alexander and in its flight heading straight for the enemy." It is peculiar that Aristander is wearing a *chlanis* (χλανίς), since that is usually a woman's garment. Other military seers in Greek art, as noted above, wear a helmet and carry a sword as they perform the *sphagia*. Was Aristander to have no part in the actual fighting? Was he following the conventions of his native Telmessus, a Carian city?

The fact that this incident was described by the court historian Callisthenes of Olynthus, the nephew of Aristotle, should not be a cause of skepticism, even if we are told that the troops were greatly encouraged by the appearance of the eagle. Alexander was deeply religious, but he also knew how to exploit the propaganda value of religion. He surely trusted in the abilities of his and his father's seer, but he also knew how to exploit his employment of that seer. Callisthenes, for his part, is projecting the image of Alexander that the king himself wanted disseminated throughout the Greek world and for posterity. He seems to have written up Alexander's campaign as a great Panhellenic crusade, surely with his patron's approval.[65] The eagle both confirms Alexander as son of Zeus and validates the imminent victory as god's will. In this battle, father and son will fight together against the enemy common to all Greeks.

In addition to Aristander, two other seers are mentioned by name as serving Alexander.[66] Both Aristander and Cleomantis the Lacedaemonian were ordered by Alexander to sacrifice on behalf of Cleitus in response to a portent that prefigured

---

65. See Pearson 1960: 33–38, 48; Hamilton 1969: liii–liv; Pédech 1984: 51–65; Prandi 1985; and Devine 1994: esp. 97–98.
66. See King 2004: 54–58.

his death.[67] After Aristander's death, Demophon appears as the leading seer at the court. He advised Alexander not to attack the city of the Malians,[68] and went with Ptolemy to the temple of Serapis in order to inquire after Alexander's health during his fatal illness.[69] Several incidents are recorded, however, that imply that a larger number of seers attended the expedition than just the three who happened to be named.[70] On occasion other seers, or even unnamed bystanders, interpret a phenomenon incorrectly, but Aristander alone gets it right.[71]

These anonymous seers are obviously being used as a foil to Aristander, and this smacks of being a literary motif and is perhaps attributable to the court historian Callisthenes of Olynthus. Nevertheless, I think we can accept it as a fact that Alexander had attracted a considerable number of seers who perhaps competed for his attention and favors. But no other seer, at least in the tradition that has come down to us, could fill the void caused by Aristander's death in c. 328/7.[72] Perhaps the loss of the trusted seer helps to explain some of Alexander's subsequent actions and behavior, both in terms of his military strategy and of his increased obsession with superstition. One suspects, but alas cannot prove, that Alexander relied heavily on Aristander psychologically and that his death removed a stabilizing factor in his life. If this is true, then his relationship with Aristander would be analogous to that of Nicias with Stilbides.[73]

It is worth stressing that for earlier periods as well our sources seem to indicate that more than one seer might be present with an army, and not only if that army was composed of contingents from various cities. Nor was Alexander the only person of eminence to have seers in his personal retinue. Polycrates of Samos had several at his court who attempted to dissuade him from accepting an invitation to meet the Persian governor Oroetes at Magnesia in c. 522 B.C. (Hdt. 3.124). He took one

67. Plut. *Alex.* 50.3.

68. Curt. 9.4.27–29; Diod. 17.98.3–5.

69. Arr. 7.26.2.

70. Arr. 3.2.2 and 4.15.7–8; Plut. *Alex.* 24.5, 26.6, and 57.5.

71. Arr. 1.11.2 and Plut. *Alex.* 2.3 (at the court of Philip II). Aristander alone understands the proper meaning of an omen at Plut. *Alex.* 14.5. Bystanders do not accept his prediction at Plut. *Alex.* 25.1–2.

72. Aristander disappears from the historical record after the death of Cleitus in 328 (except for a story told by Aelian, who is notoriously unreliable, at *VH* 12.64), and most scholars assume that he died c. 327. King (2004: 52–54, 231), however, suggests that he had a falling out with Alexander as a result of their disagreement about crossing the Jaxartes (Tanais) when the sacrifices were unfavorable.

73. See Plut. *Nic.* 23.5–6.

of these seers with him on that fatal trip, a man who was later delivered from his captivity at Susa by the Greek doctor Democedes of Croton (Hdt. 3.132). So too Pelopidas before the battle of Leuctra communicated a dream to the seers in his camp (Plut. *Pelop.* 21), and Timoleon took seers with him when he set sail for Sicily (Plut. *Tim.* 8). Indeed, a variety of sources indicate that numerous seers were to be found in armies, in cities, and in the households of the great. Aeschylus seems to imagine that "prophets" (*prophētai*) and "dream interpreters" were a regular component of a king's household (*Ag.* 409; *Cho.* 32–41), and a century later we still hear of the seers who served the tyrant Dionysius II of Syracuse (Plut. *Dion* 24).

In the next chapter I will discuss a very important passage of Xenophon's *Anabasis,* in which he says (6.4.12–16): "The generals were sacrificing, and the seer was Arexion the Arcadian (for Silanus the Ambraciot had already run away, having hired a boat from Heracleia)." The implication is that Silanus was the chief seer on this expedition and, had he still been present, would have been the one to conduct this sacrifice; but because he was not present, another seer stepped in. Likewise, the principal seer serving Mardonius at Plataea was Hegesistratus of Elis, but his Greek allies had their own seer in addition, Hippomachus of Leucas. And there is that famous passage of Thucydides in which the seers advise Nicias to wait twenty-seven days before leaving Syracuse. If we put that passage together with Plutarch's account, we might infer that Stilbides' opinion would have been decisive had he still been alive.[74] Common sense dictates that more than one seer be present on an expedition in case the general's favorite grew ill or was killed in battle. Moreover, that passage of Xenophon cited above (and quoted more fully in chapter 5) suggests that a number of experienced seers might be present in an army, ready to step forward just in case the opportunity arose.

When more than one seer, indeed several seers, were present on a campaign, how did that affect the dynamic between seer and client? Although Alexander's expedition provides the clearest examples, it is possible, on occasion, to infer competition between seers in other contexts as well. Might this perspective yield a new way of looking at some otherwise familiar incidents?

A political explanation is usually given for the actions of the Boeotarchs (the chief officers of the Boeotian Confederacy) in disrupting the sacrifice of Agesilaus at Aulis in 396 B.C.[75] Agesilaus was en route to Asia Minor ostensibly in an attempt to free the Greeks of Asia from Persian control, but in reality to impose Spartan con-

74. See the discussion in chapter 4.
75. On this episode, see Hamilton 1969: 30–32 and Shipley 1997: 124–28.

trol there; and that was something that the Thebans, as well as the Athenians and Corinthians, strongly opposed. The act of sacrificing at Aulis, as had Agamemnon before him, obviously had significant symbolic capital in terms of Panhellenic ideology. It is obvious too that the Thebans in particular would not have wanted Agesilaus to profit politically from what would we call a publicity stunt. But perhaps there was a supplementary explanation for their objections at the personal and religious level. Xenophon gives a very succinct narrative of what happened, merely saying that when the Boeotarchs discovered that Agesilaus was sacrificing, they sent horsemen who threw his victims from the altar (*Hell*. 3.4.3—4).

Plutarch (*Ages*. 6), in a much fuller account, provides the detail that shows that Agesilaus was technically in the wrong. Although it was the right of the seer appointed by the Boeotians to perform the sacrifices there, Agesilaus employed his own seer, thus transgressing the laws and customs of the Boeotians. Even if the Thebans had not been opposed to Agesilaus's expedition on political grounds, fearing as they did the expansion of Spartan power in Asia Minor, the local seer could hardly have endured this insult to his honor and prerogatives. And there may have been a religious consideration as well. Would anyone but the shrine's designated *mantis* have the requisite knowledge of local ritual to ensure that the sacrifice was performed in a way pleasing to the deity?

When the general won a victory, the seer shared in the credit. As discussed previously, this was true to an extent greater than one would imagine to have been the case. But it is not so clear that he also took some responsibility for a defeat. As long as he merely indicated that the gods gave approval for battle or for a particular course of action, then the responsibility for defeat lay with the general alone. And thus it might well have been the case that a seer's reputation could survive a major defeat that permanently destroyed the career of the general whom he served, and that realization might also have increased whatever tensions may have existed between the two. Yet there were dangers in this line of occupation, especially insofar as death in battle for the seer was a real possibility.

A DANGEROUS PROFESSION

The archetypal seer who foresaw his own death and yet determined to fight anyway was Amphiaraus. Even though he could foresee that the expedition against Thebes would end in his own death, he was compelled by the deception of his wife to participate (Hom. *Od*. 15.244—47). As Aeschylus has him say (*Sept*. 587—89): "I for my part shall fatten the soil of this country, a seer covered over by an enemy land. Let us fight. I expect a not dishonorable death." No Greek could have been unfamiliar with the story of Amphiaraus's death, first told perhaps in the epic *Thebaid* (*EGF* F 9), that as he was fleeing from Thebes in his chariot, Zeus, with a clap of thunder, caused the earth to open beneath him and to swallow him up. That spot was still pointed to in Pausanias's day (1.134.1–2), and there was a famous and much-consulted oracle of Amphiaraus at Oropus where the method of consultation was by incubation.[76]

Amphiaraus proved to be a fitting mythical paradigm for later seers who went into battle in full knowledge that they might perish in the fighting. In this respect as in others life imitated art. Megistias chose to stay and perish with his Spartan employers at Thermopylae (Hdt. 7.221, 228). Herodotus relates that during the night before the final struggle, before any other information had been received, "the seer Megistias, having looked into the entrails (*hiera*), proclaimed the death that would come for them at dawn" (7.219). Hegesistratus, who had been Mardonius's seer at Plataea in 479, at some later date was captured by the Spartans while he was serving as a seer on the island of Zacynthus. He had once before escaped execution by the Spartans, but this time they managed to kill him (Hdt. 9.37–39). From Athens we have a casualty list of the Erechtheid tribe from 460 or 459 B.C. that lists the seer Telenikos among the dead (two generals also fell in that season's fighting).[77] A casualty list from Argos of about 400 B.C. lists the name of a seer prominently near the top of the inscription.[78] Indeed, this Argive inscription, perhaps more than any other piece of material evidence, testifies to the public recognition of the seer's importance. Underneath the heading "The following died," four individuals were listed by office in a single column in a prominent position at the top of the stone, whereas below these names everyone else was listed by phratry in four columns. Although the names are missing, the titles have survived: *probasileus* (a magistrate who acted in place of a king), seer, general, and, last of all, priest. If these are listed in order of importance, the implication is that being a seer, at least for the Argives, was more important than being a general or a priest.

Lysander's seer fell with him before the walls of Haliartus in Boeotia in 395 B.C. (Plut. *Lys.* 28.5). And the Athenian seer who took the omens for the democrats who fought the Thirty at Munychia in 404 accurately predicted that he would be the first to die in the battle (Xen. *Hell.* 2.4.18). Since a seer performed the *sphagia* in full view

76. In general, see Schachter 1981: 19–26.
77. ML 33 = Fornara 78.
78. *SEG* 29.361.

of the army in the moments before the opposing armies engaged, he was perhaps close to the front when the actual fighting began. Indeed, Thucydides (6.69.2) refers to the seers "bringing forward the customary sacrifices" after the skirmishing of light-armed troops had already begun. This was a dangerous position to be in, and it is no wonder that the "model" seers both of myth and of real life were described as being "good with the spear."

Dangers and pressures aside, individuals were willing to undertake this line of work because the rewards for success could be extremely high. Cyrus the Younger gave his seer Silanus three thousand gold darics, or ten talents, because he had accurately predicted that the King would not fight within the previous ten days (*Anab.* 1.7.18). The Iamid seer Callias assisted Croton in its war with Sybaris in 510 and was richly rewarded with select estates (Hdt. 5.44–45). Mardonius paid a high price for the Elean seer Hegesistratus who served him at Plataea in 479 (Hdt. 9.38). If Deiphonus was contracting work throughout Greece, he must have been making huge sums of money (Hdt. 9.95). Isocrates claims that Thrasyllus, a native of the small island of Siphnos, inherited books on divination from his guest-friend, the childless seer Polemaenetus. He then taught himself the art of divination, became a wandering seer, left illegitimate children throughout the Greek world, and acquired so great a fortune that when he retired to Siphnos he was the wealthiest of the citizens and married into the island's most respected family (*Aeginet.* 19.5–9). If one measures success in terms of wealth and prestige, the rewards were well worth the risks. It would be wrong to give the impression, however, that most of those who turned to divination as a livelihood necessarily became wealthy. It is all too easy to be misled by the success stories. In most professions there are a number of very highly paid and much-sought-after individuals at the upper end of the market.

An Athenian by the name of Lysimachus, who was the grandson of the famous fifth-century Athenian statesman Aristides, was a very poor man who made his living by working a dream-interpreting tablet (Plut. *Arist.* 27.3, citing Demetrius of Phalerum who knew him). Such perhaps was the fate of most would-be diviners, even if dream interpretation was the least esteemed of the mantic arts. It also seems that if one wanted to hire a seer, that is just any seer, it was easy enough to find one. Xenophon (*Anab.* 7.1.33–41) relates that when the Ten Thousand were in Byzantium they were approached by a Theban named Coeratadas, "who was traveling about not as an exile from Greece, but desiring to be a general and advertising himself in case some city or people should be in need of a general." He indeed persuaded the Ten Thousand to make him their general and came to an agreement with them that he would appear on the next day having "sacrificial victims, a seer, and food and drink for the army." As it turned out, he could provide neither favorable omens from sacrifice nor enough food even for a single day, and so "he went away, taking his victims and renouncing his generalship." There is a lot worth commenting on in this passage, but the procurement of victims and a seer is what concerns us here.[79] Did he get these in Byzantium? Aristotle (*Oec.* 1346b) claims that the people of Byzantium, being short of funds, place a one-third tax on the income of wonder-workers, seers, and the sellers of drugs. It is hard to tell whether this indicates that such individuals were making a good living or were targeted as undesirables. In any case, Coeratadas could probably have hired a seer in Byzantium without too much difficulty. The point is that if one wanted to hire the best possible seer, an Iamid for instance, the cost might be very high indeed, and the supply was undoubtedly limited.

I am going to end this chapter in an unusual way, or at least with an unusual story. The third-century B.C. poet Rhianus, who came from Bene in Crete, wrote an epic poem with the title *Messeniaca* on the Second Messenian War. The poem is no longer extant, but it apparently formed the basis of Pausanias's account of the Second Messenian War of c. 650 B.C. (4.16–23), or at least Pausanias claims it as his source (4.6.1–3). This poem had no value as political history.[80] At best, Rhianus took a bare outline of events from the fourth-century historians Callisthenes of Olynthus and Ephorus of Cyme, who themselves could have had little authentic information about the history of Messenia in the seventh century. Rhianus's story, as retold by Pausanias, is interesting because of the prominent role given to seers. Even if the whole poem is pure literary invention, it is interesting what kinds of things Rhianus has his seers doing. It is not what one finds in Homer, and for that reason I want to suggest that Rhianus gives his seers the kinds of roles and functions that he thought that they would have had in the seventh century, and that, in turn, is based on the roles that he knew them actually to have had in the classical period. Rhianus and the other "inventors" of early Messenian history were creating a pseudohistory that was meant to be credible as history: the gods do not intervene as they do in Homeric epic, and the setting is not the age of heroes, but within what most Greeks (including Ephorus) considered to be the historical period. And so what do we find the seers doing?

The seer on the Lacedaemonian side is Hecas, while the Messenians were served by Theoclus and his son Manticlus, who were members of the mantic family of the

79. See further Parker 2004: 142–43.
80. See Pearson 1962 and Figueira 1999: 226–27.

Iamidae. Hecas and Theoclus sacrifice before battle (4.16.1), which is what one would expect in real life, even if it is never found in Homer. But then things become interesting. Theoclus has supranormal vision: he warns the Messenian leader Aristomenes not to pursue the enemy beyond a pear tree in the plain, because the Dioscuri were sitting on it (4.16.4). He accurately interprets a riddling Delphic oracle pertaining to the eventual defeat of the Messenians (4.20.3). He and his son Manticlus have a role in leading the troops; in fact, Theoclus seems to be second in command of the whole army. He ends his life by plunging into the ranks of the Lacedaemonians (4.21.2–12). And after the Messenians are finally defeated, Manticlus becomes the cofounder of a colony in Sicily (the refoundation of Zancle as Messene), where he founds the temple of Heracles Manticlus (4.23.2–9).

Hecas, for his part, interprets an omen, devises the strategy that leads to the defeat of the Messenians, and gives orders to the Lacedaemonian army (4.21.7–12). In effect, the seers do more than just sacrifice and interpret signs of various kinds; they take an active part in devising strategy and leading the troops into battle. This portrait is idealized to be sure, but (as we have seen) there are parallels for each of these functions in historical texts, whereas no previous work of Greek poetry had given seers such authoritative and varied roles. Rhianus has simply put all of the known historical roles together, and in so doing he reveals what a Greek of the third century B.C. thought that a seer of heroic status was capable of.

> When the seer Eucleides saw the omens from sacrifice,
> he said that he was persuaded that Xenophon did
> not have any money. "But I know," he said, "that
> even if money should ever be about to come to you,
> some obstacle always appears—if nothing else, your
> own self."
>
> XENOPHON, *Anabasis*

The seer Eucleides obviously felt comfortable enough with his client to deliver a pretty blunt judgment. How did seers and clients usually interact? Were there established modes of conduct and etiquette? To what degree did a successful divinatory session depend on having a thorough knowledge of one's client's particular problems and the social context of those problems? Let me begin with a brief summary of how I think that a seer performed the ritual of sacrificial divination, and then I will attempt to answer these questions.

The seer, in a white tunic and wearing a garland, would place one or more victims near the altar. He would then utter a prayer and direct a question to a specific divinity, such as Zeus the King or Heracles the Leader. After slaying the victim (with or without an attendant to assist), he would remove the entrails and examine the liver. The liver was the palette on which the gods encoded their messages. The seer would have learned the art of reading, or decoding, this message, which was written in the symbolic system used by the gods, as an apprentice to a master, perhaps supplemented in the later classical period by book learning.

The Greek seer did not have access to the great libraries and omen collections of the ancient Near East, but this does not mean that there were no rules to his art, or that it was entirely based on subjective free association. Unwritten and orally transmitted codes and symbolic systems can be quite complex. Indeed, "social anthropology has amply demonstrated that extraordinary feats of classification and manipulation of symbols in highly complex interlocking systems are also very common, even in societies which are much less sophisticated than were those in ancient Mesopotamia."[1] One's client, or other interested parties, might look on and ask to see the liver, but interpretation was not, as it can be in some societies, a communal undertaking.[2] Finally, I want to stress something that has already been argued in earlier chapters. Extispicy was no empty, mundane ritual, but a high-stakes performance before an audience of mortals and gods, in which success could bring the seer fame, high status, and great wealth.

We actually have very little direct information about how the seer and his client might interact and negotiate both a suitable interpretation of signs and a response to those signs. Apart from merely declaring that a sacrifice or omen was favorable or unfavorable, a seer often must have given some advice and guidance. This process of negotiation might have been nuanced and subtle. Yet the scanty evidence at our disposal, however fragmentary and elusive it may be, can be put into a fruitful interpretative context and fleshed out for its implications by turning to the discipline of social anthropology.

Recent work in the field of anthropology has revealed several different aspects of divination. On the one hand, it is a form of ritual, "a formal procedure that trained practitioners follow in order to provide clients with advice or help for solving what might be or become a problem."[3] This ritual aspect of divination lays emphasis on the traditional nature of what the seer says and does. That is, during a consultation the seer follows a traditionally prescribed pattern of verbal and physical action. On the other hand, divination not only was a form of ritual; it was also a performance.[4] This realization, of course, should elicit no surprise, since public ritual is by its very nature performative.[5] Divination is merely a particular kind of ritual performance.

Every seer seeks to establish a special relationship or rapport with his clients and to persuade those clients of his expertise. If every diviner acted like every other,

---

1. Cryer 1994: 199.

2. Such as among the Me'en ethnic group of southwestern Ethiopia (Abbink 1993: 722): "Although acknowledged experts take the lead in interpreting the entrails, they cannot claim any firm authority on the basis of their expertise. Instead, they let the inferential process run its course."

3. Hallen 2000: 168. For case studies, see Bascom 1969 and Devisch 1993.

4. See Drewal 1991, 1992, 1994; and Peek 1991a. Fortes (1987: 15) says of divination among the Tallensi: "A divining session follows a set procedure. It is a dramatic dialogue in speech, gesture and expression with the use of a specialized but not esoteric vocabulary."

5. See Rappaport 1979: 175–76 and Tambiah 1979.

there would be no means of distinguishing oneself, of setting oneself apart as having a special gift or skill. Thus individuality, creativity, and flexibility are also important aspects of the seer's craft. Finally, in addition to the ritual and performative aspects of divination, there is one other dimension that should not be overlooked: "the intellectual prowess of the diviner."[6] The seer practiced a traditional craft, but he practiced it successfully by applying his intelligence to the situation at hand and by putting on a performance that served to establish confidence in his abilities and skills.

In sum, when a seer conducts a rite of divination there are three major components to his activity: he is engaged in a ritual activity, he is acting out a performance, and he is employing his ingenuity and intelligence. All three of these facets—ritual, performance, and intelligence—are evident in the case studies that can be extracted from our ancient sources.

Greek society demanded that experts in all fields repeatedly and publicly demonstrate their expertise.[7] It is characteristic of the performance culture of ancient Greece that even physicians found it necessary to put on a performance, often a public one before patients and their families and friends, and had to persuade patients of their competence in competition not only with magical healers, but with other physicians. What has been said of the physician was equally true of the seer: "In the performance of his art, the physician was always on stage."[8] The performance of both medicine and divination was a type of public spectacle.

The role of performance and intelligence in a seer's activity comes out in a story told by Xenophon, in what is indeed the first appearance of divination in the *Anabasis* (1.7.18). Xenophon tells us that Cyrus was marching with his entire army in battle order because "he believed that the King would fight on this day." When the King did not appear, "Cyrus summoned the Ambraciot seer Silanus and gave him three thousand gold darics, because when sacrificing eleven days previously, he had said to him that the King would not fight within ten days. Cyrus had said: 'Then he shall not fight at all if he shall not fight within these days. If you should prove to

6. Hallen 2000: 169.

7. On the importance of performance in democratic Athens, see the collection of essays in Goldhill and Osborne 1999 (and esp. the contribution of Jameson on Athenian religion). But note too the shrewd observations of Pelling (2005: 83): "What, anyway, is 'performance,' and where does it stop? Most of our behaviour is ritualized in some way; most of it plays up to, or plays off, roles that are expected or constructed. It is all too easy for these categories to broaden in such a way that they are drained of interpretative value."

8. Jouanna 1999: 75–85.

be speaking the truth, I promise you ten talents.' At that time he gave him the gold, since the ten days had passed."

Why did Silanus predict that ten days would pass without a battle? Because Xenophon, in order to heighten the dramatic effect, reports his prediction at the time it was fulfilled, rather than at the time it was made, the reader is left to guess the original context. That context was probably the campground sacrifice, which would have taken place as Cyrus's army was breaking camp for the day's march. All that Silanus need have said was that the signs were propitious for marching out, or, more boldly, that the King would not fight on that particular day. Obviously, he took a gamble of sorts and told Cyrus what he thought that the prince wanted to hear. And this gamble paid off extremely handsomely: ten talents was a huge fortune, making Silanus the equivalent of a millionaire in today's world. The gamble, if we can call it that, was not irrational. There was a good chance that the King would withdraw to Persia in order to muster a larger army and that Cyrus would proceed unchallenged to Babylon.[9]

A successful performance, enacted with intelligence and creativity, must not be taken as an indication of cynical manipulation of the signs by the seer. The seer was far more concerned with maintaining his own position by playing a positive role in the community than he was to take advantage of the presumed gullibility of his clients for his own personal advantage.[10] In any case, to explain the actions of seers in terms of a self-serving conscious manipulation, either of their own devising or at the behest of their commanders, is far too simplistic and grossly misconstrues the function of divination in Greek society. In fact, there is absolutely no warrant to doubt the sincerity of the Greek seer, any more than of the shaman in contemporary societies that practice shamanism. Being a self-aware performer is in no way inconsistent with sincerity: indeed, modern ethnographic studies have demonstrated that among shamans even "a charlatan may come to actually believe in the magical powers attributed to him by the audience, and to take his powers seriously."[11]

We cannot recover the actual psychological processes by which a Greek seer inspected and interpreted the omens, and it is certainly the case that almost all methods of divination are open to manipulation, whether conscious or unconscious, on the part of the diviner.[12] The degree of such manipulation will of course vary from

9. See Plut. *Arta.* 7.
10. For this as a valid observation cross-culturally, see Sweek 2002: 45.
11. Lindholm 1990: 210 n. 6. See also Nordland 1962 for American Indian shamans who have become Christians and yet still insist on the reality of their shamanistic experiences.
12. See Collins 1978: 237.

one individual to another and will be conditioned by the nature of the divinatory procedures that are employed. But we can say that the Greek seer represented himself as divining by virtue of his art and by aid of his innate prophetic gifts. When the seer sacrificed the victim and then interpreted the entrails, he was engaged in a public performance before an audience of mortals and of gods; both his immediate success and his prospects for future employment depended on how well and how convincingly he played his role as expounder of the divine will.[13] His value to society as the practitioner of a socially useful craft in turn depended on his human audience's faith in his ability properly to interpret the signs sent by the gods.[14] There was always the potential, however, for an additional aspect to this interaction. When members of the audience, such as Xenophon, know enough about divination to act as a check on the seer's interpretation, then they become participants in the rite as well as mere witnesses.

To talk of manipulation, moreover, is to seriously misunderstand the role of the diviner in the act of divination. If divination is to be socially useful, if it is to assist the client to resolve his or her particular problems, and, more generally, if it is to assist in relieving social conflicts in the wider community, then the diviner must be aware of the social context of the questions submitted to divination. It is not enough simply to ask a question, and then to expect a diviner to be able to answer it. Should I join the expedition? Should I marry this particular woman? Should I buy a house in the city or in the country? Should I enter into this business arrangement? In order to answer these and similar queries, the seer must have social knowledge about his client. In other words, for the diviner to do his job properly he needs to know not only his client's particular problem, but also the social context for that problem. As one anthropologist has succinctly stated this state of affairs, "the possible interpretations of a given situation are limited, not by the formal properties of the oracle or the meanings assigned to individual combinations but by the diviner's ability to con-

13. I disagree with Jameson (1999: 323), who asserts that the performance of sacrifice in divination requires witnesses rather than an audience.

14. For the social function of divination, see Park 1963 and the important collection of articles in Peek 1991a. For the performative aspects, see also LaGamma 2000 and Pemberton 2000. Zeitlyn (1990: 659–60) criticizes the sociological analyses of Park (1963), who treats divination as a procedure for legitimating decisions, and Beattie (1964), who sees it as a procedure for providing therapeutic benefits to the consultants. Such emphases on the social consequences of divination, while valid and illuminating in my opinion, omit an equally important subject (as pointed out by Zeitlyn): the interaction between diviner and client as well as that between diviner and different methods of divination.

struct his answers in response to typical problems and solutions."[15] So when, for instance, the seer examines the entrails before battle, for him to divine successfully and meaningfully, he needs to have an understanding both of the general strategic situation and of his general's particular concerns. It is a misnomer, and a misunderstanding of the essential nature of the divinatory act, for us to deride that as conscious manipulation.

It is possible to demonstrate this point by turning once again to Xenophon's interaction with the seer Silanus in the *Anabasis* (5.6.15–19, 28–30). When the Ten Thousand were near Sinope on the Black Sea, Xenophon conceived the idea of founding a colony.[16] But before mentioning this possibility to the soldiers, he decided to sacrifice first. Xenophon, however, apparently did not feel competent to perform this sacrifice himself. Rather, he summoned Silanus to do it for him. This had an unintended consequence. Silanus did not want Xenophon's plan to succeed, because he desperately wanted to get back to Greece with the three thousand darics that he had been given by Cyrus. So he leaked Xenophon's scheme to the army, adding that Xenophon wanted to acquire a great name and power for himself, and not surprisingly that got Xenophon into a great deal of trouble.

Why did not Silanus save himself, and everyone else, a great deal of time and trouble, by simply telling Xenophon that the omens were unfavorable for discussing a colony? If the observation of sacrificial signs is a purely subjective business, Silanus certainly was motivated to read them in a negative way. When Xenophon explained himself to the army, we are given the reason why Silanus had been unable to lie. According to Xenopon (*Anab.* 5.6.29), "Silanus the seer responded with respect to the most important point that the omens from sacrifice were favorable. For he knew that I too was not inexperienced on account of my always being present at sacrifices. But he said that treachery and a plot against me appeared in the omens, since he indeed knew that he himself was plotting to slander me to you."

This is a good example of what can happen when seer and client have conflicting interests, even if the seer understands the social context of his client's question. Silanus knew all too well what was at stake, but instead of lying he told the truth. There was indeed treachery and a plot against Xenophon, devised by Silanus himself. It is also highly ironic that Silanus went on to fulfill his own prophecy; or, rather, he successfully predicted his own actions. If we wish to rationalize this incident, it is easy enough to conjecture that he was trying to frighten Xenophon into

15. Jules-Rosette 1978: 556–57. For another example, see Lienhardt 1961: 68–69.
16. See Malkin 1987: 102–3 on this episode.

abandoning his scheme; but that is not the way that Xenophon, the insider in this system of belief, presents the situation. Rather, Silanus is depicted as being simultaneously a very bad man and a very good seer.

A spectacular example of a self-conscious theatricality in combination with a perhaps unconscious manipulation is found in an incident recorded by Xenophon in his *Hellenica* (2.4.18–19). Thrasybulus, who was in command of the Athenian democrats who had seized Munychia in Piraeus, had just finished addressing his troops. But instead of attacking the forces of the Thirty, he made no move. Why did he hesitate? Xenophon explains:

> For the seer had ordered them not to attack until one of their own number had either been killed or wounded. He had said: 'When this happens, we shall lead the way, and there will be victory for you who follow, but for me, as I think, death.' And he did not speak falsely. But when they took up their arms, just as if he was being led on by a certain fate, he was the first to spring forward, and, falling upon the enemy, he was killed. He is buried at the ford of the Cephisus River.

Xenophon himself seems uncertain as to why this seer sacrificed himself in this way. Had he planned it all in advance, or did he succumb to a sudden impulse to charge the enemy? If the whole thing was staged in the sense that he had purposefully set out to stage his own death and thus fulfill his own prophecy, it was an act that could only be performed once. The reward was a prominent burial (at public expense, one wonders?) and remembrance of his deed, if not of his name. For some reason Xenophon chose not to record his name for posterity.

There was probably a difference in how a seer interacted with his employer when meeting in private and before an audience of spectators. This difference comes out very clearly in Plutarch's account of the seer Miltas, who had studied at Plato's Academy. As discussed previously, an eclipse of the moon took place just before Dion's expedition to Sicily in 357 B.C. was about to set sail, an expedition that was intended to overthrow Dionysius II, tyrant of Syracuse. According to Plutarch (*Dion* 24), Dion and his friends understood that eclipses were caused by the earth's shadow falling on the moon; but since the soldiers were greatly disturbed, Miltas stood in their midst and encouraged them, interpreting the eclipse as a favorable sign sent by god. But he also had something to say to Dion and his inner circle in private, something not meant for the common soldiers to hear: "As for the bees that were seen settling in swarms on the sterns of Dion's ships, he indicated in private to Dion and his friends that he was afraid that Dion's undertakings would prove to be successful, but after flowering for a short time, would wither away." If this story is true, and there is no *prima facie* reason to reject it, Miltas's interpretation nicely mirrors the anxieties that Dion must have been feeling and that indeed proved justified. After initial success, he was assassinated, and Dionysius II returned to power as tyrant of Syracuse.

One way in which divination works is by discovering a correspondence between a client's immediate problem and something unusual or difficult in that client's social environment. In a case of this kind, the seer's task is to discover, explain, and predict the structure of this correspondence. Obviously, if diviner and client do not share a basic social knowledge, then a correspondence cannot be found, and divination cannot offer a resolution to the client's current difficulties. The anthropologist James Fernandez describes his own consultation in 1965 of a Zulu whistling diviner about the health of his ailing father.[17] At the time he felt that she did not offer him a satisfactory divination (her advice, that he should endeavor to be in better contact with his father, seemed rather obvious). It was only later that he came to the realization that "the whistling diviner was suddenly confronted with a member of another culture about whom neither she nor her method could presume very much and who otherwise offered little information to go on in the framing of questions."

Fernandez subsequently had much more success with Zulu dream diviners because they had got to know him over a matter of months, and that gave them considerable contextual knowledge of him and his situation. They also had the advantage of using a method of divination that gave greater scope for interpretation, inasmuch as they had his dream to work with. After he related his dream in which he saw his father waving to him from a window, they counseled him to phone his father in America (advice that he found disappointing at the time), since they had "divined" his own suppressed worries. But at that time he did not appreciate their insight "into the human condition" and his place in it. His own unexamined positivist attitudes had prejudiced his perceptions: "While I was, I think, listening carefully to the discourse in other arenas of African religious life, for some reason I conceived of divination as an arena of rather mechanical, probably fraudulent, communication between gods and men and between diviners and clients. I focused on the recommendations contained in the divination and not on the complexities of the communication itself."

A skilled seer, by eliciting the necessary information from his client, is able to

---

17. See Fernandez 1991: 213–15.

establish a social context for the specific problem at hand and thus to discover the appropriate correspondence. "He asks the client himself to diagnose the problem by presenting all of the likely variables and the context of their appearance in his daily life. The diviner then establishes a new context of explanation drawn from the descriptions and synthesized by the immediate social context in which they appear: the divining séance."[18]

An example of how this dynamic between seer and client worked in the social context of classical Greece appears near the end of Xenophon's *Anabasis*. It is worth quoting this passage in full, since it is perhaps the most detailed and vivid scene that we possess of a "historical" (that is, nonpoetic) consultation between a seer and his client (7.8.1–6):

> From there they sailed into Lampsacus, and Eucleides, a Phliasian seer, the son of the Cleagoras who had painted the inner walls in the Lyceum, encounters Xenophon. He was delighted that Xenophon had returned safely, and he asked him how much gold he had. But Xenophon told him on oath that he would not have sufficient travel money for the journey home if he did not sell his horse and his personal belongings. Eucleides did not believe him. But when the people of Lampsacus sent gifts of hospitality to Xenophon and he was sacrificing to Apollo, he had Eucleides stand next to him. When Eucleides saw the *hiera* (omens/entrails), he said that he was persuaded that he did not have any money. "But I know," he said, "that even if money should ever be about to come to you, some obstacle always appears—if nothing else, your own self." Xenophon agreed with this. Then Eucleides said: "Zeus Meilichios is an obstacle to you," and he asked him if he had already sacrificed to him, "just as at home," he said, "I used to sacrifice for you and offer whole victims." But Xenophon said that he had not sacrificed to this god from the time when he had left home. And so Eucleides advised him to sacrifice just as he was accustomed, and he said that it would turn out for the better. On the next day Xenophon, having gone to Ophrynium, sacrificed and burnt whole pigs in the way that was customary for his family, and he obtained good omens. And on this day Bion and Nausicleides arrive for the purpose of giving money to the army, and they are entertained by Xenophon. They redeemed and gave back to him the horse that he had sold in Lampsacus for fifty darics, suspecting that he had sold it because of need, since they heard that he took pleasure in the horse. And they were not willing to be reimbursed for its price.

18. Jules-Rosette 1978: 557.

Now this passage, it must be conceded, is not completely transparent, since the author has an apologetic purpose for inserting it at this point in his narrative. In the preceding narrative Xenophon had delivered a lengthy speech to the Thracian king Seuthes, refuting the charge of his own soldiers that he had received money and gifts from Seuthes while his own men had not been paid in full for their services (7.7.37–47). In this scene Xenophon proves his innocence by providing a divine validation of his claims. But the fact that it was convenient and rhetorically useful for Xenophon to place this incident near the end of the *Anabasis* does not mean that he invented it. And even if he has shaped the scene in a certain way in order to prove a particular point, the depiction of his interaction with his seer is intended to be plausible to his contemporary audience. In other words, his intended audience was meant to recognize this scene as being not untypical of how a seer and his client might interact.

Eucleides had not seen Xenophon since he had set out on Cyrus's expedition, some two years earlier, in 401. The seer had assumed, it seems, that Xenophon would have made a great deal of money in the course of his adventure, and at first he was incredulous that Xenophon was now so destitute that he would have to sell his horse and personal possessions in order to afford the trip home to Athens. Eucleides was now so far removed from Xenophon's social environment and circumstances that he could no longer relate to his former client's problems. When he came to realize that Xenophon actually was destitute, he then needed to discover a correspondence between the problem (Xenophon's poverty) and something unusual in Xenophon's social environment. The correspondence that he hit upon was not between his poverty and some aspect of the circumstances of Xenophon's recent employment, but between his poverty and a ritual fault—that is, his failure to sacrifice to Zeus Meilichios.

The crucial feature of this correspondence is that the seer has made the connection on the basis of his own social knowledge about Xenophon. He knew that Xenophon used to sacrifice to this particular manifestation of Zeus when back at home, and thus it was natural to attribute his current financial distress to his failure to sacrifice to this deity. Since Xenophon assumes that his readers understand Greek cult, he understandably leaves it unsaid that Zeus Meilichios was Zeus in his capacity as the gracious and gentle recipient of propitiatory sacrifices. That Eucleides had correctly diagnosed the cause of Xenophon's troubles was verified on the very next day when he was able to retrieve what must have been his most valuable and prized possession, the horse that he had been forced to sell for the fabulous sum of fifty gold darics.

An excellent example of the resilience of prophecy to refutation is the story with which Xenophon chooses to end his *Anabasis* (7.8.8–23*)*. Xenophon quite obviously, and innocently I think, gives this incident as an exemplum of the truth of divination. Yet a modern reader, with a different perspective and worldview, might be more inclined to read it, against Xenophon, as a demonstration of the falsehood of divination. While at Pergamum, Xenophon was given information that if he acted quickly he could capture a wealthy Persian with his family and possessions. As he always did in such circumstances, "Xenophon sacrificed, and Basias, the Elean seer who was present, said that the omens were especially favorable for him and that the man was easy to capture." It indeed did turn out, after a narrow escape in which nearly half of his six hundred troops were wounded, that the Persian, his family, and possessions were captured. Xenophon ends the account with these simple words: "And in this way the previous omens came to pass."

The *Anabasis* itself, moreover, neatly ends with a sentiment that brings the narrative full circle to Xenophon's initial encounter with the seer Eucleides. After they had returned to Pergamum with the Persian and his possessions, we are told: "There [in Pergamum] Xenophon greeted the god [i.e., hailed him as truly Meilichios, or "gracious"]. For the Laconians, the company commanders, the other generals, and the soldiers cooperated so that he could take the pick of the plunder—horses and oxen and the other things. Consequently, he was now capable even of assisting someone else." So what would appear to a modern reader as a dangerous and nearly fatal adventure that turned out successfully despite heavy casualties was for Xenophon the validation of the predictions of two different seers, a justification for his decision to have set out in the first place, and a confirmation that the gods, Zeus Meilichios in this case, do indeed care for those individuals who pay them reverence.

As one can infer from Xenophon's relationship with Eucleides, the seer might know (and indeed need to know) a great deal about his client's personal circumstances. When the Greeks reached the vicinity of Sinope, the army offered the supreme command to Xenophon (as discussed in chapter 3). This passage is, to be sure, important evidence for the use of divination in decision making, but it also reveals a great deal about the role of the seer as personal attendant and adviser. So let us look at this passage not from the point of view of Xenophon, as we did earlier, but from that of the seer who had escorted Xenophon on his way to meet Cyrus (6.1.22):

Since Xenophon was at a loss what to decide, it seemed best to him to consult the gods; and having placed two victims next to himself, he proceeded to sacrifice to Zeus the King, the very god that had been prescribed to him by the oracle at Delphi. And he believed that he had also seen the dream from this god, the dream that he saw at the time when he began to take joint charge of the army. And he remembered that at the time when he was setting out from Ephesus for the purpose of being introduced to Cyrus, an eagle was screeching on his right; it was sitting, however, and the seer who was escorting him said that although it was a great omen,[19] one that did not pertain to a private individual and indeed signified glory, it nevertheless indicated distress. For other birds especially attack the eagle when it is sitting. However, the omen did not portend making money; for it is rather while the eagle is flying about that it gets its provisions. And so when he sacrificed, the god quite clearly indicated to him neither to ask for the command in addition nor, if they should elect him, to accept it.

This passage provides a particularly noteworthy example of a seer in action. Xenophon does not tell us his name, but I think that I can guess. Was he the Phliasian seer Eucleides, the seer who had served Xenophon back in Athens? Had he then waited for Xenophon at Lampsacus? Whoever he was, his job seems to have been to escort Xenophon from Ephesus (and perhaps from Athens) to Cyrus at Sardis. Along the way he would have been expected to interpret the significance of any ominous signs and to sacrifice victims if the occasion warranted it. Why did he interpret the omen of the sitting and screeching eagle in the way that he did? It was clearly a good sign that the eagle, Zeus's own bird, was on Xenophon's right-hand side. But it was sitting, not flying, and that indicated trouble for the reasons that he gave. Was this seer forced by the rules of his art to give this omen a mixed positive/negative interpretation?[20]

He could not have known that Xenophon would have a great deal of difficulty ahead of him because he could not possibly have guessed the real purpose behind Cyrus's expedition nor have foreseen Xenophon's involvement in leading the troops back to Asia Minor. Xenophon and his fellow Greeks, including all of their commanders except for Clearchus, had been told by Cyrus that he was leading them on an expedition against the Pisidians, and they were extremely displeased when

19. Or "bird of prey," since *oiōnos* has both meanings.
20. As Dillon (1996: 110) points out, "it is interesting to note that the features of the omen are interpreted in the light of knowledge of the behavioural characteristics of the eagle: clearly bird divination was at least partly a *technē*, skill, based on observation of animal behaviour."

they eventually discovered that the expedition was actually directed against the King of Persia.[21] Perhaps this seer felt uneasy about Xenophon getting involved with Cyrus for the same reason that Socrates did; for Cyrus had given substantial aid to Sparta during the Peloponnesian War, and the Athenians were likely to disapprove of any dealings with him.[22] Yet strangely, the last part of the seer's prediction was not quite true, for Xenophon, as we have seen, did make money at the end of his adventure when he captured the wealthy Persian mentioned above.

There is one other striking feature of this passage, one that leads us back to looking at it from the narrator's point of view. Xenophon here reverses the usual procedure, well known from the royal inscriptions of the Assyrian kings Esarhaddon and Ashurbanipal, of good omens reinforcing each other. Indeed, Xenophon himself a little later on in the *Anabasis*, encourages his men to join battle with the enemy by pointing out that all three types of omen are favorable (6.5.21): "the omens from sacrifice (*hiera*) are favorable, the bird omens are propitious, and the *sphagia* are excellent. Let us go against the enemy."[23] It has been remarked about the passage that we have been discussing that "the Delphic oracle, a dream, the call of a bird and the sacrificial victims are all invoked to guarantee the authenticity of the result of the sacrifice."[24] Nonetheless, the result is essentially negative. Xenophon's seer, of course, could not have known about the dream (which lay in the future) when he interpreted the eagle portent, although it would not be surprising if he had been told about Xenophon's consultation of the Delphic oracle. Ultimately, it is not a professional seer but Xenophon himself who combines four different divinatory experiences that took place at different times in order to justify his decision not to take the command that was being offered to him.

Finally, it is worthwhile to look once again at the events that took place at Calpe harbor. Although this incident has been much discussed, there is still something to be learned from it about the position of the seer in Greek society. This incident (*Anab.* 6.4.12–5.2) is always considered from the point of view of Xenophon. But what of Arexion, the presiding seer? The seer Silanus had by now hired a ship and run away, the army was nearly out of provisions, and the generals asked Arexion to sacrifice concerning their departure by land. He should have known, or could have guessed, that the army had long suspected that Xenophon was inclined to found a

21. *Anab.* 1.2.1 and 1.3.1.
22. *Anab.* 3.1.5.
23. See Jameson 1991: 206.
24. Bowden 2004: 236.

colony along the Black Sea and that this was an ideal spot. Did he also realize that if the Greeks marched out they were likely to face fierce enemy resistance? Xenophon had just told the troops that "the enemy had regained their courage" and that they should be prepared to fight. This must have been a very delicate situation, the very type of situation that a seer dreaded. As it turned out, the sacrifices were not favorable for a departure. The soldiers, or at least some of them, then alleged that Xenophon had bribed Arexion. In order to diffuse this situation and to reestablish confidence in his seer, Xenophon invited any seers who happened to be in the army to join in observing the sacrifices on the following day.

But on the next day the victims were unfavorable even after three attempts, despite the fact that the soldiers had now run out of food. Xenophon then decided to sacrifice, not for a departure, but for foraging for provisions. Nonetheless, three attempts did not produce favorable omens. The troops were so exasperated that they went to Xenophon's tent and told him that they were out of food. But he said that he would not lead them out without favorable omens. On the following day, the third day in this story, the sacrifices were still not favorable. Had the troops lost confidence in Arexion at this point? For some reason, not explained in the text, Xenophon asked one of his fellow generals, Cleanor, "to take special care if there should be something in the sacrifice."[25] Obviously, this was intended to deflect suspicion away from Xenophon himself, and perhaps from Arexion too.

Despite the fact that the gods were unwilling to give their permission for the army to leave camp, Neon, who was one of the generals, led out two thousand men on his own initiative. Five hundred of them were cut down by a cavalry force that, unbeknown to the Greeks, had been sent by the Persian satrap Pharnabazus. Xenophon performed *sphagia* and went to the rescue.[26] On the following day, the fourth day of

25. I am retaining the manuscript reading *prothumeisthai* in *Anab.* 6.4.22. Parker (2004: 145) accepts the emendation *prothuesthai*, which would mean that Xenophon asked Cleanor to "initiate the sacrifice." Since the text makes sense as it stands, I see no reason to change it.

26. Jameson (1991: 206) explains Xenophon's *sphagia* in this passage in these terms: "Note that the performance of *sphagia* here is explained by the failure of previous *hiera*. For him they had essentially the same function." I do not think that this is right. Xenophon was in a hurry to help Neon's men, and *sphagia* undoubtedly could be performed much more quickly than *hiera*. But the more important consideration was that he knew that he had to set out and that he could not risk unfavorable omens. Although it is true that *sphagia* could be unfavorable at the first attempt (the clear implication of *Anab.* 6.5.8), the chances of failure must have been much less than when performing *hiera*. In this case Xenophon clearly intends that the reader understand these *sphagia* to be propitiatory, and that is why he does not say whether they were favorable or not. He had no time to lose, he was determined to fight, and he is propitiating the gods rather than seeking their permission.

this incident, the Greeks fortified a base camp on the Calpe peninsula, and a boat arrived bringing food and sacrificial victims. Now that the Greeks had a secure position to which to retreat in case of a defeat, knew that a substantial force sent by Pharnabazus was supporting the local people, and had received provisions, the victims proved favorable on the very first attempt. "Xenophon rose early in the morning and sacrificed for marching out, and the sacrifices were favorable with the first victim. When the sacrifices were just about over, Arexion the seer sees an auspicious eagle, and he bids Xenophon to lead the way."

Is this coincidence too great for us to take seriously?[27] Was Arexion told to give this particular performance? Or, to put it differently, did he script this performance himself, as the actor in his own play, or was it scripted for him by Xenophon? It has been inferred that "generals nervous about the wisdom of an advance would inevitably have sensitized their seers to the smallest defect in a victim's liver."[28] The best that we can say is that Xenophon expected his readers to believe that Arexion was, as we would say, a free agent; that he was a professional who exercised a specialized skill, and that he was able, by virtue of his knowledge and training, to read the signs sent by the gods accurately and without deceit. And Arexion must have presented himself to his employers and to the army in just this way. To me at least, Arexion did not need Xenophon to tell him what to say or what to see. He was the seer whom the generals had chosen to replace Silanus precisely because he could be counted on to interpret the sacrifices correctly in accordance with what the gods and the situation called for.

As discussed previously, Xenophon is a source of great value because he writes of his own personal experiences. Nonetheless, it is his voice that we hear, not that of the seers whose activities he describes; moreover, incidents are narrated from his point of view. A passage more than a hundred years later than the writings of Xenophon gives us a unique opportunity to hear a seer, in his own voice, offering an interpretation. Here the usual situation, in which it is the consultant who is the narrator, is reversed. It is the seer who speaks, and not just any seer, but the learned and prolific Philochorus whom we have met before as the author of a book called *On Divination*. In a fragment of his *Atthis* (a local history of Attica) he says:[29]

---

27. Zucker (1900: 42–51) sees this as an example of generals tricking their impetuous troops by seercraft, and Parker (2004: 144–46) seems to concur. For another view, see Popp 1957: 67 n. 86.
28. Parker 2004: 145–46.
29. *FGrH* 328, F 67 (quoted at Dion. Hal. *Din.* 3).

When this year had ended and the next was beginning, an omen occurred on the Acropolis. A dog entered the temple of Athena Polias and, going into the Pandroseion, climbed onto the altar of Zeus Herkeios under the olive tree and lay down. It is a tradition among the Athenians that dogs should not go up to the Acropolis. At about the same time, a star was visible in the sky for a time during the day, though the sun was shining and the weather was fine. We were asked about the meaning of the omen and the apparition, and we said that both portended the return of exiles, not as a consequence of revolution but under the existing constitution. And this interpretation turned out to be fulfilled.

When asked his opinion about strange and uncanny portents, Philochorus related them to the likely return of the partisans of Demetrius of Phalerum, which probably took place in 292/1 B.C.[30] Of course, Philochorus is writing this down after he had proven to be correct. Had he been wrong, we would never have known about it.

One other prose text is worth looking at before turning to the world of Greek tragedy. If only this incident were as historically reliable as those reported by Xenophon, it would be an invaluable piece of evidence. But even if it is a literary fiction of a much later time than the purported dramatic date, it still can tell us something about how seers were thought to act. Plutarch cites Phainias of Eresus, who was a student of Aristotle, for the following story.[31] As Themistocles was sacrificing alongside the admiral's trireme just before the battle of Salamis in 480 B.C., three handsome and splendidly attired prisoners of war were brought to him, who happened to be nephews of Xerxes. "When Euphrantides the seer saw them, since at one and the same moment a great and conspicuous flame shot up from the sacrificial victims and a sneeze was heard on the right, he clasped Themistocles by the hand and ordered him to consecrate the youths and sacrifice all of them to Dionysus Omestes [the eater of raw flesh], while praying to the god; for thus would there be both safety and victory for the Greeks." Themistocles was terrified, but "the crowd dragged the prisoners to the altar and compelled the sacrifice to be made, as the seer had commanded."

30. See Parker 1996: 281. Although Philochorus says "we," the plural probably stands for the first person singular "I" (as translated by Parker) and is a "plural of modesty" (Smyth 1008). If, however, it is a genuine plural, it will not refer to an official board of seers (for which there is no evidence); rather, it is possible that the advice of several seers was sought on this particular occasion (on a purely ad hoc basis), and that Philochorus was one of the seers thus consulted.

31. *Them.* 13; cf. *Arist.* 9.2 and *Pel.* 21.3.

Although this story is clearly an invention (the historical context has been shown to be inaccurate), it just as clearly reveals what a seer was thought capable of doing as well as the influence that he could wield.[32] Euphrantides recognizes the omen, interprets its significance, and, moreover, directs what course of action needs to be taken in order to accommodate it. His commander hesitates, but the common soldiers comply with the seer's commands.

So much for the evidence for how one might consult a seer successfully. But that is only one side of the coin. There are plenty of examples in Greek literature, particularly in Homer and tragedy, of where this system of interaction and negotiation has broken down and led to strife between client and diviner. Might it be possible to infer from these scenes of mutual recrimination how a successful interaction might have proceeded? Is it possible that such scenes as those between Teiresias and Oedipus in the *Oedipus Tyrannus* (284–462), Teiresias and Creon in the *Antigone* (988–1115), and Agamemnon and Calchas in the *Iliad* (1.68–120) represent the inverse of the norm, or rather a travesty of usual practice? We could then read these scenes in such a way as to reconstruct usual, accepted, and successful procedures. This perspective might also help us to interpret a scene in the *Antigone* that seems illogical (988–1115).

Let us begin with the *Antigone*. When Teiresias first enters, Creon treats him with respect, even if the dynamic between them seems rather stiff. For example, when Creon asks him what is going on, he merely says; "I will teach, and you obey the seer." Creon is certainly ready to obey and is shaken when the seer tells him that he is standing "on the razor's edge of fortune." Teiresias then describes his recently failed attempt at divination in vivid detail: how when he attempted to observe the movement of birds from his special seat, he could hear the birds tearing at each other with bloody claws; how when he then attempted a burnt sacrifice, the victim would not burn on the altar; how a dank slime oozed from the thigh bones and the fat dissolved from them; and how the gall bladder sprayed high into the air. This scene was so memorable that it is probably depicted on an Attic red-figure calyx krater by the Kleophon painter, dating to between 440 and 410 B.C. (see figs. 16 and 17).[33]

Now despite these spectacularly adverse omens, when Teiresias continues to

---

32. It is judged unhistorical by Frost (1980: 150), Henrichs (1981: 208–24), Jameson (1991: 216), Hughes (1991: 111–15), and Strauss (2004: 149–50), as well as in every major history of the Persian Wars.

33. See Jameson 1986.

address Creon he seems to imply that all will be well if Creon will only give Polyneices a proper burial. As he says (1031–32), "I am well disposed to you, and my advice is good; and it is most sweet to learn from one who gives good advice, if his advice brings profit." Yet only a few moments later, after Creon has scorned his advice and impugned his honesty, Teiresias gives a prediction of utter doom to Creon, prophesying the death of Creon's own son.

How can one explain Teiresias's dire prophecy in terms of the logic of Greek divination? Is Sophocles asking his audience to suspend belief because the scene does not actually correspond to the logic of everyday religious practice, or has Creon brought this second prophecy upon himself because he has not negotiated Teiresias's first response according to the normal rules of interaction between a seer and his client? This is not to say that Teiresias has the supernatural power to cause events. He is angry, and that anger provokes him to reveal things that were better left unsaid: "In my anger, like an archer, I have discharged such sure arrows at your heart (for you cause me distress), the sting of which you will not escape" (1084–86). Rather than causing Creon's imminent misfortune, he has the leeway to interpret and then to reinterpret the same set of signs in relation to changing circumstances.

Alternatively, it is also possible that a new perception of events has entered his mind in relation to a new decision on the divine plane: just as Creon's response has angered Teiresias, so too it has simultaneously angered the gods whose will Teiresias is able to read by virtue of his innate faculty of divination. Just before he delivers his prophecy to Creon he says: "You will incite me to indicate the things in my mind that ought to be left alone." These things are called *ta akinata*, which can be translated either as "undisturbed/unrevealed" or as "not to be disturbed or revealed."[34] The ambiguity may be purposeful, and so too it is left unclear just how long Teiresias has known these dark secrets. Were they contingent on Creon's initial reaction to his advice or on the gods' reactions to Creon's impious response to Teiresias?[35]

In any case, because Creon did not accept Teiresias's initial interpretation of the signs and immediately reverse his unholy decisions concerning the corpse of Polyneices, the seer makes a prediction that is predicated upon Creon's initial refusal.

34. The former translation is offered by Griffith (1999: 305 [note on line 1060]); the latter by Jebb (1906) and Lloyd-Jones (Loeb edition).
35. The impiety partly lay in the way that he speaks (1039–41): "You shall not conceal him [Polyneices] in a grave, not even if Zeus's eagles, snatching up the body, wish to carry the meat to Zeus's throne." Even though Creon believes that "no human being has the power to stain the gods" (1043–44), his outburst is nonetheless impious and rash.

FIGURE 16.

Divination from the burning of entrails. The tall bearded man standing over the altar may be holding a gallbladder in his right hand,
which he is about to squeeze in order to direct the bile into the fire
on the altar. Omens were probably taken by examining the color of
the sprayed bile and then by noting how the bladder itself reacted
when placed directly in the fire. To the right of the altar a boy holds
a double spit with a bundle of entrails at its end, while behind the
altar a youth holds a tray with a cake upon it. Is the seated bearded
figure the seer Teiresias? Jameson (1986), who believes that it is,
plausibly argues that the painter drew this figure with a blind eye
and that the pupil was wrongly restored when the vase was reconsti-
tuted from fragments. Red-figure calyx-krater, Kleophon painter,
440–430 or 420–410 B.C. The State Hermitage Museum, St. Petersburg, Inv. no. B-1658 (formerly 774, Stephani 1636).

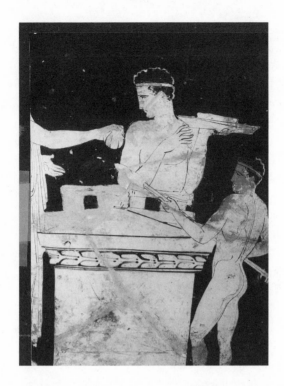

FIGURE 17.
Detail of figure 16, showing the figures at the altar.
The State Hermitage Museum, St. Petersburg.

When Teiresias departs and the chorus subsequently convinces Creon to release his niece Antigone and grant proper burial to Polyneices, it is then too late to reverse Teiresias's prediction.

In the *Oedipus Tyrannus*, Oedipus summons Teiresias so that the seer can tell him who the slayers of Laius were.[36] The scene opens in a very problematic way. What kind of seer, when summoned in a crisis, would say to his client "Sorry, I know something important, but I just can't tell you"? But when Teiresias unexpectedly refuses to give Oedipus any information, the king loses his temper. Teiresias is then forced by Oedipus to reveal that Oedipus himself is the accursed murderer. The

36. The bibliography on this scene is immense, but note in particular Moreau 1993; Ugolini 1995: 120–42; Edmunds 2000; and Struck 2003. For a general treatment of oracles and seers in Sophocles, see Jouanna 1997.

king, of course, does not take this lightly but accuses the seer of being a fraud who had been bribed by Creon. The scene ends with the seer revealing both the past, that Oedipus had killed his father and married his mother, and the future, that he will be driven out of Thebes as a blind vagabond.

Obviously, this interchange is the inverse of how a consultation should take place. A seer should not be forced to read the signs, his interpretation should not be dismissed out of hand, his integrity should not be questioned, and he should not storm off while making dire predictions for the inquirer. This is not to say that the audience would have placed "blame" on either Oedipus or Teiresias for having acted inappropriately, but they would have recognized that the breakdown in the process of consultation and negotiation in itself signified and portended the evils that were about to befall the house of Laius. It is striking that in both plays the protagonists initially greet Teiresias in highly eulogistic terms. Creon admits that he had personally benefited by consistently following the seer's counsel (*Ant.* 991–95), and Oedipus even addresses him as "lord" (*anax*) and "the only champion and savior whom we can find" (*OT* 303–4). It is only when they receive advice that they do not wish to hear or to accept that they viciously turn against Teiresias, accusing him of venality and of accepting bribes. And yet their initial declarations of trust fatally undercut their subsequent skepticism.

It is unlikely that any historical inquirer would address his seer as "lord" or praise his abilities in such hyperbolic terms, or that any historical statesman or general would lose his cool in public to the same extent. Yet we saw an example where Xenophon distrusted his seer, even though it was a seer in whom Cyrus had put great trust. So the mythical/legendary story of Teiresias is a template that simultaneously mirrors and inverts contemporary practices and concerns.

The last extant tragedy in which the character of Teiresias plays a role is Euripides' *Bacchae* (215–369), and here too he has a major confrontation with the ruler of Thebes. Yet this scene is very different from anything in Sophocles. It begins with Pentheus ridiculing his grandfather Cadmus and the seer Teiresias for wearing fawn skins and holding fennel wands, and this then leads to an accusation of a type that we saw in Sophocles (255–57): "You persuaded these things, Teiresias. By introducing this new divinity [Dionysus] to humankind you wish to watch the birds and to take payment for burnt offerings." Teiresias does not respond, however, by appealing to his mantic art or by revealing a prediction of evils to come. Rather, he delivers what might be called a sophistic argument and engages in theological speculations, arguing, for instance, that the infant Dionysus was not literally sown into the thigh of Zeus.[37] The scene ends with Pentheus ordering one of his servants to destroy and desecrate the seat where the seer "watches for birds of omen." This scene presents a variation on a theme: it is a kind of consultation, but one in which the seer presents arguments based on reason rather than on divination.

The prototype for the consultation gone awry is the famous scene at the beginning of Homer's *Iliad* (1.1–120). The Achaean army has suffered through nine days of plague, and on the tenth day Achilles, on his own initiative, calls an assembly and brings forth Calchas to explain the reason for Apollo's anger. The seer then duly explains that the cause was Agamemnon's dishonorable treatment of the priest Chryses and that the remedy would be to restore the priest's daughter without a ransom. Agamemnon then explodes at Calchas, exclaiming (106–8): "Seer of evil things: never yet have you told me anything good. Always the evil things are dear to your heart to prophesy, but no excellent word have you yet spoken or accomplished." Nonetheless, he acquiesces in the seer's interpretation and agrees to return his prize, the priest's daughter. The problem, of course, is that Agamemnon demands to be given a substitute prize, another female captive, for the one he must return. And this reaction and demand prompt the wrath of Achilles and thus the rest of the story.

In the *Agamemnon*, the interaction between Calchas and Agamemnon is rather different. When the winds prove adverse and the expedition is unable to set sail for Troy, Calchas proclaims as a remedy the sacrifice of the king's daughter Iphigenia. Agamemnon reluctantly accepts this, "putting on the yoke of necessity" (218), all the while "not finding fault with any seer" (186). It would seem then that Sophocles, in constructing the scenes in his *Oedipus Tyrannus* and *Antigone*, has taken the possibilities for conflict a step further. It is part of the dynamic of those two plays that disregarding the advice of Teiresias is tantamount to disregarding the word of Apollo himself with all the consequences that such impiety would entail. Just before Teiresias's entrance in the former play the chorus says (284–85): "I know that he whose sight is closest to that of the lord Phoebus is the lord Teiresias."

If we wish to recover how a divinatory consultation was supposed to work, in the sense that the cooperation between diviner and client was personally and socially advantageous, then we need to turn away from poetic texts to the world of prose.

37. See Roth (1984), who argues that Euripides' portrait of Teiresias has the appearance of being a parody of a "theological sophist," of which Euthyphro (as depicted in Plato's *Euthyphro* and *Cratylus*) would be a historical example.

And, as we have seen, our prose sources may be supplemented by comparative material. Yet there is one passage in tragedy that proves the rule that relations between political and religious authorities tend to be adversarial rather than cooperative in that particular genre. In real life, clients, and particularly those exercising military command, needed to rely on their seers, and differences of opinion needed, for obvious reasons, to be concealed from the rank and file. But even in the case of private individuals, no one consulted a seer in order to have a wrangle.

The relationship between seer and client might be not only mutually advantageous, but even intimate, as we saw in the case of Xenophon and Eucleides. A passage in Sophocles' *Ajax* is perhaps unique in Greek literature for showing the compassion of the seer. In the *Iliad* (1.74) Calchas is described as being "well-meaning" (*euphroneōn*, which could also mean "well-judging") when he addressed the assembled Achaeans. In the *Ajax* he goes far beyond this. As reported in a messenger speech (748–83), he left a meeting of the royal council, approached Teucer alone, and "kindly-minded (*philophronōs*) he placed his right hand in Teucer's hand" and urged him not to let his brother Ajax leave his tent for that day if he wished to see him alive again. There then follows a sermon on the dangers of thinking thoughts that are too great for a man and the dangers involved in insulting the gods. It is hard to escape the impression that Calchas here speaks for Sophocles himself, and this is in keeping with the general observation that the only sources of knowledge about divine intentions in Sophocles are seers and oracles.[38] Those who doubt them are invariably proved false.

This brings us full circle to the story that Xenophon told about the advice given to him by the seer Eucleides. In that passage we see the relationship between seer and client at its best. The seer, relying on his knowledge both of his client's personal circumstances and of the broader social context of the consultation, helps the client to discover the root cause of his difficulties and proposes a reasonable remedy. The client complies, and he experiences a complete reversal in his fortunes, adversity quickly being replaced by success. If only Creon or Pentheus had similarly listened to Teiresias. The seer can make a difference both in the "real" world represented in historical texts and in the imaginary one enacted on the stage.

38. So Parker 1999, esp. 17–19: "It may seem that the argument thus far can be summed up as 'cherchez le *mantis*': real insight into the will of the gods in Sophocles comes only from the interpretation by oracles and seers embedded in the plays" (19).

EIGHT

Not Just a Man's Profession

The Female Seer

> I told you in the course of this paper that Shakespeare
> had a sister; but do not look for her in Sir Sidney Lee's
> life of the poet. She died young—alas, she never wrote
> a word.
>
> VIRGINIA WOOLF, *A Room of One's Own*

Actually, William Shakespeare had a sister who lived to be rather old—seventy-seven, in fact. Teiresias, on the other hand, had two daughters, and we even know their names—they were Manto and Daphne. Neither they nor their father is likely to have been a "real" person, but that does not really matter. In the Greek imagination they were the first in a long line of female seers who were mortal, unlike Themis or Phoebe, the first prophetesses at Delphi, who were goddesses.[1] Daphne, according to one late tradition, was actually a prophetess at Delphi, and she was so accomplished at composing oracles that Homer appropriated many of her verses as his own.[2]

The best-known of all female seers was the Pythia at Delphi, who served as the mouthpiece of the god Apollo. The god was thought to possess her and to speak directly through her; the voice was hers, but the words were his.[3] Thus the Pythia saw all time and space as one. For Apollo, as Pindar expresses it (*Pyth.* 3.29), "has the mind that knows all things."[4] The assumption of most modern scholars is that all female seers were of this type; they were the passive agents of mediumistic possession. There is reliable, if scanty, evidence, however, that some of the migrant

1. Aes. *Eum.* 1–8.
2. Diod. 4.66, perhaps drawing on a Hellenistic source.
3. So Dodds 1951: 70.
4. For the panoptic vision of the gods, see Manetti 1993: 15.

charismatic seers were female, and that they performed so-called technical divination. Their activities are mostly not recorded by our sources because they did not participate in military ventures. Warfare, however, was not the only sphere of activity in which mantic assistance might be sought and paid for. For one thing, the female seer was involved in those rites of purification and healing that were also part of the seer's craft. Melampus, according to myth, had healed the daughters of Proteus of their madness by means of purifications. The Cretan "holy man" Epimenides is said to have purified Athens after the sacrilege of the Cylon affair in c. 632 B.C.[5] And Plato talks of seers who could release one from blood-guilt by incantations and prayers.

Every reader of Plato's *Symposium* is surely struck by the figure of Diotima, who Plato says delayed the onset of the plague at Athens by ten years (201d). Whether Diotima was a real person is not at issue here.[6] What is important is that she represents a type of individual who was recognizable to Plato's contemporaries. That such a type really existed, and is not a literary fiction, is remarkably confirmed by an iconographically unique grave stele found, coincidentally enough, in Mantinea (see fig. 18). It dates from the late fifth century and depicts a woman holding a liver in her left hand.[7] What else could she be other than a seer? Whoever this woman was and whatever the range of her expertise, she is represented as a practitioner of divination by hepatoscopy. This is a striking image and the only reference, literary or artistic, to a woman's engaging in that particular mode of divination. In the world of myth, Teiresias had a daughter named Manto, who was the mother of the seer Mopsus, but our sources do not indicate what manner of divination she practiced.

This woman from Mantinea, whether she called herself priestess or seer (or indeed both) is laying claim to expertise in a method of divination that was particularly associated with warfare and thus within the male sphere of activity. The literal field of battle, however, was not the only venue in which a seer might perform sacrificial divination. We can easily imagine a context in which a woman might interpret the entrails of a sacrificial animal within a domestic setting—for instance, on

---

5. See Arist. *Ath. Pol.* 1; Plut. *Sol.* 12; Diog. Laert. 1.110. Plato (*Leg.* 642d), however, places his visit to Athens in 500 or 490 B.C. Aristotle (*Rh.* 1418a23–26) calls him a "seer," whereas Plato refers to him as a "holy man" (ἀνὴρ θεῖος).

6. On her literary depiction in Plato, see Halperin 1990: 113–51 and Hunter 2004: 81–82.

7. The only detailed study is Möbius 1967. It is disputed whether this stele is a grave monument or a votive dedication (see Ridgway 1981: 141–42 for the arguments), but the former seems more likely to me.

FIGURE 18.

A female seer holding a liver. The stele of "Diotima" from Mantinea. This large grave relief is of a woman in an Argive peplos, standing facing right and holding a liver in her left hand. In front of her feet is the lower trunk of a palm tree (which indicates her connection to Apollo). Found in Mantinea in 1887, it is the work of an Argive sculptor of c. 420–410 B.C. Height 1.48 m, width 0.80 m. National Archaeological Museum Athens, inventory number 226. Kaltsas 2002: 132, no. 254. Photograph by Gösta Hellner. German Archaeological Institute, Neg. 1 DAI-ATH-NM 5912.

the occasion of her client leaving home for war or travel or seeking to know whether a particular business venture or marriage was advantageous.

It is dangerous, if exceedingly tempting, to infer too much from a unique representation. But new evidence confirms the impression made by this stele. From Larissa in Thessaly we have the epitaph, dating to the third century B.C., of Satyra, who is called a seer (*mantis*).[8] A contemporary poem suggests that this Satyra was not the only female seer. The recently published collection of epigrams attributed by modern scholars to the Hellenistic poet Poseidippus of Pella (mid-third century B.C.) contains a group of fifteen epigrams dealing with bird augury. One of them refers to the activities of a female seer:[9]

> To acquire a house slave the dusky heron is an excellent bird-sign,
> whom Asterie the seer summons to her rites;
> heeding this omen, Hieron obtained one slave for the fields
> and one with the lucky foot for the house.

The phrase "summons to her rites (*hiera*)" may refer to the setting up of a station for the purpose of observing the flight of birds, the very sort of action that is attributed to Teiresias in Greek tragedy.[10] Poetry does not necessarily reflect real life in any direct way, and one certainly would not want to argue that Asterie was a historical person. Yet the point of the poem does not require the seer to be female, and it would be oddly gratuitous to introduce a female seer if none existed in real life. The two other seers named in this collection are both male: Damon and Strymon.[11] The epitaph and the poem taken together also prove something else—that a woman might be allowed the appellation "seer" in her own right.[12]

Like her male counterpart, the female seer had distinctive apparel that set her apart from ordinary people. In the *Agamemnon* (1264–70), Cassandra refers to her scepter and to the fillets of divination (μαντεῖα στέφη) that she wore around her neck, as well as to the "prophetic garb" (χρηστηρίαν ἐσθῆτα) that she imagines

---

8. *SEG* 35.626. The epitaph of Satyra is inscribed on a fragment of a gray-white marble stele and reads: "Satyra the seer" (Σατύρα ἁ μαντίς).

9. Poem 6 in Acosta-Hughes, Kosmetatou, and Baumbach 2004.

10. Soph. *Ant.* 998–1022 is the fullest description.

11. See poems 14 and 15 in Acosta-Hughes, Kosmetatou, and Baumbach 2004.

12. Here I disagree with Parker (2005: 121), who suggests: "Details remain vague, but it seems that, as 'seer' is the main generic term for a male religious professional, so 'priestess' is its female equivalent."

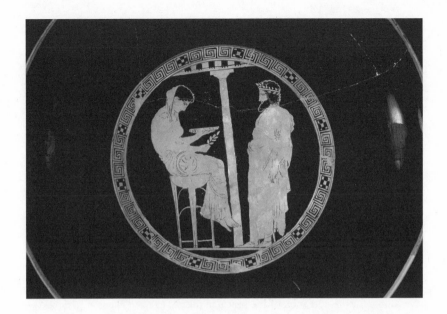

FIGURE 19.
Themis sits on Apollo's tripod at Delphi, while Aegeus, king of Athens, stands before her. According to myth, Themis delivered oracles at Delphi at a time before the oracle came under Apollo's control. Athenian vase, attributed to the Codrus painter, c. 440 B.C. Antikensammlung, Staatliche Museen zu Berlin, Berlin. Photo Bildarchiv Preussischer Kulturbesitz / Art Resource, NY.

that Apollo is removing from her body, apparently a robe of some sort. The inside of an Attic red-figure kylix (drinking cup) of c. 440 B.C. shows Themis (a mythical forerunner of the Pythia) seated on a tripod and holding a spray of laurel (see fig. 19). In this case, it is the tripod and laurel spray, the necessary and emblematic accoutrements of Delphic prophecy, that tell the viewer that she is a prophetess.

THE PYTHIA AND HER ORACLES

No aspect of Greek divination has drawn as much scholarly attention as Delphic oracles. The classic problem is whether the Pythia herself delivered intelligible oracles or whether she spoke unintelligibly, and her words were put into order either by attendant male priests or by professional versifiers. A subset of this problem is whether the verse oracles that are preserved by Herodotus (whether formulated by the Pythia or by her male attendants) are authentic. By "authentic" I mean that the oracles were delivered as we have them before the events that they refer to.

Needless to say, this is an ideologically charged set of problems, since basic issues of gender roles and of the nature of religious authority are at stake. There has been a strong positivist tendency to rationalize Delphic responses by asserting *a priori* that all oracles that exhibit clairvoyance or that seem accurately to predict the future must be fictitious in the sense of being made up after the fact.[13] More subtly, it has been argued that they are part of an evolving oral tradition, and that traditional notions of authorship cannot be applied to them.[14] It has also been proposed that the Pythia gave simple responses in prose (often in the form of "it would be (or would not be) more profitable and better to do x"), which were subsequently turned into verse by poets working for the shrine. These poets, so it is argued, were commissioned to produce collections for publication, the purpose of which was to give grandeur and authority to Delphic oracles.[15] All of these positions suffer from serious defects, not least of which is that they must reject the explicit testimony of our most authoritative source for the operation of the oracle in the archaic and classical periods, the historian Herodotus, who consistently depicts the Pythia speaking in verse directly to her inquirers.

But perhaps one could say that the application of a positivist methodology to the study of the Pythia and her oracles is not in itself inappropriate, but rather the error has been to begin from the supposition that no woman could possibly have delivered the type of verse oracles that are attributed to her by Herodotus and other sources. If positivism essentially is the application of probability and rigorous argumentation, then one actually can use this method of analysis to make a strong case for the position that the Pythia was indeed the author of verse oracles. All that one really need do is to lay aside the *a priori* assumption that she could not possibly have done so.

---

13. See Parke and Wormell (1956), Crahay (1956), and Fontenrose (1978), who vainly seek criteria of authenticity in order to distinguish between not genuine and genuine oracles. Fontenrose accepts none of the Delphic verse oracles in Herodotus as authentic; yet, as Mikalson (2003: 57–58) points out, the important point is that the Greeks after Herodotus accepted the oracles in his text as he presented them.

14. Maurizio 1997. See also Maurizio 2001: 39 n. 8: "Oracular texts reflect an oral tradition in which the effect of male transmission is problematic if not impossible to evaluate. No oracles, because of their oral transmission and reformulation in writing, represent the exact words of any one Pythia." The second sentence, of course, does not necessarily follow from the first.

15. Most recently and most fully by Bowden (2005: 22–24, 33–39). For simple responses, see, for example, Fontenrose 1978: 212–24 and Morgan 1990: 155–56.

An earlier generation of scholars took it for granted, in the absence of any reliable ancient testimony, that the priestess of Apollo at Delphi (the Pythia) uttered unintelligible sounds that the male prophets (the *prophētai*) then formulated into oracles. Recent scholarship, however, has demolished this theory; the prophets may well have helped to explain Delphic oracles to the inquirers, but there is absolutely no evidence that they composed them.[16] One extremely strong piece of circumstantial evidence points to the Pythia as the author of her own oracles, whatever form those oracles may have taken. In the few cases where our sources claim that someone attempted to get a favorable oracle through bribery, it is the Pythia herself who is bribed.[17] That can make sense only if the Pythia indicated her answer in a way that was directly intelligible to the inquirer. And so Herodotus tells us (6.66) that an elite Delphian named Cobon was won over by the Spartan king Cleomenes, and that he "persuaded [i.e., bribed] Periallus the *promantis* to say the things that Cleomenes wished to be said." When this was discovered later, Cobon was sent into exile, and Periallus was deprived of her office. The Delphians held the Pythia responsible, and so should we.[18]

The Delphic priestess, moreover, was not a unique phenomenon in the Greek world, even if she was the most authoritative conduit for the divine will. Three priestesses delivered the oracles at Dodona (Hdt. 2.55). Although it is uncertain whether they spoke in an ecstatic state (as did the Pythia) or merely drew lots, they too will have acted independently of male priests.[19] There was a story that the Spartan Lysander, in an effort to change the Spartan constitution so that the kingship would be an elective office, attempted unsuccessfully to bribe both the Pythia and the priestess at Dodona.[20] The whole story is probably a fabrication, but it reveals how Greeks thought that one might go about acquiring a made-to-order oracle.[21]

Greek terminology is too imprecise to be used as a guide in distinguishing specific roles or functions. The Pythia is variously called *mantis*, *prophētis*, and *promantis*. In

<hr/>

16. See Price 1985 and Maurizio 1995.

17. A point well made by Price (1985: 142). See further Hdt. 6.75. The Athenian family of the Alcmaeonidae is also said to have bribed the Pythia: Hdt. 5.63, 90–91; 6.122.

18. *Contra* Goff (2004: 224), who seems not to realize that the verb ἀναπείθειν means "to bribe" in this context.

19. The evidence is thoroughly discussed by Parke (1967: esp. 80–93).

20. Plut. *Lys.* 24–26, 30; Diod. 14.13. Plutarch cites the fourth-century B.C. historian Ephorus of Cyme as his source at *Lys.* 25.3 and 30.3.

21. I argue that this incident is unhistorical (M. Flower 1991: 81–83).

the same passage Herodotus calls the priestesses at Dodona *promanties* and *hiereiai*. Apollo himself is *prophētēs* and *mantis*. And there are three titles for the male attendants at Delphi: *hosios*, *hiereus*, and *prophētēs*, although only the last of these appears in texts of the classical period.[22] Moreover, there are simply no objectively valid criteria by which the modern scholar, using his or her own notion of probability, can divide oracles into the categories of authentic and inauthentic. We are constrained by our own culturally determined notions of both what is "probable" and what can and cannot happen. It is my own subjective opinion that those oracles have the greatest claim to authenticity that merely refer the problem back to the client and thus force the client by the act of interpretation to construct his own response.[23] Thus I would accept the historicity of the famous oracles delivered to the Athenians in 481, for they merely set out the three policies that were being discussed in Athens at that time.[24] The Athenians were then left to provide their own answer.

On the other hand, Delphic oracles cannot be considered subject to the rules of transmission of oral literature, because they were often, perhaps usually, written down at the very moment of utterance. Herodotus, for example, says that the Athenian ambassadors who consulted Delphi in 481 and who received the famous wooden wall oracle "wrote it down for themselves" (7.142.1).[25] He also tells us that the Pisistratidae kept a collection of oracles on the Athenian acropolis (5.90.2). Even at Sparta there were provisions for preserving the exact texts of oracles. The Spartan kings each appointed two officials called Pythioi, whose job it was to consult Delphi; the texts of the oracles were then kept in the possession of the kings, although the Pythioi also had knowledge of them (6.57). Sparta was far less literate than other Greek communities and not known for preserving large quantities of written texts, so its attitude toward the transmission and recording of Delphic oracles reveals an interest in precise documentation that should have been more, not less, prevalent in other Greek cities.[26] Indeed, a remark of the sixth-century

---

22. See Maurizio 1995: 70, 83–84.

23. On this feature of oracles, see Parker 2000: 80.

24. Parker 2000: 99.

25. Cf. 1.47.1, 48.1; 8.135.2. Dillery (2005: 215–16) stresses that these are the only cases in Herodotus of oracles being put down in writing. Nonetheless, Herodotus strongly implies that it was usual procedure, at least in Sparta, for a written version to be kept.

26. The evidence, such as it is, suggests that there may also have been archives of treaties (Plut. *Lys.* 30.3). On Spartan literacy in general, which must have been minimal in my view, see Millender 2001.

Megarian poet Theognis encapsulates the general attitude of Greeks toward the words of the god (805–10):

It is necessary for the man who is a *theoros* [sacred ambassador], Cyrnus,
to be straighter than a carpenter's compass, rule, and square,
that man to whom the priestess of the god at Pytho in her response
reveals the god's voice from the rich *adyton* [inner room].
For neither adding anything would you still find a remedy,
nor subtracting anything would you avoid giving offence in the eyes of
    the gods.

A further indication of verbatim preservation is the fact that some oracles contain metrical anomalies.[27] For instance, the oracle that Herodotus quotes in relation to Leonidas's decision to remain at Thermopylae (7.220) contains an unmetrical line (ἄστυ ἐρικυδές; see further below). If such oracles were reformulated again and again as they passed through a chain of oral transmission, one would expect such an anomaly to have been removed (by changing ἄστυ to δῶμ'). The fact that it was not changed demonstrates the conservatism of the Greeks, as of other peoples, in preserving the exact wording of sacred texts. An oracle was, after all, as Theognis says above, the *very words* of a god. As such, it was sacrilegious to change or alter it.[28] It must be stressed that even if all of the Delphic oracles in verse from archaic and early classical Greece had been passed down orally for one or more generations before being written down, it would still be the case that the same rules of oral transmission do not apply to a sacred text as to a secular one. A Delphic oracle in hexameter verse does not have the same ontological status as epic poetry; in the case of the latter the precise wording might be altered in each subsequent performance by a professional bard. The former, however, was a sacred text, and as such it was simply not preserved in the same way as other species of poetry. In fact, the verse form of an oracle not only served the function of randomizing the response; it also made it easier for the precise words of the god to be remembered. Yet since sufficient evidence exists that oracles were often recorded in writing at the time of delivery, this point does not need to be pressed.[29]

27. See Todd 1939.
28. Maurizio (1997: 315–16) has trouble with this passage because it refutes her contention that the texts of oracles changed with each new "performance."
29. See Steiner 1994: 80–82.

But again, what is crucial is not whether the oracles that we still possess are the very words of the Pythia or of the attendant male priests or an after-the-fact fabrication. What matters is that the Greeks without exception, including intellectuals such as Plato, believed that the Pythia herself was capable of delivering verse oracles. But just how complex were they? Are we talking about a feat of oral composition that would have been beyond the abilities of all but the most highly educated Greeks? By the standards of ecstatic utterance that are found in other cultures, they were complex indeed, but by comparison with other forms of Greek verse, the Pythia's dactylic hexameters are fairly simple. In the context of Greek oral culture, they are not beyond the compositional ability in extempore oral composition of a Greek who had had a sustained exposure to Homer.

Of the 581 Delphic oracles to be found in the collection of Parke and Wormell, 175 are hexametric, and many others may be prose paraphrases of what were originally hexameter oracles. Many of these hexameter oracles contain epic formulas that are also found in Homer and Hesiod. The presence of epic formulas in Delphic oracles has been taken as a sure indication that the Delphic responses are the product of oral verse composition.[30] But instead of coming to the obvious conclusion that the Pythia herself improvised the verses as part of her oracular "performance," modern scholars have been quick to infer on the basis of late and suspect evidence (Strabo 9.3.5 and Plut. *Mor.* 407b–c) that male versifiers were present whose job it was to impose a hexametric form on the Pythia's utterances.[31]

To take a famous example, the first two lines of the famous tortoise and lamb soup oracle given to Croesus, comprise a commonplace sentiment. The Pythia proclaims to Croesus's envoys even before they can put their question (Hdt. 1.47.3): "I know the number of grains of sand and the measure of the sea." The same idea is found in Pindar's ninth *Pythian* of c. 474 B.C., where the Centaur Cheiron says to Apollo (44–50): "You perceive clearly how many grains of sand in the sea and rivers are beaten by the waves and by the blasts of the winds." My point is that the

30. McLeod (1961) discusses the formulas and dissects a number of examples. He explains these formulas as indicating the work of oral poets at Delphi who drew from traditional material. Crahay (1956), by contrast, argues that Delphic oracles were concocted by borrowing formulas from Homer and Hesiod. See also Dobson (1979), who supports McLeod's view.

31. Bowden (2005: 36–38) uses the alleged existence of these poets as the basis for his reconstruction of how the oracle functioned, yet he does not take the trouble to examine what Plutarch and Strabo actually say. Fontenrose (1978: 212–15) is quite right to dismiss their evidence as a later invention intended to explain the tradition of verse oracles from archaic and classical Greece: "Only Strabo and Plutarch mention these Delphic poets. And neither's remarks can be taken as good evidence of their actual presence at Delphi in former times" (215).

Pythia could have begun many different oracles with these two lines; they are a formula that aided oral composition.

Any Pythia who had been exposed to epic hexameter could have composed the oracles that have come down to us in the context of the oral performance of a divinatory séance. Confirmation can be found in the apparent fact that verse oracles had become a rarity by the last quarter of the fourth century B.C. Plutarch says that the historian Theopompus of Chios attempted to refute those of his contemporaries who did not believe that the Pythia still prophesied in verse; yet he was able to collect only a small number of verse oracles.[32] Theopompus was active during the second half of the fourth century B.C. By this time written composition had finally overtaken oral composition as the dominant means of literary production in the Greek world. It is thus no wonder that the Pythias, reflecting the general trend in Greek society, no longer had the facility to compose poetry orally.

All systems of divination employ randomizing devices, the purpose of which is to establish resistance to human manipulation and thus to insure that divination is an "objective" system of access to divine knowledge.[33] The randomizing device employed at Delphi was the versified and ambiguous language of the Pythia.[34] The poeticized, ambiguous, and metaphorical speech of the Pythia was not the language of a human woman, but of the god Apollo. By virtue of its being divine language, it was difficult for the men who consulted Delphi to interpret and understand the Pythia's words. Another randomizing device was the "spontaneous" oracle; that is, an oracle that apparently has no relation to the question being asked. There are many examples of such oracles in Greek literature, and some may well be historical. But it would be enough to support a belief in the Pythia's objectivity if it were believed, quite independently of its likelihood, that she had in the past and might again in the future pronounce an oracle that was completely unrelated to the question put to her. Thus the Pythia's demeanor, her voice, the nature of the language that she used, and even anxiety at the prospect of an unwanted oracle all were randomizing devices that established objectivity and created resistance to manipulation. From the Pythia's point of view, her role as the conduit of divine knowledge, as the spokesperson for a god, authorized her to pronounce orally and intelligibly on a wide range of private and public issues.

32. *Mor.* 403e–f = *FGrH* 115, F 336. Bowden (2005: 34) is thus incorrect in his assertion that Plutarch "is the only ancient author directly to address the question of how the Pythia spoke."
33. See Ahern 1981: 53 and Maurizio 1995: 81.
34. See Maurizio 1995: 79–83.

The presence of epic formulas in conjunction with poetic and metric infelicities may indicate that Delphic verse oracles were composed orally, but it leaves open the question of who composed them. To me the fact that the Greeks of the classical period believed that it was the Pythia who composed her own utterances is decisive, but this will hardly convince everyone. The balance of probability can be made to favor the Pythia, however, once one considers an analogous body of material that has only very recently been made easily accessible. These are the verse prophecies of the votaries of Istar that were published as a corpus only in 1997. We shall return to these later.

WHO WAS THE PYTHIA?

Although the ontological status of her speech is a fascinating topic, what can be said about the Pythia herself is particularly relevant to the topic of this study. What sort of person became a Pythia, how was she chosen, what kind of lifestyle did she have, and under what conditions did she deliver oracles? The trouble, as is well known, is that if we want to know who the Pythia was, we have to turn to late sources— that is, to authors who were writing hundreds of years after the classical period. Plutarch, who was himself a priest at Delphi in the early second century A.D. and therefore was theoretically in a position to know something about the Pythias with whom he served, wrote three dialogues dealing with the oracular shrine at Delphi. These essays, *The E at Delphi*, *The Oracles at Delphi No Longer Given in Verse* and *The Decline of Oracles* form part of the large collection of his dialogues called *Moralia* (or *Moral Essays*).[35] Diodorus Siculus, who was writing in the first century B.C., has something interesting to say about the origins of the oracle, but it is far from clear that his information is in any way reliable.

According to Diodorus (16.26.6), the Pythia was originally a young maiden. But, in what he calls "more recent times," after she was raped by an inquirer who became enamored of her, the convention changed. The Delphians then passed a law that prophecies could be given only by a woman of at least fifty years of age who wore the costume of a young maiden.[36] In Plutarch's time, she was still a woman over fifty who, even if previously married, now needed to remain chaste. Secluded from contact with strangers, she lived a simple life (*Mor.* 438c). She might come from a hum-

---

35. For a discussion of these works, see Lamberton 2002: 155–72.

36. It would be interesting to know Diodorus's source for this story. Schwartz (1903: 682), whose judgment must always be taken seriously, argues that it is a rhetorical writer of c. 100 B.C.

ble family and had no specialized training or education before she became Apollo's priestess (*Mor.* 405c–d). But even if this were true of Plutarch's time, it would be methodologically incorrect to assume it to be true of the classical period as well. A recent book on Delphi states as a fact that "the women who held the post were not particularly educated" and on the basis of this assumption concludes that "it is highly improbable that an uneducated woman would be able to extemporise verse in hexameters, since this is not a metre that is very close to normal speech."[37]

It seems doubtful that the Pythia ever was a young maiden, since Aeschylus in his *Eumenides* has her call herself "an old woman" (38), and Euripides has Ion, in the play of that name, refer to her as "mother" (1324). Diodorus's account, therefore, smacks of being a rationalizing tale meant to explain the anomaly of an older woman in a maiden's apparel. But even Plutarch, despite the fact that he was a priest at Delphi himself, must not be taken at face value. The assumption is often made that religious institutions and practices are somehow more static and resistant to innovation than other social practices.[38] That is an illusion. The heyday of Delphi was between 800 and 300 B.C. Plutarch wrote about Delphi around A.D. 100, or some four hundred years after the period that we are interested in. Surely practices, procedures, and cult personnel had undergone changes over so many centuries. Even Sparta, allegedly the most conservative of Greek states, was the scene of constant innovation in both religious and secular spheres (which were hardly separable in any case).[39] By way of modern comparison, the Roman Catholic Church is viewed by many as an inherently conservative religious institution. Yet fifty years ago the priest spoke the mass in Latin while facing away from the congregation, whereas today he speaks in the vernacular while facing the people. A thousand years ago he could marry and have children.

37. Bowden 2005: 16, 33–34. Bowden rejects outright the seminal work of Maurizio (1995 and 2001) without actually engaging with her arguments. Even Fontenrose (1978: 223–24) leaves open the possibility that some Pythias might have had the requisite skill spontaneously to compose oracles in hexameter verse. As Lloyd-Jones (1976: 67) points out (although he attributes the verses to the attending *prophētēs*): "The rapid improvisation of hexameters is less difficult than some people imagine; it is helped by practice."

38. So Bowden (2005: 18), who asserts that "all Greek ritual practices tended to be conservative, in that stress was laid on continuing to carry out activities in the way that they had always been done" and concludes that "procedures at Delphi remained more or less constant over many centuries." But the Greek emphasis on continuity of practice cannot be taken at face value as proof of actual continuity, since many allegedly traditional practices (both among the Greeks and the Romans and cross-culturally) are actually invented traditions. See H. Flower 2000; Flower 2002; and Humphreys 2004: 223–75.

39. So Flower 2002.

How then can one explain the wearing of a maiden's clothing? Is it because the Pythia was conceived of as the god's bride?[40] One group of modern scholars has argued that the possession of the Pythia by Apollo was a sexual act, and that the oracles were the offspring of this union. The Pythia, so it is argued, is less a virgin than a dedicated and properly exclusive mate of Apollo. Each oracle is a product of this sexual union, and thus the oracles are part divine and part human.[41] This way of looking at the relationship between god and human priestess has a certain resonance with modern preoccupations, but it finds absolutely no support in any ancient text. The Greeks simply had no notion that when the Pythia sat on the tripod she was about to undergo a sexual union with Apollo, or that she was being impregnated by the gaseous emissions from the chasm, real or imagined, over which she sat. Indeed, a postmenopausal woman fifty years old or older might be surprised to learn that she was about to have sex with the youthful and beautiful Apollo.

Herodotus (1.182) records a custom at Patara in Lycia whereby the prophetess (*promantis*) is shut up by night in the temple so that she can have sex with the god Apollo. Some have taken this as evidence that the Pythia, at least in early times, was conceived of as the god's concubine and that both Apollo himself, as well as this notion of priestess as concubine, came to Greece from Anatolia.[42] Herodotus, however, saw this cult as a bizarre foreign ritual.[43] In any case, the tripod at Delphi was not a bed, and the Pythia was not cloistered in the temple at night with the god.[44] The closest mythic parallel is the story of Cassandra, but her possession by Apollo is a substitute for the sexual union that she had falsely promised him, not a manifestation of it.[45] And in Euripides' *Trojan Women*, Hecuba refers to her daughter Cassandra in terms that imply that she was not considered Apollo's bride or concubine (251–58). Hecuba has just been told by the Greek herald that Cassandra is to be Agamemnon's concubine, and she exclaims: "Do you mean the virgin of Phoebus, to whom the gold-haired god gave a life without marriage as a special privilege?" Phoebus Apollo, in other words, granted her perpetual virginity, something that Agamemnon has deigned to take away. Sometimes an earlier generation of scholars, despite their Victorian bias, had it right, and this is one of those cases. The

40. As argued by Fehrle 1910: 75–111 and Latte 1940.

41. See Sissa 1990: esp. 33–40 and Maurizio 1998: 155.

42. Latte (1940: 17), however, thinks that by the classical period hardly a trace of the original rite was left and the Pythia became the instrument of the god and no more.

43. See Parker 1983: 93.

44. This point is made by Sissa (1990: 39) herself.

45. Note esp. *Ag.* 1202–12.

Pythia's abstention from sexual intercourse was a matter of ritual purity and nothing more.[46]

The biographical profile of the Pythia has, I maintain, been seriously distorted by the tendency of modern scholars to rely on the testimony of late sources. The trouble is that the authors of the classical age record precious few details about her. Yet even so it may be possible to derive more information from them than is commonly thought possible, especially if this information is combined with a wholly neglected source of non-Greek contemporary information—the Neo-Assyrian prophets and prophetesses of the goddess Istar. But first let us look at the contemporary Greek evidence. We know the names of only two historical Pythias, and only because Herodotus chose to record their names. One was Aristonice, who delivered the oracles to the Athenians in 481 B.C. (7.140); the other was Periallus, notable because she had been bribed through the instigation of the Spartan king Cleomenes and subsequently was removed from her office (6.66).

Herodotus, we may surmise, mentions these two Delphic priestesses because the historical circumstances were extraordinary. The Athenians refused to accept the first oracle, and so Aristonice gave them a second one, which was the famous oracle about the wooden wall. As for Periallus, there cannot have been many Pythias who were publicly disgraced. The same explanation holds when Herodotus names the priestesses at Dodona—Promeneia, Timarete, and Nicandra—for the foundation myth of the oracle there, that a black dove flew all the way from Egyptian Thebes to Dodona in northern Greece, alighted on an oak tree, and with a human voice ordered that an oracle center be established (2.54–57). Herodotus himself does not accept this story at face value but argues for the Egyptian version that the oracle had been established by an abducted Egyptian priestess. It may be controversial exactly why he names these Dodonean priestesses: whether it was because the story was not well known and he fears that his audience will not believe him, or because it is a device to establish his credentials as a serious inquirer.[47] If, as has been argued, the story of the dove establishing the oracle was told by Pindar, then the lat-

---

46. Parke and Wormell 1956: vol. 1, 35: "This deliberate selection of women who thereafter renounced all sexual relations need not be taken as implying any view that the Pythia was the bride of Apollo. Such an idea is nowhere expressed. The sole motive appears to have been ritual purity."

47. On this incident, see esp. Parke 1967: 57–59, 206–9; Fehling 1989: 65–70; Pritchett 1993: 71–75; Nesselrath 1999; and Munson 2005: 67–69. Fehling characteristically claims that Herodotus has invented his conversations with the priests at Thebes in Egypt and with the priestesses at Dodona. If that were true, then we would be left with a Herodotus who is so clever (and so postmodern) that he deconstructs as false the very story that he himself has invented. On the problem of Herodotus's source citations, see esp. Luraghi 2001.

ter explanation is the more likely. In either case, the general principle holds that the name of a prophetic priestess is given only under unusual circumstances.

According to Plutarch, in the heyday of the oracle there were two Pythias on active duty, taking it in turn to give prophecies, and one held in reserve (*Mor.* 414b). Prophecies were given on the seventh of each month, except for the three winter months when Apollo was away (*Mor.* 292d–f). It is again necessary to point out that scholars tend to assume that religious conventions are conservative and unchanging. Real life is not that simple, and the number of priestesses may never have been precisely fixed, nor the number of days each month that were available for consultations. Nine days a year might have been sufficient for Plutarch's time, when consultations were considerably less frequent, but probably not for the archaic and classical periods. What should be absolutely clear, however, is that at all periods the Pythia, who sat on Apollo's tripod while prophesying, was responsible for her own oracles. She entered into a self-induced altered state of consciousness, perhaps aided by subterranean gaseous emissions, and then, believing herself to be possessed by Apollo, she spontaneously composed hexameter verse. The type of spirit possession manifested by the Pythia most closely resembles what one anthropologist recently has called Patterned Dissociative Identity. This phenomenon takes place when an individual's identity is dissociated and he or she manifests an alternative identity that is culturally patterned—that is, determined and shaped by the society in which it occurs.[48]

The theory found in Plutarch that the Pythias of the classical period were under the influence of gaseous emissions, although long dismissed by scholars as the invention of a later age, has recently been revived.[49] Yet if the Pythia was indeed under the influence of ethylene gas, this would have served as a relaxant and mild clarificatory stimulant; she was not what we would call "high."

---

48. This term is put forward by Klass (2003: 118–19) and is a subset of his general category "Human Dissociative Phenomena." He proposes it as a universally applicable replacement for the terms "spirit possession" and "altered states of consciousness." Other important studies of spirit possession are Sargant 1973 and Lewis 1986, and the classic work: Lewis 1989.

49. De Boer, Hale, and Chanton (2001) argue that the temple of Apollo was purposely built over an area of cross-faulting in order to enclose hydrocarbon gases (their theories have been popularized by Broad 2006). This is a radical challenge to traditional scholarship about Delphi. The authors maintain that the emission of light hydrocarbon gases (especially ethylene), traces of which can be found in travertine rock and spring water, induced the prophetic trance of the priestess. Yet, as pointed out to me by my student Emma Ljung, the samples provided by the authors are very small, travertine rock is very porous, and the Pythia would have needed to inhale very

SOME CROSS-CULTURAL COMPARISONS

There is no exact anthropological parallel for this process that will decisively persuade the skeptic that a peasant woman, or indeed any Greek woman, could generate, on the spur of the moment, the type of verse oracles recorded by Herodotus and other sources. The closest modern parallel is the Chief State Oracle of Tibet, located at the monastery of Nechung until the Chinese annexation of Tibet, and now functioning at the reestablished Nechung monastery in exile at Dharamsala in northern India.[50] The Nechung oracle, a male priest, is called the Kuden (which means "receiving body") and acts as the mouthpiece of the counseling spirit Dorje Drakden ("the Renowned Immutable One"). He works himself into an altered state of consciousness, aided by the stimuli of incense; the sound of horns, cymbals, and drums; heavy clothing and armor weighing more than seventy pounds; controlled respiration; and the chanting of invocations and prayers by a choir of monks. After he enters an altered state of consciousness, a huge helmet is placed on his head, weighing some thirty pounds.

Questions were, and are, usually put to the Kuden directly, but the means of response is variously recorded. A Tibetan source, himself the son of a Chief State Oracle who served in approximately 1912–18, claims that the oracle would answer through his secretary, who apparently was the only one able to hear the response. The secretary wrote down exactly what he heard without providing any interpretation of his own, and then gave the response to the questioner.[51] The American journalist John Avedon, however, describing a consultation that took place in Dharmasala on February 14, 1981, and citing as his source the abbot of the monastery, writes: "His voice is startling. Each word is crisply enunciated, yet in an ethereal, halting, hollow tone suggesting immense age and distance." And: "The message itself is delivered in a lilting metered verse. Each line is prefaced by a high, wailing 'eh' sound that trails off into the short stops of the following words."[52]

---

large amounts of gases that are very unstable. I find it highly unlikely, on the basis of the evidence submitted so far, that the levels of hydrocarbon gases were significant enough to have had much of an effect on the Pythia.

50. The similarities were first noticed by Arnott (1989), whose article should be read by anyone with an interest in Delphi. For a general treatment of Tibetan oracles, see Nebesky-Wojkowitz 1956: 409–54.

51. This is the account of the Tibetan lama Lobsang Lhalungpa, the son of the Chief State Oracle who served in approximately 1912–18, as provided in an interview to Lipsey (2001: 262–63).

52. 1984: 196–97.

Finally, the current Dalai Lama, in his autobiography of 1990, describes his own direct consultations of the Nechung oracle: "There follows an interchange between Nechung and myself, where he makes ritual offerings to me. I then ask any personal questions I have for him. After replying, he returns to his stool and listens to questions put by members of the Government. Before giving answers to these the *kuten* begins to dance again, thrashing his sword above his head. He looks like a magnificent, fierce Tibetan warrior chieftain of old."[53] All agree that at the end of the session the Kuden collapses and loses consciousness. Perhaps these different accounts reflect the proclivities of different Nechung oracles, something that should be kept in mind when discussing the mode and style of the pronouncements of the Pythia.

Although we cannot recover the psychological state of the Pythia and do not have the evidence to reconstruct how she entered into an altered state of consciousness, this surely provides a compelling parallel. Analogy, to be sure, does not constitute proof.[54] What the Tibetan example does prove, however, is that a human being, without the use of mind-altering stimulants, is able to enter a deep state of trance, and while in that state to utter intelligible, and sometimes enigmatic, prophecies in verse. If the Kuden could do this, then so could the Pythia.

Spirit possession can be found in many cultures, ancient and modern. Though few classical scholars seem to be aware of it, the Pythia had her contemporary counterparts in the ecstatic prophetesses of Istar at Arbela in Assyria. It was only in 1997 that the corpus of these oracles became available in a modern edition (with a facing English translation), and thus their relevance to Delphic poetry has not been fully explored. Twenty-nine oracles addressed to the Assyrian kings Esarhaddon (681–669) and Ashurbanipal (668–626) comprise the collection. The majority of these oracles had apparently been proclaimed in the temple of Istar at Arbela and were then transmitted to the king in oracle reports written by professional scribes. The individual reports were then copied onto eleven tablets for permanent deposit in the royal archives at Nineveh. The texts include the names of nine female and four male prophets (including two who seem to be bisexual, probably castrated transvestites). These prophets composed their oracles orally, and in so doing they utilized a rich poetic tradition, drawing freely on the language and ideas of myths

53. 1990: 236.
54. A point well made by Arnott (1989: 152): "Analogy admittedly is not argument, and the individual reader must judge for himself the applicability of the evidence."

and religious hymns, as well as of royal and cultic poetry. But the prophecies them-selves require little in the way of interpretation. They straightforwardly and directly offer support to the reigning king. A typical example is the following:[55]

> [Esarh]addon, king of the lands, fear [not]!
> What wind has risen against you, whose wing I have not broken? Your enemies
> will roll before your feet like ripe apples.
> I am the Great Lady; I am Istar of Arbela, who cast your enemies before your
> feet.
> What words have I spoken to you that you could not rely upon?
> I am Istar of Arbela. I will flay your enemies and give them to you.
> I am Istar of Arbela. I will go before you and behind you.
> Fear not! You are paralysed, but in the midst of woe I will rise and sit down
> (beside you).
> By the mouth of Issar-la-tasiyat of Arbela.

There is not much to complain about, or indeed to interpret, in this prophecy. Such oracles are half prose and half poetry and employ religious imagery, mytho-logical allusions, metaphors, and similes. They were written down from oral per-formances and apparently were not edited before being reported to the king.[56] Yet, given their allusions to various Near Eastern myths and genres of cultic poetry, they seem not to be the products of untrained ecstatics, but rather of individuals who were regular members of the community of devotees of Istar and who shared in the same educational background.[57] Indeed, the name of the prophet who gave the ora-cle quoted above means "Do not neglect Istar!" If that was her birth name, it may suggest that her parents had also been devotees of Istar.[58]

Like the Pythias at Delphi, these prophets prophesied in an altered state of con-sciousness and acted as the direct mouthpieces of the god. And like Delphic oracles, these oracles were considered valid for all time, and thus they were copied for

---

55. Parpola 1997: no. 1.1.

56. Nissinen (2000b: 98), however, raises the possibility of scribal reformulation of the oracles: "An open question is to what extent the literary parallels between prophecies and cultic literature go back to the scribes by whom the prophecy reports were formulated." I accept Parpola's judg-ment that the oracles "were written down from oral performance and apparently not subjected to any substantial editing" (1997: XLVII).

57. Parpola 1997: XLVII–VIII and LXVII.

58. Parpola 1997: L.

deposit in the royal archives. They were considered the word of god with enduring significance.[59] Yet despite the similarities, there are also striking differences.

In contrast to its Assyrian counterpart, what is so exceptional about Delphic prophecy is its sophistication in terms of its poetic range and polyvalent meaning. The prophets of Istar employed a limited and somewhat formulaic inventory of structural and thematic elements, which could be freely combined.[60] The king is told not to be afraid because the god or goddess is with him and that he will overcome his enemies, and this message is delivered again and again in stereotypical language drawn from traditional material.[61] In short, Neo-Assyrian prophecies are remarkably monotonous, and their primary function is to bolster royal ideology.

Delphic verses, although sometimes disjointed and jarring, are considerably less formulaic. Nonetheless, even if Delphic oracles display a far greater degree of polyvalence, there is something important to be learned by the comparison. The prophets, who were votaries of Istar and who prophesied in her temple, had a socioreligious role in Assyrian society that was the result of education and training in a specific environment.[62] Their prophecies show familiarity with a broad range of cultic literature. These were not untrained ecstatics. And despite the fact that "their thematic repertory is somewhat limited and formulaic," it is still the case that "their literary quality can have been achieved only through conscious striving for literary excellence, and their power of expression reflects the prophets' spiritual assimilation to the Goddess who spoke through their lips."[63] Should we then assume, as so many classical scholars do, that the Pythia was an untrained and uncultured cipher for the male priests who supplied the actual verse oracles, someone with no poetic ability of her own? Or should we infer that professional verifiers were responsible for turning her mundane prose responses into ambiguous verse?

If in Plutarch's time the Pythia was an ordinary woman with no special training or education, that was probably not true of classical Greece. Unfortunately, we do not know how a Pythia was chosen. It is, however, possible to make an informed guess. Cross-cultural comparisons indicate that self-selection is a regular feature of individuals who specialize in spirit possession. If a woman could not become a Pythia until she had reached the age of fifty, it is easy to imagine a long apprenticeship in a

59. See van der Toorn (2000), who compares Old Babylonian and Neo-Assyrian prophecy.
60. Parpola 1997: XLVIV and XLVII.
61. Grabbe 2000: 27–30.
62. Nissinen 2000b: 109.
63. Quoting Parpola 1997: LXVII.

community of believers (the already serving Pythias, the female temple staff, and the various male priests and attendants). During that apprenticeship she would internalize the requirements and become well versed in Delphic traditions and procedures.[64]

The modern study of shamanism can perhaps be used to fill out some of the gaps in our evidence for how the Pythia became practiced in her art. It has been shown that "learning is central in attaining shamanic status as initiates are taught to act *as if* entranced as a road to actually *becoming* entranced." Furthermore, "the study of trance states shows that repeated engagement in trance seems to change the capacity of the brain, allowing the individual easier access to primary process thought, and a more vivid expression of emotions."[65] And even while in a state of ecstatic trance the shaman maintains a degree of detachment: "he is both caught up in, and yet outside of, the trance; a self-conscious actor, as well as the enraptured participant."[66] Although the precise psychological state of the Pythia, who was experiencing spirit possession (or patterned dissociation of identity), *may* have been different from the trance state of the shaman, it would not be at all surprising if her training and psychological conditioning were somewhat similar.[67] The claim that the Pythia had no specialized training and was just any old peasant woman off the farm (so to speak) is a rhetorical strategy meant to underscore the fact that it was Apollo, and not human art, that was the source of oracular responses. Even if by Plutarch's time she received less formal training than in earlier centuries, we still should not take his assertions at face value.

Was the Pythia only powerful and influential in Greek society because she was the passive, and thus the unconscious, instrument of the god? In other words, was she empowered to speak out publicly to an audience of men precisely because it was not she who was speaking? This makes sense in the context of a patriarchal society, in which

64. See Parke and Wormell 1956: vol. 1, 35–36 and esp. Goff 2004: 222–25.

65. Lindholm 1990: 167

66. Lindholm 1990: 161. See further Peters 1982.

67. Goff (2004: 280–82) accepts Plutarch's representation of the Pythia as active, engaged, and self-monitoring and argues that the experience of possession is "usually structured and learned." The difference, however, between trance and spirit possession is stressed by Klass (2003: 118–19), who maintains that in the latter "consciousness is not lost by the individual, as in the varieties of trance, but is instead exhibited by one or more alternative identities. Thus, Dissociative Identity Phenomena are characterized by the manifestation of *alters*, while trance is characterized by non-traumatic, non-sleep eclipse of consciousness, though the individual may, upon resuming consciousness, *report* (but not *manifest*) encounters with other entities." Matters are complicated, however, by the fact that the term "trance" is used by scholars in various disciplines to cover a wide range of different mental states (see Morris 2006: 19).

virtually all political and religious power was exercised by men. Yet perhaps this picture, although fitting well with modern notions of Greek society, is too simple and monolithic. As Herodotus tells the tale (1.91), when Croesus sent his chains to Delphi with the complaint that Apollo had deceived him, it was the Pythia who gave the four-part explanation for what had happened. Even though Herodotus distances himself from this narrative with the words "it is said that the Pythia spoke as follows," he need not have used her as the shrine's spokesperson. Indeed, if the Pythia was considered to be nothing more than the god's mouthpiece, it would be odd for Herodotus to represent her as discussing the intentions both of Apollo and of the Fates.

It is possible, moreover, to argue by analogy from what Herodotus tells us about his encounter with the priestesses at Dodona. They expressed to Herodotus their own speculations about the origins of the gods (2.53) and were well informed about the mythical origins of Dodona (2.55): "The priestesses of Dodona said these things, of whom the oldest was Promeneia, the next Timarete, and the youngest Nicandra. And the other Dodoneans who are involved with the temple agree with them." It is important to stress that it is to the authority of the priestesses that Herodotus appeals, whereas the male personnel are referred to in the most vague terms, and they merely confirm what the priestesses told Herodotus. If Herodotus is telling us the truth about his own experience (by which I mean that he did go to Dodona and did converse with the priestesses on the said topics), then these were highly articulate and well-educated women who had the freedom to converse with visitors. The Pythias of classical Greece may have been of the same stamp. If so, then that might be the most immediate explanation, and one that Plutarch himself was unable to grasp, as to why the Pythia prophesied in verse in archaic and classical Greece but no longer did so in later periods when the nature of her training and education had changed.

The best evidence for how the Pythia both acted and perceived herself comes not from Diodorus or Plutarch, who are simply too late to be strictly relevant to the classical period. Rather, the opening scene of Aeschylus's *Eumenides* depicts a Pythia who is about to enter the temple of Apollo for the purpose of giving oracles. Although, as stated before, Greek tragedy does not give an unmediated view of social reality, this is at least a contemporary representation, and, moreover, there is no obvious dramatic reason for depicting the Pythia in a way other than how she actually conducted herself. Just before she enters the temple she proclaims (30–33): "I take my seat as seer upon my throne, and now may the gods grant me far better fortune than in my previous goings in, and if any of the Greeks are present, let them enter in order of the lot, as is the custom; for I prophesy as the god may lead me."

This passage supports an interpretation of Delphic prophecy whereby the Pythia herself takes center stage and is responsible for her own oracles. It also nicely meshes with the picture of the Pythia that one finds in the pages of Herodotus, where she always speaks for herself without an intermediary and often speaks in verse.[68] Moreover, her prayer for better success may not simply be a standard formula but may hint at the dangers inherent in spirit possession—that is, the danger of the kind of bad experience that led to the death of a Pythia as described by Plutarch almost five hundred years later in his essay *The Decline of Oracles* (*Mor.* 438b).

In this much-cited passage Plutarch writes that when the sacrificial victim (a goat) did not respond to being sprinkled with water, the priests were so eager to please a foreign delegation that they literally drenched it. They then apparently forced the Pythia to go ahead with the session:

> She went down into the oracular chamber unwillingly, they say, and halfheartedly; and at her first responses it was immediately clear from the harshness of her voice that she was not responding properly and was like a laboring ship, as if she was filled with an inarticulate and evil spirit. Finally she became completely hysterical and with a frightful shriek rushed toward the exit and threw herself down, with the result that not only the members of the deputation but also the prophet Nicander and the cult officials that were present fled. However, after a little while, they went in and took her up, still conscious; and she lived on for a few days.

This particular Pythia was obviously not in the right mental state to undergo possession and was surely influenced by the fact that the omens were so clearly unfavorable and artificially forced. How usual, one wonders, could a situation like this have been? Did the attending priests have the authority to compel a Pythia to give a prophecy if she felt unready? If other deaths had occurred in the course of the sanctuary's history, would not Plutarch have alluded to them? Or would such deaths have been purposefully forgotten, since it would have profited no one to remember them? These are not questions that we can answer.

In sum, a series of interlocking propositions supports the authenticity of Delphic oracles in verse. Apart from a few late sources (Plutarch, Strabo, Libanius), all of our evidence points to the conclusion that the Pythia was the author of her own ora-

---

68. The evidence for Herodotus's depiction of a consultation with the Pythia is nicely collected and summarized by Compton 1994.

cles without the mediation of a male priest or bard. The inquirer, and not some priest or bard, wrote down the response; the inquirer was expected not to tamper with the response, since to do so would have been an act of impiety (Theognis). In Sparta, and probably in other states as well (for Sparta is unlikely to have been unique in this respect), official archives were kept of Delphic oracles; and even in those cases where oracles were preserved only orally, inasmuch as they were sacred texts, they were not subject to the usual vagaries of oral transmission.

When the Pythia so wished, she was capable of giving explicit advice in plain language. But when she was dealing with a particularly difficult or delicate problem, she composed verse responses in which were embedded a variety of possible recommendations and a range of possible consequences.[69] As Heraclitus observed, "the Lord whose oracle is in Delphi neither speaks nor conceals but gives a sign (σημαίνει)."[70] So too Aristotle assumes that ambiguity is often typical of oracles, and cites as an example the oracle that was given to Croesus that he would destroy a mighty empire.[71] Nor is Herodotus the only source for examples of ambiguous verse oracles. According to Diodorus Siculus, Philip II of Macedon, shortly before his assassination in 336 B.C., asked the Pythia "if he would conquer the King of the Persians," and in response he received a single disjointed hexameter line: "Wreathed is the bull; all is done; there is the one who will sacrifice him." Although Philip found the oracle "ambiguous," he interpreted it as foretelling that the Persian King would be sacrificed like a sacrificial victim.[72] Philip, as it soon unfolded at his daughter's wedding, was the "bull."

The purpose of such ambiguity, or interpretative polyvalence, was not evasion. For ambiguity is not necessarily evasive. Rather, oracular ambiguity served to define the limits of the problem and the range of possible solutions, and then to refer the problem back to the inquirer. The inquirer, through the act of interpretation, then provided his own answer.[73] But it must be stressed that this answer was not the only

---

69. Even though she does not believe that any extant oracle represents the exact words of any one Pythia, Maurizio (2001: 53) is correct in seeing the Pythia herself as the source of oracular ambiguity: "The historical Pythias, I have argued, adopted and embellished an ambiguous style of oracular pronouncement in order to address the spiritual and social needs that their earliest clients, colonists and tyrants, brought to the divinatory session."

70. Diels-Kranz F 93 = Plut. *Mor.* 404d. For the translation "indicates through signs," see Romeo 1976.

71. *Rh.* 1407a32–37.

72. Diod. 16.91.2–4. The oracle is also quoted at Paus. 8.7.6.

73. See Parker 1985: 301–2; Price 1985: 148–49; Morgan 1990: 156–57; and Maurizio 1995: 85–86 and 2001: 41–46. Bowden (2005: 49–51) rejects the notion that any oracles were deliberately

possible answer, because many such oracles were open to being interpreted in different ways. Thus the advice that the Pythia gave was not simply to do x, but was of the sort "you could do x, or you could do y, and here are the consequences of each choice." I would imagine (based on the "wooden wall" oracle) that the act of interpretation, whether conducted individually or collectively, entailed an initial decoding of each grammatical unit of an oracle, which was then followed by an analysis that attempted to explain the whole response.

A CASE STUDY

Let us now look at a specific example of how this process might have worked. In 481 B.C. four oracles were delivered to the Greeks by the Pythia on the subject of the imminent Persian invasion led by Xerxes. Herodotus quotes all four of them, probably some forty to fifty years after they were first spoken. He treats these oracles as essential evidence for understanding the motives and decisions of the Greeks, and he artfully places them at key points in his narrative. Indeed, one might even say that he uses them to help structure the narrative in book 7 of his history. One oracle was given to the Argives, one to the Spartans, and two to the Athenians. No one seems to have commented on this before, but the style and imagery of these four oracles are strikingly similar; so similar in fact that I want to suggest that all four were composed by the Pythia whose name was Aristonice. It is also possible that all four were delivered on the same occasion, since, as mentioned above, in Plutarch's day at least oracles were given only on one day each month. The oracle to the Spartans runs as follows (Hdt. 7.220):

But as for you, oh inhabitants of spacious Sparta,
either your great very famous city is plundered by the descendants of Perseus,
or not, but the land of Lacedaemon shall mourn for a slain king, from the race
    of Heracles.
For neither the strength of bulls, nor of lions, shall stop him face to face;
for he possesses the strength of Zeus. And I say that he shall not be stopped
until one or the other of these things he has utterly torn and divided.

---

ambiguous, but he fails to mention the evidence of Heraclitus, Aristotle, and Diodorus cited-above. Morgan (1990: 157), however, has some difficulty accepting the social utility of ambiguous oracles:"responses that were regularly hard to interpret would undoubtedly have diminished the value of the oracle as a tool for problem-solving within the community." The opposite seems to me to be the case: their value lay in letting the community construct its own solution.

This may be a very clever prophecy, but it is certainly very bad poetry. It might seem outlandishly subjective to pass such a judgment, but Plutarch has one of his speakers make this very point in his dialogue *The Oracles at Delphi No Longer Given in Verse*. One of the professional guides has just read out a verse response that was recorded on stone, and this prompts the visiting philosopher Diogenianus to comment that he had often wondered at the barrenness and cheapness of the verses in which the oracles are delivered (*Mor.* 396d): "Although the god is leader of the Muses, . . . we observe that most of the oracles are full of metrical and verbal errors and barren diction."

Literary quality aside, the oracle is clever because it refuses to succumb to a single interpretation. Either a Spartan king will die or the city will be sacked; but when and by whom is left intentionally unclear. The "descendants of Perseus" could be either Persians or Argives, inasmuch as the Persians claimed Perses, the son of Perseus of Argos, as their ancestor (or so Xerxes claimed).[74] The Persians and the Argives were Sparta's two bitterest and most powerful enemies at this time, and the oracle can be taken to refer to either of them. But who is it that has the strength of Zeus? The "him" (τὸν) in line 5 is grammatically obscure: it might refer to the king of Persia, but not necessarily so. As in the oracle given to the Athenians that is quoted below, it could refer to "fierce Ares." Obscurity and polyvalence are features that can help to render an oracle socially and politically useful. Nonetheless, this is poetry of a very low order (as explained in the note below).[75]

How can one best explain these stylistic features of the oracle, and in particular the banality of the language? It is not, I would argue, by positing the existence of a second-rate male poet, who should have had the time and the training to produce something rather more polished. The most economical explanation is that these are

74. Hdt. 7.150; cf. 1.125.3 and 7.61.3, with Georges 1994: 66–71.

75. Consider the phrase "very famous city" in the second line. According to a standard commentary on Herodotus, "the synizesis in ἄστυ ἐρικυδές is intolerable," and it is asserted that the original wording must have been the more metrical δῶμ᾽ ἐρικυδές, with ἄστυ being a gloss (How and Wells 1912: vol. 2, 227, citing Richards 1905: 345; but see Todd 1939). Synizesis is the union in pronunciation of two adjacent vowels into one syllable without forming a diphthong. Yet despite the phonetic awkwardness, this emendation is completely arbitrary and unnecessary— "house" makes no sense; it was the "city" that was endangered. The fact is that the poetry is not very good, and it only gets worse. Lines 5–7 of the oracle display a remarkable poverty of vocabulary. The word for "strength," μένος, is used both of the defender and of the invader. And the three different uses and forms of the verb ἔχειν, which is used to mean "to hold/possess/stop," respectively (σχήσει, ἔχει, σχήσεσθαι), is extraordinary in light of the richness of Greek poetic vocabulary (so Macan 1908: 326).

the words of a person in a high state of mental agitation: the thought is disjointed, the syntax obscure, the meter rough, and the vocabulary both simple and repetitious. If these are not the precise words of the Pythia in 481 B.C., then they are a superb imitation of what a genuinely ecstatic woman would have uttered. The closest parallel in literature is Aeschylus's Cassandra in her long exchange with the chorus at *Agamemnon* 1072–1330. While possessed she sings in lyrics but reverts to iambics (the meter of everyday speech) when in a normal mental state. Aeschylus has modeled her dialogue upon the type of disjointed speech uttered by the historical Pythias of his own time, but with this difference. Cassandra's speech may be vivid and difficult to understand in terms of image and syntax, but the poetry is of a high order, and her vocabulary is extremely rich and varied. Herodotus's Pythia reveals to us what prophetic speech was like in practice.

The opening words of this oracle to the Spartans ("But as for you/to you") suggest that it follows closely upon another response. The most obvious candidate is the first of the two oracles that were given to the Athenians, since the stylistic and emotional registers of these two oracles are indeed very similar. The authenticity of the second oracle to the Athenians, the one that mentions the wooden wall, is doubted by most modern scholars. But the language of the oracle suggests otherwise. For instance, it contains the phrase "the land of Cecrops" (an early king of Athens), which is similar to "the land of Lacedaemon" (the hero after whom the land and city were named) in the oracle given to the Spartans.[76] However that may be, let us concentrate on the first Athenian oracle, quoted by Herodotus at 7.140:[77]

Oh wretched ones, why do you sit here? Flee to the ends of the earth,
abandoning your homes and the topmost head of your city round like a wheel.
For neither the head remains fixed nor the body,
nor the feet below nor indeed the hands, nor is some part of the middle left,
but they are unenviable.
For fire and fierce Ares are casting it down, driving a Syrian chariot.
He shall also destroy many other fenced cities and not yours alone;
and many temples of the immortal gods he shall give to ravenous fire,
those that somewhere now stand streaming with sweat,

76. As Maurizio (1997) well points out, the second oracle did not invalidate or replace the first one; it simply added to it. Dillery (2005: 217), however, claims that Herodotus saw the second oracle as being more definitive than the first one and as replacing it.

77. Important treatments of these oracles include Evans 1982; Georges 1986; Holladay 1987; Robertson 1987; and Giuliani 2001: 55–69.

quivering with fear, but black blood has been poured down over the
 topmost roofs,
having foreseen the necessity of evil.
But go out of the inmost shrine, and spread your heart over with evils.

This is another example of a famous oracle whose poetic quality is spectacularly dismal. In particular, several features of the syntax and grammar are arresting and peculiar. First of all, there is the alteration between singular, plural, and dual (referring to two people) in the way that the Pythia addresses the inquirers. This cannot be a matter of metrical convenience; rather, it is indicative of a mind that is in an elevated state of consciousness and is not focused on the physical presence of the inquirers themselves. Second, there is a rapid and not quite logical or grammatical switch of striking images, from burning temples to sweating statues to dripping blood that can foresee the future. That last image is so bizarre and illogical that scholars have suggested that "fore-seen" (προϊδόν) must be a confusion for "fore-shown" (προφαῖνον).[78] Blood can serve as a portent that reveals in advance some evil, but can it also foresee that evil? In the logic of everyday speech and action it cannot, but in the logic of oracular speech and image it obviously can.

The much shorter oracle that was delivered to the Argives bears comparison to its longer companions (Hdt. 7.148):

Hateful to your neighbors, but dear to the immortal gods,
holding the spear within, sit, being on your guard,
and guard the head. The head shall preserve the body.

Here again the poverty of vocabulary (the verb meaning "to guard" is used twice: πεφυλαγμένος/πεφύλαξο), as well as the obscurity of the subject of the main verb, is striking. Who is the addressee? Is it Argos personified as a male person, holding a spear, sitting on the ground, and protecting his head? Or is it the body politic, the political community, that is being personified? If the latter, then this metaphor of the body politic is repeated from the first oracle given to the Athenians. If we had a larger body of oracles from the early fifth century, we would probably see the Pythia using a repertoire of images and expressions that were appropriate to certain situations. They would leave the poetic fingerprint of a particular prophetess, whose name might well have been (indeed probably was) Aristonice.

78. So Macan 1908: 188 and many others, following Stein 1889: 130.

Not all Pythias, of course, would have been equally good at versifying extemporaneously while in an altered state of consciousness. That fact may alone be sufficient to explain why verse oracles were more common at some times and periods than at others. However far-fetched a conclusion this may seem to modern Western scholars, it too is corroborated by the oracle centers of modern Tibet. The Tibetan lama and scholar Lobsang Lhalungpa, himself the son of a former Chief State Oracle, when asked about the language of the responses, said: "Most ordinary oracles spoke in a simple local dialect, whatever it was. But the Chief State Oracle and some of the high oracles—there were quite a number of them—often answered in versified form. Some of the Chief State Oracles are known for their poetic answers. Others were less poetic, but they all tended to be. I have compared some of the sayings or answers of Chief State Oracles. One was so eloquent, so beautiful—really poetic. Others were poetic, but not to the same degree. Individual traits do come out."[79]

79. Lipsey 2001: 262–63.

He is prosperous and happy who knows all these
things and does his work without offence to the
immortal gods, interpreting omens from birds and
avoiding transgressions.

HESIOD, *Works and Days*

In a society in which public displays of expertise and knowledge were ubiquitous, the performance of the seer in the context of the rituals of divination was in at least one respect unique. Doctor, sophist, orator, and general all gave performances before audiences of various kinds and sizes, but the knowledge that they claimed to impart was their own. The poet, to be sure, could claim knowledge through divine inspiration that came from the Muses, the daughters of Zeus and of Memory. Nonetheless, it was the seer who acted as the critical bridge between the limited and partial knowledge of mortals and the superior knowledge of the gods. Regardless of what type of divination was being enacted, it was up to the seer to recognize and to decode, and in some cases to transmit, the signs and messages that the gods were willing to vouchsafe to mortals.

The social role and divinatory expertise of the seer was important both at times of crisis and in the routine dilemmas of everyday life. The advice of seers was essential to the efficient running of the *polis* in peace and in war, as well as to the solving of personal problems in the private sphere. No general would leave camp or begin battle without first consulting his seer. And the whole gambit of life's problems and uncertainties was brought to the attention of the expert diviner, the seer. Before one married or entered a business arrangement or accused a neighbor of theft or moved houses, one had recourse to divination. Indeed, Socrates, according to Xenophon, said that anyone who proposed to run a household or a city efficiently needed the help of divination. Those with the time and the money might travel to an oracular center, but for most Greeks the easiest access to the will of the gods was through the self-employed seers who traveled from city to city.

In the Greek world seers were the most authoritative experts in all matters pertaining to religion. Their competence was exceptionally broad, encompassing many different forms of divination, as well as healing and purification. The seer (*mantis*) was not a priest (*hiereus*), but some seers, such as the Iamidae and Clytiadae, who worked Zeus's oracle at Olympia, had some of the functions of priests. The priests of civic cults were not professionals in our sense of the word. They managed the sanctuaries of the gods and performed the traditional sacrifices on behalf of the community, but this position required no special skill or charisma, as is demonstrated by the fact that many priesthoods were obtained by lottery or sale.

A seer, by contrast, was a professional, and not just any person could hope to become one. But unlike other professional occupations, such as that of doctor, artist, or architect, it was also a high-status occupation, and many of the most sought-after seers came from elite, famous, and ancient families. Success at seercraft could also be the key to acquiring great fame and wealth. It is no coincidence that the only outsider to be granted full Spartan citizenship during the classical period was a seer (with the proviso that he also obtained citizenship for his brother).

The high status of being a seer comes into sharper relief as soon as we realize something that the modern misunderstanding of Aristophanes and the scholia to his comedies has obscured. To slander a seer was to call him something else: an oracle-collector (*chrēsmologos*) or a wizard (*magos*) or a beggar-priest (*agurtēs*). A seer (*mantis*), however, would not have desired either to be called or to call himself by those appellations. In a society in which status anxiety was prevalent, what people called you was as important as what you called yourself.

The Greek seer was responsible for the interpretation both of solicited signs (such as were derived from sacrifice) and of unsolicited signs (such as an eclipse or an earthquake). Some seers, such as the Pythia, also became possessed by a god and acted as the god's mouthpiece. Typologies of divination, as articulated from Plato to the present day, tend to be overly rigid and to obscure the overlap between these different methods of divination, especially by positing a strict opposition between "natural/inspirational" divination and "artificial/technical" divination. The cross-cultural study of divination, however, reveals that such distinctions fail to capture the rich complexity of what seers actually do in practice, of how they perceive themselves, and of how they are perceived by others. Whatever the particular type of divination that was being deployed, Greek seers often claimed that they performed under the influence of divine inspiration, although this "inspiration" might manifest itself in different ways.

Any individual, of course, could attempt to interpret a sign or indeed could sacrifice an animal. Strictly speaking, an expert, whether priest or seer, was not needed in the performance of private, as opposed to public, rituals. But it was safer, and more authoritative, to entrust the rites of divination to an expert. And where did one find this expert? The Pythia, who acted as a god's mouthpiece, was an obvious choice but was not accessible for most Greeks. There were, to be sure, various other oracular centers on the Greek mainland, although only Dodona in Epirus could equal the prestige of Delphi. Yet to consult them took time, trouble, and money. Closer to hand were the self-employed seers. Some of them were the citizens of one's own community, but others wandered from city to city in the quest for clients and money. Anyone, to be sure, could call himself or herself a seer. It was up to the client to find one with a reputation for accuracy and, just as important, for honesty.

In order to gain clients and to acquire a good reputation, seers needed to advertise themselves and their accomplishments. One important and traditional means of advertisement was to claim membership in a famous family of seers, especially a family that claimed descent from an eponymous ancestor who had acquired prophetic power either as the gift of a god or by some other supernatural means. This was important because mantic skill was seen as something that could be inherited; the original divine gift was still potent in a seer's descendants. The construction of a persona was not only important as a means of self-advertisement and for the projection of an image. It was also a means whereby the seer simultaneously constructed an identity for himself, an identity that he internalized even as he projected it to others.

The symbiotic relationship between the worlds of real life and high literature also played a role in constructing both identity and image. Historical seers might model themselves on the seers of epic and tragedy in the hope of creating an aura of infallibility. Teiresias, Calchas, and Melampus may have clashed with their employers, but their predictions were always proven true in the end. Scenes of confrontation in high literature could serve as a sort of cautionary tale of how client and seer should not interact, while simultaneously confirming the ability of seers to convey accurate information that actually served the best interests of their employers. At the same time, the wide audience and civic context for theatrical and rhapsodic performances guaranteed that seers would retain a prominent place in the collective Greek imagination.

Once success was achieved, statues at Panhellenic centers and elaborate grave monuments could enhance an individual's or a family's reputation. And then there was what was perhaps the most potent ingredient for success—the one thing that was most essential for attracting and retaining clients. That was personal charisma. The power of charisma was such that it could entice a Persian prince, Cyrus the Younger, to promise, on a whim, to pay his seer a fortune if his prediction should prove true. It could even induce the Spartans, who were so covetous of their special status, to extend citizenship as the price of employment.

Charisma was far more important in the cultural milieu of the Greek seer than book learning or technical expertise. In the ancient Near East, divination was a science to be mastered. In the Greek world, it was an art that found its expression in a performance to be staged. All ritual acts, of course, have a performative aspect, and one would not want to deny that Babylonian, Assyrian, and Etruscan diviners also "performed" the rituals of divination. What is at issue here is a matter of emphasis and degree in terms of culturally patterned behavior. The divinatory performance of the Greek seer was highly theatrical and rhetorical inasmuch as it needed to convince its human audience of its validity without the aid of a scholarly apparatus that could substantiate its claims to objectivity.

If we had the books on divination that circulated in the late classical period, it is highly unlikely that they would be in any way comparable to the Babylonian and Assyrian divinatory texts that have been recovered by archaeologists. The Greek books would have set out some basic principles of interpretation, but they were not comprehensive works of reference or instruction. The Greek seer, certainly, needed some technical knowledge, principally when it came to the interpretation of entrails and bird signs; but he was not a scholar. His expertise was not based on book learning, but rather on observation and practice. Many practicing seers, and especially those who belonged to elite mantic families (such as the Iamidae and Melampodidae), must have provided some sort of apprenticeship to their members. It was this apprenticeship, the ability to name one's "teachers," that served as one's credentials.

The successful seer was able to give a persuasive performance before an audience of mortals and, from their perspective at least, of gods. What made that performance "successful"? From the seer's point of view success might be measured in terms of prestige, status, and career advancement. From the client's point of view a successful divinatory session was one that resulted in resolving a dispute, relieving uncertainty and anxiety, or reaching a difficult decision. Divination, as some moderns like to emphasize, can validate in the eyes of the masses decisions already taken by an elite. But that is not its primary function. Its primary function, the one that makes it socially and politically efficacious, is its ability to help individuals and groups make decisions that are particularly difficult, stressful, contentious, or consequential.

Seers were well paid because they performed an essential function in Greek society by facilitating decision making at all levels. Regardless of whether one's methodological orientation toward the study of religion tends to be positivist or relativist, one thing is clear and indisputable. Seers were in demand because the vast majority of Greeks of every social stratum both believed that their expertise could be useful and actually found it to be so over time. The criticisms of seers that occur in our sources from Homer to Euripides do not contradict this conclusion. If anything, such criticisms reveal an anxiety that is present in all societies that depend on seers. The community places its trust in individuals who are often outsiders and who claim to have a special access to supernatural knowledge. Skepticism served the important function of supporting the divinatory system of knowledge and belief by providing an escape valve in cases of failure. If a decision taken on the basis of divination leads to a disadvantageous result or even to catastrophe, one can attribute this to the incompetence or dishonesty of the seer who had been consulted rather than to a fault in the system itself. Thus divination, as a means of communication between supernatural powers and human beings, cannot easily be falsified within a community that practices it.

Calling the practice of divination a performance should not be taken to imply that Greek seers were frauds or charlatans, or, to put it in morally neutral terms, were simply pretending. Ethnographic studies have sufficiently demonstrated that being a self-aware performer is not at all psychologically incompatible with taking one's own powers seriously. Although we can never know what any particular seer was actually thinking as he or she engaged in the rites of divination, we can say that the functioning of this system as well as it did over such a long period of time presupposes a genuine belief in its efficacy by both practitioner and client. The charisma of the performer continually reassures the client that he is dealing with someone whose abilities, pronouncements, and advice he can trust. At the same time, the pressure on the seer to perform well, given that his continued employment depended on the success and confidence of his clients, must have been tremendous.

Clients, however, were not naive, even when dealing with seers that they otherwise trusted. The example of Xenophon shows that there was calculation involved in how and when one used divination and in the types of questions that one asked. In a society in which the rituals of divination were commonly employed, both seer and client developed strategies for using this system in a way that was most advantageous and beneficial for their respective interests. If this counts as "manipulation," it was a species of manipulation that was not at all inconsistent with a genuine belief in the objective validity of divination.

I have argued in this book that both the practice of divination and the consultation of seers were pervasive in the Greek world. Would the Greeks have behaved and acted differently, both individually and collectively, without seers and oracles to guide them? If we could somehow extract divination from their experience, what would Greek history and Greek culture look like?

It would be difficult, and perhaps not very meaningful, to try to answer that question directly, for no simple answer could be given. One could argue, for example, that if Nicias had not consulted his seers about the eclipse of the moon in 413 B.C., the Athenian armada would have escaped from Syracuse, and, as a consequence, the Athenians would have had the necessary resources to win the Peloponnesian War. But one might just as easily argue that if his personal seer, Stilbides, had still been alive at the time, he would have persuaded an otherwise reluctant Nicias to leave Syracuse at the time of the eclipse. So it was not the presence or absence of divination per se that was decisive for the eventual result, but the way that divination was used. But there is more to it than that. Even though Nicias's personal attitude toward divination was historically consequential in the sense that he followed the recommendation of the seers who were present, the fact that these seers were consulted at all was not a matter of his personal choice. It was not an elective action. Divination was so embedded in the structure of Greek politics and warfare that neither Nicias nor any other leader could simply ignore an occurrence that his troops took to be ominous.

The deep embeddedness of divination is usually not recognized by classical scholars, perhaps because the centrality and ubiquity of divination reveal a mentality that is profoundly alien and foreign when viewed through the lens of post-Enlightenment positivism and rationality. Nonetheless, without divination Greek "religion" itself would be fundamentally altered, since divination was an integral part of the whole nexus of relationships, rituals, and beliefs that comprised the religious system of the Greeks. Moreover, one simply could not remove divination from the fabric of Greek culture without expecting other areas of experience to be affected as well. Religious beliefs, like all beliefs, do not exist in a vacuum; rather, they are surrounded and supported by other beliefs in what may be called a "doxastic neigborhood."

Finally, if this question were addressed to Xenophon, someone who routinely and, as far as we can tell, genuinely sought divine guidance, he would not answer in the same vein as so many modern students of antiquity. As scholars we tend to give greater objective value to the inferred social or symbolic function of an institution or practice than to the purpose that its actual practitioners assign to it. Xenophon, I am convinced, would not say that the primary purpose of divination was to confirm his resolve to do things that he had already decided to do or to boost his morale at times of uncertainty, even if it sometimes served those ends. He certainly would not have admitted that divination could function as a self-consciously constructed pretext or justification for controversial or contested decisions, or as a means for the elite to control the masses. Rather, he would firmly assert that the purpose of divinatory rituals was to ascertain the will of the gods in reference to proposed courses of action, and that gods had given him advice that had helped him avoid mistakes and achieve success. In this respect there is a marked continuity of belief from the time of Hesiod in c. 700 B.C. to the time of Xenophon in the early fourth century and beyond. Of course, correctly interpreting the coded messages that the gods sent by implanting them on the entrails of an animal or by manipulating the flight of a bird or by causing abnormal phenomena was not easy. And that is why one always needed the services of an experienced seer.

The experience of a Greek such as Xenophon, who was a well-educated member of the elite and who had been a follower of Socrates, tells us something exceptionally important about Greek attitudes. Xenophon confirms that the routine consultation of seers and oracles was considered to be normative behavior among his contemporaries. And in Xenophon's case those contemporaries were not just Athenians and Spartans, but his fellow mercenaries from a large number of Greek cities, all of whom seem to have put as much trust in divination in general, and in the particular expertise of seers, as he did. What was considered unusual and worthy of comment in Greek society was the behavior of individuals who either mocked divination as useless or were, as we might say, compulsively obsessed with it.

Divination in Greece, as well as in the ancient world generally, was something so essential and routine that it is easy to imagine that its sudden disappearance would have caused a severe disruption of both political and private life. Seers could be found in the entourage of the wealthy, as their confidants and traveling companions; they accompanied generals on campaign and participated in state enterprises, such as colonization; they frequented the cities and houses of any who were willing to pay for their services. The "blameless" seer, the charismatic companion who could give unerring advice that would lead to success at home and abroad, this was a person that almost any Greek would have looked hard to find and paid much to employ. The fact that we know the names of only some seventy "historical" seers does not in any way indicate the unimportance or low status of such individuals, but rather, their ubiquity. When a seer does something so out of the ordinary as to be named, it is often an action of such historical consequence that only a figure of considerable influence could have achieved it.

Three stone pillars, each inscribed with a verse epigram, were set up at Thermopylae in commemoration of those Greeks who had fallen there in 480 B.C. (Hdt. 7.228). One was for the Peloponnesians, another for the Spartans, and a third for the seer Megistias. The first two pillars were an official dedication by the Amphictyons (a body who administered a local shrine of Demeter), but the third was a private dedication by the poet Simonides of Ceos for his guest-friend Megistias (quoted in chap. 3). Simonides obviously felt that his friend had done something to deserve such special and personal commemoration (no other Greek was identified by name on these pillars), and who are we to disagree?

BIBLIOGRAPHY

Abbink, J. 1993. "Reading the Entrails: Analysis of an African Divination Discourse." *Man*, n.s., 28: 705–26.

Acosta-Hughes, B., E. Kosmetatou, and M. Baumbach, 2004. *Labored in Papyrus Leaves: Perspectives on an Epigram Collection Attributed to Posidippus (P.Mi.Vogl. VIII 3009)*. Washington, D.C.

"Actes du IIe Colloque International du C.E.R.G.A. sur 'Oracles et mantique en Grèce ancienne.'" *Kernos* 3 (1990).

Ahern, E. M. 1981. *Chinese Ritual and Politics*. Cambridge.

Amandry, P. 1975. *La mantique apollinienne à Delphes: Essai sur le fonctionnement de l'oracle*. Paris.

Anderson, J. K. 1970. *Military Theory and Practice in the Age of Xenophon*. Berkeley.

———. 1974. *Xenophon*. London.

Andrewes, A. 1974. "The Arginousai Trial." *Phoenix* 28: 112–22.

Argyle, A. W. 1970. "Χρησμολόγοι and Μάντεις." *CR* 20: 139.

Arnott, W. G. 1989. "Nechung: A Modern Parallel to the Delphic Oracle?" *GRBS* 36: 152–57.

Asad, T. 1993. *Genealogies of Religion: Discipline and Reasons of Power in Christianity and Islam*. Baltimore.

Avedon, J. F. 1984. *In Exile from the Land of Snows*. New York.

Badian, E. 1981. "The Deification of Alexander the Great." In *Ancient Macedonian Studies in Honor of Charles F. Edson*, edited by H. J. Dello, 27–71. Thessaloniki.

Baldriga, R. 1994. "Mopso tra Oriente e Grecia : Storia di un personaggio di frontiera." *QUCC* 46: 35–71.

Banton, M., ed. 1966. *Anthropological Approaches to the Study of Religion*. London.

Barnes, M. H. 2000. *Stages of Thought: The Co-evolution of Religious Thought and Science*. Oxford.

Barton, T. S. 1994. *Ancient Astrology*. London.

Bascom, W. 1969. *Ifa Divination: Communication between Gods and Men in West Africa*. Bloomington.

Baumbach, M., and K. Trampedach. 2004. "'Winged Words': Poetry and Divination in Posidippus' Oionoskopika." In *Labored in Papyrus Leaves: Perspectives on an Epigram Collection Attributed to Posidippus (P.Mi.Vogl. VIII 3009)*, edited by B. Acosta-Hughes, E. Kosmetatou, and M. Baumbach, 123–60. Washington, D.C.

Baumgarten, R. 1998. *Heiliges Wort und Heilige Schrift bei den Griechen: Hieroi Logoi und verwandte Erscheinungen*. Tübingen.

Baynham, E. 1998. *Alexander the Great: The Unique History of Quintus Curtius*. Ann Arbor.

Beard, M. 1986. "Cicero and Divination: The Formation of a Latin Discourse." *JRS* 76: 33–46.

Beard, M., and J. North, eds. 1990. *Pagan Priests*. London.

Beattie, J. H. M. 1964. "Divination in Bunyoro, Uganda." *Sociologus* 14: 44–61.

———. 1966. "Consulting a Diviner in Bunyoro: A Text." *Ethnology* 5: 202–17.

———. 1967. "Consulting a Nyoro Diviner: The Ethnologist as Client." *Ethnology* 6: 57–65.

Becher, I. 1985. "Tiber überschwemmungen: Die Interpretation von Prodigien in Augusteischer Zeit." *Klio* 67: 471–79.

Berve, H. 1926. *Das Alexanderreich auf prosopographischer Grundlage*. 2 vols. Munich.

Blenkinsopp, J. 1996. *A History of Prophecy in Israel*. Louisville.

Bloch, M. E. F. 1998. "What Goes Without Saying." In *How We Think They Think: Anthropological Approaches to Cognition, Memory, and Literacy*, 22–38. Boulder.

Bloch, R. 1984. *La divination dans l'antiquité*. Paris.

———. 1991. *La divination*. Paris.

Bobzien, S. 1998. *Determinism and Freedom in Stoic Philosophy*. Oxford.

Bonfante, L. 2006. "Etruscan Inscriptions." In *The Religion of the Etruscans*, edited by N. T. De Grummond and E. Simon, 9–26. Austin.

Borger, R. 1956. *Die Inschriften Asarhaddons, Königs von Assyrien*. Graz.

Borthwick, E. K. 1976. "The Scene on the Panagjurischte Amphora: A New Solution." *JHS* 96: 148–51.

Bosworth, A. B. 1977. "Alexander and Ammon." In *Greece and the Eastern Mediterranean in History and Prehistory*, edited by K. H. Kinzl, 51–75. Berlin.

———. 1988. *From Arrian to Alexander*. Oxford.

———. 1996. *Alexander and the East: The Tragedy of Triumph*. Oxford.

———. 2003. "Plus ça change . . . : Ancient Historians and Their Sources." *CA* 22: 167–98.

Bottéro, J. 1992. *Mesopotamia: Writing, Reasoning, and the Gods*. Translated by Zainab Bahrani and Marc Van De Mieroop. Chicago.

———. 2001. *Religion in Ancient Mesopotamia*. Translated by Teresa Lavender Fagan. Chicago.

Bouché-Leclercq, A. 1879–82. *Histoire de la divination dans l'antiquité*. 4 vols. Paris.

Bourdieu, P. 1987. "Legitimation and Structured Interests in Weber's Sociology of Religion." In *Max Weber, Rationality and Modernity*, edited by S. Whimster and S. Lash, 119–36. London.

Bousquet, J. 1975. "Arbinas, fils de Gergis dynaste de Xanthos." *CRAI (Comptes rendus de l'Académie des Inscriptions et Belles-Lettres)* Jan.–March: 138–48.

———. 1992. "Les inscriptions du Létôon en l'honneur d'Arbinas et l'épigramme grecque de la stèle de Xanthos." In *Fouilles de Xanthos IX: La region nord du Létôon—les sculptures—les inscriptions gréco-lyciennes*, edited by H. Metzger, 155–87. Paris.

Bowden, H. 2003. "Oracles for Sale." In *Herodotus and His World*, edited by P. Derow and R. Parker, 256–74. Oxford.

———. 2004. "Xenophon and the Scientific Study of Religion." In *Xenophon and His World*, edited by C. Tuplin, 229–46. Historia Einzelschriften 172. Stuttgart.

———. 2005. *Classical Athens and the Delphic Oracle: Divination and Democracy*. Cambridge.

Bowie, F. 2000. *The Anthropology of Religion*. Oxford.

Bremmer, J. N. 1993. "Prophets, Seers, and Politicians in Greece, Israel, and Early Modern Europe." *Numen* 40: 150–83.

———. 1996. "The Status and Symbolic Capital of the Seer." In *The Role of Religion in the Early Greek Polis*, edited by R. Hägg, 97–109. Stockholm.

———. 1999. "The Birth of the Term 'Magici.'" *ZPE* 126: 1–12. (Repr. in *The Metamorphosis of Magic from Late Antiquity to the Early Modern Period*, ed. Jan N. Bremmer, Jan R. Veenstra, and Brannon Wheeler, 1–11 and 267–71 [Leuven, 2002].)

Brenk, F. 1977. *In Mist Apparelled: Religious Themes in Plutarch's 'Moralia' and 'Lives.'* Mnemosyne Supplement 48. Leiden.

Broad, W. 2006. *The Oracle: The Lost Secrets and Hidden Message of Ancient Delphi.* New York.

Brodersen, K., ed. 2001. *Studien zur Funktion von Zukunftsvorhersagen in Literatur und Geschichte seit der Antike.* Hamburg.

Bruit Zaidman, L., and P. Schmitt Pantel. 1992. *Religion in the Ancient Greek City.* Translated by P. Cartledge. Cambridge.

Burkert, W. 1962. "GOHS: Zum griechischen 'Schamanismus.'" *RhM* 105: 36–55.

———. 1983. "Itinerant Diviners and Magicians: A Neglected Element in Cultural Contacts." In *The Greek Renaissance of the Eighth Century B.C.: Tradition and Innovation*, edited by R. Hägg, 115–19. Stockholm.

———. 1985. *Greek Religion.* Cambridge, Mass.

———. 1991. *Oedipus, Oracles, and Meaning: From Sophocles to Umberto Eco.* The Samuel James Stubbs Lecture Series. Toronto.

———. 1992. *The Orientalizing Revolution: Near Eastern Influence on Greek Culture in the Early Archaic Age.* Translated by M. E. Pinder and W. Burkert. Cambridge, Mass.

———. 1996. *Creation of the Sacred: Tracks of Biology in Early Religions.* Cambridge, Mass.

———. 2005. "Signs, Commands, and Knowledge: Ancient Divination between Enigma and Epiphany." In *Mantikê: Studies in Ancient Divination*, edited by S. I. Johnston and P. T. Struck, 29–49. Leiden.

Buxton, R. 1994. *Imaginary Greece.* Oxford.

———, ed. 2000. *Oxford Readings in Greek Religion.* Oxford.

Callaway, H. 1871–72. "On Divination and Analogous Phenomena among the Natives of Natal." *Journal of the Royal Anthropological Institute* 1: 163–85.

Caquot, A., and M. Leibovici, eds. 1968. *La divination.* 2 vols. Paris.

Carne-Ross, D. S. 1979. "Weaving with Points of Gold: Pindar's Sixth Olympian." In *Instaurations: Essays in and out of Literature, Pindar to Pound*, 29–60. Berkeley.

Carney, E. 2000. "Artifice and Alexander History." In *Alexander the Great in Fact and Fiction*, edited by A. B. Bosworth and E. J. Baynham, 263–85. Oxford.

Carp, T. 1983. "*Venus Utraque:* A Typology of Seerhood." *CW* 76: 275–85.

Casevitz, M. 1989. "Les devins des tragiques." In *Transe et théâtre*, edited by P. Ghiron-Bistagne, 115–29. Lyon.

———. 1992. "Mantis: Le vrai sens." *REG* 105: 1–18.

Cavanaugh, M. B. 1996. *Eleusis and Athens: Documents in Finance, Religion, and Politics in the Fifth Century B.C.* Atlanta.

Cawkwell, G. L. 2005. *The Greek Wars: The Failure of Persia.* Oxford.

Chadwick, N. K. 1942. *Poetry & Prophecy.* Cambridge.

Chantraine, P. 1968–80. *Dictionnaire étymologique de la langue grecque.* 4 vols. Paris.

Charpin, D. 1985. "Les archives du Devin Asqudum dans la Résidence du 'Chantier A.'" *M.A.R.I.* 4: 453–62. Paris.

Chirassi Colombo, I. 1985. "Gli interventi mantici in Omero: Morfologia e funzione della divinazione come modalità di organizzazione del prestigio e del consenso nella cultura greca arcaica e classica." In *Soprannaturale e potere nel mondo antico e nelle società tradizionali,* edited by M. Fales and C. Grottanelli, 141–64. Milan.

Christidis, A.-Ph., S. Dakaris, and I. Vokotopoulou. 1999. "Magic in the Oracular Tablets from Dodona." In *The World of Ancient Magic,* edited by D. R. Jordan, H. Montgomery, and E. Thomassen, 67–72. Bergen.

Clairmont, C. 1970. *Gravestone and Epigram: Greek Memorials from the Archaic and Classical Period.* Mainz on Rhine.

Clinton, K. 1974. *The Sacred Officials of the Eleusinian Mysteries.* Philadelphia.

Collins, J. J. 1978. *Primitive Religion.* Totowa, N.J.

Compton, T. 1994. "The Herodotean Mantic Session at Delphi." *RhM* 137: 217–23.

Connor, W. R. 1963. "Two Notes on Diopeithes the Seer." *CP* 58: 115–18.

Crahay, R. 1956. *La littérature oraculaire chez Hérodote.* Paris.

Cryer, F. H. 1994. *Divination in Ancient Israel and Its Near Eastern Environment: A Socio-historical Investigation.* Sheffield.

Dalai Lama. 1990. *Freedom in Exile: The Autobiography of His Holiness, the Dalai Lama of Tibet.* London.

Dale, A. M., ed. 1967. *Euripides, Helen.* Oxford.

Daux, G. 1958. "Notes de lecture: Le devin Cléoboulos." *BCH* 82: 364–66.

Dawe, R., ed. 1982. *Sophocles: Oedipus Rex.* Cambridge.

Dean-Jones, L. 2003. "Written Texts and the Rise of the Charlatan in Ancient Greek Medicine." In *Written Texts and the Rise of Literate Culture in Ancient Greece,* edited by H. Yunis, 97–121. Cambridge.

De Boer, J. Z., J. R. Hale, and J. Chanton. 2001. "New Evidence for the Geological O of the Ancient Delphic Oracle (Greece)." *Geology* 29.8 (August): 707–10.

De Grummond, N. T. 2005. "Prophets and Priests." In *The Religion of the Etruscans,* edited by N. T. De Grummond, and E. Simon, 27–44. Austin.

Dein, S. 1997. "Lubavitch: A Contemporary Messianic Movement." *Journal of Contemporary Religion* 12.2: 191–204.

Denyer, N. 1985. "The Case against Divination: An Examination of Cicero's *De divinatione.*" *PCPS* 31: 1–10.

Detienne, M. 1967. *Les maîtres de vérité dans la grèce archaïque.* Paris.

———. 1996. *The Masters of Truth in Archaic Greece.* New York.

Devine, A. M. 1994. "Alexander's Propaganda Machine: Callisthenes as the Ultimate Source for Arrian, *Anabasis* 1–3." In *Ventures into Greek History,* edited by I. Worthington, 89–102. Oxford.

Devisch, R. 1993. *Weaving the Threads of Life: The Khita Gyn-Eco-Logical Healing Cult among the Yaka.* Chicago.

Dickie, M. W. 2001. *Magic and Magicians in the Greco-Roman World.* London.

Dickson, K. 1992. "Kalkhas and Nestor: Two Narrative Strategies in *Iliad* 1." *Arethusa* 25: 327–58.

Dillery, J. 1995. *Xenophon and the History of His Times.* London.

———. 2005. "Chresmologues and *Manteis:* Independent Diviners and the Problem of Authority." In *Mantikê: Studies in Ancient Divination,* edited by S. I. Johnston and P. T. Struck, 167–231. Leiden.

Dillon, M. 1996. "*Oionomanteia* in Greek Divination." In *Religion in the Ancient World: New Themes and Approaches,* edited by M. Dillon, 99–121. Amsterdam.

Di Sacco Franco, M. T. 2000. "Les devins chez Homère: Essai d'analyse." *Kernos* 13: 35–46.

Dobson, M. 1979. "Herodotus 1.47.1 and the *Hymn to Hermes:* A Solution to the Test Oracle." *AJP* 100: 349–59.

Dodds, E. R. 1951. *The Greeks and the Irrational.* Berkeley.

———. 1973. *The Ancient Concept of Progress and Other Essays on Greek Literature and Belief.* Oxford.

———. 1977. *Missing Persons: An Autobiography.* Oxford.

Dover, K. J. 1973. "Some Neglected Aspects of Agamemnon's Dilemma." *JHS* 93: 58–69.

———. 1988. "Thucydides on Oracles." In *The Greeks and Their Legacy: Collected Papers,* edited by K. J. Dover, 65–73. Oxford.

Drewal, M. T. 1991. "The State of Research on Performance in Africa." *African Studies Review* 34 (3): 1–64.

———. 1992. *Yorba Ritual: Performers, Play, Agency.* Bloomington.

———. 1994. "Embodied Practice/Embodied History: Mastery of Metaphor in the Performance of Diviner Kolawole Ositola." In *The Yorba Artist: New Theoretical Perspectives on African Arts,* edited by R. Abiodun, H. J. Drewal, and J. Pemberton, III, 171–90. Washington, D.C.

Dunbar, N., ed. 1995. *Aristophanes, Birds*. Oxford.

Durand, J.-L., and F. Lissarrague. 1979. "Les entrailles de la cité—Lectures de signes: Propositions sur la hiéroscopie." *Hephaistos* 1: 92–108.

Dürrbach, F. 1893. "L'apologie de Xénophon dans l'Anabase." *REG* 6: 343–86.

Easterling, P. E. 1989. "City Settings in Greek Poetry." *PCA* 86: 5–17.

Edmunds, L., ed. 2000. "The Teiresias Scene in Sophocles *OT*." *Syllecta Classica* 11: 33–73.

Ehrenberg, V. 1948. "The Foundation of Thurii." *AJP* 69: 149–70.

Eichler, F. 1950. *Die Reliefs des Heroon von Gjölbaschi-Trysa*. Vienna.

Eitrem, S. 1938. "Mantis und Σφάγια." *SO* 18: 9–30.

Evans, J. A. S. 1982. "The Oracle of the 'Wooden Wall.'" *CJ* 78: 24–29.

Evans-Pritchard, E. E. 1937. *Witchcraft, Oracles, and Magic among the Azande*. Oxford.

———. 1956. *Nuer Religion*. Oxford.

———. 1965. *Theories of Primitive Religion*. Oxford.

———. 1976. *Witchcraft, Oracles, and Magic among the Azande*. Abridged version by E. Gillies. Oxford.

Faraone, C. A., and D. Obbink, eds. 1991. *Magika Hiera: Ancient Greek Magic and Religion*. New York.

Feeney, D. 1998. *Literature and Religion at Rome*. Cambridge.

Fehling, D. 1989. *Herodotus and His 'Sources': Citation, Invention, and Narrative Art*. Translated by J. G. Howie. Leeds.

Fehrle, E. 1910. *Die kultische Keuschheit im Altertum*. Giessen.

Fernandez, J. W. 1991. Afterword to *African Divination Systems: Ways of Knowing*, by P. M. Peek. Bloomington.

Ferrari, G. 2003. "Myth and Genre on Athenian Vases." *CA:* 37–54.

Festinger, L., H. W. Riecken, and S. Schachter. 1956. *When Prophecy Fails*. New York.

Figueira, T. J. 1986. "Population Patterns in Late Archaic and Classical Sparta." *TAPA* 116: 165–213.

———. 1999. "The Evolution of the Messenian Identity." In *Sparta: New Perspectives*, edited by S. Hodkinson and A. Powell, 211–44. London.

Flower, H. 1991. "Herodotus and Delphic Traditions about Croesus." In *Georgica: Greek Studies in Honour of George Cawkwell*, Institute of Classical Studies, University of London, Bulletin Supp. 58, edited by M. A. Flower and M. Toher, 57–77. London.

———. 2000. "The Tradition of the *Spolia Opima:* Marcus Claudius Marcellus and Augustus." *CA* 19.1: 34–64.

Flower, M. A. 1991. "Revolutionary Agitation and Social Change in Classical Sparta." In *Georgica: Greek Studies in Honour of George Cawkwell*, Institute of Classical Studies, University of London, Bulletin Supp. 58, edited by M. A. Flower and M. Toher, 78–97. London.

———. 1994. *Theopompus of Chios: History and Rhetoric in the Fourth Century B.C.* Oxford.

———. 1997. *Theopompus of Chios: History and Rhetoric in the Fourth Century B.C.* Oxford. Paper edition with postscript.

———. 1998. "Simonides, Ephorus, and Herodotus on the Battle of Thermopylae." *CQ* 48: 365–79.

———. 2000. "From Simonides to Isocrates: The Fifth-Century Origins of Fourth-Century Panhellenism." *CA* 19: 65–101.

———. 2002. "The Invention of Tradition in Classical and Hellenistic Sparta." In *Sparta: Beyond the Mirage*, edited by A. Powell and S. Hodkinson, 193–219. London.

———. 2008a. "The Iamidae: A Mantic Family and Its Public Image." In *Practitioners of the Divine: Greek Priests and Religious Officials from Homer to Heliodorus*, edited by B. Dignas and K. Trampedach. Cambridge, Mass.

———. 2008b. "Athenian Religion and the Peloponnesian War." In *Athenian Art in the Peloponnesian War*, edited by O. Palagia. Cambridge.

Flower, M. A., and J. Marincola, eds. 2002. *Herodotus, Histories, Book IX*. Cambridge.

Fontenrose, J. 1978. *The Delphic Oracle*. Berkeley.

Fortes, M. 1987. *Religion, Morality, and the Person: Essays on Tallensi Religion*. Cambridge.

Fowler, R. 2000. "Greek Magic, Greek Religion." In *Oxford Readings in Greek Religion*, edited by R. Buxton, 317–43. Oxford.

Frankfurter, D. 2002. "Dynamics of Ritual Expertise in Antiquity and Beyond: Towards a New Taxonomy of 'Magicians.'" In *Magic and Ritual in the Ancient World*, edited by P. Mirecki and M. Meyer, 159–78. Leiden.

Frazer, J. G. 1888. "The Language of Animals." *The Archaeological Review* 1: 166–81.

Freyburger, G., and J. Scheid, 1992. *Cicéron, De la divination*. Paris.

Frost, F. J. 1980. *Plutarch's Themistocles: A Historical Commentary*. Princeton.

Gagarin, M. 2002. *Antiphon the Athenian: Oratory, Law, and Justice in the Age of the Sophists*. Austin.

Gager, J. G. 1992. *Curse Tablets and Binding Spells from the Ancient World*. Oxford.

Gantz, T. 1993. *Early Greek Myth: A Guide to Literary and Artistic Sources*. Baltimore.

Garland, R. 1982. "A First Catalogue of the Attic Peribolos Tombs." *ABSA* 77: 125–76.

———. 1984. "Religious Authority in Archaic and Classical Athens." *ABSA* 79: 75–122.

———. 1990. "Priests and Power in Classical Athens." In *Pagan Priests*, edited by M. Beard and J. North, 73–91. London.

Geertz, C. 1983. "Centers, Kings, and Charisma." In *Local Knowledge*, edited by C. Geertz, 121–46. New York.

Georges, P. 1986. "Saving Herodotus' Phenomena: The Oracles and Events of 480 B.C." *CA* 5: 14–59.

———. 1994. *Barbarian Asia and the Greek Experience*. Baltimore.

Georgiadou, A. 1997. *Plutarch's Pelopidas : A Historical and Philological Commentary*. Stuttgart.

Giuliani, A. 2001. *La città e l'oracolo*. Milan.

Goff, B. 2004. *Citizen Bacchae: Women's Ritual Practice in Ancient Greece*. Berkeley.

Goldhill, S. 1991. *The Poet's Voice: Essays on Poetics and Greek Literature*. Cambridge.

Goldhill, S., and R. Osborne, eds. 1999. *Performance Culture and Athenian Democracy*. Cambridge.

Goode, W. J. 1949. "Magic and Religion: A Continuum." *Ethnos* 14: 172–82.

Gould, J. 2003. "Herodotus and the 'Resurrection.'" In *Herodotus and His World*, edited by P. Derow and R. Parker, 297–302. Oxford.

Gourinat, J.-B. 2005. "Prédiction du futur et action humaine dans le traité de Chrysippe *Sur le destin*." In *Les Stoïciens*, edited by G. Romeyer-Dherbey and J.-B. Gourinat, 247–73. Paris.

Grabbe, L. L. 1995. *Priests, Prophets, Diviners, Sages: A Socio-Historical Study of Religious Specialists in Ancient Israel*. Valley Forge.

———. 2000. "Ancient Near Eastern Prophecy from an Anthropological Perspective." In *Prophecy in Its Ancient Near Eastern Context: Mesopotamian, Biblical, and Arabian Perspectives*, edited by M. Nissinen, 13–32. Atlanta.

Graf, F. 1995. "Excluding the Charming: The Greek Concept of Magic." In *Ancient Magic and Ritual Power*, edited by M. Meyer and P. Mirecki, 29–42. Leiden.

———. 1997. *Magic in the Ancient World*. Cambridge, Mass.

———. 2002. "Theories of Magic in Antiquity." In *Magic and Ritual in the Ancient World*, edited by P. Mirecki and M. Meyer, 93–104. Leiden.

Green, P. 1970. *Armada from Athens*. London.

Greenwalt, W. S. 1982. "Macedonian Mantis." *AncW* 5: 17–25.

Griffith, J. G. 1974. "The Siege Scene on the Gold Amphora of the Panagjurischte Treasure." *JHS* 94: 38–49.

Griffith, M., ed. 1999. *Sophocles, Antigone*. Cambridge.

Griffiths, A. 1999. "Euenios, the Negligent Nightwatchman (Herodotus 9.92–96)." In *From Myth to Reason? Studies in the Development of Greek Thought*, edited by R. Buxton, 169–82. Oxford.

Grottanelli, C. 2003. "Evenius Becomes a Seer (Herodotus 9. 93–95): A Paradoxical Initiation?" In *Initiation in Ancient Rituals and Narratives: New Critical Perspectives*, edited by D. B. Dodd and C. A. Faraone, 203–18. London and New York.

Guinan, A. G. 2002. "A Severed Head Laughed: Stories of Divinatory Interpretation." In *Magic and Divination in the Ancient World*, edited by L. Ciraolo and J. Seidel, 7–30. Leiden.

Haack, M.-L. 2002. "Haruspices publics and privés: Tentative d'une distinction." *REA* 104: 111–33.

———. 2003. *Les haruspices dans le monde romain*. Bordeaux.

Hahn, R. A. 1973. "Understanding Beliefs: An Essay on the Methodology of the Statement and Analysis of Belief Systems." *Current Anthropology* 14 (3): 207–29.

Hainsworth, B. 1993. *The Iliad: A Commentary*. Vol. 3: Books 9–12. Cambridge.

Hallen, B. 2000. *The Good, the Bad, and the Beautiful: Discourse about Values in an African Culture*. Bloomington.

Halliday, W. R. 1913. *Greek Divination*. London.

Halperin, D. 1990. *One Hundred Years of Homosexuality*. London.

Hamilton, J. R. 1969. *Plutarch, Alexander: A Commentary*. Oxford.

Hankinson, R. J. 1988. "Stoicism, Science, and Divination." *Apeiron* 21: 123–60.

Harris, E. M. 1995. *Aeschines and Athenian Politics*. Oxford.

Harrison, T. 2000. *Divinity and History: The Religion of Herodotus*. Oxford.

Harvey, F. D. 1991. "Herodotus 1,78 and 84: Which Telmessos?" *Kernos* 4: 245–58.

Heintz, J-G., ed. 1997. *Oracles et prophéties dans l'antiquité*. Actes du Colloque de Strasbourg, 15–17 juin 1995. Strasbourg.

Henrichs, A. 1981. "Human Sacrifice in Greek Religion: Three Case Studies." In *Le sacrifice dans l'antiquité*, 195–235. Fondation Hardt pour l'étude de l'antiquité classique, Entretiens 27. Geneva.

———. 2003. "Writing Religion: Inscribed Texts, Ritual Authority, and the Religious Discourse of the Polis." In *Written Texts and the Rise of Literate Culture in Ancient Greece*, edited by H. Yunis, 38–58. Cambridge.

Hepding, H. 1914. "Iamos." *RE* IX.I: 685–89. Berlin.

Herman, G. 1989. "Omissions in Thucydides." *CQ* 39: 83–93.

Herskovits, M. J. 1938. *Dahomey*. 2 vols. New York.

Heurgon, J. 1957. "Influences grecques sur la religion étrusque." *REL* 35: 106–26.

———. 1961. *La vie quotidienne chez les Étrusques*. Paris.

———. 1964. *Daily Life of the Etruscans*. New York.

Holladay, A. J. 1986. "Religious Scruples in Ancient Warfare." *CQ* 36: 151–60.

———. 1987. "The Forethought of Themistocles." *JHS* 107: 182–87.

Hornblower, J. 1981. *Hieronymus of Cardia*. Oxford.

Hornblower, S. 1991, 1996. *A Commentary on Thucydides*. 2 vols. Oxford.

———. 1992. "The Religious Dimension to the Peloponnesian War, or, What Thucydides Does Not Tell Us." *HSCP* 94: 169–97.

———. 1994. *Greek Historiography*. Oxford.

Horton, R. 1967. "African Traditional Thought and Western Science." *Africa* 38: 50–71, 155–87. (Repr. in Horton 1993: 197–258.)

———. 1993. *Patterns of Thought in Africa and the West: Essays on Magic, Religion, and Science*. Cambridge.

How, W. W., and J. Wells. 1912. *A Commentary on Herodotus*. 2 vols. Oxford. (Repr. with corrections, 1928.)

Huffmon, H. B. 2000. "A Company of Prophets: Mari, Assyria, Israel." In *Prophecy in Its Ancient Near Eastern Context: Mesopotamian, Biblical, and Arabian Perspectives*, edited by M. Nissinen, 47–70. Atlanta.

Hughes, D. 1991. *Human Sacrifice in Ancient Greece*. London.

Humphreys, S. C. 2004. *The Strangeness of Gods: Historical Perspectives on the Interpretation of Athenian Religion*. Oxford.

Hunter, R. L. 2004. *Plato's Symposium*. Oxford.

Hutchinson, G. O. 2001. *Greek Lyric Poetry: A Commentary on Selected Larger Pieces*. Oxford.

Immerwahr, H. R. 1966. *Form and Thought in Herodotus*. Cleveland.

———. 1990. *Attic Script: A Survey*. Oxford.

Jacoby, F. 1949. *Atthis, the Local Chronicles of Ancient Athens*. Oxford.

Jameson, M. H. 1986. "Sophocles, *Antigone* 1005–1022: An Illustration." In *Greek Tragedy and Its Legacy: Essays Presented to D. J. Conacher*, edited by M. Cropp, E. Fantham, and S. E. Scully, 59–65. Calgary.

———. 1991. "Sacrifice before Battle." In *Hoplites: The Classical Greek Battle Experience*, edited by V. D. Hanson, 197–228. London.

———. 1999. "The Spectacular and Obscure in Athenian Religion." In *Performance*

Culture and Athenian Democracy, edited by S. Goldhill and R. Osborne, 321–40. Cambridge.

Jastrow, M. 1912. *Die Religion Babyloniens und Assyriens*. Vol. 2. Giessen.

Jebb, R. C., ed. 1906. *Sophocles, Antigone*. Cambridge.

Jehne, M. 1995. "Die Funktion des Berichts über die Kinadon-Verschwörung in Xenophons *Hellenika*." *Hermes* 123: 166–74.

Jeyes, U. 1978. "The 'Palace Gate' of the Liver: A Study of Terminology." *JCS* 30: 209–33.

———. 1980. "The Act of Extispicy in Ancient Mesopotamia: An Outline." In *Assyriological Miscellanies* 1, Institute of Assyriology, edited by B. Alster, 13–32. Copenhagen.

———. 1989. *Old Babylonian Extispicy: Omen Texts in the British Museum*. Istanbul.

Johnson, D. 1999. *Hume, Holism, and Miracles*. Ithaca, N.Y.

Johnston, S. I. 2005. "Introduction: Divining Divination." In *Mantikê: Studies in Ancient Divination*, edited by S. I. Johnston and P. T. Struck, 1–28. Leiden.

Jong, I. J. F. de. 2001. *A Narratological Commentary on the* Odyssey. Cambridge.

Jordan, B. 1979. *Servants of the Gods: A Study in the Religion, History, and Literature of Fifth-Century Athens*. Hypomnemata 55. Göttingen.

———. 1986. "Religion in Thucydides." *TAPA* 116: 119–47.

Jouan, F. 2004. *Euripide, Tragédies, tome VIII, 2e partie: Rhésos*. Paris.

Jouanna, J. 1997. "Oracles et devins chez Sophocle." In *Oracles et prophéties dans l'antiquité*, edited by J-G. Heintz, 283–320. Actes du Colloque de Strasbourg, 15–17 juin 1995. Paris.

———. 1999. *Hippocrates*. Translated by M. B. DeBevoise. Baltimore.

Jules-Rosette, B. 1978. "The Veil of Objectivity: Prophecy, Divination, and Social Inquiry." *American Anthropologist*, n.s., 80: 549–70.

Kaltsas, N. 2002. *Sculpture in the National Archaeological Museum, Athens*. Los Angeles.

Kannicht, R. 1969. *Euripides, Helena*. 2 vols. Heidelberg.

Karp, A. 1998. "Prophecy and Divination in Archaic Greek Literature." In *Mediators of the Divine: Horizons of Prophecy, Divination, Dreams, and Theurgy in Mediterranean Antiquity*, edited by R. M. Berchman, 9–44. Atlanta.

Katz, J. T., and K. Volk. 2000. "'Mere Bellies'? A New Look at *Theogony* 26–8." *JHS* 120: 122–31.

Keightley, D. N. 1978. *Sources of Shang History: The Oracle-Bone Inscriptions of Bronze Age China*. Berkeley.

Kerferd, G. B. 1981. *The Sophistic Movement.* Cambridge.

Kett, P. 1966. "Prosopographie der historischen griechischen Manteis bis auf die Zeit Alexanders des Grossen." Diss., Erlangen-Nürnberg.

Kindt, J. 2001. "Von Schafen und Menschen: Delphische Orakelsprüche und soziale Kontrolle." In *Prognosis: Studien zur Funktion von Zukunftsvorhersagen in Literatur und Geschichte seit der Antike,* edited by K. Brodersen, 25–38. Münster.

King, C. J. 2004. "Divination in the Alexander Historians: Dreams, Omens, and the Seer Aristander of Telmessus." PhD diss., Brown University.

Kingsley, P. 1995. *Ancient Philosophy, Mystery, and Magic.* Oxford.

Kirk, G. S. 1985. *The Iliad: A Commentary.* Vol. 1: Books 1–4. Cambridge.

———. 1990. *The Iliad: A Commentary.* Vol. 2: Books 5–8. Cambridge.

Klass, M. 2003. *Mind over Mind: The Anthropology and Psychology of Spirit Possession.* New York.

Klees, H. 1965. *Die Eigenart des griechischen Glaubens an Orakel und Seher: Ein Vergleich zwischen griechischer und nichtgriechischer Mantik bei Herodot.* Tübinger Beiträge zur Altertumswissenschaft 43. Stuttgart.

Koch-Westenholz, U. 2000. *Babylonian Liver Omens: The Chapters Manzāzu, Padānu, and Pān tākalti of the Babylonian Extispicy Series Mainly from Aššurbanipal's Library.* Copenhagen.

Körte, G. 1905. "Die Bronzeleber von Piacenza." *RömMitt* 20: 348–77.

Kossatz-Deissmann, A. 1981. "Nestor und Antilochus: Zu den spätarchaischen Bildern mit Leberschau." *AA:* 562–76.

Kovacs, D. 2003. *Euripidea Tertia.* Leiden.

Krammenhuber, A. 1977. *Orakelpraxis, Träume und Vorzeichenschau bei den Hethitern.* Heidelberg.

Kugel, J. L., ed. 1990. *Poetry and Prophecy: The Beginnings of a Literary Tradition.* Ithaca, N.Y.

Kuhrt, A. 1995. *The Ancient Near East.* Vol. 2. London and New York.

Laeyendecker L., et al., eds. 1990. *Experiences and Explanations: Historical and Sociological Essays on Religion in Everyday Life.* Leeuwarden.

LaGamma, A. 2000. *Art and Oracle: African Art and Rituals of Divination.* New York.

Lambert, W. G. 1967. "Enmeduranki and Related Matters." *JCS* 21: 126–38.

———. 1998. "The Qualifications of Babylonian Diviners." In *Festschrift für Rykle Borger zu seinem 65. Geburtstag am 24. Mai 1994: Tikip santakki mala basmu,* edited by M. Maul, 141–58. Groningen.

Lamberton, R. 2002. *Plutarch.* New Haven.

Latacz, J. 1989. *Homer: Der erste Dichter des Abendlands*. 2d ed. Munich.

————. 2000. *Homers Ilias: Gesamtkommentar*. Band I.2: Erster Gesang. Munich.

————. 2003. *Homers Ilias: Gesamtkommentar*. Band II.2: Zweiter Gesang. Munich.

Lateiner, D. 1993. "The Perception of Deception and of Gullibility in Specialists of the Supernatural (Primarily) in Athenian Literature." In *Nomodeiktes: Greek Studies in Honor of Martin Ostwald*, edited by R. Rosen and J. Farrell, 179–95. Ann Arbor.

Latte, K. 1940. "The Coming of the Pythia." *HTR* 33: 9–18.

Lavelle, B. M. 1991. "The Compleat Angler: Observations on the Rise of Peisistratos in Herodotus (1.59–64)." *CQ* 41: 317–24.

Leavitt, J., ed. 1997. *Poetry and Prophecy: The Anthropology of Inspiration*. Ann Arbor.

Lebrun, R. 1990. "Quelques aspects de la divination en Anatolie du sud-ouest." *Kernos* 3: 185–95.

Lessa, W. A., and E. Z. Vogt. 1979. Introduction to Chapter 7 in *Reader in Comparative Religion*, edited by W. A. Lessa and E. Z. Vogt, 332–34. 4th ed. New York.

Leszl, W. 1996. "I messaggi degli dei e i segni della natura." In *Knowledge through Signs: Ancient Semiotic Theories and Practice*, edited by G. Manetti, 43–85. Bologna.

Lévy, E. 1997. "Devins et oracles chez Hérodote." In *Oracles et prophéties dans l'antiquité*, edited by J-G. Heintz, 345–65. Actes du Colloque de Strasbourg, 15–17 juin 1995. Paris.

Lewis, I. M. 1986. *Religion in Context: Cults and Charisma*. Cambridge.

————. 1989. *Ecstatic Religion: A Study of Shamanism and Spirit Possession*. 2d ed. London.

Lienhardt, R. G. 1961. *Divinity and Experience: The Religion of the Dinka*. Oxford.

Lieshout, R. G. A. van. 1980. *Greeks on Dreams*. Utrecht.

Linderski, J. 1982. "Cicero and Roman Divination." *P&P* 36: 12–38.

————. 1986. "Watching the Birds: Cicero the Augur and the Augural Templa." *CP* 81: 330–40.

Lindholm, C. 1990. *Charisma*. Oxford.

Lipsey, R. 2001. *Have You Been to Delphi? Tales of the Ancient Oracle for Modern Minds*. Albany.

Lissarrague, F. 1989. "The World of the Warrior." In *A City of Images: Iconography and Society in Ancient Greece*, edited by C. Bérard et al., 39–52. Princeton.

————. 1990. *L'autre guerrier: archers, peltastes, cavaliers dans l'imagerie attique*. Paris.

Lloyd, G. E. R. 1979. *Magic, Reason, and Experience*. Cambridge.

————. 1987. *The Revolutions of Wisdom*. Berkeley.

————. 2002. *The Ambitions of Curiosity: Understanding the World in Ancient Greece and China*. Cambridge.

Lloyd-Jones, H. 1976. "The Delphic Oracle." *G&R* 23: 60–73.

Loewe, M. 1994. *Divination, Mythology, and Monarchy in Han China*. Cambridge.

Loewe, M., and C. Blacker, eds. 1981. *Oracles and Divination*. Boulder.

Löffler, I. 1963. *Die Melampodie: Versuch einer Rekonstruktion des Inhalts*. Meisenheim am Glan.

Lonis, R. 1979. *Guerre et religion en Grèce à l'époque classique*. Paris.

Lossau, M. 1990. "Xenophons Odyssee." *A&A* 36: 47–52.

Luraghi, N. 1997. "Un *mantis* eleo nella Siracusa di Ierone: Agesia di Siracusa, Iamide di Stinfalo." *Klio* 79: 69–86.

————. 2001. "Local Knowledge in Herodotus' *Histories*." In *The Historian's Craft in the Age of Herodotus*, edited by N. Luraghi, 138–60. Oxford.

Lyons, D. 1998. "Manto and *Manteia*: Prophecy in the Myths and Cults of Heroines." In *Sibille e linguaggi oracolari*, edited by I. C. Colombo and T. Seppilli, 227–37. Pisa.

Maass, M. 1996. *Delphi: Orakel am Nabel der Welt*. Sigmaringen.

Macan, R. W. 1908. *Herodotus: The Seventh, Eighth, and Ninth Books*. 2 vols. in 3. London.

MacBain, B. 1982. *Prodigy and Expiation: A Study in Religion and Politics in Republican Rome*. Collection Latomus 177. Brussels.

MacGaffey, W. 1983. *Modern Kongo Prophets: Religion in a Plural Society*. Bloomington.

Malkin, I. 1987. *Religion and Colonization in Ancient Greece*. Leiden.

Manetti, G. 1993. *Theories of the Sign in Classical Antiquity*. Translated by C. Richardson. Bloomington.

————. 1996. *Knowledge through Signs*. Brepolis.

Mantis, A. 1990. *Problemata tes eikonografias ton iereion kai ton iereon sten archaia ellenike techne*. Athens.

Marinatos, N. 1981. "Thucydides and Oracles." *JHS* 101: 138–40.

Mason, P. G. 1959. "Kassandra." *JHS* 79: 80–93.

Mastrokostas, E. I. 1966. "Epistēmata ek Myrrinountos." In *Charistērion eis Anastasion K. Orlandon*, 3: 281–99. Athens.

Mastronarde, D. J. 1986. "The Optimistic Rationalist in Euripides." In *Greek Tragedy and Its Legacy: Essays Presented to D. J. Conacher,* edited by M. Cropp, E. Fantham, and S. E. Scully, 201–11. Calgary.

Maurizio, L. 1995. "Anthropology and Spirit Possession: A Reconsideration of the Pythia's Role at Delphi." *JHS* 115: 69–86.

———. 1997. "Delphic Oracles and Oral Performances." *CA* 16: 308–34.

———. 1998. "Narrative, Biographical, and Ritual Conventions at Delphi." In *Sibille e linguaggi oracolari,* edited by I. C. Colombo and T. Seppilli, 133–58. Pisa.

———. 2001. "The Voice at the Centre of the World: The Pythia's Ambiguity and Authority." In *Making Silence Speak: Women's Voices in Greek Literature and Society,* edited by A. Lardinois and L. McClure, 38–54. Princeton.

McLeod, W. E. 1961. "Oral Bards at Delphi." *TAPA* 92: 317–25.

McSweeney, B. 1974. "The Priesthood in Sociological Theory." *Social Compass* 2: 5–23.

Meier, J. P. 1994. *A Marginal Jew: Rethinking the Historical Jesus.* Vol. 2. New York.

Melton, J. G. 1985. "Spiritualization and Reaffirmation: What Really Happens When Prophecy Fails." *American Studies* 26.2: 82.

Metzler, D. 1990. "Der Seher Mopsos auf den Münzen der Stadt Mallos." *Kernos* 3: 235–50.

Meyer, J. W. 1987. *Untersuchungen zu den Tonlebermodellen aus dem Alten Orient.* Kevelaer.

Mikalson, J. D. 1983. *Athenian Popular Religion.* Chapel Hill.

———. 1991. *Honor Thy Gods: Popular Religion in Greek Tragedy.* Chapel Hill.

———. 2003. *Herodotus and Religion in the Persian Wars.* Chapel Hill.

———. 2004. *Ancient Greek Religion.* London.

Millender, E. G. 2001. "Spartan Literacy Revisited." *CA* 20: 121–64.

Moberly, R. W. L. 2006. *Prophecy and Discernment.* Cambridge.

Möbius, H. 1967. "Diotima." In *Studia Varia: Aufsätze zur Kunst und Kultur der Antike mit Nachträgen,* 33–46. Wiesbaden.

Montiglio, S. 2005. *Wandering in Ancient Greek Culture.* Chicago.

Moreau, A. 1993. "Les prophéties de Tirésias: Un devin trop humain (*Oed. Roi,* 300–462)." In *Sophocle, le texte, les personages,* edited by A. Machin and L. Pernée, 219–32. Aix-en-Provence.

Morgan, C. 1990. *Athletes and Oracles: The Transformation of Olympia and Delphi in the Eighth Century B.C.* Cambridge.

Morris, B. 2006. *Religion and Anthropology: A Critical Introduction.* Cambridge.

Morris, S. P. 1992. *Daidalos and the Origins of Greek Art.* Princeton.

Morrison, J. S. 1981. "The Classical World." In *Oracles and Divination*, edited by M. Loewe and C. Blacker, 87–114. Boulder.

Munson, R. V. 2001. *Telling Wonders: Ethnographic and Political Discourse in the Work of Herodotus.* Ann Arbor.

———. 2005. *Black Doves Speak: Herodotus and the Languages of Barbarians.* Cambridge.

Murray, O. 2001. "Herodotus and Oral History Reconsidered." In *The Historian's Craft in the Age of Herodotus*, edited by N. Luraghi, 314–25. Oxford.

Murray, P. 1981. "Poetic Inspiration in Early Greece." *JHS* 101: 87–100.

Myers, F. W. H. 1921. "Greek Oracles." In *Essays Classical & Modern*, 1–105. London.

Nabokov, P. 2002. *A Forest of Time: American Indian Ways of History.* Cambridge.

Näf, B. 2004. *Traum und Traumdeutung im Altertum.* Darmstadt.

Nagy, G. 1990. "Ancient Greek Poetry, Prophecy, and the Concepts of Theory." In *Poetry and Prophecy: The Beginning of a Literary Tradition*, edited by J. L. Kugel, 56–64. Ithaca, N.Y.

Nebesky-Wojkowitz, R. de. 1956. *Oracles and Demons of Tibet: The Cult and Iconography of the Tibetan Protective Deities.* London.

Nesselrath, H. G. 1999. "Dodona, Siwa und Herodot—ein Testfall." *MH* 56: 1–14.

Neugebauer, O., and H. B. van Hoesen. 1959. *Greek Horoscopes.* Philadelphia.

Nilsson, M. P. 1940. *Greek Popular Religion.* Oxford.

———. 1948. *Greek Piety.* Oxford.

———. 1955–67. *Geschichte der griechischen Religion.* Vol. 1, 3d ed. Vol 2, 2d ed. Munich.

Nissinen, M. 1998. *References to Prophecy in Neo-Assyrian Sources.* Helsinki.

———, ed. 2000a. *Prophecy in Its Ancient Near Eastern Context: Mesopotamian, Biblical, and Arabian Perspectives.* Atlanta.

———. 2000b. "The Socioreligious Role of the Neo-Assyrian Prophets." In *Prophecy in Its Ancient Near Eastern Context: Mesopotamian, Biblical, and Arabian Perspectives*, edited by M. Nissinen, 89–114. Atlanta.

Nock, A. D. 1972. "Religious Attitudes of the Ancient Greeks." In *Essays on Religion and the Ancient World*, edited by Z. Stewart, 2: 534–50. Oxford.

Nordland, O. 1962. "Shamanism as an Experiencing of 'the Unreal.'" In *Studies in Shamanism*, edited by C. Erdsman, 166–85. Stockholm.

North, J. 1990. "Diviners and Divination at Rome." In *Pagan Priests*, edited by M. Beard and J. North, 49–71. London.

Nougayrol, J. 1955. "Les rapports des haruspicines étrusque et assyro-babylonienne et le foie d'argile Falerii veteres (Villa Giulia 3786)." *CRAI:* 509–20.

———. 1966. "La langue des haruspices babyloniens: À propos d'un foie d'argile inédit." *CRAI:* 193–202.

Oberhelman, S. M. 1993. "Dreams in Greco-Roman Medicine." *Aufstieg und Niedergang der Römischen Welt* II.37,1: 121–56. Berlin.

Oliver, J. H. 1950. *The Athenian Expounders of the Sacred and Ancestral Laws.* Baltimore.

Olson, S. D., ed. 1998. *Aristophanes, Peace.* Oxford.

Oppenheim, A. L. 1977. *Ancient Mesopotamia: Portrait of a Dead Civilization.* Rev. ed. Chicago.

Opsomer, J. 1996. "Divination and Academic 'Scepticism' according to Plutarch." *Studia Hellenistica* 32: 165–94.

Osborne, M. J. 1970. "Honours for Sthorys (*IG* ii².17)." *BSA* 65: 151–74.

———. 1981, 1982. *Naturalization in Athens.* 2 vols. Brussels.

Ostwald, M. 1986. *From Popular Sovereignty to the Sovereignty of Law.* Berkeley.

Overholt, T. W. 1989. *Channels of Prophecy: The Social Dynamics of Prophetic Activity.* Minneapolis.

Pailler, J.-M. 1988. *Bacchanalia: La répression de 186 av. J.-C. à Rome et en Italie.* Rome.

Pallottino, M. 1982. *Etruscologia.* Milan.

Papademetriou, J. 1957. "Ὁ θειος του Αισχινου Κλεοβουλος ὁ Μαντις." *Platon* 9: 154–62.

Park, G. K. 1963. "Divination and Its Social Contexts." *Journal of the Royal Anthropological Institute* 93: 195–209.

Parke, H. W. 1967. *The Oracles of Zeus.* Oxford.

———. 1985. *The Oracles of Apollo in Asia Minor.* London.

Parke, H. W., and D. E. W. Wormell. 1956. *The Delphic Oracle.* 2 vols. Oxford.

Parker, R. 1983. *Miasma.* Oxford.

———. 1985. "Greek States and Greek Oracles." In *Crux: Essays in Greek History Presented to G. E. M. de Ste. Croix on His 75th Birthday,* edited by P. A. Cartledge and F. D. Harvey, 298–326. London. (Repr. in Buxton 2000, 76–108.)

———. 1988. "Spartan Religion." In *Classical Sparta: Techniques behind Her Success,* edited by A. Powell, 142–72. London.

———. 1996. *Athenian Religion: A History.* Oxford.

———. 1998. "Pleasing Thighs: Reciprocity in Greek Religion." In *Reciprocity in Ancient Greece,* edited by C. Gill, N. Postlethwaite, and R. Seaford, 105–25. Oxford.

————. 1999. "Through a Glass Darkly: Sophocles and the Divine." In *Sophocles Revisited: Essays Presented to Sir Hugh Lloyd-Jones,* edited by J. Griffin, 11–30. Oxford.

————. 2000. "Sacrifice and Battle." In *War and Violence in Ancient Greece,* edited by Hans van Wees, 299–314. London.

————. 2004. "One Man's Piety: The Religious Dimension of the *Anabasis.*" In *The Long March: Xenophon and the Ten Thousand,* edited by R. Lane Fox, 131–53. New Haven.

————. 2005. *Polytheism and Society at Athens.* Oxford.

Parpola, S. 1997. *Assyrian Prophecies.* Helsinki.

Pearson, L. 1960. *The Lost Histories of Alexander the Great.* Philadelphia.

————. 1962. "The Pseudo-History of Messenia and Its Authors." *Historia* 2: 397–426.

————. 1987. *The Greek Historians of the West: Timaeus and His Predecessors.* Atlanta.

Pease, A. S. 1911. "The Omen of Sneezing." *CP* 6: 429–43.

Pédech, P. 1984. *Historiens compagnons d'Alexandre.* Paris.

Peek, P. M., ed. 1991a. *African Divination Systems: Ways of Knowing.* Bloomington.

————. 1991b. "The Study of Divination, Present and Past." In *African Divination Systems: Ways of Knowing,* edited by P. M. Peek, 1–22. Bloomington.

Pelling, C. B. R. 2002. *Plutarch and History.* London.

————. 2005. "Tragedy, Rhetoric, and Performance Culture." In *A Companion to Greek Tragedy,* edited by J. Gregory, 83–102. Oxford.

Pemberton, John, III, ed. 2000. *Insight and Artistry in African Divination.* Washington, D.C., and London.

Pendrick, G. J., ed. 2002. *Antiphon the Sophist: The Fragments.* Cambridge.

Peters, L. 1982. "Trance, Initiation, and Psychotherapy in Tamang Shamanism." *American Ethnologist* 9: 21–46.

Pfeffer, F. 1976. *Studien zur Mantik in der Philosophie der Antike.* Meisenheim.

Pfiffig, A. J. 1975. *Religio etrusca.* Graz.

Piepenbrink, K. 2001. "Prophetie und soziale Kommunikation in der homerischen Gesellschaft." In *Prognosis; Studien zur Funktion von Zukunftsvorhersagen in Literatur und Geschichte seit der Antike,* edited by K. Brodersen, 9–24. Münster.

Pongratz-Leisten, B. 1999. *Herrschaftswissen in Mesopotamien: Formen der Kommunikation zwischen Gott und König im 2. und 1. Jahrtausend v.Chr.* Helsinki.

Popp, H. 1957. "Die Einwirkung von Vorzeichen." Diss., Erlangen.

Powell, C. A. 1979. "Religion and the Sicilian Expedition." *Historia* 28: 15–31.

Prandi, L. 1985. *Callistene: Uno storico tra Aristotele e i re macedoni.* Milan.

Pratt, L. 1994. "*Odyssey* 19.535–50: On the Interpretation of Dreams and Signs in Homer." *CP* 89: 147–52.

Price, S. R. F. 1984. *Rituals and Power.* Cambridge.

———. 1985. "Delphi and Divination." In *Greek Religion and Society,* edited by P. Easterling and J. V. Muir, 128–54. Cambridge.

———. 1999. *Religions of the Ancient Greeks.* Cambridge.

Pritchett, W. K. 1971. *The Greek State at War.* Vol. 1. Berkeley.

———. 1979. *The Greek State at War.* Vol. 3. Berkeley.

———. 1993. *The Liar School of Herodotus.* Amsterdam.

Radermacher, L. 1898. "Euripides und die Mantik." *RhM* 53: 497–510.

Rappaport, R. A. 1979. *Ecology, Meaning, and Religion.* Richmond, Calif.

Rawson, E. 1978. "Caesar, Etruria, and the *Disciplina Etrusca.*" *JRS* 68: 132–52.

Redfield, J. M. 1975. *Nature and Culture in the* Iliad. Chicago.

Reinhardt, K. 1957. "Die Sinneskrise bei Euripides." *Die neue Rundschau* 68: 615–46. (Translated as "The Intellectual Crisis in Euripides," in *Oxford Readings in Classical Studies: Euripides,* ed. J. Mossman, 16–46 [Oxford, 2003].)

Reynolds, J. J. 2004. "Inquiries into Signs and Sign-Inference in Greek Literature before Aristotle." PhD diss., Princeton University.

Richards, H. 1905. "Notes on Herodotus, Books IV–IX." *CR* 19: 340–46.

Ridgway, B. 1981. *Fifth Century Styles in Greek Sculpture.* Princeton.

Rigsby, K. J. 1976. "Teiresias as Magus in *Oedipus Rex.*" *GRBS* 17: 109–14.

Ritz, U. 1988. *Das Bedeutsame in den Erscheinungen: Divinationspraktiken in traditionalen Gesellschaften.* Frankfurt.

Robertson, N. 1987. "The True Meaning of the 'Wooden Wall.'" *CP* 82: 1–20.

Rochberg, F. 2004. *The Heavenly Writing: Divination, Horoscopy, and Astronomy in Mesopotamian Culture.* Cambridge.

Romeo, L. 1976. "Heraclitus and the Foundation of Semiotic." *Versus* 15: 73–90.

Romilly, J. de. 1992. *The Great Sophists in Periclean Athens.* Translated by J. Lloyd. Oxford.

Rosivach, V. J. 1997. Review of *Eleusis and Athens* by M. B. Cavanaugh 1996. *Bryn Mawr Classical Review* 97.2.22.

Roth, P. 1982. "*Mantis:* The Nature, Function, and Status of a Greek Prophetic Type." PhD diss., Bryn Mawr College.

————. 1984. "Teiresias as Mantis and Intellectual in Euripides' *Bacchae*." *TAPA* 114: 59–69.

Roux, G. 1964. "Meurtre dans un sanctuaire sur l'amphore de Panagjuriste." *AntK* 7: 30–41.

————. 1976. *Delphes, son oracle et ses dieux*. Paris.

Rudhardt, J. 1958. *Notions fondamentales de la pensée religieuse et actes constitutifs du culte dans la Grèce classique: Étude préliminaire pour aider à la compréhension de la piété athénienne au IVème siècle*. Geneva.

Rüpke, J. 1996. "Controllers and Professionals: Analyzing Religious Specialists." *Numen*: 241–62.

————. 2004. "Roman Religion." In *The Cambridge Companion to the Roman Republic*, edited by H. I. Flower, 179–95. Cambridge.

Russo, J. 1992. *A Commentary on Homer's Odyssey*. Vol. 3: Books 17–24. Oxford.

Saler, B. 1993. *Conceptualizing Religion: Immanent Anthropologists, Transcendent Natives, and Unbounded Categories*. Leiden.

————. 2001. "On What We May Believe about Beliefs." In *Religion in Mind*, edited by J. Andresen, 47–69. Cambridge.

Sanders, L. J. 1997. "What Did Theopompus Think of Dion?" *SCI*: 20–31.

Sargant, W. 1973. *The Mind Possessed: A Physiology of Possession, Mysticism, and Faith Healing*. London.

Schachter, A. 1981. *Cults of Boiotia*. Vol. 1. London.

————. 2000. "The Seer Tisamenos and the Klytiadai." *CQ* 50: 292–95.

Scheer, T. 1993. *Mythische Vorväter: Zur Bedeutung griechischer Heroenmythen im Selbstverständnis kleinasiatischer Städte*. Munich.

Schepens, G. 1994. "Politics and Belief in Timaeus of Tauromenium." *AncSoc* 25: 249–78.

Schmitt, A. 1990. *Selbständigkeit und Abhängigkeit menschlichen Handelns bei Homer: Hermeneutische Untersuchungen zur Psychologie Homers*. Akademie der Wissenschaften und der Literatur, Abhandlungen der geistes- und sozialwissenschaftlichen Klasse, Bd. 5. Mainz-Stuttgart.

Schofield, M. 1986. "Cicero for and against Divination." *JRS* 76: 47–65.

Schwartz, E. 1903. "Diodoros." *RE* V.I: 663–704. Berlin.

Sedley, D. 1998. "The Etymologies in Plato's *Cratylus*." *JHS* 118: 140–54.

Shapiro, H. A. 1990. "Oracle-Mongers in Peisistratid Athens." *Kernos* 3: 335–345.

Sharpe, E. J. 1987. *Comparative Religion: A History*. 2d ed. London.

Shaw, R. 1991. "Splitting Truth from Darkness: Epistemological Aspects of Temne

Divination." In *African Divination Systems: Ways of Knowing*, edited by P. M. Peek, 137–52. Bloomington.

———. 1996. "The Politician and the Diviner: Divination and the Consumption of Power in Sierra Leone." *Journal of Religion in Africa* 26: 30–55.

———. 1998. "The Praying Diviner: Debating Islam and Divination in Postcolonial Sierra Leone." In *Afrika und das Andere: Alterität und Innovation*, edited by Heike Schmidt and Albert Wirz, 32–41. Hamburg.

Shipley, D. R. 1997. *Plutarch's Life of Agesilaus*. Oxford.

Simon, E. 1992. "Mopsos II." *LIMC* VI.1. Zurich.

Sissa, G. 1990. *Greek Virginity*. Cambridge, Mass.

Sluiter, I. 1997. "The Greek Tradition." In *The Emergence of Semantics in Four Linguistic Traditions*. Amsterdam and Philadelphia.

Smith, N. D. 1989. "Diviners and Divination in Aristophanic Comedy." *CA* 8: 140–58.

Sokolowski, F. 1955. *Lois sacrées d'Asie Mineure*. Paris.

———. 1969. *Lois sacrées des cités grecques*. Paris.

Sordi, M., ed. 1993. *La profezia nel mondo antico*. Milan.

Sourvinou-Inwood, C. 1997. "Tragedy and Religion: Constructs and Readings." In *Greek Tragedy and the Historian*, edited by C. Pelling, 161–86. Oxford.

———. 2000a. "What is Polis Religion?" In *Oxford Readings in Greek Religion*, edited by R. Buxton, 13–37. Oxford.

———. 2000b. "Further Aspects of Polis Religion." In *Oxford Readings in Greek Religion*, edited by R. Buxton, 38–55. Oxford.

———. 2003. *Tragedy and Athenian Religion*. Lanham, Md.

Sperber, D. 1996. *Explaining Culture: A Naturalistic Approach*. Oxford.

———. 1997. "Intuitive and Reflective Beliefs." *Mind and Language* 12: 67–83.

Spiro, M. E. 1973. "Religion: Problems of Definition and Explanation." In *Anthropological Approaches to the Study of Religion*, edited by Michael Banton, 85–126. ASA Monographs 3. London.

Stadter, P. A. 1989. *A Commentary on Plutarch's Life of Pericles*. Chapel Hill and London.

Stählin, R. 1912. *Das Motiv der Mantik im antiken Drama*. Giessen.

Starr, I., ed. 1990. *Queries to the Sungod: Divination and Politics in Sargonid Assyria*. Helsinki.

Starr, J. 1974. "The 'baru' Rituals." PhD diss., Yale University.

———. 1983. *The Rituals of the Diviner*. Malibu.

Stein, H., ed. 1889. *Herodotos, Buch VII*. Berlin. (6th ed., 1908.)

Steiner, D. T. 1994. *The Tyrant's Writ: Myths and Images of Writing in Ancient Greece*. Princeton.

Steinhauser, K. 1911. *Der Prodigienglaube und das Prodigienwesen der Griechen*. Ravensburg.

Stengel, P. 1886. "Σφάγια." Hermes 21: 307–12.

———. 1896. "Prophezeiung aus den Σφάγια." Hermes 31: 478–80.

———. 1920. *Die griechischen Kultusaltertümer*. Munich.

Stephenson, F. R., and L. J. Fatoohi. 2001. "The Eclipses Recorded by Thucydides." *Historia* 50: 245–53.

Stockinger, H. 1959. *Die Vorzeichen im homerischen Epos*. Munich.

Storey, I. C. 2003. *Eupolis: Poet of Old Comedy*. Oxford.

Strauss, B. 2004. *The Battle of Salamis: The Naval Encounter That Saved Greece—and Western Civilization*. New York.

Struck, P. T. 2003. "The Ordeal of Divine Sign: Divination and Manliness in Archaic and Classical Greece." *ANDREIA: Studies in Manliness and Courage in Classical Antiquity*, edited by R. M. Rosen and I. Sluiter, 167–86. Leiden.

———. 2004. *Birth of the Symbol: Ancient Readers at the Limits of Their Texts*. Princeton.

Stylianou, P. J. 1998. *A Historical Commentary on Diodorus Siculus, Book 15*. Oxford.

Suárez de la Torre, E. 1992. "Les pouvoirs des devins et les récits mythiques: L'example de Mélampous." *Les Études Classiques* 60: 3–21.

Sweek, J. 2002. "Inquiring for the State in the Ancient Near East: Delineating Political Location." In *Magic and Divination in the Ancient World*, edited by L. Ciraolo and J. Seidel, 41–56. Leiden.

Szymanski, T. 1908. "Sacrificia graecorum in bellis militaria." Diss., Marburg.

Tadmor, H., B. Landsberger, and S. Parpola. 1989. "The Sin of Sargon and Sennacherib's Last Will." *SAAB* 1989: 4–51.

Talbert, R. J. A. 1974. *Timoleon and the Revival of Greek Sicily, 344–317 B.C.* Cambridge.

Tambiah, S. J. 1979. *A Performative Approach to Ritual*. Oxford.

Taplin, O. 1992. *Homeric Soundings: The Shaping of the Iliad*. Oxford.

Thiel, J. H. 1994. *Studies in Ancient History*. Edited by H. T. Wallinga. Amsterdam.

Thomas, R. 1989. *Oral Tradition and Written Record in Classical Athens*. Cambridge.

———. 2000. *Herodotus in Context: Ethnography, Science, and the Art of Persuasion*. Cambridge.

Thomassen, E. 1999. "Is Magic a Subclass of Ritual?" In *The World of Ancient Magic*, edited by D. R. Jordan, H. Montgomery, and E. Thomassen, 55–66. Bergen.

Thulin, C. O. 1905–9. *Die etruskische Disziplin.* 3 vols. Götenburg. (Repr. 1968, Darmstadt.)

Todd, O. J. 1939. "An Inelegant Greek Verse." *CQ* 33: 163–65.

Towler, R. 1974. *Homo Religiosus: Sociological Problems in the Study of Religion.* London.

Trampedach, K. 2003a. "Platons Unterscheidung der Mantik." In *Philosophie und Lebenswelt in der Antike*, edited by K. Piepenbrink, 52–66. Darmstadt.

———. 2003b. *Politische Mantik: Studien zur Kommunikation über Götterzeichen und Orakel im klassischen Griechenland.* Habilitationsschrift. Konstanz.

———. 2008. "Authority Disputed: The Seer in Homeric Epic." In *Practitioners of the Divine: Greek Priests and Religious Officials from Homer to Heliodorus*, edited by B. Dignas and K. Trampedach. Cambridge, Mass.

Tuplin, C. 2003. "Heroes in Xenophon's *Anabasis*." In *Modelli eroici dall' antichità alla cultura europea*, edited by A. Barzanò, C. Bearzot, F. Landucci, L. Prandi, and G. Zecchini, 4: 115–56. Rome.

Turner, V. 1968a. *The Drums of Affliction: A Study of Religious Processes among the Ndembu of Zambia.* Oxford.

———. 1968b. "Religious Specialists: An Anthropological View." In *International Encyclopedia of the Social Sciences*, 13: 437–44. New York.

Ugolini, G. 1995. *Untersuchungen zur Figur des Sehers Teiresias.* Munich.

van der Meer, L. B. 1979. "Iecur Placentium and the Orientation of the Etruscan Haruspex." *BABesch* 54: 49–64.

———. 1987. *The Bronze Liver of Piacenza: Analysis of a Polytheistic Structure.* Amsterdam.

van der Toorn, K. 2000. "Mesopotamian Prophecy between Immanence and Transcendence: A Comparison of Old Babylonian and Neo-Assyrian Prophecy." In *Prophecy in Its Ancient Near Eastern Context. Mesopotamian, Biblical, and Arabian Perspectives*, edited by M. Nissinen, 71–87. Atlanta.

Vannicelli, P. 2005. "Da Platea a Tanagra: Tisameno, Sparta e il Peloponneso durante la Pentecontaetia." In *Erodoto e il 'modello erodoteo': Formazione e trasmissione delle tradizioni storiche in Grecia*, edited by M. Giangiulio, 257–76. Trento.

Vansina, J. 1985. *Oral Tradition as History.* Madison.

Van Straten, F. T., ed. 1995. *Hiera kala: Images of Animal Sacrifice in Archaic and Classical Greece.* Leiden.

Vernant, J.-P., ed. 1974. *Divination et rationalité.* Paris.

———. 1991. "Speech and Mute Signs." In *Mortals and Immortals,* 303–17. Princeton.

———. 2001. "Forms of Belief and Rationality in Greece." In *Agon, Logos, Polis: The Greek Achievement and Its Aftermath,* edited by J. P. Arnason and P. Murphy, 118–26. Stuttgart.

Versnel, H. S. 1991. "Some Reflections on the Relationship Magic-Religion." *Numen* 38: 177–97.

Wach, J. 1944. *Sociology of Religion.* Chicago.

Weber, M. 1963. *Sociology of Religion.* Translated by Ephraim Fischoff. Introduction by Talcott Parsons. Boston.

———. 1978. *Economy and Society: An Outline of Interpretative Sociology.* Edited by G. Roth and C. Wittich. 2 vols. Berkeley. (Translation of *Wirtschaft und Gesellschaft.*)

Wees, H. van. 1996. "Heroes, Knights, and Nutters: Warrior Mentality in Homer." In *Battle in Antiquity,* edited by A. B. Lloyd, 1–86. London.

Weniger, L. 1915. "Die Seher von Olympia." *Archiv für Religionswissenschaft* 18: 53–115.

West, M. L. 1978. *Hesiod, Works and Days.* Oxford.

———. 1997. *The East Face of Helikon: West Asiatic Elements in Greek Poetry and Myth.* Oxford.

West, S. 1988. *A Commentary on Homer's Odyssey.* Vol. 1: Introduction and Books 1–8, edited by A. Heubeck, S. West, and J. B. Hainsworth. Oxford.

Westenholz, J. G. 1997. *Legends of the Kings of Akkade.* Winona Lake, Ind.

Whittaker, C. R. 1965. "The Delphic Oracle: Belief and Behaviour in Ancient Greece—and Africa." *HTR* 58: 21–48.

Wilamowitz-Moellendorff, U. von. 1931. *Der Glaube der Hellenen.* Vol. 1. Berlin.

Woodruff, P. 2004. "Antiphon, Sophist and Athenian." In *Oxford Studies in Ancient Philosophy,* edited by D. Sedley, 26: 323–36. Oxford.

Wright, M. 2005. *Euripides' Escape Tragedies.* Oxford.

Yunis, H. 1988. *A New Creed: Fundamental Religious Beliefs in the Athenian Polis and Euripidean Drama.* Hypomnemata 91. Göttingen.

Zahan, D. 1979. *The Religion, Spirituality, and Thought of Traditional Africa.* Chicago.

Zaidman, B. L., and P. Schmitt Pantel. 1992. *Religion in the Ancient Greek City.* Translated by P. Cartledge. Cambridge.

Zeitlin, F. I. 1986. "Thebes: Theater of Self and Society in Athenian Drama." In *Greek Tragedy and Political Theory,* edited by J. P. Euben, 101–41. Berkeley.

Zeitlyn, D. 1990. "Professor Garfinkel Visits the Soothsayers: Ethnomethodology and Mambila Divination." *Man*, n.s., 25: 654–66.

Zeusse, E. M. 1987. "Divination." In *The Encyclopedia of Religion*, edited by M. Eliade. New York.

Zucker, A. 1900. *Xenophon und die Opfermantik in der Anabasis*. Nürnberg.

Zuntz, G. 1960. "On Euripides' *Helena:* Theology and Irony." In *Entretiens sur l'antiquité classique*, vol. 6: *Euripide*, 199–241. Geneva.

INDEX

Page references in italics refer to illustrations.

Alexander the Great *(continued)*
172; divinity of, 178, 180; hepatoscopy
concerning, 131; interpretation of
omens, 114; murder of Cleitus, 80,
179, 181n72; mutiny against, 174;
obedience to omens, 174; seers of,
59, 80, 113, 126, 129, 130–31, 178–81;
superstitiousness of, 129, 178–79; use
of sacrificial divination, 126, 127
Alexandria, Aristander on, 179
Amphiaraus (seer): family of, 42; oracle
in Boeotia, 64, 148, 151; prediction of
his death, 93, 183–84; in *Seven against
Thebes*, 19, 23, 97, 120–21, 183–84;
use of ornithomancy, 92
Amphilochus (seer), family of, 42
Amphilytus *(chrēsmologos)*, 64; prophecy
of, 79
Anaxagoras of Clazomenae, 119, 180
Anaxibius, disregarding of omens, 172
Animals, sacrificial, 162. *See also*
Extispicy; Hepatoscopy
Anthropology: belief systems in, 105;
comparative, 105; native informants
in, 15; study of religion, xv, 11; view
of divination, xiv, 4, 10n22, 85, 86–87,
145, 189
Antigonus, seers of, 131
Antiochus I of Commagene, horoscope
of, 127n58
Antiphon: on dream interpretation, 52–
53, 125; as *teratoskopos*, 125
Antiphon (oligarch), 126
Apollo: in Greek tragedy, 18; male
prophets of, 89; oracle at Clarus, 43,
45, 89; oracle at Thebes, 24, 89; possession of Pythia, 1, 24, 89, 211, 226,
230, 231, 237; union with priestesses,
224; wrath of, 36. *See also* Oracles,
Delphic
Apollodorus (commander under Alexander), use of divination, 130–31
Apollonius Rhodius, 51

Arbela, temple of Istar at, 228
Arexion (seer): at Calpe, 143, 200–202;
performance of *sphagia*, 156, 161, 182
Argives, Delphic oracles delivered to,
235, 238–39
Argive women, healing of, 27, *28*, 212
Arginusae, battle of: seers at, 167–69
Aristander of Telmessus, 93, 172; aver-
sion of omens, 80; death of, 181; extis-
picy by, 179; influence of, 179; on por-
tents, 52; sacrifice for Cleitus, 180;
skills of, 35
Aristarchus of Samothrace, 61
Aristobulus, on seers, 131
Aristonice (Pythia), 225, 238
Aristophanes: *chrēsmologoi* in, 12, 62–63,
139; seers in, 60, 62, 103, 123, 151;
Thouriomanteis in, 123n40
Aristotle: on Antiphon, 125; on augury,
135; on oracles, 234; on seers, 186
Armies, purification of, 99
Arrian: on Alexander's seers, 130–31; on
disregarding of omens, 172; on Indian
mutiny, 174
Artaxerxes (king of Persia), 166
Asad, Talal, 67
Ashurbanipal: extispicy under, 32n31;
knowledge of divination, 49–50;
library of, 31–32, 200; oracles
addressed to, 228
Asqudum (seer), 50; in military expedi-
tions, 96
Assembly (Athens): debate on oracles,
58, 139n7; seers attending, 122
Assent, Locke on, 11
Asterie (female seer), 214
Astrology, Hellenistic, 127
Astyphilus of Poseidonia (seer), 177
Athens: Council of 500, 62; Delphic oracles for, 58, 75, 76, 218, 225, 235, 237–
38; oligarchic coup (411), 126; oracle
collections at, 218; performance in,
190n7; relations with Chalcis, 62;

return of exiles to, 203; seers in, 3n5, 122–26; Sicilian expedition (415-13), 64–65, 114–19, 177, 245

Augury (bird signs): Aristotle on, 135; Cicero on, 113; in Ephesus inscription, 113; epigrams on, 214; in Hesiod, 51; in Homer, 25, 79; in *Oedipus Tyrannus*, 136; in *Prometheus Bound*, 90; seers' use of, 24; skepticism concerning, 137; as *technē*, 199n20; Xenophon's use of, 15. *See also* Divination, artificial

Auspices (bird signs), 8; Cicero on, 128

Authority: charismatic, 59n98; mantic, 4; of oracles, 145, 217; Pythia's, 217; religious, 24, 30; of seers, 12, 24, 30, 58, 59, 87, 241; Teiresias's, 30

Autocleides, 52, 117; interpretation of dreams, 116

Avedon, John, 227

Azande people; sing. Zande (Sudan), 10n22; poison oracles of, 6, 101n51, 105, 145, 149, 161; rituals of, 20, 105; witch doctors of, 13, 145–46, 149–50

Bārûs (Assyrian seers), 30–31, 46; social status of, 50

Basias (seer), 198

Beattie, J. H. M., 13n38, 192n14

Belief: intuitive, 11n27; reflective, 11n27; theories of, 10–11

Belief, religious: in Greek society, 10; in Greek tragedy, 18

Belief systems: anthropological study of, 105; divination as, 105–6, 107–8; social purpose of, xiv; Stoic, 107

Blindness, among seers, 37, 51

Bloch, M E. F., 11n28

Boeotia, oracles of, 2, 148, 151

Bosworth, A. B., 17n50

Bottéro, Jean, 1

Bowden, H., 125n47, 144n20; on Delphic oracle, 122, 220n31, 221n32, 223n37; on Diopeithes, 125n51; on oracles,

235n73; on ritual, 223n38; on tragedy, 20n57

Bowie, F., 81n23

Bronze Age, hepatoscopy in, 33

Burkert, Walter, 29

Calchas (seer): in *Ajax*, 210; artificial divination by, 88, 91; artists' depictions of, 48, *49*; contest with Mopsus, 44, 45, 151; intuitive divination of, 88, 91, 95; prophecies by, 88

Calchas (Homer): and Agamemnon, 80, 133–34, 204, 209; augury of, 25; on future knowledge, 78

Callaway, Henry, 7

Callias (seer): assistance to Croton, 156, 185; family of, 38

Callicratidas (general), 168

Callisthenes of Olynthus, 17; on Alexander, 80, 181; Panhellenism of, 180; on prebattle omens, 175

Calliteles (seer), 46

Calpe, omens at, 143, 170, 200–202

Campground sacrifice. *See Hiera*

Carp, T., 37n42

Cassandra: in *Agamemnon*, 89, 214–15, 237; costume of, 214–15; prediction of her death, 93; prophetic possession of, 89, 92; skill of, 86; use of verse, 237; virginity of, 224–25

Cato the Elder, on *haruspices*, 47

Cecrops, 95, 237

Chalcis (Euboea), relations with Athens, 62

Charisma: importance in Greek culture, 243; of seers, 29, 30, 59, 70, 243, 246

Cheirisophus (general), 101

Chrēsmōdoi (oracle chanters), 62

China, divination in, 9, 40, 83n26

Chrēsmologoi: in Aristophanes, 12, 62–63, 139; Athenians' anger with, 138–39; decline of, 64–65, 139; in Euripides, 61; in Herodotus, 63, 65; itinerant, 125;

divination, 129; seers of, 70; Silanus and, 103, 185, 190–91

Dalai Lama, 13th, 7
Dalai Lama, 14th (Tenzin Gyatso), on oracles, 1, 7, 228
Damon (seer), 214
Daphne (female seer), 211
Deiotarus (tetrarch of Gallograecia), 8, 128
Deiphonus (seer), 37, 71; ancestors of, 45
Delphi: male priests at, 215, 217, 218, 220, 230; Navarchs monument, 95; Plutarch's service at, 222, 223; temple staff of, 231. *See also* Oracles, Delphic
Demaenetus (seer), 95, 96
Dēmioergoi (public workers), 23
Democedes of Croton, 182
Demon, *On Sacrifices*, 52
Demophon (seer), and Alexander, 181
Demosthenes, at siege of Syracuse, 115, 116
Dercylidas, assault on Cebren, 171
Dickie, M. W., 26n16, 66n119
Dillery, J., 3n5, 64n112; on Lampon, 123n41; on oracles, 218n25
Dillon, M., 199n20
Dinka people, religion of, 67, 108n8, 150
Diodorus Siculus: on battle of Arginu-sae, 167–69; on battle of Mantinea, 166; on omens, 166, 175; on seers, 167–69; on siege of Syracuse, 118; sources of, 126, 166, 167; on Thurium, 123n40; on Timoleon, 111n15
Diogenianus (philosopher), 236
Dion of Syracuse: assassination of, 195; and Miltas, 178, 194–95; seers of, 110, 194–95; Sicilian expedition of, 110, 118, 194–95
Dionysius II (tyrant of Syracuse): Dion's expedition against, 110, 118,

194–95; seers of, 110, 182; Timoleon's mission against, 111
Dionysus: Egyptian cult of, 25; possession by, 89
Dionysus Omestes, sacrifice to, 203
Diopeithes (*chrēsmologos*), 65n114; departure from Athens, 125n52; and Nicias, 177; political activity of, 124–25
Diotima (female seer), 29, 89, 212; stele of, *213*
Disposition theory (belief), 10n24
Dissociative Identity Phenomena, 231n67
Divination: alternatives offered by, 75; ancient definition of, 73; anthropological view of, xiv, 10n22, 85; apotropaic action following, 69, 79, 80–84; apprenticeship in, 38, 70; arbitrating function of, 75; Ashurbnipal's knowledge of, 49–50; and Athenian democracy, 122–26; authoritative, 87, 101, 104–5; as belief system, 105–6, 107–8; books on, 37, 51–53, 129, 154, 188; Chinese, 9, 40, 83n26; Chrysippus on, 73, 106n2; Cicero on, 73, 84–85, 90, 106n2; on clay tablets, 31–32; comparative study of, 9–10; as craft, 72; cross-cultural study of, 26, 241; cultural usefulness of, 153–54; defining function of, 75; demystification of, 129; direction of future through, 76–80; discourse of, 12; discovery of analogies in, 144–45; failures of, 107–8; falsification of, 122; fillets worn in, 214; flexibility of, 174; functions of, 75, 243–44; in Greek literature, 14–21; in Greek tragedy, 14, 17–19; in *Harry Potter*, 22; hereditary faculty of, 27, 37; in Hippocratic corpus, 12, 28, 113; in the *Iliad*, 35–36; impromptu, 70; in industrialized societies, 5; in inscriptions, 21; interpretation in, 14,

Divination *(continued)*
24, 72–73, 85, 113–14; as knowledge system, 2, 6, 132, 165, 244; legitimation of, 72; long-distance, 130–31; *versus* madness, 84; manipulation of, 5, 70, 153–54, 173, 174–76, 191, 221, 244–45; and medicine, 12; methodology for study of, 9–12; modern attitudes toward, 5, 12–14; Naskapi, 75n9; objectivity concerning, 6, 153, 154–55, 243; in oratory, 21; origins of, 24–26, 37; ox tails in, 53; performative aspects of, 4, 146, 155, 189, 190–91, 194, 240, 243, 244; Plutarch's attitude toward, 17; positivist attitude toward, 195, 244, 245; as primitive, 13; and prophecy, 30; psychology of, 9; public, 69; question and answer in, 53, 100–103, 244; randomizing devices in, 165, 221; rationality of, 13–14; reliance of Greek society on, 17, 132; resilience to refutation, 198; ritual aspects of, 189, 190; role in decision-making, 6, 244; scholarship on, 3; skepticism concerning, 5, 8, 12, 104, 132–37, 147, 151–52, 244; social context of, 192–93; social function of, xiv, 74–80, 116, 117, 146, 192; and sophistic teaching, 125; sources for, 14–21; at Sparta, 42, 125, 160; spider, 55n91; sub-Saharan, 9, 10n22, 75n9, 86n31, 145; by Tallensi people, 190n4; teaching of, 129; as threat to power, 128; Thucydides on, 16, 61; typology of, 24, 84–91, 241; ubiquity of, 245, 246; unforeseen consequences of, 19; validity of, xiv, 106, 117, 132; warriors' belief in, 101; in Western society, 18–19; wisdom, 88n34; Yoruba, 75n9; Zulu, 195

Divination, artificial, 24; by Calchas, 88, 91; Hellenistic, 130; inspiration in, 87, 91; *versus* natural, 84–91; noninspirational, 23; randomizing devices in, 90;

Teiresias's, 92; by women, 29–30, 212. *See also* Augury; Extispicy; Hepatoscopy

Divination, Hellenistic: military, 126–31; as *technē*, 130

Divination, military: at battle of Arginusae, 167; at battle of Cunaxa, 165; consequences of, 147; decline of, 126; guarantees in, 165–69; Hellenistic, 126–31; purpose of, 128; reassurance through, 75; sacrifical, 126, 127; Thucydides on, 127. *See also* Hiera; Seers, military; *Sphagia*

Divination, natural: *versus* artificial, 84–91; Calchas's, 88, 91, 95; innate faculty of, 37, 38, 87–88; by military seers, 90; in *Oedipus Tyrannus*, 91; prophecy in, 88–89; role of heredity in, 27, 37; by seers, 24, 90; types of, 88–89. *See also* Consciousness, altered; Spirit possession

Divination, Near Eastern, xv, 24, 30–37, 72, 243; Assyrian, 31–32, 34, 45–46; Babylonian, 33, 34; hepatoscopy in, 33, *34, 35*; Mesopotamian, 32n19; royal service in, 31

Divination, sacrificial, 24, 25, 66; Alexander's use of, 126, 127; by Clytiadae, 41n54; disruption of, 183; frequency of, 83, 170; private, 53n87; question and answer in, 100; by Spartan kings, 160; technical aspects of, 161–62; usefulness of, xiv; validity of, 172–73; in vase painting, *206, 207*; Xenophonic system of, 126. *See also* Hiera; *Sphagia*

Divination, technical. *See* Divination, artificial

Diviners. *See* Seers

Dodds, E. R., 6–7, 111; on Croesus, 148n29

Dodona: lead tablets from, 2n2, 102. *See also* Oracles, of Zeus at Dodona

Dorje Drakden (counseling spirit, Tibet), 227

Dover, K. J., 142n17, 155n9

Dream interpretation, 3n6, 22; Antiphon on, 52–53, 125; cultural components of, 111; by Lysimachus, 185; by seers, 24; Zulu, 195

Dreams: in Timoleon's mission, 112–13; Xenophon's, 15n43

Dunbar, N., 125n47

Duris of Samos, 125n50

Dürrbach, F., 15n43

Earthquakes, as omens, 114

Eclipses, as omens, 114

Eclipses, lunar, 52, 53; during Dion's expedition, 118; interpretation of, 110, 194; in Sicilian expedition, 114–19, 245; soldiers' reaction to, 115

Ecstatic states. *See* Consciousness, altered; Spirit possession

Eleusinian Mysteries, 111; priests of, 59

Eleusis, First Fruits decree at, 123n40

Elis, seers from, 38, 46

Emar (Mascana), hepatoscopic models from, *35*

Empedocles, 81n23; healing by, 27

Empyromancy (burning of entrails), 24; at Olympia, 40; by Teiresias, 92

Enmeduranki, King: Tablet of the Gods, 45–46, 50

Ennius, on *haruspices*, 47

Epaminondas, manipulation of omens by, 175

Eperastus (seer): statue at Olympia, 99; self-advertising by, 130

Ephesus, augury inscription from, 113

Ephorus of Cyme, 16; Diodorus's use of, 111n15, 166, 167; Plutarch's use of, 217n20

Epicharmus, 52n84

Epimenides (wonder-worker), 27

Esarhaddon, King, 200; extispicy under,

32n31, 148–49; oracles addressed to, 228, 229

Etruscans: *haruspices*, 47–49, *48*; hepatoscopy by, 33

Eucleides (seer), 188; advice to Xenophon, 196–97, 198, 199, 210

Euenius of Apollonia (seer), 14, 19, 93; descendants of, 45; Herodotus on, 44; innate faculty of divination, 37, 38

Eumolpidae, 59

Euphrantides (seer), 203

Eupolis (playwright), 62, 63

Eupompidas, Theanetus and, 157

Euripides: *Bacchae*: —seer-client relationships in, 208–9; —Teiresias in, 19, 136, 208–9; *Children of Heracles*, *chrēsmologoi* in, 61; *Electra*, hepatoscopy in, 100; *Helen*, seers in, 138, 140, 145; *Iphigenia among the Taurians*, seers in, 136; *Iphigenia at Aulis*, seers in, 136, 138; *Philoctetes*, seers in, 138; *Phoenissae*: fate in, 76–77; Teiresias in, 95, 146; rationalism of, 141n13; religious attitudes of, 140; *Rhesus*, seers in, 140–41; skepticism of, 5, 137; *Trojan Women*, Cassandra in, 224

Eurymachus (*Odyssey*), 135

Euthyphro, as seer, 142

Evans-Pritchard, E. E., 11n28, 12, 13; on Zande ritual, 20, 105; *Witchcraft, Oracles, and Magic among the Azande*, 6, 149–50; on witch doctors, 145–46

Expiation, rituals of, 83

Extispicy (entrail examination), 24, 188; by Aristander, 179; Assyrian, 32, 148–49; Babylonian, 120, 149; Cicero on, 113; Clearchus's use of, 162; consequences of, 189; depiction of old men in, 54, 55, *55*, *56*, *57*, 57–58; by female seers, 212, 214; frequency of, 83; by mantic families, 154; by Me'en people, 190n2; Neo-Assyrian, 161; objectivity in, 154–55; origins of, 25, 44;

Extispicy *(continued)*
    performative aspects of, 192; place
    in *poleis*, 69; possession in, 88n34;
    Roman belief in, 9; in vase paintings,
    26, 53–58, *54, 55, 56, 57*; by warriors,
    54, 54–55, *56, 57*, 57–58; Xenophon's
    knowledge of, 55, 129, 193; Xeno-
    phon's use of, 15, 74. *See also* Divina-
    tion, artificial; Hepatoscopy

Families, mantic, 37–50, 70, 71; competi-
    tion among, 146; extispicy by, 154;
    individuality within, 99. *See also*
    Clytiadae; Iamidae; Melampodidae;
    Telliadae
Fate, 93, 194, 232; Greek conception of
    76–79
Fehling, D., 225n47
Fernandez, James, 195
Ferrari, G., 54n90
Figueira, T. J., 158n11
Fontenrose, J., 60n100, 216n13, 220n31,
    223n37
Fortes, Meyer, 108, 154n4, 189n4
Frankfurter, D., 63n110
Frazer, James G.: on magic and religion,
    4n8, 67–68
Friezes, depiction of *sphagia* on, 163–64,
    164
Future: Greek conception of, 76n15;
    knowledge of, 75–76, 78

Gagarin, M., 126n56
Gager, J. G., 68n124
Generals: choice of seers, 128; disagree-
    ment with seers, 169–76; knowledge
    of divination, 129–30; partnership
    with seers, 176–83; relationship with
    seers, 153, 155–57, 159, 169–76, 183,
    193, 202, 240
Gods: appeasement of, 82–83; Chrysip-
    pus's conception of, 106, 107; human
    offspring of, 178; omniscience of, 150–

51; punishment of disobedience, 120;
    reciprocity with mortals, 106–7; seers'
    negotiation with, 83–84; will of, 79–
    80, 82, 165, 245; Xenophon's concep-
    tion of, 106. *See also* Communication,
    divine
Goff, B., 231n67
Gould, J., 108n8
Green, P., 117n25
Guinan, Ann, 73nn4–5, 109n10; "A Sev-
    ered Head Laughed," 113–14
Gyges, Delphic oracle of, 77

Hagesias of Syracuse (seer), Pindar on,
    39, 40n50, 97
Hahn, R. A., 11n24
Halistherses (seer), 134–35
Halliday, W. R., 4n8
Harrison, T., 10n22
Haruspices, 47–49, *48*; political influence
    of, 47n70; social aspirations of, 49
Healing, by seers, 27, *28*, 212, 241
Hector (Homer), ignoring of omens,
    120, 133–34, 135, 136, 138
Hegesistratus (seer), 14; death of, 184;
    family of, 38; Mardonius and, 185;
    name of, 47; at Plataea, 170, 182;
    prophecies of evil, 80–81
Hellenica Oxyrhynchia, 167
Hepatoscopy (inspection of liver), 25;
    Assyrian, 32, 33; Bronze Age, 33; in
    campground sacrifice, 102; concerning
    Alexander, 131; in *Electra*, 100; Etrus-
    can, 33; by female seers, 212, *213*; fore-
    telling of death, 130–31; manipulation
    of, 176; Near Eastern, 33, *34, 35*; place
    in *poleis*, 69; in *Prometheus Bound*, 91.
    See also Extispicy; Liver
Hephaestion, divination concerning,
    130–31
Heracleidae, return of, 166n29
Heracles: divinity of, 178; Spartan kings'
    descent from, 125

Heraclitus, on Delphic oracles, 234
Heredity, role in divine inspiration, 27, 37
Hermogenes, gods' communication with,
106, 112–13
Herodotus: on Callias, 156; on *chrēsmologoi*, 63, 65; on Deiphonus, 71; on Delphic oracle, xiii, 112; on Euenius, 44; on *magoi*, 66n118; on Melampus, 25, 43; Mycale in, xiii; on omens, 109–10, 166, 172; on oracle of Zeus at Dodona, 24, 25, 232; on oracles, 15n41, 60n102, 148, 215, 218n26, 235; on Pisistratus, 69n20; on Plataea, xiii, 170, 176–77; on Pythia, 93, 216, 225, 232, 233, 237; seers in, 14–15, 16, 19, 39, 93; on seers' initiative, 156–57; on Simonides, 94; source citations in, 225n47; on Tisamenus, 14, 41–42, 93-94
Hesiod: on bird signs, 51; future knowledge in, 78; on Melampus, 25; Mopsus in, 44; self-representation of, 78n19
Hiera (campground sacrifice), 24, 159–65; at assault on Cebren, 170–71; at battle of Cunaxa, 165; hepatoscopy, 102; performative aspect of, 191; purpose of, 160; *versus sphagia*, 162–63, 166, 201n26. *See also* Divination, military; *Sphagia*
Hierocles (*chrēsmologos*), 61, 62, 63; public maintenance of, 123, 124n44
Hieronymus of Cardia, 126
Hipparchus (son of Pisistratus), 63–64
Hippocratic corpus, divination in, 12, 28, 113
Hippocratic oath, 38
Hippomachus of Leucas (seer), 47; at Platea, 169, 182
Histories, Greek: divination in, 14; seers in, 14–17
Homer: conception of gods, 106; *Iliad*: —bird augury in, 25; —divination in, 35–36; —omens in, 120, 133–34, 135, 136, 138; seer-client relations in,

20; *Odyssey*: —bird augury in, 79; —fate in, 76; —Melampodidae in, 42; seers in, 134–35; skepticism about seers, 133–35
Homeric Hymn to Pythian Apollo, divination in, 76
Hoplites. *See* Warriors
Hornblower, S., 16n45
Horoscopes, invention of, 127
Horton, R., 13n38, 67n123
Human Dissociative Phenomena, 226n48
Hume, David, 6n16

Iamidae (mantic family), xv, 38; branches of, 40; descent from, 43; Pindar on, 39, 40; Rhianus on, 187; stewardship of Olympian oracle, 40, 59, 241
Iamus (seer), 38; historicity of, 42; in Pindar, 39, 40; on temple of Zeus, 40, *41*
Immerwahr, H. R., 47n68
Inscriptions: concerning seers, 40n50, 95, 96, 97, *98*, 99–100; divination in, 21; omens in, 32–33; as source for Greek religion, 92n39
Inspiration. *See* Divination, natural
Isocrates, on seers, 26, 27
Iphigenia, 138, 219
Istar (goddess), priestesses of, 225, 228–29

Jameson, 160n16, 192n13, 206; on *sphagia*, 201n26
Jehoshaphat (king of Judah), 81
Johnston, S. I., 3n6

Karp, A., 11n27
Kerykes (family), 59
Kigaanira people (Uganda), divination by, 86n31
King, C. J., 181n72
Kings: mantic authority of, 4; service of seers to, 30–31

Melampodidae (mantic family), 38; descent from, 43; in Homer, 42

Melampus (seer), 14–15, 38; descendants of, 42, 100; healing by, 27, 28, 212; Herodotus on, 43; Hesiod on, 25; historicity of, 42; payment for, 146

Mental state theory (belief), 10n24

Mesopotamia: divination in, 32n19; hepatoscopic models from, 34; priests of, 46

Messene, refoundation of, 187

Messenian War, Second: Delphic oracle on, 187; seers in, 186–87

Methone, payment of tribute by, 124

Micaiah (prophet), 81

Mikalson, J. D., 20n57, 92n39; on oracles, 216n13

Miltas (seer), 110, 118; and Dion of Syracuse, 178, 194–95; interpretation of eclipse, 194–95

Miracles, credibility of, 6n16

Moirai (fates), 76

Mopsus (seer): contest with Calchas, 44, 45, 151; Hesiod on, 44; historicity of, 43–45; quasi-divine knowledge of, 91

Morgan, C., 235n73

Munychia, battle of: seers at, 93, 184–85

Musaeus, oracles of, 64

Muses, divine inspiration from, 240

Mycale, battle of, xiii, 37

Myers, F. W. H., 148n29

Myth, importance in Greek culture, 159

Nagy, G., 22n1

Naram-Sin and the Enemy Hordes (Babylonian epic), 120

Naskapi people, divination by, 75n9

Nathan (prophet), 30

Navarchs monument (Delphi), 95

Near East: divination in, xv, 24, 30–37, 72, 243; extispicy in, 161; omen collections of, 31–32, 33, 51, 188; oracles of, 148, 228–29. *See also* Seers, Near Eastern

Nechung (Tibet), oracle at, 227–28

Neon of Asine, disregarding of omens, 144, 201

Nicander (prophet), 233

Nicandra (priestess at Dodona), 225

Nicias: accountability of, 118; belief in omens, 115, 116; and Diopeithes, 177; seers of, 103, 117, 245; at siege of Syracuse, 115, 116; and Stilbides, 116, 177, 181, 245

Nineveh, royal archives of, 31-32

Nissinen, M., 229n56

Oath taking, 33n35

Old Comedy, seers in, 60, 61, 103

Old men, depiction in extispicy, 54, 55, 55, 56, 57, 57–58

Oligarchy, Spartan: divination during, 125

Oliver, J. H., 61n104

Olson, S. D., 62, 124n44

Olympia: empyromancy at, 40; inscriptions from, 40n50; statues of seers at, 99; oracle of, 2, 40, 59, 241; temple of Zeus at, 40, 41

Omens: Assyrian texts, 31–32, 51; attending crises, 110–11; aversion of, 80–84; in Babylonian texts, 33, 51; at battle of Cunaxa, 166–67; at battle of Leuctra, 175; at Calpe, 143, 170, 200-202; classification of, 32; disregarding of, 119–22, 133–35, 136, 144, 170–71, 172; dogs in, 203; formation of, 109; Hector's ignoring of, 120, 133–34, 135, 136, 138; Herodotus on, 109–10, 166, 172; in inscriptions, 32-33; manipulation of, 5, 70, 176, 191–92; Plutarch on, 110; recognition of, 73; reinforcement among, 200; seers' interpretation of, 72–73, 240; self-evident, 112; signifying power of, 73, 114; sneezing, 112;

Omens *(continued)*
solicited and unsolicited, 241; in
Sophocles, 121; Theopompus of Chios
on, 110; in Timaeus of Tauromenium,
110; in Xenophon, 80, 166, 170-71,
172, 173, 175, 193, 200-202; from Zeus,
112

Onomacritus (*chrēsmologos*), 63, 64

Onasander, on seers, 129

On Regimen in Acute Diseases (Hippocratic corpus), divination in, 12

Oracles: on Agesilaus, 124–25; alternatives offered by, 75; of Apollo Ptous,
24, 89; Aristotle on, 234; Athenian
Assembly on, 58, 139n7; authority
of, 145, 217; authorship of, 4, 216–22,
226, 233–34; Azande, 6, 101n51, 105,
145, 149, 161; Boeotian, 2, 148, 151; at
Clarus, 43, 45, 89; collections of, 60,
218, 220, 234; ecstatic utterance of, 58;
functions of, 76; in Greek literature,
18, 92; Herodotus on, 15n41, 60n102,
148, 215, 218n25, 235; interpretation
of, 14, 84, 235; in *Libation Bearers*, 18;
at Mallus, 43; manipulation of, 217;
Mardonius's consultation of, 151; of
Musaeus, 64; Near Eastern, 148, 228–
29; in *Oedipus Tyrannus*, 18, 19, 122,
136–37; oral tradition of, 216n14, 219;
Plato on, 149; Plutarch on, 220n31,
236; poison, 6, 101n51, 105, 145, 149,
161; political importance of, 125, 139;
polyvalence of, 234; positivist analysis
of, 216; randomizing devices in, 221;
recipients' use of, 4–5; reformulation
by scribes, 229n56; simultaneous questioning of, 151; in Sophocles, 18, 19,
122, 136-37; spontaneous, 221; termite,
145; testing of, 150–51; of Trophonius, 105; in verse, 219, 220–21;
of Zeus Ammon, 151, 178. *See also*
Chrēsmologoi

Oracles, Assyrian: literary qualities of,
229–30; spirit possession in, 228–29;
validity of, 229–30

Oracles, Delphic, 1–2; for Athens, 235,
237–38; authenticity of, xiii, 216, 233;
collections of, 218, 220, 234; for Croesus, 77, 83–84, 91, 220, 232; Croesus's
testing of, 147–48, 149, 150–51; delivered to Argives, 235, 238–39; Gyges',
77; in Herodotus, xiii, 112; in Homeric
Hymns, 76; importance to Athenian
democracy, 122n34; interpretation
of, 14, 236; literary quality of, 236;
in *Oedipus Tyrannus*, 18, 19, 122, 136–
37; for Philip of Macedon, 234; Plutarch on, 102n54, 222, 223, 231n67;
polyvalent meaning of, 230, 236;
recording of, 218–19; reformulation
by male priests, 215, 217, 220, 230;
role of gaseous emissions in, 226n48;
on Salamis, 112; on Second Messenian
War, 187; for Spartans, 235–38;
synizesis in, 236n75; timing of, 226;
Tisamenus's consultation of, 18, 40–
41, 93; tripod in, 224; verse responses
of, 215–16, 223n37, 230, 233, 236;
wooden wall, 58, 75, 76, 218, 225, 235,
237–38; Xenophon's consultation of,
15, 200; on Xerxes, 235–39. *See also*
Pythia

Oracles, of Zeus at Dodona, 2; establishment of, 225; Herodotus on, 24, 25,
232; origins of, 232; prestige of, 242;
priestesses of, 24, 217, 218, 225, 232;
questioning of, 102, 103

Oracles, Olympian, 2; stewardship of,
40, 59, 241

Oracles, Tibetan, 9–10, 149; altered
consciousness in, 227; Dalai Lama
on, 1, 7, 228; verse delivery of, 239

Oral culture, Greek, 220

Oratory, divination in, 21

Ornithomancy, 86; place in *poleis*, 69; by
Teiresias, 92. *See also* Augury

Oroetes (Persian governor), 181
Orthagoras (seer), 178
Overholt, T. W., 86n31, 108n5
Ox tails, in divination, 53

Pagondas (general), 127
Panagjurischte Amphoras, conspiracy of
  Pelopidas on, 157–58, *158*
Parke, H. W., 45; and Wormell, D. E. W.,
  216n13, 220, 225n46
Parker, Robert, 15n43, 20n56, 126n57, 145,
  210n38; on belief, 153n3; on female
  seers, 214n12; on poison oracle,
  101n51; on sacrifice, 83n26, 102n52
Parpola, S., 229n56
Patterned Dissociative Identity, 226
Pausanias (general): descent from Zeus,
  155; seers of, 122, 160, 166n29
Pausanias (travel writer): on Amphia-
  raus, 184; on second Messenian War,
  186; on seers, 64, 95; on Theaenetus,
  177; on Thrasybulus, 99; on Tropho-
  nius, 105
Pearson, L., 17n47
Peek, Philip, 5, 10n22; on ecstatic states,
  86
Peithagoras (seer), 130–31
Pelling, C. B. R., 17n50, 190n7
Pelopidas: conspiracy of, 157–58, *158*;
  dream of, 182
Peloponnesian War: prophecies on, 139;
  seers in, 16, 95, 139
Pendrick, G. J., 126n56
Perdiccas, seers of, 131
Performance. *See* Divination, performa-
  tive aspects of
Periallus (Pythia), 217, 225
Pericles, seers of, 119, 122–23, 178
Perinthus, siege of, 166n29
Peripatetics, belief in clairvoyance, 7
Persephone: priestesses of, 111–12
Perses (ancestor of Persians), 236
Pharnabazus (satrap), 201, 202

Pherecydes of Samos, 44
Philip of Macedon: Delphic oracle of,
  234; seers of, 126
Philochorus (seer): divination works of,
  52, 53, 202–3; employment as seer,
  202–3; on siege of Syracuse, 116–17
Phineus (seer), blindness of, 37
Phoebe (prophetess), 211
Pindar: on Dodona, 225; on Hagesias, 39,
  40n50, 97; on Iamus, 39, 40; seers in,
  23
Pisistratus, 69n20; use of prophecy, 79
Plastromancy (turtle shell divination), 40
Plataea, battle of: Herodotus on, xiii, 170,
  176–77; Hippomachus of Leucas at,
  169; sacrifices preceding, 166; seers
  at, 94, 102, 121, 122, 155, 157, 169–70,
  182; *sphagia* at, 155; Tisamenus at, 3,
  19, 94–95, 122, 141, 155, 157, 166, 169,
  177
Plato: on *chrēsmologoi*, 60n103; Diotima
  in, 212; on divination, 7–8, 12; doctors
  in, 87; on madness, 84, 88; on magicians, 65, 68; on oracles, 149; on purification, 212; on religion, 68; on seer-
  general relationships, 155; on seers, 23,
  28–29, 68, 69–70, 85, 103, 139n9, 140,
  142; on types of divination, 85–86, 87,
  90, 241
Pliny the Elder, 52
Pliny the Younger, on divination, 8–9
Plutarch: on Agesilaus, 183; on Alexander, 178; attitude toward divination,
  17; on Delphic oracle, 102n54, 221n32,
  222, 223; on Diopeithes, 124; on
  eclipses, 118, 119; on Miltas, 194–
  95; on omens, 110, 166; on oracles,
  220n31, 236; priesthood at Delphi,
  222, 223; on Pyrrhus, 127–28; on
  Pythia, 222, 223, 226, 231n67, 233;
  on seers, 16; on Sicilian expedition,
  177; on siege of Syracuse, 116–17,
  118; on Theocritus the seer, 157–58;

Plutarch *(continued)*
on Timoleon, 111; use of Ephorus of
Cyme, 217n20; use of Theopompus of
Chios, 114n26
Poetry, and prophecy, 78n19
Poets: seers and, 22; societal function of,
78
Polemaenetus (seer), 26–27, 53, 185;
name of, 47
Poleis. See City states
Polles (seer), 48
Polybius: and divination, 126; on
Timaeus of Tauromenium, 17, 127
Polycrates of Samos, seers of, 181–82
Polypheides (seer), family of, 42
Portents, seers' interpretation of, 24. *See
also* Omens
Poseidippus of Pella, 214
Positivism: view of divination, 195, 244,
245; view of oracles, 216
Poulydamas (Homer), 133, 138
Preturnaturalists, 5n11
Price, S. R. F., 10n22
Priestesses: of Istar, 225, 228–29; of
Persephone, 111–12; union with
Apollo, 224; of Zeus at Dodona, 24,
217, 218, 232
Priests: beggar, 28, 29, 66, 67, 241; at
Delphi, 215, 217, 218, 220, 230; of
Eleusinian Mysteries, 59; in *Leviticus*,
50–51; Mesopotamian, 46; official
capacity of, 58; *versus* seers, 58–60,
69–70, 241
Pritchett, W. K., 27n20, 154, 160n16
Promanteia, 2
Promeneia (priestess of Dodona), 225,
232
Prometheus, establishment of divination,
25, 91
Prophecies: Calchas's, 88; and divina-
tion, 30; failed, 108; inspired, 84;
in natural divination, 88–89; Neo-
Assyrian, 72, 230n59; on Pelopon-

nesian War, 139; poetry and, 78n19; by
seers, 78–80
Prophets: in Aeschylus, 182; of Apollo,
89, Hebrew, 30, 81; Native American,
5n11; versus diviners, 23, 85
Purification, 22; for Alexander, 179; of
armies, 99; Near Eastern, 31; Plato
on, 212; by seers, 27, 212, 241; in
Xenophon, 27
Pyrrhus (king of Epirus), seers of, 99,
127–28
Pythia, 215–22; age of, 222; altered
consciousness of, 79, 226, 228, 231;
apprenticeship of, 230–31; authority
of, 217; bribing of, 151, 217; as bride
of Apollo, 224; chastity of, 222, 225;
choice of, 222, 230; composition of
oracles, 4, 216–22, 226, 233–34; costume of, 222, 224; on Croesus, 77, 83–
84, 91, 147–48; cross-cultural comparisons to, 227–30; death of, 233; education of, 223, 230, 232; effect of gaseous emissions on, 226; in *Eumenides*,
86, 223, 232–33; Heraclitus on, 234;
Herodotus on, 93, 216, 225, 232, 233,
237; identity of, 222; influence of, 231;
objectivity of, 221; Plutarch on, 222,
223, 226, 231n67, 233; possession by
Apollo, 1, 24, 89, 211, 226, 230, 231,
237; and priestesses of Istar, 225, 228–
29; questioning of, 102; social status
of, 50, 222–23; testing of, 150–51;
and Tibetan oracle, 9–10, 227–28;
on Tisamenus of Elis, 18, 40–41, 93;
titles of, 217; use of cleromancy, 86;
verse responses of, 216, 220, 221–22,
223n37, 239. *See also* Oracles, Delphic
Pythioi (Spartan officials), 218

Regimen in Acute Disease (Hippocratic
treatise), divination in, 113
Regulus, M. Aquilius, 9
Religion: anthropology of, xv, 11; Dinka,

67, 108n8, 150; and magic, 4n8, 65–71, 81; neutrality in study of, 11; persuasive power of, 67–68; sociology of, xv, 63; teleological view of, 13; world *versus* primitive, 13n36

Religion, Greek: of city-states, 67, 68–69, 108; in Greek literature, 143; in *Memorabilia*, 89–90; Plato on, 68; role of divination in, 245

Rhianus (poet), on seers, 186–87

Rituals: apotropaic, 80, 82–83; Azande, 20, 105; conservatism in, 223n38; of expiation, 83; in Greek tragedy, 92n39; magical, 68n124, 81; private, 242; of purification, 179, 212; skepticism concerning, 104

Rochberg, F., 127n58

Roman Catholic Church, conservatism of, 223

Roth, P., 23n2, 142n19

Rowling, J. K., 22

Rüpke, J., 63n110

Sacrifice: apotropaic, 69, 83; human, 203; nondivinatory, 162; propitiatory, 160; Xenophon on, 83n26, 160. *See also* Divination, sacrificial; *Hiera*; *Sphagia*

Salamis, battle of: *chrēsmologoi* on, 65; Delphic oracle on, 112; seers at, 203, 204; Themistocles at, 203

Saler, B., 10n24

Samas (Assyrian god), 45

Samuel (prophet), 30

Sardis, fall of, 77

Satyra (female seer), 214

Satyrus (seer), 178n53

Saul (king of Israel), need for omens, 120

Scapulimancy, 75n9

Seercraft. *See* Divination

Seers: access to divine knowledge, 2, 5, 139; in Aeschylus, 27, 90-91, 209; altered consciousness of, 23, 24, 79, 84-91; apprentices of, 38, 70; aristo-

cratic, 22; in Aristophanes, 60, 62, 103, 123, 151; Aristotle on, 186; Athenian, 3n5, 122–26; authority of, 12, 24, 30, 58, 59, 87, 241; belief in, 3–4; blameless, 97; blind, 37, 51; charismatic, 29, 30, 59, 70, 243, 246; charlatanism charges against, xiv, 5, 28–29, 147, 152, 155, 191; and *chrēsmologoi*, 60–65, 241; in comedy, 19, 60, 61, 103; competition among, 182; in conspiracies, 157–58, *158*; costume of, 164, 180, 188; demand for, 146; diversion of evils, 69, 79, 80–84; divine inspiration of, 26, 90, 241–42; dream interpretation by, 24; ecstatic utterances by, 24, 79, 84–91; employers of, 19–20; employment in city states, 69, 240; Etruscan, 47–49, *48*; evidence for, 9–10; good omens from, 80, 82; greed of, 135–36, 140, 146, 147, 176; in Greek literature, 13–17, 21; in Greek tragedy, 19, 92, 94, 122, 135–36, 242; healing by, 27, *28*, 212, 241; in Herodotus, 14–15, 16, 19, 39, 93, 156–57; in Hippocratic corpus, 28; independence of, 30; initiative-taking by, 156–59; inscriptions concerning, 40n50, 95, 96, 97, *98*, 99–100, 242–43, 247; intellectual prowess of, 191; interpretation of omens, 72–73, 240; legitimacy of, 63; in literary texts, 10; and magicians, 65–71, 241; manipulation of omens, 5, 70, 191–92; monuments to, *48*, 95, 99, 242–43, 247; names of, 47; negotiation with gods, 83–84; objectivity of, 153; origins of, 4n8; payments for, 123n37, 146, 185, 244; Plato on, 23, 28–29, 68, 69–70, 85, 103, 139n9, 140, 142; and poets, 22; predictions concerning themselves, 132; pressures on, 155, 244; prestige of, 58, 243; *versus* priests, 58–60, 69–70, 241; prophecies by, 78–80; prophecies of death, 93, 183;

Seers *(continued)*
public maintenance of, 122–24; purification by, 27, 212, 241; qualifications for, 50–58; questioning of, 53, 100–103, 244; rationalizing view of, 153; relationships with clients, 188–90, 192–202, 204–10, 242, 244; religious authority of, 24, 30; respect for, 6; Rhianus on, 186–87; rivalry among, 146; role in divine communication, 2, 5, 139; in scholia, 60–61; self-advertisement by, 42, 130, 242; self-awareness of, 191; self-confidence of, 70; self-image of, 92–100; self-representation of, 4, 6, 192; social position of, 145, 200–201, 241; societal function of, 2, 5–6, 78, 85, 86, 146, 153, 240; soldiers as, 144–45; statues of, *41*, *48*, 95, 99, 100, 130, 177, 178, 242; successful, 70–71, 243; taxation of, 186; testing of, 147–52; types of, 22–23; in vase paintings, *28*, 204–5, *206*, 207; and will of gods, 82. *See also* Divination; Families, mantic

Seers, archaic, 12; healing by, 27; in Homer, 36; influence of, 126; societal importance of, 31

Seers, classical, 12–13; effect of literature on, 19; eponymous ancestors of, 42–43; functions of, 186; intellectual backgrounds of, 123n38; political activities of, 123, 126, 139; technē of, 23

Seers, female, 29–30; artificial divination by, 212; costume of, 214–15; epigram on, 214; extispicy by, 212, 214; hepatoscopy by, 212, *213*; spirit possession of, 85, 211; stele of "Diotima," 212, *213*; in vase painting, *215*

Seers, Hellenistic, 126–31; Alexander's, 59, 80, 113, 126, 129, 130–31, 178–81; of King Pyrrhus, 99, 127–28

Seers, historical: identity of, 246; *versus* literary, 92–94; literary models of,

242; *versus* mythical, 2. *See also* Seers, classical; Seers, military

Seers, itinerant, 29, 147, 241, 242; as mobile priests, 59, 69–70; from Near East, 42; oral knowledge of, 31; wealth of, 26

Seers, military, 93, 95–97, 99; Babylonian, 96; at battle of Arginusae, 167–69; at battle of Mantinea, 166; choice of, 128–29; at Cnidus, 103; credit for victory, 183; death in battle, 183–84; Diodorus on, 167–79; Dion's, 110, 194–95; disagreement with generals, 169–76; divine inspiration of, 90; on eclipses, 114–19; garb of, 164; influence on morale, 176; natural divination by, 90; partnership with generals, 176–83; Pausanias's use of, 122, 160, 166n29; in Peloponnesian War, 16, 95, 139; at Plataea, 94, 102, 121, 122, 155, 157, 169–70, 182; promises of victory, 165–69; relationship with generals, 153, 155–57, 159, 169–76, 183, 193, 202, 240; reporting of omens, 92; role in success, 94; at Salamis, 203, 204; in Second Messenian War, 186–87; in Sicilian expedition (415-13), 114–19, 133, 141, 145, 245; as strategists, 187; at Thermopylae, 46, 94, 122, 184. *See also* Divination, military

Seers, mythical, 14–15; in Euripides, 19, 95, 136, 137, 138, 140, 141–42, 145; families of, 38–39; *versus* historical, 2; historicity of, 42–45; in Homer, 133n2, 134–35; relations with clients, 242; in Sophocles, 19, 66, 92, 135, 136–37, 140, 210. *See also* Calchas; Teiresias

Seers, Near Eastern: Assyrian, 30–31, 46, 50; Babylonian, 50, 96; migration to Greece, 42; service to kings, 30–31; social status of, 49–50; use of adoption, 46

Sennacherib (Assyrian king), extispicy by, 148

Seuthes (king of Thrace), 74; offer to Xenophon, 100, 101

Shakespeare, William, 211

Shamanism: altered consciousness in, 231; American Indian, 191n11; self-belief in, 191; Siberian, 81

Shapiro, H. A., 65n114

Sibyls, as seers, 24

Sicilian expedition (415-13), 64–65; lunar eclipse during, 114–19; Plutarch on, 177; seers in, 114–19, 133, 141, 145, 245

Silanus (seer): and Cyrus the Younger, 103, 185, 190–91; defection of, 143, 182, 200; relationship with Xenophon, 173, 193–94

Simonides of Ceos: commemoration of Megistias, 94, 247; on Tisamenus, 169n35

"Sin of Sargon" (Akkadian text), 148

Siwah oasis (Libya), oracle of Zeus Ammon at, 151, 178

Sneezing, as omen, 112

Society, Greek: performative culture of, 191; questioning of norms in, 132; reliance on divination, 17, 132; religious belief in, 10; seers in, 2, 5–6, 31, 78, 85, 86, 146, 153, 240

Society, Western: divination in, 18–19

Socrates: on divination, 73n6, 240–41; in Xenophon, 73n6, 89, 102, 107, 240

Solon, on seers, 24, 82

Soothsayers. *See* Seers

Sophists: contests between, 151, 179–80; itinerant, 147

Sophocles

Ajax, seers in, 210

Antigone: omens in, 121; seer-client relationships in, 209; Teiresias in, 19, 92, 204–5, 208, 209

Oedipus Tyrannus: divination in, 136–37; intuitive divination in, 91; omens

in, 121; oracles in, 18, 19, 122, 136–37; seer-client relationships in, 204–5, 207–8; Teiresias in, 19, 66, 92, 135, 136–37, 140, 144, 204–5, 207–8, 209

Sorcerers (*goai*), 55, 65, 66, 67

Soudinus (seer), 176

Sparta: Delphic archives at, 234; Delphic oracles for, 235–38; divination at, 42, 125, 160; influence in Asia Minor, 183; royal succession at, 124

Spartans: versus Lacedaemonians, xv–xvi

Sperber, D., 11n27

Sphagia (battle-line sacrifice), 24, 159–65; Arexion's performance of, 156, 161, 182; attire for, 163–65; at battle of Cunaxa, 165; depiction on friezes, 163–64, *164*; versus *hiera*, 162–63, 166, 201n26; at Munychia, 184–85; at Plataea, 155; purpose of, 160; Thucydides on, 16n45, 127; in vase painting, *163*; by warriors, *163*; Xenophon's performance of, 160, 201, 202. *See also* Divination, military; *Hiera*

Spirit possession, 9, 22, 24; as craft, 86; by Dionysus, 89; in extispicy, 88n34; of female seers, 85; passivity of, 89; of women, 85, 89. *See also* Consciousness, altered; Divination, natural; Pythia, possession by Apollo

Spiro, M. E., 67n123

Statues. *See* Seers, statues of

Sthorys of Thasos (seer): Athenian citizenship of, 122, 141; at battle of Cnidus, 103; payments to, 123n37; public maintenance of, 123

Stilbides (seer), 117; death of, 116, 182, 245; and Nicias, 116, 177, 181, 245

Stoics: belief in clairvoyance, 7; belief system of, 90, 107

Strabo: on Mopsus, 44; on oracles, 220n31

Struck, P. T., 20n57, 121n32

Strymon (seer), 214

Suda, Diopeithes in, 125n52

Sweek, J., 31n27

Symmachus (seer), 97

Synizesis, in oracles, 236n75

Syracuse, Athenian siege of, 114–19

Tablets, oracular, 2n2, 102

Tallensi people, divination by, 190n4

Teachers, adoption of students, 38

Teiresias (seer), 15; artificial divination by, 92; blindness of, 37; daughters of, 211, 212; in Euripides, 19, 95, 136, 146, 208–9; intuitive divination by, 91; military victory of, 95; religious authority of, 30; in Sophocles, 19, 66, 92, 135, 136–37, 140, 144, 204–5, 207–8, 209; in vase painting, 204–5, *206*, 207

Telenikos (seer), 184

Telliadae (mantic family), 38; descent from, 43

Tellias (seer), 38; strategems of, 157

Tellias (seer), historicity of, 38, 42

Telmessus (Caria), seers of, 46–47

Theaenetus (seer): statue of, 177; and Tolmides, 46, 177

Theanetus (seer), and Eupompidas, 157

Thebaid, seers in, 97

Thebes, oracle of Apollo Ptous at, 24, 89

Themis (prophetess), 211; depiction in vase paintings, *215*

Themistocles, at Salamis, 203

Theoclus (seer), 186–87

Theoclymenus (seer), 78–79; family of, 42

Theocritus (seer), in conspiracy of Pelopidas, 157–58, *158;* at Leuctra, 158, 175

Theodotus (seer), 127

Theognis, on oracles, 219

Theophrastus, superstitious man of, 112

Theopompus of Chios, 17; on Delphic oracle, 221; historical method of, 111n14; on omens, 110; Plutarch's use of, 114n26

Thermopylae: commemorative pillars at, 247; seers at, 46, 94, 122, 184

The Sacred Disease (Hippocratic corpus), seers in, 28

Thibron (Spartan), 75

Thiel, J. H., 114n26

Thomassen, E., 68n124

Thrasybulus (seer), 127; death of, 194; military service of, 97, 99; statue of, 99; self-advertising by, 130

Thrasyllus (general), 168

Thrasyllus (seer), 26, 53; wealth of, 185

Thucydides: on *chrēsmologoi*, 61; on divination, 16, 61, 127; on seers, 138–39, 182, 184; on siege of Syracue, 115, 118; on *sphagia*, 16n45, 127

Thurium, founding of, 123

Tibet, oracles of, 7, 9–10, 149, 227–28, 239

Timaeus of Tauromenium, 17; omens in, 110, 127

Timarete (priestess of Dodona), 225, 232

Timoleon: seers of, 178, 182; Sicilian mission of, 111–12

Tisamenus of Elis (seer), 14–15, 40–42; and Calchas, 93, 95; consultation of Delphic oracle, 18, 40–41, 93; divine sanctioning of, 42; family of, 38, 177; in Herodotus, 41–42, 93–94; name of, 47; at Plataea, 3, 19, 94–95, 122, 141, 155, 157, 166, 169, 177; self-advertisement by, 42; Simonides on, 169n35; Spartan citizenship of, 146, 241; victories of, 177n51

Tisamenus (seer, great-grandson of Tisamenus), 157

Tolmides, and Theaenetus, 46, 177

Tragedy, Greek: divination in, 14, 17–19;

oracles in, 18; religious belief in, 18,
144; rituals in, 92n39; seers in, 19, 92,
94, 122, 135–36, 242
Trampedach, K., 31n28
Trauma, omen perception following,
109
Triremes, sacred, 111
Trophonius, oracle of, 105
Truth, in Western discourse, 6
Tulkus (reincarnate lamas), 7
Tuplin, C., 112n17
Turtle shells, divination with, 40
Tyet (term for Dinka diviners), 67, 150

Van Straten, F. T., 57n92
Vase paintings: divination in, *206, 207*;
extispicy in, 26, 53–58, *54, 55, 56, 57*;
female seers in, *215*; seers in, *28*, 204–
5, *206*, 207; *sphagia* on, *163*
Vernant, J.-P., 10n22, 13n37, 76n15
Vulci, bronze mirror from, 48, *49*

Wach, J., 63n110
Warriors: belief in divination, 101; extispicy by, *54*, 54–55, *56, 57*, 57–58; as
seers, 144–45; *sphagia* by, *163*
Weber, Max: *Sociology of Religion*, 63; on
charismatic authority, 59n98
West, M. L., 51n77
Wilamowitz-Moellendorff, U. von, 33n34
Witch doctors, Azande, 13, 145–46; testing of, 149–50
Women, spirit possession of, 85, 89. *See
also* Priestesses; Seers, female
Wooden wall oracle, 58, 75, 76; authenticity of, 237; choices in, 235; delivery
of, 225; poetic quality of, 238; recording of, 218. *See also* Oracles, Delphic
Woodruff, P., 126n56

Xenocritus, 123n40
Xenophanes of Colphon, 8

Xenophon
Anabasis: battle of Cunaxa in, 165;
Coeratadas in, 185–86; divination
in, 15, 190–91, 198; frequency of
sacrifice in, 83n26; omens in, 166,
170–71, 193, 200–202; purification
in, 27; seer-client relations in, 196–
97; seers in, 14, 60, 143–44; Socrates
in, 102, 240; *sphagia* in, 156, 160,
201, 202
conception of gods, 106
consultation of Delphic oracle, 15,
200
Cyropaedia: Croesus in, 149; divination
in, 106; omens in, 173
Eucleides' advice to, 196–97, 198, 199,
210
Hellenica: Agesilaus in, 183; apotropaic
ritual in, 82; battle of Arginusae in,
167; *chrēsmologoi* in, 65; *hiera* in,
170–71; manipulation of omens in,
175; Munychia in, 93; omens in, 80,
173, 175
Hipparchicus: divination in, 73; sacrifice
in, 172–73
knowledge of divination, 129–30,
192
knowledge of extispicy, 55
Lacedaemonion Politeia, *hiera* in, 160
Memorabilia: divination in, 76, 106,
107; religion in, 89–90; Socrates in,
73n6, 107
obedience to omens, 170–71
performance of *sphagia*, 160
piety of, 15
on prebattle sacrifice, 127
questioning of entrails, 100–101, 102
relationship with seers, 196–202
relationship with Silanus, 173, 193–94
religious beliefs of, 73n6, 167
sacrifices to Zeus, 75, 196, 197, 198–99
on seers, 3, 245

Xenophon *(continued)*

   Symposium: divination in, 106; Hermogenes in, 112

   use of divination, 15–16, 74–75, 100–
101, 246

   use of extispicy, 15, 74

   on validity of omens, 172

Xerxes: Delphic oracles on, 235–39;
Onomacritus and, 64

Yoruba people, divination by, 75n9

Zandeland. *See* Azande people (Sudan)

Zeitlyn, F. I., 55n91

Zeus: omens from, 112; temple at Olympia, 40, *41. See also* oracles, of Zeus at
Dodona

Zeus Ammon, oracle of, 151, 178

Zeus Meilichios, sacrifice to, 196, 197,
198–99

Zeusse, E. M., 88n34

Zulus: belief in clairvoyance, 7; divination by, 195

INDEX LOCORUM

Plutarch *(continued)*

Aristides

9.2	203
15.1	166
17–18	166n20
18	155n10, 166n29
18.2	166
27.3	185

Artaxerxes

7	191n9

Cimon

18	115, 154n5, 177

Dion

22–27	178
24	110, 182, 194, 118n26
54.5–7	17n48

Lycurgus

22	160n16
22.4	160

Lysander

22.5–6	125n51
24–26	217n20
25.3	217n20
28.5	184
30.3	217n20, 218n26

Moralia

214f	176n49
290d	27n20, 99n49
292d	1n1
292d–f	226
396d	236
403b	151
403e–f	221
404d	234n70
405c–d	223
407b–c	220
414b	226
431e–33	7n21
438b	233
438c	222
575b–598f	157

Nicias

4	103n56
4.2	177
13	139, 151, 177
13.1	177
13.1–4	177
14	151
23.5	177
23.5–6	116, 181n73
23.9	52n81

Pelopidas

21	182
21–22	158
21.3	203

Pericles

6	119
6.2	123n39
32.2	124

Pyrrhus

6.5	127n59
29.4	135n3
30.3	127n59
30.5	154n5

Solon

12	212n5

Themistocles

13	203n31

Timoleon

4	178n53
8	111, 111n15, 182

Polyaenus

4.20	176, 176n49

Polybius

10.23.4	17

Posidippus (Acosta-Hughes,
Kosmetatou, and
Baumbach 2004)

6	214n9
14, 15	214n11

Text	10.25/14 Fournier
Display	Fournier
Compositor	BookMatters
General Index	Roberta Engleman
Index Locorum	Adam Gitner
Printer and binder	Thomson-Shore, Inc.